22

D0588318

BEYOND BLACK AND WHITE

From Civil Rights to Barack Obama

MANNING MARABLE

VERSO

London · New York

This edition published by Verso 2016
First published by Verso 1995
© Manning Marable 1995, 2009, 2016

1 3 5 7 9 10 8 6 4 2

Verso
UK: 6 Meard Street, London W1F 0EG
US: 20 Jay Street, Suite 1010, Brooklyn, NY 11201
versobooks.com

Verso is the imprint of New Left Books

ISBN-13: 978-1-78478-766-0
ISBN-13: 978-1-78478-768-4 (US EBK)
ISBN-13: 978-1-78478-767-7 (UK EBK)

British Library Cataloguing in Publication Data
A catalogue record for this book is available from the British Library

Library of Congress Cataloging-in-Publication Data
A catalog record for this book is available from the Library of Congress

Typeset by illuminati, Grosmont
Printed in the US by Maple Press

CONTENTS

ACKNOWLEDGEMENTS

The following essays, several of which have been revised for this collection, have been previously published: "Black America in Search of Itself" first appeared in *The Progressive*, vol. 55, no. 11 (November 1991). "Race and Realignment in American Politics" was published originally in Mike Davis, Fred Pfeil and Michael Sprinker, eds., *The Year Left: An American Socialist Yearbook*, vol. 1 (London: Verso, 1985). "At the End of the Rainbow" first appeared in *Race and Class*, vol. 34, no. 2 (October–December 1992). "Race and Class in the US Presidential Election of 1992" was published originally in *Race and Class*, vol. 34, no. 3 (January–March 1993). A shorter version of "Politics, Personality and Protest in Harlem: The Rangel–Powell Congressional Race" was published in *The Village Voice*, September 13, 1994. "Clarence Thomas and the Crisis of Black Political Culture" first appeared in an anthology edited by Toni Morrison, *Race-ing Justice, En-Gendering Power: Essays on Anita Hill, Clarence Thomas, and the Construction of Social Reality* (New York: Pantheon Books, 1992). "Blueprint for Black Studies" was presented at a conference on African-American Studies at the University of Wisconsin-Madison, in April 1991, and was later published in *The Black Scholar*, vol. 22, no. 3 (Summer 1992). "Black Studies, Multiculturalism and the Future of American Education" first appeared in the June–September 1995 issue of *Items*, the newsletter of the Social Science Research Council, New York. "Malcolm as Messiah: Cultural Myth versus Historical Reality" first appeared in *Cineaste*, vol. 19, no. 4 (1993). "Memory and Militancy in Transition: The 1993 March on Washington" first appeared in *Race and Class*, vol. 35, no. 3 (January–March 1994). An earlier version of "Benjamin Chavis and the Crisis of Black Leadership" was published in *Blueprint for Social Justice*, vol. 18, no. 2, October 1994. "Black Intellectuals in Conflict" first appeared in *New Politics*, vol. 5, no. 3 (Summer 1995). "African-American Empowerment in the Face of Racism: The Political Aftermath of the Battle of Los Angeles" first appeared in the *Black Collegian*, vol. 23, no. 1 (September–October, 1992). "Beyond Racial Identity Politics: Toward a Liberation Theory for Multicultural Democracy" first appeared in *Race and Class*, vol. 35, no. 1 (July–September 1993). "The Divided Mind of Black America: Race, Ideology and Politics in the Post-Civil-Rights Era" was written in the winter and spring of 1994 in collaboration with Leith Mullings, Professor of Anthropology at the City University of New York Graduate School, and was published originally in *Race and Class*, vol. 36, no. 1 (July–September 1994). "History and Black Consciousness: The Political Culture of Black America" was published in *Monthly Review*, vol. 47, no. 3 (July–August 1995). "Harlem and the Racial Imagination: Reflections on the Million Youth March" first appeared in *Souls*, vol. 1, no. 1 (1999). "The Political and Theoretical Contexts of the Changing Racial Terrain" first appeared in *Souls*, vol. 4, no. 3 (2002). "Reparations and the Politics of Black Consciousness" first appeared in the *Free Press* (8 August 2002) under the title "Reparations, Black Consciousness, and the Black Freedom Struggle." "Katrina's Unnatural Disaster: A Tragedy of Black Suffering and White Denial" first appeared in *Souls*, vol. 8, no. 1 (2006). "Racializing Justice, Disenfranchising Lives: Toward an Anti-Racist Criminal Justice" first appeared as the preface to an anthology edited by Manning Marable, Keesha Middlemass and Ian Steinberg, *Racializing Justice, Disenfranchising Lives: The Racism, Criminal Justice and Law Reader* (New York: Palgrave Macmillan, 2007). "Blackness beyond Boundaries: Navigating the Political Economies of Global Inequality" first appeared as the introduction to an anthology edited by Manning Marable and Vanessa Agard-Jones, *Transnational Blackness: Navigating the Global Color Line* (New York: Palgrave Macmillan, 2008). "Barack Obama, the 2008 Presidential Election and the Prospects for a 'Post-Racial Politics'" first appeared in *The Black Commentator*, no. 306 (8 January 2009) under the title "Racializing Obama: The Enigma of Post-Black Politics and Leadership."

The storm is rising against the privileged minority
of the earth, from which there is no shelter in isolation
or armament. The storm will not abate until a just distribution
of the fruits of the earth enables men everywhere to live in
dignity and human decency. The American Negro ... may be
the vanguard of a prolonged struggle that may change the shape
of the world, as billions of deprived shake and transform the
earth in their quest for life, liberty, and justice.

Martin Luther King, Jr.

PREFACE TO THE FIRST EDITION

B*eyond Black and White* was written largely in the four years between 1991 and 1995, when I was employed at the University of Colorado at Boulder and, after 1993, at Columbia University. Because the volume is a collection of political and social essays, written at different times and in response to various events, from the Senate Judiciary Committee hearings regarding the nomination of Clarence Thomas to the US Supreme Court to the Los Angeles civil uprising of April–May 1992, there is a certain amount of repetition and restatement of political ideas. As the book was being written, I was forced to reassess many of my older ideas about the character and relative permanence of "race," and its impact within American politics. But despite the diversity of topics considered within the essays, there is a conjunctural and theoretical unity expressed within the work as a whole.

The main thesis of the book is that "race" as it has been understood within American society is being rapidly redefined, along with the basic structure of the economy, with profound political consequences for all sectors and classes. The massive flood of both legal and undocumented workers from Third World countries seeking low-wage employment, for example, has sharply transformed the ethnic, cultural and social composition and character of thousands of urban working-class neighborhoods and communities. Against this changing social background, our notions of the social categories which convey the day-to-day meaning of "black" and "white" have also begun to change, especially within the major cities of the USA. Because this social transformation is occurring at a political conjuncture dominated by conservative ideology and a retreat from welfare state policies, race relations and racial discourse are reflected within an altered debate about the character of discrimination, the nature of prejudice, and invented notions about who the "real victims" of inequality are. A new generation of white Americans, born largely after the civil-rights movement, felt little or no historical responsibility or social guilt for being the beneficiaries of institutional racism. Racism was described increasingly in the media as a problem of the historical past, not a contemporary problem of inequality with practical consequences for the oppressed. The political discourse in the 1990s which has focused on controversial issues of public policies such as affirmative action, welfare reform and the rights of undocumented immigrants, directly reinforced the perception that white elite males somehow had become the most oppressed social class in the country.

The fact that the political definition of "racial discrimination" has been rapidly transformed in a fairly short period of time should not be surprising to anyone. Race is essentially a social construction, not a permanent fact of biology or genetics. It is dynamic and constantly being renegotiated along the boundaries of color. Race relations shifted in the period between 1954 and 1968, with the passage of the Civil Rights Act of 1964 and the Voting Rights Act of 1965, and the massive social protest mobilizations which desegregated American society to a considerable degree. What did *not* change in the 1960s was the long-held characterization that the quintessential core of the racial problematic was a social conflict between black and white. The events of the 1990s have greatly transformed this simplified biracial framework.

This book is also about the transformation of African-American leadership since the civil-rights movement. In the 1960s, when young African-Americans were asked the question "What do you want?", we frequently replied: "A black face in a high place." What we meant by this was that the goal of the civil-rights movement should be the expansion of African-Americans in positions of authority, power and privilege within the established social order. We calculated the gains of the movement by the percentage of black Americans represented in the political system, as well as in professional, managerial and legal positions of authority. This model of symbolic representation clearly broke down in the 1980s. Blacks were elected as mayors of major cities, who aggressively pursued policies, such as increasing sales tax on the public and reducing taxes on corporations, which directly went against the best interests of black working-class communities. The elevation of Clarence Thomas to the US Supreme Court dramatically revealed the inherent contradictions and limitations of simplistic, racial-identity politics.

One of the chapters in Part I of this volume, "Race and Realignment in American Politics," was actually written ten years ago, in the depressing aftermath of Ronald Reagan's landslide re-election as president, and in the context of what some scholars have termed "the Second Cold War." I have included it here because in many respects the essay addressed the factors and personalities behind the subsequent resurgence of white mass conservatism in the 1990s and the political backlash against civil rights and affirmative action. It predicted the emergence of Speaker of the House Newt Gingrich as a potential leader for the extreme right within national politics. "Black America in Search of Itself," published originally in 1991, explored the impact of Reaganism and the collapse of the welfare state within urban black culture and race relations. Institutional racism, the disinvestment of capital from central cities with the loss of millions of industrial and manufacturing jobs, the rapid expansion of the informal sector or underground urban economy, cutbacks in welfare and social programs for the poor, and the proliferation of markets for both illegal drugs and deadly weapons, all contributed to a highly destructive social environment. The quality of the urban environment and public life – what we take for granted as we work, or seek health care, education, public transportation, and culture – has undergone a profound change in the USA in only a decade. These two earlier essays essentially set the framework for my subsequent work written during the next three to four years.

Another element which became increasingly influential within black civil society in the early to mid 1990s was the resurgence of black nationalism. In many respects, the renaissance of African-American demands for racial separatism, group solidarity and a rejection of coalition politics, was directly related to the decline and virtual collapse of Jesse Jackson's Rainbow Coalition in the late 1980s. For a series of complex personal motives and political reasons, Jackson refused to build a political and social protest movement independent of the Democratic Party, which could have transcended the ethnic and racial divisions paralyzing efforts for progressive change. The essay "At the End of the Rainbow" outlines Jackson's strengths and weaknesses as a national leader. The failure to establish a progressive, multicultural and democratic alternative left a vast political vacuum, not only within black civil society but throughout left-of-center politics for the entire nation. Seizing the political space, separatist organizations like the Nation of Islam grew rapidly, reaching a new generation of alienated and angry African-American youth. Inside the academy, a parallel development occurred with the growing popularity of various interpretations of "Afrocentrism." The essays "Blueprint for Black Studies" and "Black Studies, Multiculturalism and the Future of American Education" represent my evolving approach toward the relationship between culture, education and the democratic restructuring of American society.

Louis Farrakhan's politics of petty entrepreneurial capitalism, social conservatism and racial isolationism are, of course, nothing new: Booker T. Washington's agenda was virtually identical a century ago, except for the Tuskegeean's sycophantic rhetoric which appealed to the white power structure of his time. Washington appeased white America by falsely claiming that we could be "as separate as the fingers, yet one as the hand in all things essential to mutual progress." Farrakhan embraces the same racial separatism and social conservatism, but translates that agenda from a necessary evil to a positive good. Despite the media's widespread denunciations of Farrakhan and other racial separatists, it is clear that they largely serve the interests of the white political and corporate establishment, by fragmenting oppressed communities and poor people by "race." The widespread appeal of the Nation of Islam's agenda today reflects the inability of mainstream black leadership to address in a constructive and progressive manner both the rage and energies of the hip-hop generation and the most oppressed sectors of urban black America. Benjamin Chavis had the potential for bridging the political gap between the civil-rights establishment and the black nationalist sentiment within the hip-hop generation and urban youth activists. But his failure, or, perhaps more pointedly, the political campaign to discredit and to oust him from the NAACP leadership, once again made the goal of constructing a coherent and unified black progressive alternative difficult to achieve.

The significance of the failure to develop a new progressive paradigm which could transcend the theoretical and programmatic basis for the civil-rights movement of a generation ago is directly related to the rise of the far right in the 1990s. The great gift of black folk to American politics and society has been that we have consistently fought for a more inclusive and humanistic definition of democracy, the relationship between people and the state. From slavery through Reconstruction, and from the nadir of racial segregation through the desegregation movement in the South, we have consistently challenged the limited definitions of what democracy should be about. As we have struggled, others within the society have been influenced by our vision and sacrifices, and have joined the fight to expand the boundaries of democracy. The inability of the black movement to develop new theories and models of political intervention during the era of Reaganism and the conservative domination of Congress under Gingrich has meant that the entire spectrum of social forces left of center has fallen into disarray. White liberals, labor, feminists, and others, have not produced a coherent statement to halt

PREFACE TO THE FIRST EDITION

the movement to the right, because in the end that alternative must be articulated by the most oppressed sectors of our society for it to have a fundamental impact upon the social order. In short, the struggles of black people, in conjunction with other racial minorities and the poor, will prove decisive in the continuing battle to redefine the nature and character of democracy. Definitions of what blackness will mean in the future, for example, are directly related to the evolving construction of the American national identity, and its relationship to the broader currents of world cultures and political institutions. This is why an analysis of black political and civil society, its leadership and competing ideologies, is linked to the development of a broader understanding of

e.

:tempts to speak to the
y, the battle for public
pment, and the political
democratic movement
)lution to the problems
)rs of black and Latino
ruction of strong social
erything from consumer
and private education,
;hborhood associations,
improve public life for
fensive steps, there must
les, a series of intensive
sed constituencies across
es, which can generate
nocratic activism. The
failure of democracy to
found in the leadership

and insights of the most oppressed members of our society. The "lived experiences" of the oppressed, the materiality of their daily lives, reveal practical lessons of survival and struggle. That collective experience can be theorized to create part of the political strategy for community activity, mobilization and resistance. The older models of social reform, largely reflecting the perceptions and class interests of the black (and other minority) middle class, locked in incrementalist notions of gradual change, no longer make sense to the hip-hop generation. That generation has lost faith in the ability of the "system" to speak to their needs or aspirations. Therefore, we must anchor a new black and progressive politics in the struggles which are currently being waged across America's fractured urban landscape, in the collective efforts to build alternative institutions, and to resist the agenda of corporate capital. The long-term solutions to the protracted problems of urban inequality will not come from above, but largely from below. They will also require the basic redistribution of resources and the democratic restructuring of power relations between those who dominate the social order and those who actually work for a living.

At the heart of this work is also a personal journey, sparked by a chronic illness which has given greater urgency to my life and research. In 1986 I was diagnosed as having sarcoidosis. The typical treatment for sarcoidosis, a steroid called prednisone, is in some respects worse than the disease itself. After stabilizing itself for several years, the illness suddenly and unexpectedly became worse in 1993. People deal with adversity in different ways. For me, there was the recognition that one's personal contributions to the political struggle are always finite and limited. Everyone must eventually face their own mortality. But when one is diagnosed with an illness of this type, one begins to reflect critically about everything that has meaning or significance. Understanding the living reality of race, and the collective struggle to overcome the burden of discrimination, is at the heart of the entire corpus of my work. And it was from this vantage point that I began to ask harder, more searching questions of myself and of my historical and political analysis. I was forced to retrace even the contours of my own memory and personal history, as related to the definition of what race "was" and what it appeared to be evolving into at the present time.

In this process, I became convinced, more than ever before, in the power of political ideas as a social force. Leaving Boulder and relocating to New York, especially in the context of a marriage which was coming to a difficult end, was also central to this personal and theoretical transition. I had come to the conclusion that I had to attempt to construct in an urban environment an academic center which was dedicated to the study of black leadership, social theory, politics and historical development, linking these critical ideas to a general rethinking and re-examination of the future of black America. Combining scholarship with social transformation in a manner paralleling Du Bois's Atlanta University project a century earlier, this new institute would bring together African-American intellectuals with progressive representatives from various sectors of the black community to explore the changing meaning of race. The result of this effort, Columbia University's Institute for Research in African-American Studies, continues to grow and develop.

Several individuals at the Institute were helpful in the development and completion of this book. Daria Oliver, my executive assistant, helped to process day-to-day office decisions and thus provided the time and space essential for me to write many of these essays. Cheri McLeod-Pearcey, the Institute's secretary, was primarily responsible for retyping, proofreading and editing the entire manuscript. Doctoral student and research assistant Johanna Fernandez read the original version of each essay, suggesting critical editorial revisions and changes, and helping to reorganize the sequence of essays. It was through my productive discussions with Johanna that the central themes for this collection took shape, which are reflected especially in the Introduction, "The Prism of Race," and the final chapter, "History and Black Consciousness."

But my greatest debt of gratitude is owed to Leith Mullings, Professor of Anthropology at the Graduate School of the City University of New York. After relocating to New York City, my transition was made easier by the unexpected development of this intellectual partnership. It was through our numerous conversations that I came to understand the centrality of culture and ideology to the construction and dynamics of politics and power. Leith was primarily responsible for the theoretical and conceptual insights which form the theses of several chapters. She has a passionate commitment to social justice, which informs her approach to intellectual work. She has an astute ability to describe what is really at the center of a group's or community's social reality, making connections between culture, political economy and the dynamics of the social structure. A woman of great intellect and rare beauty, I have learned far more from her than I can ever express in words.

Thirty years ago, civil-rights activists marched across the Edmund Pettus Bridge in Selma, Alabama, challenging racists and state troopers led by Governor George Wallace. A generation ago, the challenge of desegregation was being waged in the stark, unambiguous context of black and white. Today, as these words are being written, the politics of race has been radically transformed, often within an Aesopian language in which both victims and predators are obscured, half-hidden or inverted; affirmative action and minority set-aside programs are publicly attacked as policies of "reverse discrimination"; the televised trial of former football superstar O.J. Simpson continues to fascinate millions of Americans, with its burlesque mixture of interracial sex, double homicide, spousal abuse and police misconduct; welfare programs are under new scrutiny, with calls for mandatory work by AFDC recipients, and demands to outlaw support to unwed mothers under the age of eighteen; and new restrictions are being pushed on nonwhite immigrants, from the denial of access to public medical services to the imposition of "English Only" language requirements. "Race" continues to be central to American politics, but its definition, utilization and

social construction are being radically transformed. We can develop an
effective strategy and theory of social change appropriate to the cultural
and social terrain of America only if we recognize how ideas about race
are constantly being redefined, while still serving a fundamental role
within the hierarchies of class and state power to manage dissent and
to divide the oppressed.

As Lani Guinier recently observed in the aftermath of a series of
Supreme Court decisions that undermined both affirmative action and
majority black legislative districts, a "leadership vacuum" exists within
national political institutions. Guinier stated: "Nature abhors a vacuum,
and into that vacuum may move the most extreme voice on each side....
We are heading to some kind of social conflagration." Looking back
on the end of the twentieth century from the distant future, we will
reflect that the Los Angeles civil unrest of 1992 was not a social product
of the policies and racial divisions expressed during the 1960s, but a
harbinger of things yet to come. Our political vision must go beyond
the confrontations and narrow boundaries of what black and white has
meant, and, for many Americans, still continues to mean: racial-identity
politics essentially serve to reinforce conservative solutions to poverty,
employment and social problems. As black Americans, we cannot be
expected to forget the harsh lessons of our own history, the unique
character and meaning of our struggle for democracy, and the central
role of our labor power in building this nation. But we must also take
the lead in creating a new democratic movement which has the capacity
to reach and to inspire a majority of Americans, who are also the real
victims of inequality.

Manning Marable
New York, 6 July 1995

PREFACE TO THE
SECOND EDITION

Now in the past the American Negro has had instructive experience in the choosing of group leaders, founding thus a peculiar dynasty which in the light of present conditions is worthwhile studying. When sticks and stones form the sole environment of a people, their attitude is largely one of determined opposition to and conquest of natural forces. But when to earth and brute is added an environment of men and ideas, then the attitude of the imprisoned group may take three main forms – a feeling of revolt and revenge; an attempt to adjust all thought and action to the will of the greater group; or, finally, a determined effort at self-realization and self-development despite environing opinion. The influence of all of these attitudes at various times can be traced in the history of the American Negro, and in the evolution of his successive leaders.

W.E.B. Du Bois, 1903[1]

The fundamental impulse behind all major African-American social movements throughout US history has been the quest for freedom. During much of the long nightmare of human bondage, lasting nearly 250 years, freedom had a clear and unambiguous meaning: the shattering of shackles, the elimination of whips and chains, the reuniting of black families who had been divided and sold apart, the ownership of farms and private property by blacks, and the personal and collective feelings of safety and integrity that are guaranteed by state power and constitutional authority. Deeply embedded within these notions of black freedom, moreover, were two strategic concepts implying collective action to maximize black civic capacity. The stronger of these was the struggle for equality. Supported primarily but not solely by the African-American middle class, the diverse social movements that championed the cause of equality generally called for the outlawing of racial segregation laws,

xix

the granting of blacks' voting rights, and the guarantee of civil liberties and constitutional rights. A second concept, drawing upon greater working-class support, can be described as the social movement for collective self-determination. Many blacks perceived themselves as an oppressed national minority group, or even a nation, with a distinctive history, culture, tradition and political history. As such, they had the right to determine for themselves what kinds of political arrangements should define blacks' relationships to the US nation-state. In everyday political terms, African-American activists who favored this perspective have called themselves "black nationalists" since the nineteenth century. Tactically, black nationalist-oriented social movements have encouraged the development of black-owned enterprises, the cultivation of a black business class, the initiation of political, cultural and commercial contacts with Africa, the Caribbean and other regions of the African Diaspora, and the construction of African-centered cultural rituals and identities that reinforce an oppositional politics to the US nation-state.

There have also been historical periods when the levels of political and economic oppression against African-Americans have been so over-whelming that black leaders have emerged who promoted acquiescence and accommodation to white supremacy. The outstanding example was black educator Booker T. Washington, founder of Tuskegee Institute in Alabama, and the architect of the notorious "Atlanta Compromise" of 1895, in which blacks surrendered their civil rights, the elective franchise and racial integration in return for segregated black consumer markets, black agricultural development, vocational schools and black-owned institutions.[2] Washington aggressively opposed black participation in trade unions and rejected coalitions between working-class blacks and whites. Politically he supported white conservatives – Republicans like Theodore Roosevelt and William Howard Taft at the federal level, and conservative Democrats locally in the Deep South. From 1895 to his death in 1915, Washington deployed his influence through a network of hundreds of political operatives, government appointees, newspaper editors, and black entrepreneurs, called the "Tuskegee Machine," that favored accomodationist politics. Washington's hegemony in African-American politics was challenged by liberal and radical blacks, most powerfully by W.E.B. Du Bois and the National Association for the Advancement of Colored People (NAACP). Undoubtedly Du Bois's characterization of a black leadership that adjusts to the "will of the greater group" was a negative reference to Washington.[3]

After World War I until the beginning of the 1950s, the general trend of national black politics was usually the struggle for equality. There were of course important exceptions, for brief periods of time. One spectacular model of black nationalist activism in the 1920s, for example, was Jamaican black nationalist Marcus Garvey's Universal Negro Improvement Association, which attracted over one million followers.[4] On the left, socialist A. Philip Randolph initiated the Brotherhood of Sleeping Car Porters, the first successful African-American union, in 1925, and led the first March on Washington Movement in 1941. That movement forced President Franklin D. Roosevelt to sign Executive Order 8802 outlawing racial discrimination in hiring policies by war industries with federal government contracts.[5]

In the 1920s and 1930s, the racial domain – the predominant sets of power relations between racialized groups, and the political economy and cultural institutions that manufacture "race" – in the United States and South Africa were strikingly similar. The major events that kept the US racial formation from evolving – or degenerating – toward the terrible destiny of South Africa's 1948 election and the triumph of legal apartheid, were the political victories of the left during the Great Depression, led in part by the US Communist Party, and by the growth of an organized black freedom movement, especially in the US's northeastern and Midwestern states. The successful legal reforms of the modern civil-rights movement, such as the passage by state legislatures of civil-rights enforcement codes and nondiscrimination in employment, began in the 1940s in the North. By the late 1940s, as South Africa descended into fascist barbarism, the racially segregated US was positioned for a different political future.

From the vantage point of contemporary black history, modern African-American leadership emerged with two critical events. The first was a legal victory: the Supreme Court's decision to overturn the legality of racially segregated schools in *Brown* v. *Board of Education* in May 1954. The high court declared in its ruling "that in the field of public education the doctrine of 'separate but equal' has no place." The following year, the Supreme Court urged the adoption of desegregation plans by public schools "with all deliberate speed." The *Brown* victory was the culmination of decades of legal and political efforts by the NAACP and other civil-rights groups. Finally, over ninety years after the Emancipation Proclamation, African-Americans could demand of the federal government their constitutional rights to a quality education for their children, without the barriers and material inequities of "Jim Crow," the US version of racial apartheid.[6]

The second political event occurred in Montgomery, Alabama, on 1 December 1955, when Rosa Parks, a respected seamstress and an NAACP local activist, refused to relinquish her seat to a white man while riding on a segregated public bus. Local black labor union leader E.D. Nixon, outraged by Parks' arrest, urged the African-American community to stage a one-day boycott of Montgomery's buses. A black professional women's group, the Women's Political Council, led by educator Jo Ann Robinson, was largely responsible for the successful citywide mobilization to protest Jim Crow regulations in public transportation. On Monday, 5 December, over 95 per cent of all blacks refused to ride the buses. Six thousand black people gathered that night at Montgomery's Holt Street Baptist Church, and reached a consensus to continue the nonviolent protest indefinitely. A black coalition, the Montgomery Improvement Association, was created, which selected a young, little-known Baptist minister as its chief spokesperson – Dr. Martin Luther King, Jr. For nearly one year the boycott continued, despite hundreds of blacks being fired from their jobs for supporting civil protest. The homes of King and other African-Americans were firebombed; local police harassed and jailed boycott organizers. On 13 November 1956, the Supreme Court ruled in favor of the boycott, and struck down the city's segregation ordinance for public transportation. The modern black freedom movement had achieved a decisive victory, and the struggle had found a new spokesperson in the powerful and charismatic Dr. King.[7]

Historians who study and document the lives of political leaders frequently make the mistake of telling a story from the vantage point of "great" people's (usually men's) lives. King was great, but an unusual number of talented and extraordinary black women and men came into the public arena to push forward measures to outlaw American apartheid: the Reverend Ralph David Abernathy, King's closest friend and confidante; the brilliant tactician Bayard Rustin; Medgar Evers, the leader of Mississippi's NAACP branch, who was brutally assassinated in front of his home and family in 1963; Septima Poinsette Clark, who created the Citizenship Education program, which taught thousands of poor and illiterate blacks to read, write, and to register to vote; Robert Moses, a young mathematics teacher, who went into Mississippi to organize voter education and registration campaigns; the Vanderbilt divinity student James Lawson, who trained civil-rights activists in civil disobedience techniques and taught them the philosophy of nonviolence of Mohandas Gandhi; the courageous Ella Baker, who inspired the creation of the Student Nonviolent Coordinating Committee (SNCC) in 1960; the legendary Fannie Lou Hamer, a former cotton field laborer, who co-founded the Mississippi Freedom Democratic Party, and challenged the whites-only state delegation at the 1964 Democratic National Convention; John Lewis, who in his early twenties participated in "freedom rides" to desegregate bus routes, and led nonviolent "sit-in" demonstrations at whites-only lunch counters; Thurgood Marshall, lead attorney of the NAACP Legal Defense Fund, and later the first black Supreme Court justice; and Gloria Hayes Richardson, who led the desegregation campaign in Cambridge, Maryland.[8]

Many of the veterans of the Black Freedom Movement of the 1950s and the 1960s would later successfully move into electoral politics, such as King lieutenant Andrew Young, who was elected to Congress in 1972, subsequently appointed US Ambassador to the United Nations in 1977, and then was elected mayor of Atlanta, Georgia, in 1981. Another prominent example of public leadership is that of civil-rights attorney Marian Wright Edelman. Born in South Carolina in 1939, Edelman earned her law degree at Yale University, and worked with various civil-rights groups. In 1968, Edelman was the Congressional liaison for King's Poor People's Campaign. Five years later, she founded the Children's Defense Fund, a nonprofit agency that today is the most prominent advocate group advancing the interests of America's children, regardless of their race or ethnicity.[9]

How has the challenge of black leadership changed over the past half century? African-American politics in the twenty-first century is defined by what I call the "paradox of integration." At no previous time in American history have there been more influential and powerful black elected officials and government administrators serving in the nation's capital. Back in 1964, the year that the Civil Rights Act was signed, outlawing racial segregation in public accommodations, the number of blacks in Congress was five; the number of African-American mayors of major US cities, towns and even villages was zero; the combined total of all black officials throughout the United States in 1964 was a paltry 104. This meant, in practical terms, that the voice of black political leadership largely emanated from two sources: firstly, the African-American Christian religious community, such as the Progressive Baptist Convention, and its representatives, including leading civil-rights clergy like Dr. King, Dr. Abernathy, Wyatt T. Walker, Fred Shuttlesworth, and others. Secondly, there was the mainstream Civil Rights community, represented by NAACP national secretary Roy Wilkins, NAACP Legal Defense Fund director Thurgood Marshall, the Congress of Racial Equality leader James Farmer, and Urban League director Whitney Young. These individuals possessed radically different approaches and tactics in their efforts to challenge Jim Crow segregation. But what they all had in common was a strategic understanding about what the fight was about. Few of them entertained any illusions about trying to get themselves elected to Congress. Their goal was the vigorous advocacy of what they perceived to be blacks' interests, and to use a variety of means – nonviolent demonstrations, economic boycotts, lobbying Congress to pass legislation, etc., to pressure white leaders and institutions to make meaningful concessions.

The passage of the 1965 Voting Rights Act, and the widespread exodus of white racist "Dixiecrats" into the Republican Party, led to the rise of the African-American electorate as a central component within the national Democratic Party. The number of African-American officials soared: from about 1,100 in 1970 to 3,600 by 1983. The Congressional Black Caucus was formed in 1971 to bring greater leverage within Congress for African-American demands. In March 1972, thousands of blacks met in Gary, Indiana, to form a "National Black Political Assembly," with the explicit idea of constructing a comprehensive "Black Agenda" of public-policy issues that would guide the actions of newly elected officials across the country. Some of us involved in the Assembly even anticipated the establishment of an all-Black Independent Political Party, where blacks could exercise the greatest possible freedom in negotiating deals between white parties and institutions.[10]

During the 1980s and early 1990s, political events triggered a fundamental transformation in the internal dynamics of black leadership nationally and in the agendas it pursued. First, the rise of a powerfully assertive Congressional Black Caucus largely superseded the political influence of the NAACP and other civil-rights organizations as the chief formulators of national black public policy. Second, the dramatic electoral campaigns of Harold Washington, running successfully to be Chicago's mayor in 1983 and 1987, combined with the Reverend Jesse Jackson's Rainbow Coalition presidential campaigns of 1984 and 1988, illustrated that blacks (then exercised by President Ronald Reagan's conservative agendas) could use electoral politics as a vehicle for mobilizing masses of people of different races and classes behind a black progressive agenda. Jackson did not win the Democratic presidential nomination, but his dramatic success in garnering over seven million popular votes in 1988, and in winning numerous primary elections and caucus states, proved that a black or Latino presidential candidate could under the right set of circumstances, win the Democratic Party's presidential nomination. Although Jackson was himself a Christian minister, his electoral campaigns shifted the focus of black politics away from the black church and civil-rights groups finally into the secular electoral arena.[11] In the quarter century following the civil-rights marches of Birmingham, Selma, and Memphis, black politics had been redefined from economic boycotts, street demonstrations, the establishment of Freedom Schools, Septima Clark's Citizenship Academies, and from Black Power-inspired automobile workers creating their own revolutionary union movements in Detroit, to electoral participation within the system.

But the Jackson presidential campaigns also revealed the deep reservoir of resistance by millions of whites to black leadership at a national level. A state-by-state review of Jackson's 1988 Democratic caucus and primary results, for example, illustrated that in states where the total population of minorities was relatively low, whites were less resistant to voting for a black candidate for president. In Vermont, where African-Americans constituted less than one per cent of all voters statewide, Jackson received 35 per cent of the Democratic caucus vote. However, in Ohio, where African-Americans made up 14 per cent of the state's electorate, 17 per cent of white voters backed Jackson. In New Jersey, where blacks accounted for 20 per cent of all Democratic voters, only 13 per cent of whites voted for Jackson. It became clear to many African-Americans that the black electorate was increasingly trapped in a paradox of empowerment: despite the reality that blacks controlled mayoral offices in major cities and represented at least 20 per cent of the national Democratic Party's electorate, they lacked effective allies to dictate new directions for national public policy, or to elect a black president. This stark recognition formed the basis of the April 21–23, 1989 African-American Leadership Summit attracting 1200 delegates. Despite successfully attracting a range of public officials and traditional civil-rights bureaucrats – including NAACP director Benjamin Hooks, National Urban League director John Jacobs, Coretta Scott King, and Jackson – most delegates under age forty left dispirited and frustrated by the absence of a coherent plan of action. The refusal by middle-class integrationist leaders to dialogue with Nation of Islam leader Louis Farrakhan also generated confusion.[12]

The chaos of the 1989 New Orleans political convention and the subsequent collapse of Jackson's Rainbow Coalition as a viable national formation, created a devastating social and political vacuum within the civic culture of black America. Young people, heavily influenced by the hip-hop music, art and culture of the period, nostalgically turned the black nationalist martyr Malcolm X into their generation's political icon. Prominent black philosopher Cornel West pessimistically specu-lated about the nihilism rampant among younger African-Americans; prominent African-American Studies scholar Henry Louis Gates, Jr., criticized black anti-Semitism.[13] The Los Angeles racial uprising of April–May, 1992, highlighted the continuing economic disparities suf-fered by the urban minority underclass, yet even despite Bill Clinton's presidential victory later that year, little meaningful change occurred. Indeed, Clinton's greatest legacies towards the African-American popula-tion – the 1995 Crime Act and the 1996 Welfare Act – devastated the lives of millions of poor people. Between 1989 and 2001, the number of Americans living behind bars more than doubled, from one to two million. Under Clinton alone, the prison population soared by 700,000 in only eight years; nearly one-half of those inmates were black.[14]

It was this uncertain political environment of urban rioting and uncertainty among African-American political elites that inspired my 1995 book, *Beyond Black and White: Transforming African-American Politics.*[15] Superficially, *Beyond Black and White* was a critique of the major events and controversies that defined African-American politics between 1990 and 1994. But the book's larger purpose was a theoretical and strategic intervention: to propose a different approach for the construction of African-American social movements and the organization of black leadership and politics. First, I argued that the old ideological boundaries that had defined most African-American political debates since the middle of the nineteenth century, and especially the conflicts between black nationalists and integrationists, were no longer relevant to the bulk of the black community. The black elite had become increasingly disconnected through its growing class privileges and affluence from the terrible problems and day-to-day survival struggles of the black working poor, the unemployed and former prisoners. What was urgently required was the fostering of an unprecedented, independent coalition of blacks, Latinos, Asian Americans, other racialized minorities, workers, and poor people, to create demands on the government and the political party system for meaningful social change. To accomplish this, a new, inclusive political language had to be constructed that spoke in a meaningful way to nonblacks. African-Americans at local levels would have to learn to become comfortable with Latino coalitions and leadership, for example. Going "beyond black and white" also meant that African-American leadership would have to create a style of political expression and language that no longer was framed primarily by the culture of the Black Church. A progressive, non-race-based politics appeared to be the best hope for advancing the objectives of black social movements for the twenty-first century.

In retrospect, *Beyond Black and White* correctly anticipated several important themes that did define the subsequent evolution of African-American politics over the next fifteen years. As the ethnic demographics of the United States changed radically after the 1990s, Hispanics surpassed blacks as the nation's largest ethnic minority group. Census projections indicated that by 2042, racial and ethnic minorities collectively would become larger than non-Hispanic whites among US voters. Equally importantly, in the 1990s and early twenty-first century, there was a major liberalization of white racial attitudes towards black culture and leadership, in which the historic animus and resistance many whites displayed toward blacks was significantly reduced. The cultural contexts for multiracial, multiclass coalition politics in many cities and even at some statewide levels had become much more viable. These factors all anticipated the inevitable rise and breakout of a leader of African descent like a Barack Obama.

But *Beyond Black and White* was overly optimistic and strategically in error in its treatment of social class as a factor in the development of social protest movements. Despite my criticisms of the black elite's comprador tendencies, its support for gentrification, and its crass manipulation of racial rhetoric to occasionally mobilize blacks against their real material interests, I overestimated the weight of historic racial solidarity and black identity as positive forces in shaping new black protests. Groups such as the NAACP and the Congressional Black Caucus, for existence, stood silent for years as criminal justice laws were made draconian, with the imposition of mandatory minimum sentencing laws on felons that created extremely long prison terms for first-time minority offenders. By 2005, roughly one-third of all black men in Mississippi had lost the right to vote for life, due to felony convictions, yet this reality failed to mobilize a new national voting rights campaign among the African-American middle class. The massive disenfranchisement of hundreds of thousands of black and low-income voters that effectively gave the presidency to the loser, conservative Republican George W. Bush, should have sparked widespread demonstrations by civil-rights groups and black elected officials across the country; with the exception of civic protests in Florida, and a symbolic protest by the Congressional Black Caucus on the floor of the House of Representatives at the formal election of Bush, national African-American resistance was largely fragmented and disorganized.[16]

The publication of *Beyond Black and White* was followed on my part by a political intervention: the launching of a national left network of black American activists, the Black Radical Congress. The Congress was started by five political intellectuals with very different histories and political affiliations, responding, in part, to the Million Man March of October 1995, and the necessity for the black left to offer a viable political alternative to the patriarchal, homophobic, black nationalist politics of Louis Farrakhan.[17] It was challenging to create the political contexts to nurture trust and cooperation between black lesbian and gay activists, feminists, revolutionary nationalists, Communists, trade unionists, independent Marxists and others. Nevertheless, the sense of political crisis was so strong that most activists put aside their differences, and for several years collaborated effectively on a series of progressive local and national projects that were designed to build black civic capacity and resistance. Although the BRC was nominally a "black organization," it rejected narrow identity-based politics; Latinos, Arab-Americans, whites and others frequently attended meetings, rallies and educational forums sponsored by the group. My major involvement in the formation was my four-year role as chairperson of the United New York BRC chapter. We made valuable contributions to local black progressive struggles during this period, focusing on police brutality cases, opposing plans by the mayoral administration of Rudolph Giuliani to privatize public schools, calling for reforms in criminal justice laws, the defending of prisoners' rights, and after 9/11, opposing the Iraq War and US global militarism.

One critical weakness of the Black Radical Congress was that despite its spirited, community-based activism, and its visionary politics as represented by the group's Freedom Agenda – inspired by South Africa's anti-apartheid Freedom Charter, the Black Panther Party's Ten Point Program, and the black feminist Combahee River Collective Statement – its internal practices and ways of conducting business were excessively sectarian.[18] What was required was not an all-black network, but a more flexible, multiracial/ethnic and ideologically more pluralistic formation that reflected especially the cultural vibrancy of the hip-hop generation of urban youth. Second, the BRC never resolved the internal tension within many socialist-oriented organizations worldwide between cadre-style, ideologically rigid orientations versus a more open, democratic and pluralistic praxis. I recall one black revolutionary nationalist in the BRC bragging that "no NAACP member" would be tolerated in his BRC local. When I heard about the comment, I knew we were in trouble. Despite my serious criticisms of the NAACP, the formation still remained the most important civil-rights group, with over a half million dues-paying members. Preaching to the converted was not my idea of effective political organizing. There was a failure of creative, independent thinking, and a reluctance to learn from the resistance and creativity from hip-hop activists who had no connections with the old feuds and ideological debates between Marxists and nationalists a generation earlier. Instead of a BRC, what should have been constructed was a "neo-Rainbow Coalition," a revised, improved and independent, mass formation based on the model of Jesse Jackson's Rainbow Coalition of the 1980s. Proposed by BRC co-founder and labor activist Bill Fletcher and actor Danny Glover, a neo-Rainbow Coalition in existence in 2007–2008 would have had a powerful and progressive impact on the Barack Obama electoral mobilization.[19]

In the wake of 9/11 and the Bush administration's repression, the decline in black militancy and social protest coincided with the sudden rise of a new generation of African-American leaders – as lawyers, businessmen, civic administrators and corporate executives – who began to transform black civil society. They successfully contested for offices in municipal, state and federal politics in campaigns that were disconnected from social protests of any kind. Instead of appealing overtly to blacks on the basis of shared racial solidarity, they deemphasized the discourse of race. In public policy, the new leaders stressed the common ground shared among groups regardless of race, class, gender and religion. Michael White, the African-American mayor of Cleveland in the 1990s, was in many ways the archetype for the "post-black" elected officials – a black mayor who was far more comfortable discussing tax abatements and corporate incentives for big business investment in his city than leading a public street protest against police brutality. As the bourgeoisification of African-American politicians became more prominent, I argued for a neo-Fanonist strategy for black resistance. In *The Great Wells of Democracy: The Meaning of Race in American Life* (2002), I suggested that the so-called "Talented Tenth," the privileged social strata within black America, had lost the capacity to provide meaningful, progressive leadership for the black masses: "The Talented Tenth of its own accord, will not and cannot break its partnerships with multinational capital unless it is pressured from below by those social forces that have experienced the greatest economic and political marginalization."[20] The new leadership for democratic renewal would have to come from working-class and low-income women involved in neighborhood associations and networks, from former prisoners, inmates and their families who were fighting against the prison industrial complex, from liberal religious activists inside faith-based institutions, and from the hip-hop artistic community. All of these constituencies were necessary to spark a more meaningful national conversation about racism, a racial dialogue far more radical than that pursued by former President Clinton in 1997–1998 that collapsed beneath his own personal scandals and political contradictions.

What emerged instead, given the vacuum on the Left, was the Barack Obama mobilization, a movement led by an African-American but with a multiracial, multiclass electoral constituency. Obama ran a race-neutral, post-black campaign that rarely made references to the central American dilemma of race. The Obama campaign generated tremendous enthusiasm and involvement among African-Americans, most of whom perceived Obama as their own racial representative, a black presidential candidate who would advance their collective interests if elected. Based on Obama's liberal Democratic public policy orientation, the programs he intends to implement will indeed have a beneficial impact on racialized minorities and the poor. He embodies the hopes and aspirations of millions of black people who vividly recall the terrible assassinations and imprisonments of our leaders and the harassment and destruction of black political organizations over several centuries. But Obama will only assume that progressive role if African-Americans and the most oppressed pressure his administration from the left to implement his own political rhetoric. Franklin D. Roosevelt and the New Deal would not have existed without the pressure of the Communist Party, A. Philip Randolph, and the masses of working people. Similarly, Obama must be pressured relentlessly to carry out his own policy agenda, because those to his right will push the administration aggressively to adopt conservative positions.

So what is to be done from the left, in the United States? The basis of a new democratic, multiethnic and multiclass social protest movement must be the radical reimagining of the American city. A livable, sustainable urban space is central to the future of the planet. And demographically, in the United States, that necessary political mobilization must effectively organize people who speak different languages, and who have recently emigrated primarily from the Caribbean, Latin America, Asia and Africa into US cities. According to the US Census Bureau's American Communities Survey in 2005–2007, for the first time in US history, people of African descent, Latinos, Asian Americans and other racialized groups account for more than half of the populations of the country's largest cities. Even in small towns and many rural areas the non-Hispanic population is declining, as the proportions of Latinos and Asians increase.[21] Since writing *Beyond Black and White*, the ethnic changes that have occurred in New York City alone have been stunning. In a city of 8.2 million, between 2000 and 2008, an estimated 81,000 immigrants settled from the Dominican Republic. Chinese immigration was a close second, amounting to 77,000, with Mexican immigration at 69,000 people. The surge of Latino immigration, especially from the Dominican Republic and Mexico, made the Bronx's combined Latino population 51 per cent of that borough's total residents. Simultaneously, due to gentrification, parts of the city that historically have been identified with African-American culture are being remade. Harlem is the best example of this, where between 2000 and 2008, the white residential population has tripled. In the same years, whites' medium housing incomes in Harlem rose 52 per cent.[22] All of these changes demand an urban political agenda that promotes green technologies, small-scale business activities, inexpensive mass transportation, accessible public health institutions, and quality public education. None of these reforms are race-based, or can be achieved by mobilizing identity-based political constituencies by themselves. We must go "beyond black and white."

Manning Marable, 10 December 2008

Notes

1. W.E.B. Du Bois, *The Souls of Black Folk* (Oxford 2007), pp. 22–3.
2. Washington's "Atlanta Compromise," called the "Atlanta Exposition Address," was delivered on 18 September 1895, in Atlanta, Georgia, and reprinted in Booker T. Washington, *Up From Slavery: An Autobiography* (New York 1900). Also see Louis R. Harlan, *Booker T. Washington: The Making of a Black Leader, 1856–1901* (New York 1972); and Kevin Gaines, *Uplifting the Race: Black Leadership, Politics, and Culture in the 20th Century* (Chapel Hill 1996).
3. Du Bois, *The Souls of Black Folk*, p. 23.
4. There is a massive scholarly literature on Garvey and Garveyism. The preeminent interpreter of Garvey is Robert Hill, whose *Marcus Garvey and the Universal Negro Improvement Association Papers* volumes (Berkeley 1983 to present) are essential. Also see Randall K. Burkett, *Garveyism as a Religious Movement* (Metchen, NJ 1978); Theodore Vincent, *Black Power and the Garvey Movement* (Berkeley 1971); and Amy Jacques Garvey, *Garvey and Garveyism* (Kingston, Jamaica 1963).
5. See Jervis Anderson, *A. Philip Randolph: A Biographical Portrait* (New York 1973); and William Harris, *Keeping the Faith: A. Philip Randolph, Milton P. Webster, and the Brotherhood of Sleeping Car Porters, 1925–1937* (Urbana 1977).
6. See Mark V. Tushnet, *Making Civil Rights Law: Thurgood Marshall and the Supreme Court, 1936–1961* (New York 1994); and Juan Williams, *Thurgood Marshall: American Revolutionary* (New York 1998).
7. See Martin Luther King, Jr., *Stride Toward Freedom: The Montgomery Story* (New York 1958); and Jo Ann Robinson, *The Montgomery Bus Boycott and the Women Who Started It: The Memoir of Jo Ann Gibson Robinson*, David J. Garrow (ed.) (Knoxville 1987).
8. See Manning Marable, *Race, Reform and Rebellion: The Second Reconstruction and Beyond in Black America, 1945–2006* (Jackson 2007); David L. Lewis, *King: A Critical Biography* (New York 1970); Taylor Branch, *Parting the Waters: America in the King Years, 1954–1963* (New York 1988); and David Garrow, *Bearing the Cross: Martin Luther King and the Southern Christian Leadership Conference* (New York 1988).
9. Marable, *Race, Reform and Rebellion*, p. 165.
10. See Marable, *Race, Reform and Rebellion*, pp. 130–31; *The National Black Political Agenda* (Washington, D.C. 1972); and Komozi Woodard, *A Nation Within a Nation: Amiri Baraka (LeRoi Jones) and Black Power Politics* (Chapel Hill 1999).
11. On Jesse Jackson, see Adolph Reed, *The Jesse Jackson Phenomenon: The Crisis of Purpose in Afro-American Politics* (New Haven 1986); Sheila D. Collins,

The Rainbow Challenge (New York 1986); and Marshall Frady, *Jesse: The Life and Pilgrimage of Jesse Jackson* (New York 1996).

12. Manning Marable, *The Great Wells of Democracy: The Meaning of Race in American Life* (New York 2002), pp. 95–7.

13. See Cornel West, *Race Matters* (Boston 1993); Henry Louis Gates, Jr., "Black Demagogues and Pseudo-Scholars," *New York Times* (20 July 1992); and Henry Louis Gates, Jr., *Loose Cannons: Notes on the Culture Wars* (New York 1991).

14. See Manning Marable, Keesha Middlemass, and Ian Steinberg, eds., *Racializing Justice, Disenfranchising Lives: The Racism, Criminal Justice and Law Reader* (New York 2007).

15. Manning Marable, *Beyond Black and White: Transforming African-American Politics* (London 1995).

16. Jill Zuckman, "Black Caucus Can't Block the Final Tally," *Chicago Tribune* (7 January 2001); and Chinta Strasberg, "Congressional Black Caucus Bolts Bush's Election Vote," *Chicago Defender* (8 January 2001).

17. See Manning Marable, "After the March," *New Statesman* (27 October 1995), pp. 14–18; and Marable, *The Great Wells of Democracy*, pp. 104–10.

18. "The Freedom Agenda" of the Black Radical Congress, 1998, in Manning Marable and Leith Mullings, eds., *Let Nobody Turn Us Around: Voices of Resistance, Reform, and Renewal; An African-American Anthology* (Lanham, MD 2000), pp. 627–33.

19. See Danny Glover and Bill Fletcher, Jr., "The Case for a Neo-Rainbow Electoral Strategy," *Souls* 7: 2 (Spring 2005), pp. 51–62.

20. Marable, *The Great Wells of Democracy*, p. 192.

21. Sam Roberts, "In Biggest US Cities, Minorities Are at 50%," *New York Times* (9 December 2008).

22. Sam Roberts, "City Growing More Diverse, Census Finds," *New York Times* (9 December 2008).

INTRODUCTION

THE PRISM OF RACE

Black and white. As long as I can remember, the fundamentally defining feature of my life, and the lives of my family, was the stark reality of race. Angular and unforgiving, race was so much more than the background for what occurred or the context for our relationships. It was the social gravity which set into motion our expectations and emotions, our language and dreams. Race seemed far more powerful than distinctions between people based in language, nationality, religion or income. Race seemed granite-like, fixed and permanent, as the center of the social universe. The reality of racial discrimination constantly fed the pessimism and doubts that we as black people felt about the apparent natural order of the world, the inherent unfairness of it all, as well as limiting our hopes for a better life somewhere in the distant future.

I am a child of Middle America. I was born in Dayton, Ohio, on 13 May 1950, at the height of McCarthyism and on the eve of the Korean conflict. One of the few rituals I remember about the anti-Communist hysteria sweeping the nation in the fifties were the obligatory exercises we performed in elementary school, "ducking and covering" ourselves beneath small wooden desks in our classroom to shield ourselves from the fallout and blast of a nuclear explosion. Most of what I now recall of growing up in south-central Ohio had little to do with nuclear war or communism, only the omnipresent reality of race.

In the 1950s, Dayton was a predominantly blue-collar, working-class town, situated on the banks of the Great Miami River. Neighborhoods were divided to some extent by class. Oakwood was the well-to-do, WASP-ish community, filled with the corporate executives and professionals who ran the city's enterprises. Dayton View on the northwest side was becoming increasingly Jewish. Kettering and Centerville were unpretentiously middle class, conservative and Republican. But beneath the divisions of income, religion and political affiliation seemed to be the broad polarization rooted in race. There appeared to be two parallel racial universes which cohabited the same city, each with its own set of religious institutions, cultural activities, social centers, clubs, political organizations and schools. African-Americans generally resided west of the Great Miami River. The central core of the ghetto was located along the corridors of West Third and West Fifth Street. With the great migration of southern blacks to Dayton immediately following World War II, the African-American population became much more dense, and began to spread west, out to the city's furthest boundaries.

The black community existed largely in its own world, within the logic of institutions it had created to sustain itself. We were taught to be proud of our history and literature. Every day, on the way to Edison Elementary School, I would feel a surge of pride as we drove past the home of celebrated African-American poet Paul Lawrence Dunbar. My parents, James and June Marable, were school teachers, a solidly middle-class profession by the standards of the status-conscious Negro elite. During the fifties, my father taught at predominately black Dunbar and Roosevelt high schools during the day; after school was dismissed, he worked as a laborer in the second shift at Dayton tire factory. Although my father had a principal's certificate and a Master's degree, which qualified him to be appointed as a principal, he was constantly passed over by white administrators because of his fiercely independent spirit and self-initiative. Frustrated, my father eventually went into business for himself, borrowing the money to build a private nursery and daycare center for black children on the city's West Side.

Because of my parent's education and jobs, we were part of Dayton's Negro middle class. Our family attorney, James McGee, was elected the city's first black mayor after the successes and reforms in the wake of the civil-rights movement. Most of my parents' friends were physicians, dentists, lawyers, school teachers, entrepreneurs and professionals of various types. Despite their pretensions, most middle-class Negroes were barely two or three paychecks from poverty. Many of the businesses that sold consumer goods to blacks, which were located on West Third Street, were white-owned. Our own business sector consisted chiefly of funeral parlors, beauty salons, auto repair shops and small restaurants.

The college-educated Negro middle class had begun purchasing comfortable, spacious homes clustered high on the ridge which over-looked the West Side, not far from the mostly German farm families who lived in Jefferson Township. Poorer black families lived closer to the factories and foundries, near the dirt, smoke and industrial stench

I vividly recall even today. Social class and income stratification were not unimportant. There seemed to be striking similarities between the houses and the manner in which working and poor people were dressed on "our" side of town and in "their" working-class neighborhoods. But color was the greatest denominator of all.

On Gettysburg Avenue there were a group of small rental properties and boarding houses which were within walking distance of the Veteran's Administration Hospital on the far West Side. In the front windows of most of these buildings were small cardboard signs, reading simply "No Colored." Blacks legally could not be denied entrance into the hotels or best restaurants downtown, but they were certainly not welcomed. White taxicab drivers often avoided picking up black passengers at the train station. Very few blacks were on the local police force. Black children weren't permitted to use the public swimming pool on Germantown Pike. In most aspects of public and private life, whites acted toward African-Americans as "superiors," and usually expected to be treated deferentially. There were exceptions, certainly. At my elementary school, there were white students who were friendly. There were white teachers who displayed kindness and sincerity towards their black students. But there was always an unbridgeable distance separating us. No white students with whom I attended school ever asked to come to my home. Although my parents taught in the Dayton Public School system, most white teachers and administrators maintained a strictly professional rather than personal relationship towards them. Whites were omnipresent in our lives, frequently as authority figures: politicians, police officers, bank-loan officers, school administrators, tax auditors, grocery-store managers. Race existed as a kind of prism through which we understood and saw the world, distorting and coloring everything before us.

Despite these experiences and numerous examples of discrimination, Dayton, Ohio was never the Deep South. Although the largest department stores downtown rarely employed Negroes, I recall that black customers were usually treated with courtesy. Whites were enrolled in every school I attended. Occasionally, whites attended our black church. Public institutions were largely desegregated. The color line was at its worst where it converged with the boundaries of class inequality. Blacks were treated most differently, for example, when it was also clear that they lacked money or material resources. Conversely, middle-class African-Americans certainly experienced prejudicial behavior by whites, but often encountered a less virulent form of hatred than their sisters and brothers who were poor. The recognition of class mobility and higher education gave a small number of blacks a buffer status from the worst forms of discrimination at a day-to-day level. But despite this relative privilege, we never forgot that we were black.

Every summer, we had the opportunity to encounter a far more racially charged society. At the end of the school year, my family packed our 1957 Chevrolet and traveled south, through Cincinnati and Nashville, along highways and narrow, two-lane country roads. Often at nights we were forced to sleep in the cramped confines of the automobile, because we could find no motel which permitted black people to stay overnight. We would stop along the highway to purchase gasoline, never knowing in advance whether we would be allowed to use the gas station's toilet facilities. If we were stopped for any reason by a highway patrol officer, we had to be prepared for some kind of verbal, racist abuse, and we had absolutely no recourse or appeal against his behavior or actions. Finally, we would arrive at my father's family home, Tuskegee, Alabama, where the sense of racial hostility and discrimination against African-Americans was the central theme of local life. I knew that Tuskegee then was in the midst of a major legal struggle initiated by blacks to outlaw the political gerrymandering of the city that had in effect disfranchised African-Americans. We were taught that any open protest or violation of the norms of Jim Crow segregation was to court retaliation and retribution, personally and collectively. We learned that whites, with few exceptions, saw us as subhuman, without the rights to economic development, political expression and participation, and public accommodation which whites accepted and took for granted for themselves.

It was in Tuskegee, during my long visits to Alabama's Black Belt as a child, that many of my basic impressions concerning the relative permanence and inflexibility of race were formed. Part of that consciousness was shaped by the experiences and stories of my father. James Marable was the grandson of slaves, and the second son of thirteen children. His father, Manning Marable, had owned and operated a small sawmill, cutting pulpwood for farm households. Along with other black rural families, they experienced the prism of race in hundreds of different ways, which formed the basic framework of their existence. From being denied the right to vote to being confined to unequal, segregated schools; from being harassed and intimidated by local white police officers to being forced to lower one's eyes when being directly addressed by a white man, "race" was ingrained in the smallest aspects of Southern daily life.

My father rarely talked at length about growing up black in the Deep South. But occasionally, and especially when we were visiting his large, extended family in Tuskegee, he would reflect about his own history, and recall the hostility and rudeness of whites toward himself, his family and his people. He was trying to prepare me for what I would surely experience. One of my father's stories I remember best occurred on a cold, early winter day in 1946. World War II had ended only months before, and millions of young people were going home. My father had served as a master sergeant in a segregated unit in the US Army Air Corps. Arriving in the Anniston, Alabama bus station, he had to transfer to another local bus to make the final forty-mile trek to his family's home outside Wedowee, Alabama.

My father was wearing his army uniform, proudly displaying his medals. Quietly he purchased his ticket and stood patiently in line to enter the small bus. When my father finally reached the bus driver, the white man was staring intensely at him. With an ugly frown, the driver took a step back. "Nigger," he spat at my father, "you look like you're going to give somebody some trouble. You had better wait here for the next bus." My father was immediately confused and angry. "As a soldier, you always felt sort of proud," my dad recalls. This white bus driver's remarks "hit me like a ton of bricks. Here I am, going home, and I'd been away from the South for four years. I wasn't being aggressive."

Dad turned around and saw that he was standing in front of three whites, who had purchased tickets after him. James Marable had forgotten, or had probably repressed, a central rule in the public etiquette of Jim Crow segregation. Black people had to be constantly vigilant not to offend whites in any way. My father was supposed to have stepped out of line immediately, permitting the white patrons to move ahead of him. My father felt a burning sense of rage, which he could barely contain. "You get there some other way, nigger," the driver repeated with a laugh. The bus door shut in my father's face. The bus pulled away into the distance.

There was no other bus going to Wedowee that afternoon. My father wandered from the station into the street, feeling "really disgusted." Nothing he had accomplished in the previous four years, the sacrifices he had made for his country, seemed to matter. The rhetoric of democracy and freedom which had been popularized in the war against fascism rang hollow and empty. Although he eventually obtained a ride home by hitchhiking on the highway, my father never forgot the bitterness and hatred in the bus driver's words. Years later, he still felt his resentment and rage of that winter afternoon in Alabama. "When you go against the grain of racism," he warned me, "you pay for it, one way or another."

For both my father and myself, as well as for millions of black people for many generations, the living content of race was simultaneously and continuously created from within and imposed from without. That is, "race" is always an expression of how black people have defined themselves against the system of oppression, as well as a repressive structure of power and privilege which perpetuates an unequal status for African-Americans within a stratified social order. As an identity, race becomes a way of perceiving ourselves within a group. To be black in what seems to be a bipolar racial universe gives one instantly a set of coordinates within space and time, a sense of geographical location along an endless boundary of color. Blackness as a function of the racial superstructure also gives meaning to collective memory; it allows us to place ourselves within a context of racial resistance, within the many struggles for human dignity, for our families and for material resources. This consciousness of racial pride and community awareness gave hope and strength to my grandfather and father; it was also the prime motivation for the Edward Wilmot Blydens, Marcus Garveys and Fannie Lou Hamers throughout black history. In this way, the prism of race structures the community of the imagination, setting parameters for real activity and collective possibility.

But blackness in a racially stratified society is always simultaneously the "negation of whiteness." To be white is not a sign of culture, or a statement of biology or genetics: it is essentially a power relationship, a statement of authority, a social construct which is perpetuated by systems of privilege, the consolidation of property and status. There is no genius behind the idea of whiteness, only an empty husk filled with a mountain of lies about superiority and a series of crimes against "nonwhite" people. To be black in a white-dominated social order, for instance, means that one's life chances are circumscribed and truncated in a thousand different ways. To be black means that when you go to the bank to borrow money, despite the fact that you have a credit profile identical to your white counterpart, you are nevertheless two or three times more likely to be denied the loan than the white. To be black means that when you are taken to the hospital for emergency health-care treatment, the quality of care you receive will be inadequate and substandard. To be black means that your children will not have the same academic experiences and access to higher learning resources as children in the white suburbs and exclusive urban enclaves. To be black means that your mere physical presence and the reality of your being can trigger surveillance cameras at shops, supermarkets, malls and fine stores everywhere. To be black, male, and to live in central Harlem in the 1990s, for example, means that you will have a life expectancy of forty-nine years of age – less than in Bangladesh. Race constantly represents itself to black people as an apparently unending series of moments of inequality, which constantly challenge us, sapping and draining our physical, mental and moral resources.

Perhaps this is what most white Americans have never fully comprehended about "race": that racism is not just social discrimination, political disfranchisement and acts of extra-legal violence and terror which proliferated under the Jim Crow segregation of my father's South. Nor is racism the so-called "silent discrimination" faced by my generation of African-Americans raised during the civil-rights era, who are still denied access to credit and capital by unfair banking practices, or who encounter the "glass ceiling" inside businesses which limits their job advancement. At its essential core, racism is most keenly felt in its smallest manifestations: the white merchant who drops change on the sales counter, rather than touch the hand of a black person; the white salesperson who follows you into the dressing room when you carry several items of clothing to try on, because he or she suspects that you are trying to steal; the white teacher who deliberately avoids the upraised hand of a Latino student in class, giving white pupils an unspoken yet understood advantage; the white woman who wraps the strap of her purse several times tightly around her arm, just before walking past a black man; the white taxicab drivers who speed rapidly past African-Americans or Latinos, picking up whites on the next block. Each of these incidents, no matter how small, constructs the logic for the prism of race for the oppressed. We witness clear, unambiguous changes of behavior or language by whites toward us in public and private situations, and we code or interpret such changes as "racial." These minor actions reflect a structure of power, privilege and violence which most blacks can never forget.

The grandchildren of James Marable have never encountered Jim Crow segregation. They have never experienced signs reading "white" and "colored." They have never been refused service at lunch counters, access to hotel accommodation, restaurants or amusement parks, or admission to quality schools. They have never experienced the widespread unemployment, police brutality, substandard housing and the lack of educational opportunity which constitute the everyday lives of millions of African-American youth. For my children – eighteen-year-old Malaika, and sixteen-year old twins, Sojourner and Joshua – Martin Luther King, Jr., Medgar Evers, Fannie Lou Hamer and Ella Baker are distant figures from the pages of black history books. Malcolm X is the charismatic image of Denzel Washington from Spike Lee's film, or perhaps the cinematic impression from several recent hip-hop music videos. "We Shall Overcome" is an interesting but somewhat dated melody of the past, not a hopeful and militant anthem projecting an integrated America.

Yet, like my father before them, and like myself, my children are forced to view their world through the racial prism. They complain that their high-school textbooks don't have sufficient information about the activities and events related to African-Americans in the development of American society. In their classrooms, white students who claim to be their friends argue against affirmative action, insisting that the new "victims" of discrimination are overwhelmingly white and male. When Joshua goes to the shopping mall, he is followed and harassed by security guards. If he walks home alone through an affluent white neighborhood. he may be stopped by the police. White children have moved items away from the reach of my son because they have been taught the stereotype that "all blacks steal." Sojourner complains about her white teachers who have been hostile and unsympathetic toward her academic development, or who have given her lower grades for submitting virtually the identical level of work turned in by her white friends. As my daughter Malaika explains: "White people often misjudge you just by the way you look, without getting to know you. This makes me feel angry inside."

A new generation of African-Americans who never personally marched for civil rights or Black Power, who never witnessed the crimes of segregation, feel the same rage expressed by my father half a century ago. When they watch the beating of Rodney King on television or the trial of O.J. Simpson, they instantly comprehend the racism of the Los Angeles police officers involved in each case, and the larger racial implications of both incidents. When they listen to members of Congress complain about "welfare dependency" and "crime," they recognize the racial stereotypes which are lurking just behind the code words. They have come to expect hypocritical behavior from the white "friends" who act cordially towards them at school but refuse to acknowledge or recognize them in another context. Race is a social force which still has real meaning to the generation of my children.

But the problem with the prism of race is that it simultaneously clarifies and distorts social reality. It both illuminates and obscures, creating false dichotomies and distinctions between people where none really exists. The constructive identity of race, the conceptual framework which the oppressed create to interpret their experiences of inequality and discrimination, often clouds the concrete reality of class, and blurs the actual structure of power and privilege. It creates tensions between oppressed groups which share common class interests, but which may have different physical appearances or colors. For example, on the recent debates concerning undocumented immigrants, a narrow racial perspective could convince African-Americans that they should be opposed to the civil rights and employment opportunities of Mexican Americans, Central Americans and other Latino people. We could see Latinos as potential competitors in the labor market rather than as allies in a struggle against corporate capital and conservatives within the political establishment. On affirmative action, a strict racist outlook might view the interests of lower-class and working-class whites as directly conflicting with programs which could increase opportunities for blacks and other people of color. The racial prism creates an illusion that "race" is permanent and finite; but, in reality, "race" is a complex expression of unequal relations which are dynamic and ever-changing. The dialectics of racial thinking pushes black people toward the logic of "us" versus "them," rather than a formulation which cuts across the perceived boundaries of color.

This observation is not a criticism of the world-views of my father, my children, or myself as I grew up in Dayton, Ohio. It is only common sense that most African-Americans perceive and interpret the basic struggle for equality and empowerment in distinctly racial terms. This perspective does speak to our experiences and social reality, but only to a portion of what that reality truly is. The parallel universes of race do not stand still. What was "black" and "white" in Booker T. Washington's Tuskegee of 1895 was not identical to categories of color and race in New Orleans a century ago; both are distinctly different from how we perceive and define race in the USA a generation after legal segregation. There is always a distance between our consciousness and the movement of social forces, between perception and historical reality. "Blackness" must inevitably be redefined in material terms and ideologically, as millions of black and Hispanic people from the Caribbean, Africa and Latin America immigrate into the USA, assimilating within hundreds of urban centers and thousands of neighborhoods with other people of color. As languages, religions, cultural traditions and kinship networks among blacks in the USA become increasingly diverse and complex, our consciousness and our ideas of historical struggle against the leviathan of race also shift and move in new directions. This does not mean that "race" has declined in significance; it does mean that what we mean by "race" and how "race" is utilized as a means of dividing the oppressed are once again being transformed in many crucial respects.

At the beginning of the African presence in the Americas, an African-American culture, nationality and consciousness was constructed. Against great odds, inside the oppressive context of slavery and later racial segregation, the racial identity and perspective of resistance, a community empowered by imagination, was developed against the weight of institutional racism. That historic leap of collective self-definition and inner faith must once again occur, now inside the very different environment of mature capitalism. We must begin the process of redefining blackness in a manner which not only interprets but also transforms our world.

PART I

THE POLITICS OF RACE AND CLASS

.

ONE

BLACK AMERICA
IN SEARCH OF ITSELF

Conspiracy theories always tell you something, if not historical truth. They abound at present in the black community. Many believe that AIDS, which has struck disproportionately among people of color, is some kind of white-supremacist medical conspiracy. Many African-Americans remember the perverse medical experiment conducted by the federal government in Tuskegee, Alabama; for forty years beginning in the 1930s, 399 black men suffering from advanced stages of syphilis went untreated in this program.

In 1988, an aide to then-Mayor Eugene Sawyer of Chicago had to leave office after declaring that "Jewish doctors were infecting black babies with AIDS." In September 1990, *Essence*, a popular black women's magazine, featured an essay headed "AIDS: Is It Genocide?" When a *New York Times*/CBS News poll in August asked African-American and white residents of New York City whether AIDS "was deliberately created in a laboratory in order to infect black people," the differences in racial perceptions were striking. Only 1 per cent of all whites polled thought this statement was true, and another 4 per cent thought it could possibly be true. On the other hand, 10 per cent of all blacks accepted the statement as valid, with another 19 per cent agreeing it could be true.

When blacks were queried about the reasons for the accessibility of crack cocaine and other illegal drugs within the African-American community, the results were similar. One-fourth of all blacks questioned agreed that the federal government "deliberately makes sure that drugs are easily available in poor black neighborhoods." An additional 35 per cent thought that this assertion was "possibly true."

When millions of people are absolutely convinced that they are being systematically destroyed, whether by an onslaught of drugs, criminal violence, or medical mayhem, any nascent racial polemicist can gather a constituency around himself and acquire a degree of legitimacy. Blacks ask themselves: Why is it so much easier to obtain crack cocaine and heroin in our neighborhoods than it is to buy fresh milk, eggs, and bread? Why are so many white educators so hostile toward the introduction of African-American Studies and multicultural requirements within the core curricula of public schools and colleges?

Dr Leonard Jeffries, Jr., chair of the African-American Studies Department at New York's City College, started a firestorm in July at the Empire State Black Arts and Cultural Festival in Albany by delivering a public address that included several blatantly anti-Semitic remarks. Jeffries, whose speech was broadcast over an Albany cable-TV station, asserted that blacks were the victims of a "conspiracy planned and plotted out of Hollywood" by "people called Greenberg and Weisberg and Trigliani." He claimed that "Russian Jewry had a particular control" over the film industry and that "their financial partners, the Mafia, put together a financial system of destruction of black people." He criticized those who opposed the inclusion of African and African-American history and culture in the state's high-school curricula. He particularly condemned Diane Ravitch, assistant secretary of the Department of Education, a Bush appointee, as "a Texas Jew" and "a sophisticated debonair racist."

The response from the white political establishment, the media, and educational officials was swift. Many Democratic and Republican politicians, including New York governor Mario Cuomo, denounced Jeffries. Democratic senator Daniel Patrick Moynihan deplored the speech, noting that "conspiracy theories about 'rich Jews' are nothing new. What is new is for such things to be said by a professor at City College."

Moynihan insisted that Jeffries "ought to resign" and that if he was not removed the trustees of City College should resign. Harold Jacobs, a member of the City University board of trustees, declared that if Jeffries was "teaching bigotry in his classes, instead of African-American studies, that's consumer fraud being paid for by the state." The college's alumni association also demanded that Jeffries be fired as department head. Jewish leaders were particularly outraged. Michael Riff, local leader of the Anti-Defamation League of B'nai B'rith, said the controversial speech had "the tinge of classical anti-Semitism: to create a web of conspiracy by suggestion, innuendo and half-truths."

The Jeffries controversy generated more heat than light, because no dialogue exists between Jeffries' critics and defenders over the real issues that divide them. Neo-conservative writer Julius Lester, who is both black and Jewish, reviewed a videotape of the speech and found that the media "misrepresented some [of] Jeffries' statements." The speech certainly contained anti-Semitic assertions, but it had little to do with Jews or black–Jewish relations.

Many black scholars suspect that the condemnation of Jeffries is actually a smokescreen for a more general assault on multicultural perspectives in education. Jeffries served as principal consultant to a state-wide curriculum-review committee for public schools in New York, which recently mandated a multicultural requirement. James De Jongh, chair of City College's faculty senate, admits that those who opposed the adoption of multiculturalism "are finding it easier to attack Jeffries on an obscure speech than to confront the curriculum."

Most black educators and leaders disagree with the expressions of anti-Semitism in Jeffries' public address, but they quietly question what the dispute is really about. It is difficult to take sympathetically the appeals of Moynihan, who a quarter of a century ago authored the notorious "black matriarchy" thesis, asserting that the black family is dysfunctional because it lacks patriarchal character. Blacks suspect that calls for the firing of the tenured professor, which in any case would be extremely difficult to accomplish legally, have little to do with anti-Semitism as such, and more with white hostility to affirmative action and the educational and political agenda of the black freedom struggle.

This perception hardened into certainty when another City College professor, Michael Levin, was vindicated by a federal court. Levin had made public statements declaring that African-Americans overall are "significantly less intelligent" than whites, and college administrators had established a committee in 1990 to investigate allegedly racist state-ments in his classroom lectures. The ruling said that the administrators were in error in ordering the investigation, and also erred in failing to discipline protesters who disrupted Levin's classes. Levin's statement following this decision targeted Jeffries as well as all other African-Americans who favor greater ethnic diversity within education. "This whole subject of Black Studies," Levin said, "is a made-up subject that shouldn't be at any college anywhere"; Jeffries and others teaching it only offer students "introductory resentment, intermediate resentment, and advanced resentment."

Many Jewish and white leaders were virtually silent about the Levin case and his legal victory, a fact not lost on black activists and scholars who reject both anti-Semitism and black chauvinism. The absence of media focus on Levin also seemed to reinforce the conspiracy thesis of Jeffries and other African-American nationalists. In this context, it is not difficult for some to ignore the objectionable and even odious elements of Jeffries' address and to insist that the attack against the black educator was racially and politically motivated.

Conversely, many Jewish leaders are upset about the apparent silence of blacks over the anti-Semitic smears of Jeffries. The Anti-Defamation League has recorded a 50 per cent increase in anti-Jewish harassment and violence on university campuses since the mid 1980s. Jewish stereotypes seem to be making a comeback in Hollywood: witness the Jewish-American princesses in *White Palace*, or the untrustworthy Jewish characters in *Bonfire of the Vanities*, *Class Action*, and *Regarding Henry*. "Kill-the-Jew" computer games are now being sold in Europe. From the perspective of many Jews, the Jeffries incident is the most threatening of a series of events – including Jesse Jackson's "Hymie" smear of 1984 and the rising popularity of Black Muslim Louis Farrakhan among young inner-city African-Americans. If mainstream black leaders fail to condemn vigorously a demagogue such as Jeffries, some reasoned, it must be because they quietly embrace anti-Semitism themselves.

Simmering racial grievances finally boiled over into violence this summer in Brooklyn's Crown Heights neighborhood, where Hasidic Jews and blacks dwell in uneasy coexistence. On an evening in August, Yosef Lifsh, a Hasidic Jew, lost control of his automobile and smashed into several black children on the sidewalk, killing one seven-year-old boy. Witnesses reported to police that Lifsh had run a red light and was speeding; others spread the rumor that he had been drinking, and that ambulance attendants assisted him before they saw to the black children. Outraged, hundreds of young black people took to the streets, hurling rocks and bottles at police and Jewish residents. Apparently in retaliation, a group of twenty or so young blacks surrounded and killed a visiting Hasidic scholar from Australia, reportedly chanting, "Kill the Jew!"

To most blacks, both deaths were criminal homicides. To New York's Jewish community and most whites, the deaths were entirely different – the first a regrettable accident, the second a deliberate murder provoked by vicious black anti-Semitism. Many black activists were troubled when attorney Barry Slotnick, who had represented subway murderer Bernhard Goetz, stepped forward as a spokesman for Lifsh. When Brooklyn district attorney Charles Hynes announced that no charges of criminally negligent homicide would be filed against Lifsh, the grief and resentment of thousands of blacks turned into deep outrage.

Instead of trying to understand the origins of black anger and violence in poverty and a sense of powerlessness, many whites leaped to the conclusion that anti-Semitism and violent sentiments have acquired a mass base of support among blacks. Few white commentators were more vehement on this baseless theme than the *New York Times* column. former editor) A.M. Rosenthal. Blaming the recent upsurge of ra. violence on "the black political marauders who goad mobs into the streets against Jews," Rosenthal asserted that their "strategy is to blow up all political and emotional bridges between blacks and nonblacks." Rosenthal linked the Crown Heights incident with the earlier Jeffries controversy, which he characterized as "weirdo speeches of a Jew-baiting professor on the public payroll and by bigotry's apologists, supporters, and conveyor belts in the black press and radio." Rosenthal offered his own self-fulfilling prophecy and warning to New York mayor David Dinkins and other black elected officials, wondering aloud whether "any black will be chosen mayor for a long time" because "so many nonblacks have been antagonized."

Nowhere in Rosenthal's diatribe did he recognize that many black politicians, and especially Dinkins, have taken a principled, public stance against anti-Semitism throughout their careers. To blame them for the actions of a small minority is, in effect, a concession to the worst form of racist bigotry. Nowhere in this none-too-subtle linkage of Dinkins with Jeffries did Rosenthal acknowledge that Jewish political behavior in recent years has grown more conservative ideologically – and has specifically opposed blacks' interests on such issues as affirmative action.

The sources of genuine tension between Jews and African-Americans cannot be so simplistically attributed to the actions of anti-Semites within the black community. From the vantage point of blacks, bridges with the liberal Jewish political establishment were torched by other, far more significant events – the gradual shift in political sympathies from Israel to the Palestinians among America's black leadership and activists, the geographical flight of many Jews from the problems of the inner city to the affluent suburbs, the general Jewish hostility toward the Rainbow Coalition and Jesse Jackson.

Rosenthal's feeble appeals to interracial dialogue were disingenuous precisely because he and others like him in the white media and political institutions refuse to face the legitimate differences which have separated African-Americans and Jewish interests in the old civil-rights coalition of a generation ago. This failure is particularly difficult for blacks such as myself, who still feel a special sympathy and political kinship with the historical struggles of Jewish people and a keen opposition to all forms of anti-Semitism. Why is this happening? Why are these disturbing and disruptive social trends emerging *now*? What is their long-term significance for black politics and culture?

Deeply embedded within the fabric of black American culture is the messianic myth of Moses and the ordeal of the ancient Hebrews.

Old Testament and reshaped to fit the contours of
ons and slave society, it became a beacon of hope and
e generations of African-Americans yearning to be
d daughters of slaves saw themselves as the children
essed by a wicked and unjust power. But a gifted,
would arise from their ranks, a figure who would
embrace both the spiritual strivings and secular ambitions of his people. This black Messiah would lead his flock across the barren wilderness to the blessed banks of the River Jordan and into the golden horizon of the Promised Land.

A century ago, the Messiah's mantle rested on the shoulders of Frederick Douglass, the great abolitionist orator. A generation ago, the weight of moral leadership was borne by Martin Luther King, Jr. King recognized that his powerful presence in the lives of African-Americans was due not solely to his sonorous rhetoric, but rather to his kinship to the messianic cultural tradition of salvation and liberation. "The Bible tells the thrilling story of how Moses stood in Pharaoh's court centuries ago and cried, 'Let my people go,' King once declared. In identical fashion, he thought, the Southern desegregation movement demonstrated that "oppressed people cannot remain oppressed forever. The yearning for freedom eventually manifests itself." If the Hebrews found the courage to follow their convictions, African-Americans could do no less. But nearly a quarter of a century after the assassination of the civil-rights movement's Messiah, and after a decade of pain imposed by the Reagan–Bush conservative reaction, African-American political culture has taken a new and very disturbing direction.

The desegregation struggle had been informed by a political ideology of what I call "liberal integrationism." Its central tenets were the eradication of all legal barriers to blacks' gaining full access to civil society, economic exchange, and political institutions; an increase in the numbers of African-Americans representing their race in both real and symbolic positions of authority within the state; a strategic alliance with liberal whites, especially the national leaders of the Democratic Party, after the Great Depression. Several generations of African-American leaders were nurtured in this secular creed and unthinkingly accepted its implications. Blacks as a group could be guaranteed continued upward mobility within the system if the rules of the game were liberalized, as larger numbers of African-American elites were elevated into the federal judiciary, legislatures, and corporate board rooms.

Brown v. *Board of Education*, the 1954 Supreme Court decision outlawing segregated schools, had created the legal framework for a democratic, "color-blind" society within the structures of liberal capitalism. This liberal faith in the system was employed to justify all the sacrifices and hardships by the children of bondage. In destroying legal Jim Crow segregation, African-Americans had escaped the clutches of a dictatorial Pharaoh; their experiences since the 1960s seemed to represent a sojourn in the wilderness. But all along this bitter path, the image of a promised land of racial equality and economic democracy seemed to loom just ahead. Then the myth veered off course. The messianic figure of the former slaves was murdered several days into the difficult journey through the wilderness. None of his closest comrades and lieutenants seemed able to bear the dual burden of political emancipator and moral guide. The creed of liberal integrationism and color-blind institutions, once affirmed with Talmudic certainty, began to be perceived as strangely anachronistic and even counterproductive.

The new generation of the oppressed, born and raised not under the old Jim Crow order but in the sterility of a political wilderness, inevitably challenged the faith of their fathers and mothers. Speaking for this lost generation, Anthony Parker, writing recently in *Sojourners*, questions the future identity of African-Americans as a people. "Unlike the generation of blacks who reached maturity before and during the early 1970s," Parker writes, "my generation has no memory of credible black leaders, such as Malcolm X or Martin Luther King, Jr. But the practice of integration created the illusion of equality with the wider culture, effectively wresting control of the black freedom movement by holding it hostage to Federal good will and weakening or destroying those institutions that influenced blacks' world view."

One major factor in the demise of black consciousness and identity was the materialism and greed inherent in the existing American political economy and secular society. By asking to be integrated into the existing structures of society, rather than demanding the basic transformation of the system, blacks became hostage to their own ideological demands. "Inoculated with secular values emphasizing the individual instead of the community," Parker observes, "young blacks rarely recognize each other as brothers and sisters, or as comrades in the struggle. We're now competitors, relating to each other out of fear and mistrust."

Other black intellectuals have also sensed that African-Americans have reached a secular epiphany, a moment of self-realization and uncertainty, when the old beliefs can no longer be sustained but the new insights into social reality cannot be fully comprehended. One of black America's most perceptive critics, Professor Cornel West of Harvard University's Afro-American Studies Department, describes the contemporary spiritual crisis as a "profound sense of psychological depression, personal worthlessness, and social despair ... widespread in black America." West recognizes that "black people have always been in America's wilderness in search of a promised land. Yet many black folk now reside in a jungle with a cutthroat morality devoid of any faith in deliverance or hope for freedom."

On a national level, the mantle of leadership apparently passed to Jesse Jackson. Despite Jackson's incredible and largely unanticipated electoral success in the 1984 and 1988 Democratic presidential primaries, however, the promise of his Rainbow Coalition was never fulfilled. From its inception, the idea of the Rainbow brought together two contradictory currents: liberals who sought to make the Democrats a "social-democratic style" party, and leftists who wanted to launch a progressive third party from the bankrupt ruins of the New Deal and the Great Society.

In the wake of George Bush's election, Jackson tactically shifted to the right, siding with the liberals. He demanded and obtained the authority for his national board to veto all important political and legislative initiatives by local Rainbow chapters. In effect, the democratic grassroots leadership responsible for much of Jackson's electoral success was muzzled from above. Efforts to build a more structured membership organization with a formal dues system and a regular newspaper were silenced. The results were inevitable. In 1989–90, the Rainbow Coalition's political action committee raised $549,973; in the first six months of 1991, the PAC raised only $33,657. Jackson's refusal to run for mayor of Washington DC reinforced perceptions that the "country preacher" has no stomach for the nitty-gritty work of actual governing.

Valuable state-wide leaders of the Rainbow defected in droves. In Louisiana, progressives bolted when Jackson ordered that all local initiatives be approved by his hand-picked lieutenant. Dissidents promptly created an independent group. In Vermont, New Jersey, and Pennsylvania, core Jackson activists are building their own local alliances. Elsewhere, there is a bitter sense of frustration and betrayal. As Kevin Gray, the 1988 campaign coordinator for Jackson in South Carolina, declared, "The movement is not supposed to be a continual photo opportunity for Jesse Jackson for President, but that's what it's been."

Unlike King, Jackson never succeeded in balancing his own personal ambitions with the broader goals of the democratic protest movement that thrust him into public prominence. But the real dilemma confronting Jackson and other African-American leaders is the limitations of their own political ideology, which is liberal integrationism. Jackson never believed that the American political system could be transformed from without, via the challenge of a third party or even a quasi-independent movement like the Rainbow Coalition. He retains a deep faith that the

Democratic Party can be transformed from within into an effective vehicle for the aspirations of the poor, the working class, women, racial minorities, and others experiencing discrimination and social injustices. But what is strikingly clear after the crushing of Jimmy Carter, Walter Mondale, and Michael Dukakis in successive presidential elections, and the ideological capitulation of mainstream Democratic Party politics to many of the central tenets of Reaganism, is that American liberalism is bankrupt. The belief in an internal, progressive realignment of the Democrats is belief in a hopeless illusion never to be achieved or realized so long as the party has some utility to corporate capitalism. It is the activists themselves who become transformed.

The crisis within black political culture is also intensified by the fraying of the bonds among virtually all African-Americans. Once, segregation led to a sense of shared suffering and group identity. An artificial yet powerful wall of race had been built around our community, giving us simultaneously a sense of oppression and a collective will to resist. On Sunday mornings in the churches of my childhood, I can distinctly recall the people who came together for the ritual of spirit and unbowed faith – the school teacher and his family in the pew ahead, the automobile mechanics and sanitation workers beside me, the doctors and dentists in the pews behind. A wide range of vocations was represented, because segregation forced every class to cooperate with each other. A black lawyer looked to the black community for his or her clients. A black entrepreneur, anxiously opening a new business, had to depend on the faithful patronage of black consumers from her or his neighborhood, civic club, fraternity, and school.

Now, in the post-civil-rights era of the 1980s and 1990s, even the definition of the term "black community" is up for debate. The net result of affirmative action and civil-rights initiatives was to expand the potential base of the African-American middle class, which was located primarily outside the neighborhood confines of the old ghetto. By 1989, one out of seven African-American families had incomes exceeding $50,000 annually, compared to less than $22,000 for the average black household. Black college-educated married couples currently earn 93 per cent of the family income of comparable white couples.

But the general experience of the black working-class, low-income people, and families on welfare – the overwhelming majority of African-Americans – is one of steady deterioration. According to *African Americans in the 1990s*, a recent report by the Population Reference Bureau, the average annual income of African-Americans is only 56 per cent that of white income, significantly less than the 63 per cent ratio in 1975. Black female-headed households average less than $9,600 annually.

Stark differences in patterns of home ownership, income, and education indicate that there are "two separate worlds inhabited by poor and middle-class black children," the report says. This strongly implies that "the African-American population will become more polarized as these children mature."

Many white liberals take such statistics to mean that the source of the material and social inequities which separate the races – institutional racism – no longer exists, or at least, in the words of influential black sociologist William Julius Wilson, has "declined in significance." A shift in liberal government policy from race-based remedies to economic, class-based programs is therefore required. From the vantage point of liberal Democrats, this would solve the perception problem among millions of white males that the party's social agenda is being held hostage to the interests of blacks. Class-based programs would eliminate the argument of "reverse discrimination" because all benefits would, theoretically, be distributed in a color-blind manner.

Stuart Eizenstat, domestic policy adviser in the Carter administration, defends this thesis. So does Richard Cohen, liberal columnist for the *Washington Post*. "If economic need, not race," Cohen writes, "became the basis for what we now call affirmative action, most Americans would not object. Whites, too, could be helped.... After all, poor is poor, although a disproportionate number of them are black." When minority community leaders read such statements, most cannot help but feel a sense of outrage and repudiation. The overwhelming majority of federal programs *were* based on income, not race. Poor whites shared substantial benefits from the initiatives of the Great Society. Currently, more than one-third of all students enrolled in the Upward Bound program, designed to prepare low-income students for college, are white. One-third of the children who attend the pre-school Head Start program are white. The majority of people living in public housing or who receive public assistance, are white.

The basis of affirmative action is the recognition that, within this society, there is systemic discrimination grounded in race and gender. Despite the passage of the Civil Rights Act of 1964, outlawing discrimination in public accommodations, race is a powerful factor in determining the actual conditions of life for any person of color, regardless of income and education. My children stand a much greater likelihood of being harassed or arrested by the police, for example, than the children of my white colleagues at the university, solely because they are black. Through practical experience, African-Americans of every social class recognize this reality. To argue that a shift in affirmative action policies from race to class will benefit them seems, at best, a gross distortion.

At worst, it is taken as yet one more piece of evidence that liberal integrationism has failed as a political strategy. Black intellectuals and politicians are increasingly convinced that white liberals have turned their backs against us; both parties have repudiated our very presence at any serious debate on public policy.

Many millions of African-Americans believe that most whites live a racial double life, that whites follow a hypocritical racial etiquette in the presence of blacks which disappears whenever they are among themselves. This is the basic premiss of the recent film *True Identity*, which features a black man who dons white make-up. He discovers that whites interact very differently with each other than they do with minorities. Abundant evidence supports this thesis. Earlier this year, a study of the American Bar Association published in *Harvard Law Review* indicated that car dealers charge African-Americans and women higher prices than white males. Male and female researchers, black and white, presented themselves as middle-class car shoppers at ninety car dealerships in the Chicago metropolitan area. They used identical negotiation styles and bartered for identical automobiles. The car dealers' offers to the consumers followed a pattern of gender and racial inequity. The final offer to white men averaged $11,352, and to white women, $11,504; to black men, $11,783, and to black women, $12,237.

Affirmative action is a particular sticking point in the 1990s. In the workplace, most white males behave publicly in a race-neutral manner. Virtually no one openly calls African-American employees or supervisors "niggers." But millions of whites harbor deep resentment against black and Latino co-workers, whom they believe have been unfairly advanced and receive excessively high wages because of affirmative action and equal-opportunity programs. In one recent survey of several thousand white male corporate employees, only 10 per cent expressed the opinion that "women were getting too much help" through affirmative action. But 50 per cent stated that blacks and Hispanics unfairly gained "too much" of an advantage by affirmative action. Conversely, 55 per cent of all Latino and black employees polled stated that "too little was being done for them" through corporate affirmative action efforts. Many whites perceive the presence of people of color in their workplace as a "zero-sum game"; the additional appointment of any single black person means that the potential job pool for whites has decreased. Instead of fighting to increase the size of the economic pie, many whites now want to take away the small slice served up to Latinos and blacks through affirmative action initiatives.

Such programs forced police departments to hire and promote thousands of minorities and women, partially in an attempt to respond to the changing urban demographics of race. But many whites have never reconciled themselves to these policy changes, which they perceive as an erosion of "standards" and professionalism." This anger and alienation is projected onto black and Latino citizens, who are generally assumed to be guilty in any confrontation. For example, a public commission reviewing the Los Angeles Police Department reported several months ago that it found more than seven hundred racist, homophobic, and sexist remarks made by officers on the department's car-communications system over the previous eighteen months. Typical of the statements were: "Sounds like monkey-slapping time" and "I would love to drive down Slauson [a street in a black neighborhood] with a flame thrower. We would have a barbecue."

But the last evidence of the pervasiveness of white privilege is found in daily life. When inner-city blacks and Latinos return from work in the downtown district, they watch the striking changes in the allocation of commuter buses and trains, which shuttle upper-class whites in comfort to their suburban enclaves. They feel their worthlessness in white eyes as they wait for graffiti-scarred, filthy trains in stations pervaded with the stench of urine. They feel the anger held in check, seeing crack-cocaine merchants operate on their street corners as police cars casually drive by, doing nothing. Everything in daily life tells them that, to those with power and wealth within the system, African-American life, property, beliefs, and aspirations mean nothing.

In the ruins of ideology, bereft of messianic leadership, the African-American community reaches a moment of painful introspection. When hope of the New Jerusalem and the possibility of political liberation dies, part of the spirit dies as well. Locked in an urban abyss of poverty, drugs, and black-against-black violence, the working class and dispossessed increasingly retreat into themselves, psychologically and culturally. If the creed of liberal integrationism no longer makes sense, and if our leaders have failed to deliver us from the wilderness, then we must turn within our own group, reviving the images and symbols for survival. The temptation is to seek refuge in the narrow alleys of racial chauvinism and political parochialism.

Black America still sees itself as the litmus test of the viability and reality of American democracy. Indeed, the African-American striving for freedom and human rights embodies the country's best examples of sacrifice and struggle for the realization of democracy's highest ideals. A century ago, black scholar W.E.B. Du Bois suggested that the "concrete test of the underlying principles of the great republic is the Negro Problem." Yet this historic burden of race cannot be comprehended solely in legislative initiative or in the struggles for voting rights. This sojourn through the wilderness is a quest for full self-consciousness, a "spiritual striving of the freedmen's sons" which represents a "travail of souls whose burden is almost beyond the measure of their strength, but who bear it in the name of a historic race, in the name of this land of their fathers' fathers, and in the name of human opportunity."

It is precisely here, at the juncture of faith and political ambition, of spirit and struggle, that the black freedom movement must revive itself, casting aside the parochial chains of chauvinism and isolation. We can find value in our culture and heritage without fostering negative stereotypes and myths about other ethnic groups. We can express ourselves ethnically without resorting to the false discourse and rationales of race. In the process, we will discover that the proverbial promised land of full equality and economic equity can be achieved, but only in concert with other groups of the oppressed – especially Latinos, Native Americans, Arab Americans, Asian/Pacific Americans, and the unemployed and economically and socially disadvantaged of all ethnic backgrounds.

Ethnic pride and group awareness constitute a beginning stage, not an end in itself, for a richer understanding of the essential diversity and pluralism that constitute our America. That awareness of diversity must point toward the restructuring of the elaborate systems of ownership and power that perpetuate the unequal status of these ethnic groups and oppressed social classes. This leap of awareness depends on our willingness to define our political, educational, and social goals in a way that is truly majoritarian, that speaks for the commonwealth of the whole society, that realizes a new level of struggle for the black freedom movement.

TWO

RACE AND REALIGNMENT
IN AMERICAN POLITICS

I

The re-election of President Ronald Reagan in 1984 was not a watershed in American electoral history, but it did accelerate deep trends in popular political culture which could produce an authoritarian social order in the very near future. This chapter is an examination of various political currents and social blocs competing for power within the bourgeois state apparatus. Although there is a brief overview of the political dynamics of the Democratic Party primaries, the emergence of the Rainbow Coalition of Jesse Jackson, and the general election, my principal concern here is to examine the increased racial polarization within elements of both the American left and right as part of a broader process of electoral political realignment of the party system. Most Marxists seriously underestimate the presence of racism as an ideological and social factor of major significance in the shape of both American conservative and liberal centrist politics – in the pursuit of US foreign policies, particularly in the Caribbean and Africa, and as an impediment to the development of a mass left alternative to the Democratic and Republican parties. Although class prefigures all social relations, the burden of race is a powerful and omnipresent element that has helped to dictate the directions of contemporary politics.

An explicitly racist aspect of the Reagan agenda manifested itself domestically and internationally. Black workers suffered disproportionately from both unemployment and social-service reductions. In 1983, for example, 19.8 per cent of all white men and 16.7 per cent of all white women were unemployed at some point; for blacks, the figures were 32.2 per cent for men, and 26.1 per cent for women workers.[1]

Between 1980 and 1983, the median black family income dropped 5.3 per cent; an additional 1.3 million blacks became poor, and nearly 36 per cent of all African-Americans lived in poverty in 1983, the highest rate since 1966.[2] The Reagan administration slashed aid to historically black universities and reduced student loans, forcing thousands of black youth out of schools.[3] The US Commission on Civil Rights and Office of Federal Contracts Compliance Programs were transformed into bulwarks for racial and sexual discrimination. In its foreign affairs, the Reagan administration authorized a policy of "constructive engagement" with apartheid South Africa. In 1981 Reagan asked Congress to repeal the Clark amendment prohibiting covert military aid to Angolan terrorists; authorized the US training of South Africa's Coast Guard; and vetoed a UN Security Council resolution condemning South Africa's illegal invasion of Angola. In 1982 the Reagan administration rescinded controls on "non-lethal" exports to apartheid's military and police; voted for a $1.1 billion loan from the International Monetary Fund to South Africa; sent 2,500 electric-shock batons to the South African police; and appointed a pro-apartheid US executive, Herman Nickel, ambassador to Pretoria. The next year, the administration established offices in downtown Johannesburg to promote accelerated US investment in the regime, and granted a license for US firms to service South Africa's Koeberg nuclear power plant.[4] By 1984 about 6,350 US corporations held direct subsidiaries or did some form of business inside the racist regime. US firms supplied 15 per cent of the state's imports, and absorbed 8 per cent of its exports, amounting to $4 billion.[5]

Given the unambiguously racist, sexist, and anti-labor character of the Reagan offensive, oppositional social movements were inevitable. In September 1981 the AFL-CIO broke with tradition to stage a massive "Solidarity" march against the administration. On 12 June 1982 over one million Americans demonstrated in favor of a freeze on the production and deployment of nuclear weapons. Black middle-class formations such as the NAACP and Operation PUSH combined with black nationalist, left and peace forces, holding a march on Washington DC on 27 August 1983 that brought more than 300,000 demonstrators to the capital. Unfortunately, the Democratic Party was, for several reasons, ill-prepared to accommodate the new militancy of women, national minorities and trade unionists. For nearly half a century, the Democrats had controlled Congress, a majority of state legislatures, and most major municipal governments. Unlike the Republicans, the Democratic Party had consciously attempted to bring together a broad spectrum of social forces and classes – trade unions, small farmers, national minorities, eastern financial and industrial capitalists, southern whites, the unemployed. It was a capitalist party, in that its governing ideology of Keynesian economics and Cold War liberalism benefited sectors of the ruling class. But in the absence of a mass labor or social-democratic party, it also functioned as a vehicle for minorities' and workers' interests to be represented, if in a limited manner. This governing coalition was first seriously weakened by democratic social movements of African-Americans in the late 1950s and 1960s, which forced the destruction of legal segregation and increased the number of black elected officials from 100 in 1964 to over 5,000 in 1980. The black freedom movement combined with the anti-Vietnam War movement to contribute to the defection from the party of millions of southern segregationists and conservatives. By the late 1960s, a political backlash against social reforms developed among many white ethnic, blue-collar workers who had long been Democrats. Although the economic recession of 1973–75 and the Watergate scandal temporarily set back the Republicans and contributed to Carter's narrow electoral victory in 1976, the general trend among whites to the right in national political culture continued. This was most evident in an analysis of the racial polarization in presidential elections between 1952 and 1976. During this period, the average level of electoral support for Democratic presidential candidates among blacks was 83.4 per cent, against 43.7 per cent among white voters. The results in 1980 were even more striking: 85 per cent of all blacks and 59 per cent of Hispanics voted for Carter, while only 36 per cent of all white voters supported his re-election. Not since 1948 had a majority of white Americans voted for a Democratic presidential candidate.[6]

The defections of major electoral groups from the Democrats had reduced the party to four overlapping social blocs. The first tendency, which was clearly subordinated within the coalition, was the democratic left: African-Americans, Latinos (except Cuban-Americans), feminists, peace activists, liberal trade unionists, environmentalists, welfare-rights and low-income groups, and ideological liberals. In national electoral politics, they were best represented by the Congressional Black Caucus and a small group of white liberals in the House and Senate. To their right was the rump of the old New Deal coalition, the liberal centrists: the AFL-CIO, white ethnics in urban machines, some consumer-goods industrialists and liberal investment bankers, and Jewish organizations. This tendency's chief representative in national politics was Minnesota senator and former vice president Hubert Humphrey. Following Humphrey's death in 1977, his protégé, Walter Mondale, assumed leadership of this bloc. A third tendency, which exhibited the most independent posture toward partisan politics, comprised what some have called the "professional managerial class" and sectors of the white, salaried middle-income strata. These white "neo-liberals" tended to oppose US militarism abroad and large defense expenditures. But on economic policies, they tended toward fiscal conservatism and a reduction of social-welfare programs. They were critical of nuclear power, and favored federal regulations to protect the environment; but they also opposed "special interests" such as organized labor. This constituency was behind the unsuccessful presidential campaigns of Morris Udall in 1976 and John Anderson in 1980. Its principal spokesman in the 1984 Democratic primaries was Colorado senator Gary Hart, who as early as 1973 had proclaimed that "American liberalism was near bankruptcy."[7] At the extreme right of the party were those moderate-to-conservative southern Democrats who had not yet defected from the party, and a smaller number of midwestern and "sunbelt" governors and legislators who had ties to small regional capitalists, energy interests, and middle-income white constituencies. The most prominent stars of this tendency in the 1970s were Carter, Florida governor Reuben Askew, millionaire Texas senator Lloyd Bentsen, and Ohio senator John Glenn. All of these groups, in varying degrees, opposed the general agenda of the Reagan administration. But only the democratic left, and most specifically the African-American community, mounted a sustained series of social protests against literally every initiative of the Republican president.

In the Democratic presidential primaries of 1984, each of these tendencies was represented by one or more candidates. Conservative Democrats Glenn, Askew, and former segregationist Ernest Hollings, currently senator of South Carolina, were in the race; the "yuppies" and white neo-liberals gravitated to Hart; Mondale drew the early endorsement of the AFL-CIO, and most of the party apparatus. Three candidates split the forces of the democratic left. California senator Alan Cranston, a strong advocate of the peace movement, received support from many freeze candidates and western liberals. Former senator George McGovern drew backing from traditional liberals, some feminists and peace activists. The Reverend Jesse Jackson, president of Operation PUSH and the central political leader within the black community, was the last candidate to announce. The Jackson and Hart campaigns were far more significant than the others, including Mondale's. Jackson's decision to run was made against the advice of most of the black petty-bourgeois leadership, the NAACP and the Urban League, who had already committed themselves to Mondale. Even the Coalition of Black Trade Unionists, which on economic matters was a good deal to the left of the NAACP elite, supported Mondale.

The Jackson campaign's core constituency, which was absolutely vital to its subsequent success, was the Black Church. Nearly 90 per cent of the African-American clergy had endorsed Jackson by the end of 1983. Church leaders and members were active in every aspect of the campaign, from distributing literature to bringing black voters to the polls. The failure of most civil-rights leaders and black elected officials to get involved in the early stages of the effort permitted several thousand black nationalists, Marxists, peace activists, and feminists to gain positions in local and state-wide campaign mobilizations. Thus Jackson, who previously had been an advocate of "black capitalism" and had a history of political opportunism, was influenced by his campaign workers, aides and policy advisers to articulate an essentially "left social-democratic" program. By mid spring the Jackson campaign's foreign and domestic policy positions were clearly to the left of any Democratic candidate for national office in US history. Jackson called for a 20 to 25 per cent reduction in the defense budget; a bilateral nuclear-weapons freeze, with billions of dollars reallocated from defense programs to human needs; the normalization of US relations with Cuba, and an end to American armed intervention in Central America, the Mideast and the Caribbean. Despite limited funds and a virtual absence of television advertising, Jackson received 19 per cent of all total Democratic primary votes, about 80 per cent of all African-Americans' votes. He won primary victories in the District of Columbia, Louisiana, South Carolina, Mississippi and Virginia. Most significantly, Jackson forced the national Democratic leaders to recognize the centrality of the black electorate within the party. The dynamic race by Jackson motivated hundreds of thousands among the nation's poor and minorities to register and to participate in the political process.[8]

Jackson's success among the African-American voters denied Mondale approximately 15 to 17 per cent of the total Democratic primary voters.[9] Hart was thereby able to maintain a credible campaign against Mondale as well. The Colorado Democrat received 36 per cent of the national Democratic vote, winning victories in New England, Florida, California, Ohio and Indiana. But unlike Jackson, who attempted to create a multiracial, progressive coalition on the left, Hart ran simultaneously on the left and right against Mondale. On foreign affairs, Hart was more critical of US military intervention in Central America than Mondale. But on domestic economic matters, Hart had previously opposed the federal loan program to the nearly bankrupt Chrysler corporation on fiscal grounds; he supported a "cost-effective" nuclear arsenal and annual increases of 4 to 5 per cent in military expenditures. Pointedly condemning Mondale as the "candidate of special interests," Hart implied that he would not be subject to the mandates of organized labor. Although he did not receive his party's presidential nomination, Hart's critique was extremely effective, and it established the basis for the Reagan–Bush attack on Mondale during the general election.[10]

On balance, Mondale should have been denied the Democratic nomination in 1984. Despite the endorsements of more than 107 senators and representatives, the AFL-CIO, and the vast majority of Democratic mayors, the Minnesota centrist received only 38.7 per cent of the national primary votes. He received 45 per cent of the labor-union members' votes, 31 per cent from Democratic college graduates, and only 28 per cent of all Democratic voters aged between 18 and 34 years old.[11] But Mondale had several distinct advantages over Jackson and Hart. By the end of May, Mondale had received over $18 million in campaign contributions, against $9 million for Hart and $1.7 million for Jackson. Such spending ratios were roughly similar to the final percentage of delegates each candidate received at the Democratic National Convention in San Francisco: Mondale, 56.8 per cent; Hart 31.1 per cent; and Jackson, 12.1 per cent. A large bloc of convention delegates were directly selected by the party apparatus, virtually guaranteeing Mondale's nomination. In many states, the selection of convention delegates had little to do with the actual primary vote. For example, in Pennsylvania's primary, Jackson received 17 per cent of the state-wide popular vote to Mondale's 45 per cent. On the convention floor, however, Mondale received 117 delegate votes to Jackson's 18.[12] As a "minority" candidate, Mondale should have recognized that he had to make credible, programmatic overtures to both Hart's and Jackson's constituencies in order to build an electoral coalition to defeat the incumbent president. But throughout the long primary season, Mondale learned nothing new; Mondale delegates were in no mood to compromise. Jackson minority platform proposals calling for major reductions in defense expenditures and for placing the party "on record as unconditionally opposed to any first use of nuclear weapons" were soundly defeated. The selection of congress-woman Geraldine Ferraro as the ticket's vice-presidential running mate was a positive concession to the women's movement, although Ferraro's politics were only slightly more progressive than Mondale's, if at all. In general, African-Americans and the liberal-left supporters of Jackson left the convention without receiving even token concessions, beyond the appearance of their candidate on prime-time television for one evening. The only real factor that would later motivate these forces to support Mondale in the general election was the real fear of the ignorant demagogue in the White House.

Given Mondale's forensic ineptitude and dull demeanor, the Republican strategy was all too easy. First, the administration defended Reagan's aggressive foreign policies, including the destabilization of

Nicaragua and the illegal invasion of Grenada, while making new overtures to the Soviet Union for a resumption of arms negotiations. The administration pressured the Federal Reserve System to east the amount of currency in circulation, which helped to extend the economic recovery through the election. The 1983–84 recovery also permitted the president to claim falsely that his program of tax cuts and deregulation for corporations was the key to prosperity. More than in any previous administration, Reaganites followed the lead of Ayn Rand: they sported the word "'Capitalism' ...on [their] foreheads boldly, as a badge of nobility."[13] On domestic social programs, the president hinted at even deeper budget reductions ahead, but solemnly vowed never to diminish social-security benefits to the elderly, a major voting bloc. Like Hart, Reagan rhetorically projected himself "as a candidate of all the people, and Walter Mondale as the weak puppet of 'interest groups' and 'special interests.'" As the "special interests' accused of manipulating Mondale included women, trade unionists, blacks, Hispanics, gays, and environmentalists – that is, 70 to 80 per cent of the population – this was a rather peculiar accusation, and its success demonstrates the extent to which political life has been degraded by right-wing populism. Mondale repeatedly defended himself against such rhetoric, but "too often it was as if no one was listening."[14]

In retrospect, it almost seems that the Democrats deliberately threw the election to Reagan. Two basic themes which could have united nearly all the factions inside the Democratic Party were social "fairness" and "peace." The overwhelming majority of white low- to middle-income families had not been touched by the 1983–84 economic recovery. Millions of white workers were unemployed or underemployed. Yet throughout his campaign, Mondale focused narrowly on the issue of federal budget deficits, and on the necessity to hike income taxes on all families earning more than $25,000 annually. Instead of demanding massive federal initiatives to reduce joblessness and poverty, the Democratic candidate proposed another $29 billion cut in social expenditures in order to diminish the federal deficit. Instead of supporting a halt to the rate of massive defense spending, Mondale called for annual military increases of 3 to 4 per cent over the inflation rate – only slightly less than Reagan's budgetary projections.[15]

Mondale's central fallacy, however, was his erroneous belief that the further to the ideological right his campaign projected its image, the greater was his ability to undercut Reagan's base, especially among white ethnic blue-collar voters and white-collar professionals. The reverse proved to be the case. Mondale probably lost a section of the Hart anti-war constituency by proposing a "military quarantine" against Nicaragua and by attacking Reagan's failure to "retaliate against terrorists." Mondale applauded the invasion of Grenada, reversing his previous position, and he promised that he would even be "tougher" in negotiations with the Soviets than Reagan. African-Americans were outraged that the Democratic candidate was virtually silent on the Reagan administration's détente with apartheid. In short, Mondale took the black vote absolutely for granted, and devoted nearly his entire campaign to courting fractions of the white electorate which historically had voted for Republican presidential candidates.[16]

II

Several striking parallels exist between Reaganism and classical fascism. Most obvious is the truculently anti-communist foreign policy of the present administration. The invasion of Grenada, the deployment of US troops in Lebanon, and the covert war against Nicaragua were all projected as part of an anti-communist offensive. As Sweezy and Magdoff observed in late 1983, such aggression was not "a literal copy of what went on in the 1930s, but, given the different circumstances of the two periods, it was about as close as you could get.... Nothing could have been more reminiscent of Hitler than the Big Lies and phony excuses Reagan came up with to justify the occupation of Grenada."[17] Usually the term "fascism" is employed as a rhetorical device by leftists to condemn the actions of US conservatives or the state, and as such lacks any serious analytical meaning. But let us examine this issue more closely.

If we begin with Dimitrov's definition of fascism as "the open terrorist dictatorship of the most reactionary, most chauvinistic, most imperialist elements of finance capital," the Reagan administration clearly falls short. Since the early 1970s, however, there has been a marked degeneration of bourgeois democratic political culture, characterized in part by the breakdown of the New Deal party system and the hegemony of the far right within the leadership of the Republican party. In recent years, a new element has been added: a popular ideology of extreme national chauvinism, described by the media as the "new patriotism." The Republicans called themselves "America's Party," implying that Democrats were somehow less than patriotic. Congressman Jack Kemp charged that Democrats were "not just soft on communism – they're soft on democracy." United Nations ambassador Jeane Kirkpatrick, resurrecting her Cold War liberal past, placed the anti-communism of Reagan firmly in the political tradition of Harry Truman and Scoop

Jackson, and argued that Mondale had betrayed this heritage. Barry Goldwater, the party's 1964 presidential nominee and "old warrior" of the ultra-right, also told the convention: "And let me remind you, extremism in the defense of liberty is no vice." Nor were the racial dimensions of the convention far to seek. Only 3.1 per cent of the delegates were black.

In the platform adopted by the convention, one half-page specifically mentioned national minority affairs. The only strong statement in the party's manifesto pertaining to blacks was an explicit rejection of racial and gender quotas in hiring policies.[18] Foreign press observers were repulsed by the spectacle. The British *Guardian* correspondent noted:

> There was something distasteful, almost sinister, in the closing scenes. When the President observed that "not one inch of soil has fallen to the Communists since he took office", he provoked the first of a number of demonstrations which may have set the pulse racing of those who remember the Berlin Olympics in 1936. Clean-cut youths in gray slacks, white shirts and red bandannas lifted their arms with salutes reminiscent of fascism, mindlessly chanting "four more years, four more years". They waved the large American flags on wooden poles in a kind of mesmerized unison. This was not the fresh and encouraging patriotism of the Olympic torch as it travelled across the country, but an uglier, more menacing version.[19]

None of this is fully developed fascism. But if a road toward an American form of fascism exists, it will be predicated on the conjunction of several ideological and political factors currently visible. The "new patriotism," like fascism, is a "vehement nationalist ideology." As Togliatti commented, "fascist ideology contains a series of heterogeneous ingredients" that serve to "solder together various factions in the struggle for dictatorship over the working masses and to create a vast movement for this scope." Fascism is a "*romantic* ideology revealing the petty bourgeoisie's effort to make the world, which is moving forward toward socialism, turn back."[20] Also pivotal in both fascist ideology and the "new patriotism" is racism. In *Friendly Fascism*, Bertram Gross observes that racism "invigorated" the political dynamics of classical fascism by serving "as a substitute for class struggle and a justification of any and all brutalities committed by members of the Master Race against 'inferior' beings."[21] Ideologically, there is the need not simply to identify a public scapegoat – Jews in Hitler's Germany, national minorities in the US – but to cultivate sharply divergent racial perceptions and conceived racial interests that reinforce the drive to the right. An August 1984 national survey of the Washington DC-based Joint Center for Political Studies presented a disturbing picture of racial polarization in contemporary American political attitudes. The vast majority of blacks, 82 per cent, disapproved of "Reagan's job performance," compared to only 32 per cent of whites. Few whites described Reagan as being racially "prejudiced," while 72 per cent of all blacks defined him as a racist. In general, the poll found that "blacks and whites assess the state of the nation very differently": 48 per cent of whites but only 14 per cent of blacks were "satisfied with the way things are going in the country"; 38 per cent of all blacks but only 6 per cent of whites "think civil rights is one of the most important issues" in the 1984 presidential campaign; and 40 per cent of all blacks and 15 per cent of whites agree with the statement that "white people want to keep Blacks down."[22]

Classical fascism developed only when the internal contradictions of the society reached a point when "the bourgeoisie [were] compelled to liquidate the democratic forms." To accomplish this end, Togliatti adds, the "mobilization of the petty bourgeoisie" was imperative.[23] In the USA, the "old" right of the late 1950s was composed almost solely of conservative intellectuals, such as Russell Kirk and William F. Buckley, and a small tendency of extreme anti-communists in groups like the John Birch Society. What truly distinguishes the new right from these older formations is its commitment and capacity to build mass movement-style organizations within the American middle classes. The most prominent of these is the Reverend Jerry Falwell's Moral Majority, which has several million evangelical conservative members and supporters. The Moral Majority was instrumental in lobbying against the nuclear freeze-niks, ultralibs and unilateral disarmers." State affiliates of the Moral Majority have also been active in selecting school texts and library books, screening instructors to eliminate "subversives" and homosexuals, and lobbying to introduce evangelical training inside public classrooms. In Alabama, Moral Majority members clashed with school officials over a textbook which "failed to express adequately the merits of capitalism." In North Carolina, members created an "Index Prohibitorium" of all books "unfit for young leaders ... anti-family, anti-God, [and] anti-Bible." One particularly objectionable text was Aldous Huxley's *Brave New World*, which Moral Majoritarians characterized as "continued degradation of youth," adding for good measure that "it would make a nice bonfire."[24]

Nor can this phenomenon be dismissed as a lunatic fringe. In 1980, the Moral Majority spent $2.5 million and registered one million working-class and middle-class Christians on behalf of Reagan. Phyllis Schlafly's Eagle Forum mobilized thousands of middle-class whites to help defeat the ratification of the Equal Rights Amendment. The Conservative Caucus, directed by Howard Phillips, claims a membership of 600,000. Richard Viguerie, the "ideological godfather" of the new right, owns six communications companies, is syndicated in 550 newspapers in a weekly political column, and runs a political commentary show on more than 3,400 radio stations. After Reagan's election in 1980, new formations were created. Viguerie, Phillips, Terry Dolan (chairman of the National Conservative Political Action Committee), and Ron Godwin of the Moral Majority formed the Conservative Populist Tax Coalition (CPTC). The goals of the CPTC are to "attract new constituencies of disaffected Americans including blue collar Democrats and minorities" by advocating a 10 per cent flat federal income-tax rate, and emphasizing themes "on patriotism," a "bootstraps" economy and strong family and traditional values. Millionaire Lew Lehrman, a conservative Republican narrowly defeated by Mario Cuomo in New York's 1982 gubernatorial race, has created the Citizens for America (CFA). The CFA recruits "leaders" from the small business sector to mobilize rightists in congressional races; recently, it has also initiated a campaign to station the National Guard in "high crime areas" of major cities. Both the CPTC and the CFA, like previous fascist groups, "use an appeal to themes stressing the alienation of the 'common man.'" Both groups project Lehrman "as a national leader and a possible successor to Reagan."[25]

In Congress, right-wing Republicans led by Georgia Representative Newt Gingrich established the Conservative Opportunity Society (COS) in 1983, with the express purpose of leading an "intellectual-populist revolution" against the Democrats and "moderate" Republicans. Pivotal members of COS include Representatives Jerry Lewis of California, chair of the House Republican Research Committee; Trent Lott of Mississippi, and Vin Weber of Minnesota.[26] Providing research for these forces are several well-funded centers, chiefly the ultra-right Heritage Foundation, formed by brewer Joseph Coors and Paul Weyrich, head of the Committee for the Survival of a Free Congress. What all of these tendencies have in common, despite their nominal allegiance to the Republican Party, is an absolute contempt for the present two-party system, and a ruthless commitment to building a multi-class, conservative order. For Gingrich, the challenge of the right is to shape "a movement, a party and western civilization" impelled by the "driving force of an ideological vision." Weyrich adds: "We are no longer working to preserve the status quo. We are radicals, working to overturn the present power structure of this country."[27]

The growth of a mass radical right in the 1980s has also permitted the renaissance of even more extreme racist formations, such as the Ku Klux Klan, and the coalition of various racist political factions under more "acceptable" labels. A prime example is the development of the

"Populist Party" in 1983–84. The impetus for the new Populists came from a merger of the old American Independent Party, formed in 1968 around presidential candidate George Wallace, and the Liberty Lobby, whose weekly tabloid *The Spotlight* has a circulation of half a million. The guiding force behind the merger was a notorious racist Willis Carto, founder of the Liberty Lobby. Like Gingrich's COS, Carto has long been critical of US monopoly capitalism, which he defines as "the means of production, money banking, and the political process … controlled by a small group of oligopolist/monopolist capitalists for their personal gain," and which "inevitably degenerates to crisis and Marxism." Carto advocates the development of an authoritarian state apparatus to ensure "the primacy of nation, culture, family, people and race" and to "protect America's racial integrity."[28] Under the Liberty Lobby's leadership, over six hundred delegates from every state attended the founding convention of the Populist Party in Nashville, Tennessee on 19 August 1984. The party's charismatic candidates were selected to appeal to low- to moderate-income whites, farmers, and small businessmen who had not benefited significantly from Reagan's economic policies and who were disaffected from both major parties. For president, the choice was celebrity Bob Richards, an Olympic gold medalist at the 1956 and 1960 games. Best known for his breakfast-cereal commercials, Richards has traveled across the nation for two decades as an "inspirational lecturer" for the Chamber of Commerce and civic clubs. Vice-presidential nominee Maureen Kennedy Salaman is also a dynamic public speaker and self-described "freedom fighter." Her political base is the 100,000-member American Health Federation, which she serves as president. Richards and Salaman project a wholesome, middle-class image – ideal for Carto.[29]

Again, as in classical fascism, the Populist Party's public agenda is eclectic. As the anti-racist journal *The Hammer* comments: "Populist literature takes a four square stance against feminism, women's equality, civil rights for homosexuals, and racial equality.… The Party is extremely right-wing but it is not conservative. It emphasizes free enterprise, but it is not antiunion."[30] In their initial party documents, the Populists denounced "international parasitic capitalism," and called for tariffs to protect Americans' jobs, parity for small family farmers, and federal spending to expand public transportation facilities. They also advocated the repeal of federal income tax, and a non-interventionist foreign policy. But the heart of the Populist program was its demand that "every race" should pursue "its destiny free from interference by another race." Populist members promised to oppose "social programs which would radically modify another race's behavior, [and] demands by one race to subsidize it financially or politically as long as it remains on American soil.... The Populist Party will not permit any racial minority, through control of the media, culture distortion or revolutionary political activity, to divide or factionalize the majority of the society..."[31] With this program, party organizers initiated local clubs in forty-nine states within six months. By mid September 1984, *The Spotlight* announced that the party's major candidates would participate in the ballot under the Populist label in nine states. However, in Alabama, Tennessee, Louisiana and Mississippi, Richards and Salaman obtained ballot access as "Independents"; in Kansas, they were listed as the national candidates of the state's "Conservative Party"; and in California, they were the candidates of the American Independent Party.[32]

The actual "cadre" of the new Populist Party is nothing but a rogue's gallery of racists and anti-Semites like Carto. The first national chairman of the party was Robert Weems. In the late 1970s, Weems was Mississippi chaplain of the "Invisible Empire" Knights of the Ku Klux Klan. Other party leaders have similar histories. Dale Crowley, national party treasurer and 1984 senatorial candidate in Virginia, was a major promoter of the anti-Semitic tract *For Fear of Jews*. The Populist chairman in Wisconsin State, Joseph Birkenstock, is also a state leader of Posse Comitatus, a rural, right-wing vigilante organization. Retired US colonel, Jack Mohr, a member of the Populists' national speakers bureau, is also leader of the paramilitary Citizens' Emergency Defense System, a subgroup of the Christian Patriots' Defense League. Mohr's major contributions to the Populists is his extensive contacts in the extreme-right "Christian identity" network, groups of evangelical whites who teach that "Jews are the children of the devil" and that African-Americans are "pre-Adamic" – that is, "false starts before God achieved perfection and made a white Adam." Kansas Populist leader Keith Shive, who was also nominated for vice president at the Nashville convention, is also leader of the right-wing Farmers' Liberation Army and has connections with Posse Comitatus. Shive's speeches to low-income farm communities throughout the Midwest have blamed Jews "as the source of all the world's ills."

Two prominent North Carolina Populists are state party vice-chairman, A.J. Barker, and chairman Hal Beck. Barker is the leader of the racist National Association for the Advancement of White People; Beck is a member of the policy board of the Liberty Lobby, and has openly called for a coalition between the new party and the KKK. In Kentucky, state party chairman, Jerrold Pope, is also a member of the neo-Nazi National States Rights Party, founded in 1958. The major Klansman besides Weems in the Populist Party is Arkansas leader, Ralph Forbes, who in 1982 was a featured speaker at a Klan rally in Washington DC. As *The Hammer* observes: "the new Populist Party operation, combining the spirit of rural revolt, anti-capitalist rhetoric, and the party's slogan of 'Power to the People' is a cleverly packaged job to help Carto consolidate a much larger constituency of people who would be repelled by an open appeal to Nazism under other circumstances." But the phenomenon of US Populism has rough parallels in Western European politics on the far right: the British National Front, Spain's Fuerzas Nuevas, the National Political Union in Greece, and especially the French National Front led by Jean-Marie Le Pen, which won 11 per cent of the vote in the European Parliament elections in June 1984. Carto's *Spotlight* has praised Le Pen's National Front as "France's Populist Party," and US rightists would like to emulate the French neo-fascists' electoral successes.[33]

I am not suggesting that the Populists have any realistic prospects of becoming a major electoral force. But I am claiming that Reaganism has permitted and encouraged the involvement of blatantly racist and anti-Semitic forces in the electoral arena to an unprecedented degree; that the ideological "glue" in the appeals of these formations to low- to middle-income whites is racism; and that the inevitable social by-product of the ultra-right's mass political mobilization is terrorism and increased violence. Throughout 1984, literally hundreds of incidents of racially motivated random violence erupted across the USA, directly and in-directly provoked by these forces. Klansmen and racist vigilantes had an especially busy year. On 8 April, several hooded and robed Klansmen, passing out leaflets in Cedartown, Georgia, beat an eighteen-year-old black youth with brass knuckles; on 19 June, racists, leaving the message, "KKK: Nigger go home," burned the home of an Indianapolis black woman; on 11 August, a black family residing in a predominantly white neighborhood of Daytona Beach, Florida had a cross burned in their front yard; on 27 August, racist vandals leaving the mark "KKK" attacked a black church in a predominantly white Milwaukee suburb; on 7 October, three racist whites, in an unprovoked public assault, left a twenty-year-old black male a quadriplegic in Fontana, California.[34]

Chicago probably experienced the greatest upsurge of racist violence, especially in the aftermath of the election of Harold Washington as the city's first black mayor. The Chicago Police Department recorded 127 separate "racial incidents" in 1984, an increase of 23 per cent over 1983. The most dramatic were the firebombings of the parsonage of a black minister in suburban Hickory Hills on 26 August, and a six-hour-long stoning attack on the home of a black family by dozens of whites, who were said to be celebrating Reagan's re-election.[35] Racial brutality in the USA is hardly new. What is ominous is that such groups have openly entered the electoral arena in many states, working vigorously for independent rightists and/or conservatives in the major parties. In North Carolina, Klansmen organized white registration drives, and state leader Glenn Miller ran in the Democratic primary for governor "on an open Klan and white supremacy platform." Klansmen in Georgia and Alabama succeeded in being named as county deputy voter registrars. Although some Klansmen gravitated to the Populist Party, most worked aggressively for Reagan's re-election. The national leader of the Invisible Empire KKK, Bill Wilkinson, publicly endorsed the president.[36]

Reagan created the social space or political environment for fascist and terrorist groups to operate with relative impunity. One example was the emergence of Taiwan-backed death squads, which since 1981 have assassinated eight prominent critics of the regime inside the USA.[37] In the northwestern states, the Idaho-based "Church of Aryan Nations" has committed public beatings, robberies and several murders. Federal authorities investigating the formation have stated that the "Aryan Nations" maintains a computerized "hit list" that targets for assassination major figures in black, labor, Jewish, and Marxist organizations.[38]

The latest innovation in the right's vigilante forces is the series of bombings, threats and assaults on abortion and family-planning clinics. There were no bomb threats on such clinics between 1977 and 1980, and only four incidents during 1983. The following year, twenty-seven abortion clinics in seven states were firebombed by evangelical anti-abortionists and right-wing groups, frequently identifying themselves as the "Army of God." A total of 157 "violent incidents" were reported last year, including assault and battery, kidnapping, vandalism, death threats, and attempted arson. A few neo-fascist groups, such as the southern California-based White American Resistance (WAR), have been formed in part to halt the extension of women's legal rights to abortion. WAR leader, Tom Metzger, who ran openly as a Klansman for Congress in 1980, and for the Senate in 1982, has publicly attributed abortions to "Jewish doctors" and "perverted lesbian nurses" who "must be punished for this holocaust and murder of white children."[39] The Reagan administration's response to these bombings was revealing. A national campaign by the National Organization of Women began on 2 March 1984, demanding that the US Justice Department investigate anti-abortion terrorism. On 1 August federal authorities finally agreed to begin to monitor the violence. However, Federal Bureau of Investigation director, William Webster, declared that he saw no evidence of "terrorism."[40] Only on 3 January 1985, in a pro-forma statement, did the president criticize the series of bombings as "violent anarchistic acts," but he still refused to term them "terrorism." Reagan deferred to

Moral Majoritarian Jerry Falwell's subsequent campaign – to have fifteen
million Americans wear "armbands" on 22 January 1985, "one for every
legal abortion" since 1973. Falwell's anti-abortion outburst epitomized
Reaganism's orientation: "We can no longer passively and quietly wait
for the Supreme Court to change their mind or for Congress to pass a
law."[41] Extremism on the right was no vice, moderation no virtue. Or,
as Hitler explained in *Mein Kampf*: "The very first essential for success
is a perpetually constant and regular employment of violence."[42]

III

A preliminary anatomy of the 6 November 1984 election results seemed
to give Reagan a resounding mandate. The president received 59 per cent
of the popular vote, and carried popular majorities in 49 states. Predict-
ably, Reagan did best in constituencies controlled by the far right, or
among those who had benefited most from the administration's economic
policies. The incumbent received strong support from voters identifying
themselves as ideological conservatives (81 per cent), voters with annual
incomes between $35,000 and $50,000 (67 per cent); Mondale's core
support came from African-Americans (90 per cent), Jewish Americans
(66–70 per cent), Hispanics (65 per cent), unemployed workers (68 per
cent), lesbians and gay men (60 to 80 per cent). Reagan's re-election can
be attributed to the continued erosion of partisan loyalties among the
various segments of the Democratic coalition. One-third of the voters
who supported Hart in the Democratic primaries switched to Reagan
in the general election. Voters between the ages of eighteen and twenty-
nine, who had given Reagan only 43 per cent of their votes in 1980,
produced 58 per cent for the Republican in 1984. About 49 per cent of
all Catholic voters – who constituted 26 per cent of the total electorate
– had supported Reagan in 1980; their 1984 vote for the president
increased to 55 per cent, despite the presence of a Catholic, Ferraro, on
the Democratic ticket.[43] One of Mondale's greatest disappointments was
the inability of organized labor leaders to produce a substantial majority
for the Democrats. After exerting "maximum energy" to guarantee a
level of support of 65 per cent or more, only 57 per cent of all union
members backed Mondale. Among all blue-collar workers, union and
non-union, Reagan received 53 per cent of the vote.[44]

The most striking characteristic of the election was the racial
polarization of the electorate. Nationally, Reagan obtained 66 per cent of
the white vote, and an unprecedented 73 per cent from white Protestants.
The feminists' "gender gap" – the recent trend for a greater proportion

of women to support liberal centrist candidates – was largely irrelevant, as white women supported the incumbent by a ratio of 64:36. Electoral support for Reagan among white women in 1980 had been only 52 per cent.[45] Racial stratification in the electorate was particularly sharp in the South, where Reagan, the Moral Majority and other conservative forces nearly succeeded in creating a "white united front." Reagan's campaign speeches during the fall repeatedly reminded whites of his firm opposition to affirmative action and civil rights. In Charlotte, North Carolina, the president attacked "forced busing" for school desegregation; in Macon, Georgia, Reagan invoked the racist motto of regional segregationists by declaring: "The South will rise again!"[46] On election day, 72 per cent of all white southerners voted for Reagan.[47] Although the black voter turnout was up by 750,000 since 1980, "most goals set by black politicians went unfulfilled," noted the *Washington Post*. In the Democratic primaries, black Democratic congresswoman Katie Hall of Indiana was defeated by a white candidate. In the November elections, the number of black state legislators rose by only three, to 376 nationally. The most painful defeat occurred in Mississippi, where black Democrat Robert Clark, in a well-financed campaign, lost by over four thousand votes to conservative Republican congressman Webb Franklin. The contested congressional district had 53 per cent black voters, but a massive voter registration drive among rural whites and selective intimidation of poor black voters produced a Republican victory.[48] Most of the white democratic left, feminists and progressive trade unionists refused to acknowledge or even to discuss critically the obviously racial composition of Reagan's conservative electoral bloc; blacks, on the other hand, had no choice except to face reality. Chicago congressman Gus Savage observed that "white Americans [had] voted en masse to accept the Reagan philosophy of narrow individualism, me-tooism and greed." NAACP organizer Joseph Madison viewed the election as a "white backlash." White Americans of nearly all social classes were "probably fearful of blacks getting too big for their political breeches. They responded in a manner that reflected a fear of black political power."[49]

On closer examination, however, the Reagan "mandate" was not as definitive as it may at first appear. A few media commentators drew parallels between Reagan's victory and that of Lyndon Johnson twenty years earlier, when the Texas Democrat received a popular vote of 61.3 per cent and 486 electoral votes. Actually, the 1984 results were much closer to Dwight Eisenhower's 1956 re-election "mandate" of 57.6 per cent than to the Johnson victory. Johnson's triumph produced two-thirds Democratic majorities in both houses of Congress, while in

1956 the Democrats had retained small congressional majorities despite the Republican presidential sweep. Similar to the latter, in 1984 the Republicans gained only fourteen seats in the House and lost two Senate seats. Eight of the fourteen House seats lost had been held by southern "Boll Weevils" or conservative Democrats who were already backers of Reagan, including Representatives Jack Hightower of Texas and Elliott H. Levitas of Georgia. African-American voters provided the critical margin of support to elect three white senators and at least eight Democratic representatives. Liberal populist Tom Harkin defeated ultra-right Republican senator Roger W. Jepsen in Iowa; liberal Democrat Paul Simon received only 43 per cent of the white vote in Illinois, but with 87 per cent of the vote from blacks defeated powerful Republican senator Charles Percy. In gubernatorial elections, the Republicans gained four states against three for the Democrats.[50]

There were other anomalies as well. Reagan carried Los Angeles County with 55 per cent of the vote, but a "Jobs with Peace" referendum on the same ballot, calling for cuts in the military budget to fund jobs programs and human services, passed with 61 per cent.[51] In a few states, Communist Party candidates received their highest vote in several decades. In Arizona, a Communist candidate for state representative received 5 per cent; in Massachusetts, Communist congressional candidate Laura Ross received 15,668 votes against Democratic House speaker "Tip" O'Neill, Jr. – roughly 8 per cent of the district's electorate.[52]

The odds are that the Democrats will take back the Senate in 1986, since nearly twice as many incumbents seeking re-election that year will be Republicans. Representative Tony Coelho, chairman of the Democratic Congressional Campaign Committee, emphasized his colleagues' defiance to the re-elected president: "As of today, you are a lame duck. Accept it. Elected officials do not have you to contend with any more."[53] New-right leader Richard Viguerie agreed, predicting that "Reagan faces two years with a hostile Congress – and the likelihood of an electoral disaster in the 1986 congressional elections."[54]

For the Republicans, Reagan's re-election simply meant that the struggle for power between the moderate conservatives and the radical right would now be fought without quarter. Both tendencies had benefited from Reagan's electoral white united front, but traditional Republican conservatives sought to break the leverage of radical reactionaries inside Congress. Veteran senator Robert Dole of Kansas, denounced by Gingrich as the "tax collector for the welfare state," handily defeated new-right candidate James McClure for the post of Senate Majority Leader. Liberal Republican John Chafee of Rhode Island defeated ultra-rightist Jake Garn of Utah to become chairman of the party's

Senate Conference Committee. Pennsylvania moderate John Heinz also overcame a challenge by another Reaganite, Malcolm Wallop of Wyoming, for the chairmanship of the 1986 Republican Senate Campaign Committee. Dole and other traditional conservatives promptly indicated that they would seek to reduce federal budget deficits and Reagan's defense expenditures to 5 per cent at most. The new right sustained other blows as well. The removal of presidential adviser Edwin Meese to the post of attorney general reduced the rightists' immediate access to Reagan. The resignation of Kirkpatrick from the UN, lamented Viguerie, was "a loss from which Reagan's foreign policy will never recover."[55]

The battle to succeed Reagan is now on, and its resolution may well determine the future of the Republican Party. Currently, the best-known Republican aspirants are traditional conservatives: Dole; former Senate Majority Leader Howard Baker of Tennessee; and vice president George Bush, who is so vehemently hated on the far right that he has been popularly described as having "put his manhood in a blind trust." If Reagan remains "neutral" in the 1988 campaign, the Republican presidential nomination will probably be won by an ultra-rightist. The two leading candidates are Jack Kemp and Lew Lehrman. In 1984 Kemp campaigned personally for nearly one hundred congressional Republican candidates, and raised $220,000 on their behalf. Kemp is a favorite of the Moral Majority, is the "mentor" of Gingrich's COS, and has the powerful backing of reactionary academic and financial institutions, including the Heritage Foundation, the American Enterprise Institute, and the Smith Richardson Foundation. As of late 1984, Lehrman's CFA was established in over 225 congressional districts, and, although he has never held public office, political observers note that his private wealth is such that "there's no limit to what he can spend."[56] Closely behind these candidates and even further to the radical right is Gingrich, who may ultimately become the right's spearhead for bringing its quasi-fascist agenda into state power.[57]

As the Republican leadership has degenerated into a series of fractious squabbles, the Democrats have turned their post-election blues into a thinly veiled condemnation of blacks and other progressive currents inside the party. Georgia Democratic chairman Bert Lance argued that Mondale's loss was due to the party's inability "to move in the direction the voters are moving in," especially "in the South."[58] But which voters? Most leaders focused on Mondale's abysmal totals among white professionals, managers, and white-collar employees. Carter's domestic-policy adviser Stuart Eizenstat declared: "We must win back the middle class that has drifted from our ranks..."[59] It was "not enough just to hand the middle class a bill for new taxes," concurred party consultant Bob Squier. The moment had arrived to "unchain the ghost of Roosevelt" and to find "new solutions to old problems."[60] What is to be done? The first step proposed was to reduce the democratic access of blacks, feminists, and other insurgent social forces inside the party's governing apparatus, the Democratic National Committee, by giving state chairmen and moderate governors greater authority. Second, the party's "welfare state" image had to be scrapped. Neo-liberal *New Republic* editor Morton Kondracke suggested that the party give "maximum sway for free market competition and individual initiative."[61] Oklahoma Representative James R. Jones advanced the "slogan of passionate conservatism."[62] But most emphatically, the Democrats should "insure" that the Rainbow Coalition and Jackson do "not drive the party further left," according to Kondracke. "A minority of activists ... coalition[s] of underprivileged racial, ethnic and other groups and single-issue advocates" had for too long dominated "the national party's affairs," advised Peter Rosenblatt, head of the centrist Coalition for a Democratic Majority. "These groups do not add up to a majority of the voting population."[63] Other white Democrats unwilling to go on public record were more blunt, charging that the party was "pandering" to black voters at whites' expense, and that "they shouldn't have given Jesse Jackson everything he wanted" – ignoring the fact that the Rainbow Coalition had received virtually nothing at the San Francisco convention.[64]

The black movement was suddenly forced to confront a victorious Reagan, and, at the same time, a Democratic leadership who blamed Mondale's loss partially on the active presence of African-Americans inside the party. Instead of capitulating to the pressure, black leaders struck back in a bold and imaginative manner. Two early activists within the Rainbow Coalition campaign, US civil-rights commissioner Mary Frances Berry and executive director of TransAfrica Randall Robinson, along with Congressman Walter Fauntroy, coordinator of the 27 August 1983 march on Washington, decided to initiate a series of anti-apartheid demonstrations outside the South African embassy in Washington DC. Throughout 1984, there had been an outbreak of demonstrations inside South Africa, similar to the 1960 Sharpeville uprisings and the 1976 Soweto revolts. On November 5–6, almost one million people participated in a nationwide strike against the regime; in September and October alone, over 150 demonstrators were murdered by police, and an unknown number were detained without charge. Despite Reagan's recent "mandate," activists recognized that the administration's flagrant policies favorable to apartheid made it vulnerable to domestic criticism. In a small demonstration on 21 November, Berry, Fauntroy and Robinson were arrested. Within days, other members of the Congressional Black Caucus staged non-violent protests and were also detained, including Parren Mitchell, Ronald Dellums and Charles Hayes. Civil-rights leader Joseph Lowery, head of the Southern Christian Leadership Conference, and Rosa Parks, the initiator of the 1955 Montgomery bus boycott movement, soon followed.

Within two weeks, a new national campaign had begun, the Free South Africa Movement. Every constituency in the Rainbow Coalition, plus national figures in the more moderate centrist bloc of the Democratic Party, began to volunteer to be arrested next. Leaders of the American Jewish Congress and the Union of American Hebrew Congregations organized pickets; black nationalists, most prominently the National Black United Front led by the Reverend Herbert Daughtry of Brooklyn, staged major protests; feminists, socialists and trade unionists all joined the demonstrations. Bill Lucy, secretary-treasurer of the American Federation of State, County and Municipal Employees; AFL-CIO secretary-treasurer Thomas Donahue; Steelworkers' vice president Leaon Lynch; and Newspaper Guild president Charles Perlik, Jr. were arrested in Washington protests. Even AFL-CIO leader, Lane Kirkland, who had been mute on the question of apartheid and was a bitter opponent of the Rainbow Coalition, saw the light. In a well-publicized meeting with Secretary of State George Schultz, on 29 November, Kirkland advocated a "progressively selective ban on the importation of South African products and ... if necessary, a full boycott, barring of new investment, complete disinvestment and severance of all social, cultural and diplomatic ties."[65]

A national Free South Africa Movement steering committee quickly formed, which included Jesse Jackson, Berry, Fauntroy, Robinson, Lowery and NAACP leader, Benjamin Hooks. The strategy had been refined by early December to encourage local mobilizations with a deliberate anti-Reagan emphasis, drawing the obvious connections between domestic and international racism. Demonstrations in December and in January 1985 assumed different forms across the country. In New York, South Africa's consulate was picketed daily at 3:00 in the afternoon – by religious groups on Tuesdays, black nationalists on Mondays, youth and student groups on Wednesdays, and so forth. In San Francisco, longshoremen refused to unload South African cargo. In Mobile, Alabama, Fauntroy and Lowery led a "pray-in" protest at the house of South Africa's honorary consul on 6 December. The next day, in Berkeley, California, one thousand students held an anti-apartheid rally, blockading the administration building for three hours, resulting in thirty-eight arrests. In Cleveland, more than two hundred trade unionists, religious leaders and civil-rights activists organized a public demonstration. On 9 December, four hundred protesters in Seattle picketed the home of the honorary consul; twenty-three were arrested. FSAM proponents in electoral politics introduced divestment legislation in forty-four states; the National Conference of Black Mayors agreed to pressure all mayors and city councils to withdraw public funds from banks with apartheid connections. Reagan desperately tried to stem mounting criticisms of his policies, as administration officials announced that the demonstrations would have absolutely "no impact" on government policy. "The real losers in this are the black community," explained one aide. Such denials were immediately undercut by a group of thirty-five new-right congressional leaders, led by Gingrich, Vin Weber, and Robert Walker of Pennsylvania. In an open letter to South African Ambassador Bernardus Fourie, they warned that they would "seek sanctions" against the regime unless it moved immediately to end racial violence and "demonstrated a sense of urgency about ending segregation laws."[66]

Despite the achievement of a new level of unity among black, progressive, and centrist political forces in combating apartheid and Reagan, larger questions remain unanswered regarding the future of the Democratic Party and the necessity to build a permanent coalition of social groups capable of defeating the right. The classical strategy of developing fascism is to splinter the working class, winning over the bulk of the disconnected lower petty bourgeoisie, then enact a series of authoritarian laws constricting bourgeois democratic liberties. Appeals to the "race consciousness" of white workers were a decisive factor in Reagan's 1984 victory, especially in the South. And the administration has already prepared plans to initiate a series of "Palmer Raids" against democratic and progressive forces when the opportunity presents itself. On 4 April 1984, the president signed Executive Order 12472, which gave the Secretary of Defense the authority to seize all "telecommunications resources" in the event of a vaguely defined "national emergency," without prior congressional approval.[67] Reagan has authorized the use of "lie detectors, wiretapping, blacklisting and censoring"; has forbidden liberal critics like Coretta Scott King from speaking on the Voice of America; and has attempted to void the Freedom of Information Act.[68] During the next three years, Reagan may have the opportunity to place three to four more judges on the Supreme Court, thus guaranteeing a conservative majority for the next quarter century.[69] On 12 October, Reagan signed into law a series of "anti-terrorism" bills, mandating stiff penalties for the taking of hostages and airline sabotage, and providing cash rewards for information leading to the arrest and conviction of individuals who commit "terrorist" acts. Six days later, the new laws permitted four hundred FBI agents and New York City police to seize nine activists on the grounds that they were planning to commit jail breakouts and robberies.[70] But the Ku Klux Klan, which committed at least six hundred documented acts of racist violence between 1978 and 1984, is "not regarded as terrorist by FBI guidelines."[71] Racism, institutional and vigilante, is the essential ideological approach for the ultra-right's efforts to divide workers and to build a permanent white united front. Authoritarian legal measures are the means to ensure that the left and national minorities will be unable to fight back.

Reagan's re-election was not inevitable, and, despite the financial and organizational power of the new right, a future authoritarian order in America remains only a possibility. However, the bulk of the Democratic Party's leaders, with their eyes fixed upon the white upper middle class, are looking in the wrong direction if they seriously intend to regain power. It is true that more than 67 per cent of all Americans earning more than $35,000 annually voted for Reagan, and that this sector comprises 31 per cent of the electorate. But they also total only 16.3 per cent of the voting-age population. They are overrepresented in national elections because they are ideologically motivated to affirm their social-class interests at the polls. Of workers who earn less than $12,500 annually, 53 per cent supported Mondale; they comprise 28 per cent of the adult population, but only 15 per cent of the active electorate. Unemployed workers, 68 per cent of whom supported the Democrats, represent 3 per cent of the electorate, but 8 per cent of all adults. Had Puerto Ricans, Mexican-Americans, African-Americans, the unemployed, low-income workers and people with less than a high-school education participated in the election in identical numbers to those earning above $35,000, Mondale would have won. The weakness in this scenario is that, had these constituencies actually voted in these numbers, the Democratic Party would now no longer be the "Democratic Party," but would be forced programmatically toward a Western European Labour party model. Hence the refusal of Mondale, Glenn, Hart and company to support demands for massive voter registration and education made by the Rainbow Coalition of Jackson. Given the domination of sections of capital, Southern moderates and the trade-union bureaucracy within the party's internal apparatus, it is highly unlikely that the left and its liberal allies, led by blacks' demands, will be able to reverse the Democrats' stampede toward "compassionate conservatism."

These democratic left forces will only sustain themselves if they coalesce as an independent political entity, which may operate for a time inside the Democratic Party, but run "independent candidates' against the two major parties in local and state-wide races. To do so will take the same kind of panache displayed in Jackson's primary campaign and the FSAM demonstrations in late 1984. Fundraising and the recruitment of personnel are important factors, but not crucial to the development of this strategy, *pace* David Gordon.[72] The real challenge is the creation of a realistic social program that can actively unify blue-collar employees, semi-skilled workers, the unemployed, and other disadvantaged sectors across the color line. In March 1985, the principal organizers of the Rainbow Coalition met in Gary, Indiana to create a permanent national formation. Jackson's new thirteen-point program, which includes demands for "fair immigration policies, revitalization of cities, aid to small farmers, and revamping the tax structure," has the potential for reaching oppressed whites and Latinos who resisted participation in the 1984 primary campaign.[73] The paradox of American social history is that the activism of people of color has been the decisive component in moving the boundaries of politics further to the left for the entire society; yet "race politics" is also the central component for the far right to discipline the entire working class. Whether the Rainbow's progressive utilization of race is able to transcend the conservative racist social movement and the white working class's tendency to affirm their racial identity rather than material interests at the polls is a political question of such decisive importance for the future of democratic politics in the USA that progressives of all races and classes ignore it at their peril.

Notes

1. Victor Perlo, "Unemployment and racism," *Daily World* (30 August 1984).
2. "Reagan Bad News for Blacks," *Buffalo Challenger*, (17 October 1984).
3. See Vivian Aplin-Brownlee, "Black Colleges: On Razor's Edge," *Washington Post* (19 November 1984); and Manning Marable, "The Quiet Death of Black Colleges," *Southern Exposure* 12 (March–April 1984), pp. 31–9.
4. See *Washington Notes on Africa* (Winter 1984), published by the Washington Office on Africa.
5. Anna De Cormis, "Trading with Enslavers: How US Companies Keep Apartheid Going," *Guardian* (26 December 1984).
6. Dianne M. Pinderhughes, "The Black Vote – The Sleeping Giant," in James D. Williams, ed., *The State of Black America, 1984* (Washington DC, 1984), p. 92; and "Portrait of the Electorate," *New York Times* (8 November 1984).
7. William G. Mayer, "Running on New: The Hart Choices," in Anne Doyle Kenney, ed., *Institute of Politics* (Cambridge 1984), pp. 19–20.
8. See Manning Marable, "The Rainbow Coalition: Jesse Jackson and the

Politics of Ethnicity," *Crosscurrents*, 34 (Spring 1984), pp. 21–42; Gerald M. Boyd, "Black Churches a Mainspring of Jackson's Efforts," *New York Times* (14 February 1984); and Benjamin F. Chavis, Jr., "Theology Under the Rainbow," *The Witness* 67 (May 1984), pp. 6–9.

9. African-American voters comprised 21 per cent of the total Democratic primary vote. Mondale received less than one-fifth of the national black vote, the remainder going to Jackson. Had Jackson not been in the race, black voter turnout rates would have fallen, but at least 75 per cent of those African-Americans who voted would have chosen Mondale. Thus Mondale would probably have won the nomination with little difficulty had Jackson decided not to run.

10. David Plotke, "Reaganism and the Problem of Special Interests," *Socialist Review* 15 (January–February 1985), p. 21.

11. "Mondale and the Voters," *New York Times* (19 July 1984).

12. Marable, "The Rainbow Coalition," pp. 30–32.

13. See Ayn Rand, *Capitalism: The Unknown Ideal* (New York 1967).

14. Dennis Altman, "A New Barbarism," *Socialist Review* 15 (January–February 1985), p. 10.

15. Anna De Cormis, "Why is Mondale so Obsessed with the Budget Deficit?", *Guardian* (17 October 1984).

16. Jack Colhoun, "Mondale–Ferraro: Peace Candidates or Cold Warriors?" *Guardian* (3 October 1984); and Jack Colhoun, "How do You Debate When You Don't Really Disagree?", *Guardian* (31 October 1984).

17. Paul M. Sweezy and Harry Magdoff, "Where Are We Going?", *Monthly Review* 35 (December 1983), pp. 1–2.

18. Lorn S. Foster, "On the Scene in Dallas," *Focus* 12 (September 1984), p. 3.

19. Quoted in Tristram Coffin, "The Radical Right: From Paranoia to Power," *Washington Spectator* 10 (1 December 1984), p. 2.

20. Palmiro Togliatti, *Lectures on Fascism* (New York 1976), p. 9.

21. "Bertram Gross, *Friendly Fascism: The New Face of Power in America* (Boston 1980), p. 21.

22. "JCPS Survey of Political Attitudes," *Focus* 12 (September 1984), p. 8.

23. Togliatti, *Lectures on Fascism*, p. 3.

24. Coffin, "The Radical Right," p. 3.

25. "Beyond the Reagan Revolution: New Strategies on the Right," *Interchange Report* 5 (Summer 1984), pp. 1, 5.

26. Kris Jacobs, "The Life of the Party: GOP Moving to the 'Nouveau-Right'," *Interchange Report* 5 (Fall 1984) pp. 11–12.

27. Coffin, "The Radical Right," p. 1.

28. A brief note on Carto: Expelled from the John Birch Society for his "extreme anti-Semitism," Carto founded the Liberty Lobby in 1956. In 1968, Carto coordinated the national "Youth for Wallace"; and in the 1970s he created two political action committees, United Republicans and United Congressional Appeal, which raised funds to defeat liberal Democrats. Carto also directs the California-based Institute for Historical Review, which has asserted that the Nazi holocaust was "a myth made up by Jews to further their interests." Carto has stated that "if Satan

himself had tried to create a permanent disintegration and force for the destruction of nations, he could do no better than invent the Jews." (Kristine Jacobs, "The Populist Party," *Interchange Report* 5 [Fall 1984], p. 2.)

29. Ibid., pp. 1–2.
30. "It's Not Populism, America's New Populist Party: A Fraud by Racists and Anti-Semites," *The Hammer* 8 (Fall 1984), p. 20.
31. "When is a 'Populist' Really a Klansman?" *The Hammer* 7 (Summer 1984), pp. 14–15.
32. "It's Not Populism," p. 21.
33. Ibid., pp. 22–3, 27; and "Populists: Racists Under Cover," *National Anti-Klan Network Newsletter* (Fall 1984), pp. 1, 7.
34. "Klan, Nazi and Other Incidents From Across the Nation," *Klanwatch Intelligence Report* (July 1984), pp. 2, 6; and *Klanwatch Intelligence Report* (December 1984), pp. 2–3.
35. Kevin B. Blackstone, "Racial Violence and Harassment Escalate in Chicago Area," *Chicago Reporter* 14 (January 1985), pp. 1, 6.
36. "Klan Holds White Voter Registration Drives, Backs Candidates," *Klanwatch Intelligence Report*, p. 4.
37. Leach Nordson, "Death Squads Still Stalk US Asian Community," *Guardian* (12 December 1984).
38. John Wojcik, "Expose Racist Plans of Terror," *Daily World* (8 January 1985).
39. "Anti-Abortion Violence Increases," *The Hammer* 8 (Fall 1984), pp. 10–12, Anne Finger, "Activists Urge Fightback against the Bombers," *Guardian* (23 January 1985); Tim Wheeler, "NOW Vigils to Protest Bombings," *Daily World* (19 January 1985).
40. Editorial, "What the FBI Won't Probe," *Guardian* (12 December 1984).
41. Finger, "Activists Urge Fightback against the Bombers."
42. Quoted in Gross, *Friendly Fascism*, p. 294.
43. "Portrait of the Electorate," *New York Times* (8 November 1984); and Christine R. Riddiough, "What Happened to the Gender Gap (and Other Gaps) in the 1984 Elections?", *Socialist Review* 15 (January–February 1985), p. 24.
44. "Portrait of the Electorate"; and Bill Keller, "Unionists Reassess Mondale Support," *New York Times* (9 November 1984). The voting trends of these traditional Democratic constituencies become more apparent when viewed historically. During the five presidential elections between 1952 and 1968, the Democrats received approximately 64 per cent of the Catholic vote, 57 per cent of the blue-collar vote, 55 per cent of the votes of Americans with less than a high-school education, and 52 per cent from voters under 30 years old. Carter's 1980 totals in these groups were generally lower: Catholics, 42 per cent; blue-collar, 46 per cent; less than high-school education, 51 per cent; and voters under 40, 44 per cent. Mondale did marginally better than Carter among Catholics, fell short among youth, and received roughly the same totals in the other groups. See Kevin P. Phillips, *The Emerging Republican Majority* (New York 1970), p. 30.

45. Hanna Lessinger, "Shot Down at the Gender Gap," *Guardian* (5 December 1984).

46. Akinshiju C. Ola, "Racism Won Big in the Elections," *Guardian* (28 November 1984).

47. Studies by the Joint Center for Political Studies indicate that race was a decisive factor in Southern whites' voting behavior. Polls indicated that 73 per cent of all Southern whites "considered Reagan a strong leader"; most approved of his overall "performance" as President (62 per cent), his economic policies (57 per cent), and his opposition to "preferential treatment for black job applicants" (77 per cent). Only 26 per cent of all whites in the South were critical of "Reagan's civil rights policies." Conversely, 87 per cent of all Black Southerners polled strongly "disapproved of Reagan's economic performance," and 89 per cent of the black electorate in the region voted for Mondale. (See Thomas E. Cavanaugh, "Election Round-Up," *Focus* 12 [November–December 1984], p. 5.)

48. Ola, "Racism Won Big in the Elections"; Juan Williams and Paul Taylor, "Blacks: They Lost With Mondale and Made No Gains in Congress," *Washington Post* (19 November 1984); and Tom Wicker, "Fighting White Drift," *New York Times* (26 October 1984).

49. Ola, "Racism Won Big in the Elections." Consideration of space precludes a fuller discussion of the reasons why the white left, with few exceptions, was unwilling or unable to come to terms with the racist behavior of the bulk of white Americans. As Anne Braden, leader of the Southern Organizing Committee for Economic and Social Justice (SOC) observed: "Most of them voted squarely against their own best interests. There is no way to explain this except to acknowledge that they did it for racist reasons, subtle or otherwise. As one of SOC's staff said, 'Reagan is calling white America back to order'." (Braden, "Today's Crisis: A Pledge to Struggle," *Southern Fight-back* 10 [January 1985], p. 1.)

50. Romulo Fajardo, "Black Voters Reject Reagan," *Daily World* (8 November 1984); David S. Broder and George Lardner, Jr., "Did Anybody See a Conservative Mandate Go By?", *Washington Post* (19 November 1984); and Cavanaugh, "Election Round-Up."

51. Emily De Nito, "People's Groups: No Mandate," *Daily World* (8 November 1984).

52. Nona Bonosky, "Communist Candidates Make Gains," *Daily World* (8 November 1984).

53. Broder and Lardner, "Did Anybody See a Conservative Mandate Go By?"

54. Tim Wheeler, "Short Coattails Frustrate the Ultra-right," *Daily World* (17 January 1985).

55. Kevin J. Kelley, "'Revenge of the Moderates' has New Right Reeling," *Guardian* (26 December 1984).

56. James Dickenson, "After Reagan," *The Washington Post* (19 November 1984); and Jacobs, "The Life of the Party," p. 12.

57. Gingrich is clearly the most dangerous national figure on the right for the next decade. He has not only called for the complete "dismantling of the liberal welfare state," but has even suggested that all federally funded

public housing should be "converted into condominium apartments." Additional "prisons should be built for hard-core criminals," and inmates "must work to pay for their keep." People accused of crimes should "bear the primary burden" of proof in courts, and defense attorneys "who are particularly disruptive or exploitative of the system would suffer economically and, ultimately, professional penalties for having failed to behave in a manner beneficial to society." Gingrich argues that teenagers should be enrolled into "the workforce as apprentices laboring for a modest wage." For youngsters, "a $500 bonus" should be rewarded "for any child who enters the first grade reading at the fourth grade level." These authoritarian prescriptions may become mainstream views inside the Republican Party by the mid 1990s. (See "The Gospel According to Gingrich," *Interchange Report* 5 (Fall 1984), pp. 13–14; and Kevin J. Kelley, "But GOP's future may belong to its Newts," *Guardian* (26 December 1984).

58. James R. Dickenson, "It Seems the Democrats Can Win Anything but the White House," *Washington Post* (19 November 1984).

59. Kevin J. Kelley, "After the Deluge, How do the Democrats Rebuild?" *Guardian* (5 December 1984).

60. Bob Squier, "FDR, The Ghost of Democrats Past," *New York Times* (5 December 1984). None of these centrist Democrats or neo-liberals produced data to illustrate that the "white middle class" had abandoned the Democrats only in the past decade. Mondale's 40 per cent vote from white-collar workers was only slightly less than the average total received by other Democratic presidential candidates from 1952 to 1980 (43 per cent). His share of votes from all college graduates (40 per cent) was somewhat higher than the 1952–80 average (38 per cent), and his vote from managers and professionals was identical (37 per cent). The Democrats never *lost* the white, upper-middle-class vote; they never had it – *especially* under Roosevelt. See Philips, *The Emerging Republican Majority*, p. 30; and "Portrait of the Electorate."

61. Kelley, "After the Deluge."

62. John Herbers, "Party Looks Inward for Ways to Regain Majority," *New York Times* (8 November 1984).

63. Peter R. Rosenblatt, "Centrism is Crucial," *New York Times* (19 November 1984).

64. Tom Wicker, "A Party of Access?" *New York Times* (25 November 1984).

65. Sue Dorfman, "Struggle Scorches South Africa," *Guardian* (12 September 1984); Heinz Klug, "Bigger Than Soweto," *Guardian* (12 September 1984); Jack Colhoun, "Wider Protests, Mounting Pressures," *Guardian* (19 December 1984); and Gerald Horne, "Movement Mounts to Free South Africa," *Daily World* (4 January 1985).

66. Jack Colhoun, "South Africa's Apologists: A Vanishing Breed," *Guardian* (26 December 1984); Denise Winebrenner, "Cleveland Labor Protests Apartheid," *Daily World* (15 December 1984); Horne, "Movement Mounts to Free South Africa"; and Colhoun, "Wider Protests, Mounting Pressures."

67. *Interchange Report* 5 (Summer 1984), pp. 6–7.

68. Joan Claybrook, "Reagan Ballooned 'Big Government'," *New York Times* (1 November 1984).

69. See Howard Levine and Tim Keefe, "A Supreme Election Issue," *Guardian* (24 October 1984).

70. Akinshiju Ola, "FBI Raids: A Prelude to Another Witch-hunt?", and Eleanor Stein, "Some Bills Did Pass," *Guardian* (31 October 1984).

71. According to an FBI spokesman, the Ku Klux Klan has not committed "any act of terrorism in the last few years." (See Evelyn Newman, "Terrorism, Reagan and the Klan," *National Anti-Klan Network Newsletter* [Fall 1984], p. 5.)

72. "Up from the Ashes II: Getting Our Act Together," *The Nation* (9 February 1985) pp. 138–43.

73. "The Rainbow Will Continue as Independent 'Third Force'," *Southern Fight-Back* 10 (January 1985), p. 5.

THREE

AT THE END OF
THE RAINBOW

The Los Angeles racial uprising of April–May 1992 illustrated the current crisis of African-American politics in the United States. With relatively few exceptions, the vast majority of middle-class black leaders and Democratic Party officials did little to justify or to explain the factors behind the rage among young African-Americans. The bulk of black leadership, less than one year ago, displayed the same absence of political courage and integrity during the national debate on sexual harassment generated by the Anita Hill–Clarence Thomas Senate hearings. Throughout black America there is a sense that the political strategies, tactics and leadership are profoundly flawed. Part of the problem can be attributed to the basic strategy for black politics, which can be characterized as "liberal integrationism." But the other troubling factor is the level of opportunism and ideological chaos which characterizes major African-American leaders. A brief examination of the curious behavior of Jesse Jackson since the 1988 presidential campaign provides the most graphic illustration of the current crisis of leadership.

For much of the twentieth century, and especially since the Second World War, the "strategic vision" for the vast majority of the black middle class and its mainstream leadership could be accurately described as "liberal integrationism." Liberal integrationism, in brief, is an approach towards political action which calls for the deconstruction of institutional racism through liberal reforms within the state, and the assimilation of black Americans as individuals within all levels of the labor force, culture and society. At root, this strategy for political change is based on what I term "symbolic representation" – that is, a belief that if an African-American receives a prominent appointment to government, or within the private sector or the media, black people as a group are symbolically empowered. This was essentially the argument of many black liberals who defended the nomination of Republican conservative Clarence Thomas to the Supreme Court. Despite his reactionary ideology, it was argued, Thomas is nevertheless racially "black"; he shares our experiences of oppression, and will "sympathize with our concerns once he's appointed to a lifetime job." This thesis was largely true during the era of Jim Crow segregation. Black professionals were connected with black working-class and poor people by innumerable linkages. Black doctors depended upon black patients; black college professors taught in historically black colleges; black lawyers usually had black clients, maintained their offices in black neighborhoods, and lived next to other black people. The police didn't inquire about an African-American's socioeconomic background or level of educational attainment if she/he was in violation of Jim Crow laws. But in the post-civil-rights era, the structures of accountability on the black professional middle class began to erode. A new type of African-American leadership emerged inside the public and private sectors which lived outside the black community and had little personal contact with African-Americans. "Symbolic representation" no longer works with bureaucrats and politicians like Clarence Thomas, who feel no sense of allegiance to the black freedom struggle.

Liberal integrationism's chief economic assumptions were those of expansive, liberal capitalism and Keynesianism. Two generations ago, when the NAACP and black liberal political leadership were integrated into the New Deal coalition as junior partners, the economic basis of unity was liberal capitalism – the belief that the economic "pie" could expand indefinitely. Today's black leadership in the Democratic Party holds many of the same economic assumptions, despite the radical transformation, deindustrialization and destruction of the US political economy in the past thirty years. The dire economic condition of African-Americans cannot be addressed by liberal reforms, tinkering at the margins of a system in the midst of structural crisis. Poverty in the black community will not be reduced significantly by minority economic set-asides, urban "enterprise zones," or by neo-Booker T. Washington-style black capitalism.

Moreover, since the 1960s, the vast majority of black liberal integrationist leaders have defined "politics" almost solely as "electoralism." Electing more African-Americans to Congress, state legislatures and city councils is perceived as increasing the political power of blacks as a group. There are at least two major problems with this notion of politics. As previously mentioned, symbolic representation only works when there exist institutions of structural accountability, the power to reward and to punish, between leaders and those whom they supposedly represent. Moreover, African-American leaders currently minimize tactics which a generation ago were at the heart of the black freedom movement – sit-ins, teach-ins, selective buying campaigns or boycotts, civil disobedience, strikes and demonstrations of all types. It is significant to note that neither Martin Luther King, Jr., nor Malcolm X, nor Paul Robeson, nor Fannie Lou Hamer nor A. Philip Randolph were elected officials; and none of them drew their political authority from the electoral arena. King's chief political practice was going to jail to assert his political and moral beliefs. Somehow, black leadership today has forgotten the tactics and lessons of the past, and has invested heavily in an electoral process which was never really designed to articulate black grievances or demands.

Finally, liberal integrationism has at its core a blind loyalty to the Democratic Party. Since the Walter White regime at the NAACP fifty years ago, the bulk of the national black leadership has perceived itself as an essential part of the political coalition behind national Democratic Party candidates for the presidency and Congress. Even Jesse Jackson's break from this mainstream position, challenging Walter Mondale and Michael Dukakis inside the Democratic presidential primaries in the 1980s, was, in retrospect, a maneuver to articulate black grievances inside the framework of the existing system.

The most progressive and potentially radical mass movement in electoral politics since 1980 was the Rainbow Coalition, a united front of liberal integrationists and socialists, trade unionists and feminists, and dozens of other constituencies, around the presidential candidacy of Jesse Jackson. Four years ago, Jackson was the leader of a massive liberal-left electoral protest current within the Democratic Party. Jackson received nearly seven million popular votes in the 1988 Democratic primaries, even more than the amount earned four years before by Democratic primary victor Walter Mondale. Massachusetts governor Michael Dukakis, the 1988 primary winner, was forced to negotiate with Jackson from a position of weakness. Thousands of black Democratic Party officials and the civil-rights establishment looked to Jackson to implement their "liberal integrationist" strategy.

However, there were two rival tendencies within the Rainbow Coalition throughout the 1980s. The moderate "liberal integrationist" groups, represented by 1988 campaign director Ron Brown, drew support from black elected officials, civil-rights officials and black entrepreneurs. They favored staying within the Democratic Party, and opposed radical or socialist public-policy positions, such as Jackson's support for the

US recognition of Castro's Cuba. The more radical activist tendency, represented by black political theorist/writer Jack O'Dell and Rainbow Coalition leader Ron Daniels, advocated a break with the Democrats and the creation of an independent, left social-democratic formation. Jackson oscillated between these two ideological poles, and finally came down hard against the left. In the winter of 1989, Jackson called for the right to appoint all Rainbow Coalition leaders at the congressional district level. In effect, he wanted to block democratic elections of Rainbow local leadership, muzzling socialist and radical black nationalist dissenters from above. Ron Daniels left the Rainbow, as did thousands of local and community-based activists who were disillusioned with Jackson's autocratic tactics. Ron Brown was quickly named national chairman of the Democratic Party, as he unveiled a pragmatic and moderate political posture. Jackson began to move away from his radical rhetoric towards a more accommodating orientation.

Yet Jackson's shift to the right didn't satisfy white critics in the Democratic Party. Many conservative Democrats blamed Jackson's liberal politics for Dukakis's defeat in 1988, and for their troubles in attracting middle-income white voters. Since 1964, for example, about 60 per cent of the white electorate have consistently voted Republican in presidential elections. Support for the Republicans grows to 70 per cent among white southern voters and Americans who earn more than $50,000 annually. Arkansas governor Bill Clinton, along with Tennessee senator Al Gore and Virginia governor Charles Robb (President Lyndon Johnson's son-in-law) became the nucleus of those wishing to move the Democratic Party to the political "center." Establishing the Democratic Leadership Council (DLC), they launched an aggressive strategy to seize control of their party's national apparatus. With Jackson on the political sidelines in the 1992 Democratic primaries, the DLC-sponsored presidential candidate, Bill Clinton, began his successful march to win the party's nomination. Clinton won a majority of African-American voters' support largely due to his backing by a number of black leaders. African-American advocates of Clinton included former Urban League leader Vernon Jordan, Los Angeles congresswoman Maxine Waters, Atlanta Congressman and former civil-rights leader John Lewis, and former Houston congresswoman Barbara Jordan. Barbara Jordan, now a law professor at the University of Texas, was the key "theoretician" of his neo-accommodationist/liberal-integrationist trend. She called upon blacks to lower their expectations of government programs, and supported pro-business efforts in the ghettos.

Increasingly isolated, Jackson felt ignored as black America's central leader, and was worried by Clinton's overt appeal to white, middle-class, suburban voters. Matters became much worse between the two men over a videotaped incident in March 1992. Clinton responded with a stream of hostile invectives when told erroneously that Jackson had endorsed another candidate for president; the taped incident was aired nationally. Despite Clinton's subsequent apology, Jackson was deeply stung by this videotaped statement, and he belatedly tried to reassert himself in the presidential contest but without actually becoming a candidate.

This helps to explain Jackson's sudden fascination with billionaire Ross Perot. Jackson had known Perot for about a decade. In 1983–84, Perot had privately financed Jackson's attempts at Middle Eastern diplomacy in Lebanon. When the eccentric billionaire announced in March that he might consider launching an independent presidential campaign, one of the first leaders consulted was Jackson. Throughout the spring, Jackson continually praised Perot to his closest allies and sycophants at his Washington DC office. He proclaimed that Perot was actually "to the left" of Clinton. Jackson ignored any evidence contradicting this bankrupt thesis. All of Perot's top strategists were white, affluent males. His chief campaign manager, Ed Rollins, had been Ronald Reagan's campaign manager in 1984. Jackson neglected to inform his supporters that Perot's former company, Electronic Data Systems (EDS), had a terrible record of affirmative action under his supervision. When Perot finally sold EDS to General Motors, for example, only 1 per cent of the company's managers and supervisors were minorities.

The Jackson–Clinton hostilities finally erupted into open warfare in June 1992, when the Arkansas governor was invited to speak before a national meeting of the Rainbow Coalition in Washington. Clinton used the speech to denounce controversial rap artist Sister Souljah, who had been invited to appear at the Rainbow meeting. Sister Souljah had been quoted in the *Washington Post* as encouraging black gangs not to murder other African-Americans but to vent their anger against whites. Clinton characterized Souljah's speech as black "racism," as odious as that of former Ku Klux Klan leader David Duke's appeals to white racism. Jackson was stunned. Clinton had previously caucused with Jackson privately before his speech, without uttering any warning about the political bombshell he planned to explode. Even worse, Clinton's aides had privately alerted members of the press before the speech about its contents. Jackson and the Rainbow Coalition had been cunningly manipulated, in effect, to illustrate the Democratic candidate's "independence" from blacks in general and from Jackson in particular.

Jackson's first instinct was to retaliate with all the resources at his disposal. He went on a series of national news programs, insisting that the Sister Souljah incident had revealed a "profound character flaw" in

Clinton. Jackson declared that Clinton was seeking to "distance himself" from blacks and trade unionists, the traditional base of all Democratic presidential candidates. In private, Rainbow supporters were told that Clinton was "the enemy." Many Rainbow Coalition activists began to call for a coalition with Perot. One prominent, progressive black political scientist privately proposed a "Perot-Jackson" independent ticket in the fall 1992 elections. Jackson associate Rev. Calvin Butts, New York City's most prominent African-American minister, signed on as the Perot campaign co-chairperson for New York state. Then, only two days before the opening session of the Democratic national convention in New York City, Jackson surprised everyone by giving a lukewarm endorsement of Clinton. Many of his oldest supporters, veterans of the 1984 and 1988 presidential campaigns, were shocked and dismayed by Jackson's televised endorsement.

Why did Jackson capitulate to Clinton? There were three decisive reasons. First was the central role of former Jackson protégé and lieutenant Ron Brown. Brown agreed with the DLC drive to move the party ideologically to the center. Brown told his former boss that Jackson would not be permitted to speak to the convention, or to a national television audience, unless he endorsed Clinton, the party's nominee for the presidency. The endorsement was "the price of admission" to New York's Madison Square Garden. Jackson did deliver a rhetorically brilliant address, arguing that the Democrats should not seek the "political center" but the nation's "moral center." Nevertheless, Jackson's public endorsement meant that Rainbow activists across the country were being ordered to march to Clinton's conservative tune.

Second, despite his constant flirtations with Perot, Jackson recognized his heavy investment in the Democratic Party, and feared any rupture from party bureaucrats and officials. The Rainbow Coalition's key activist had been prepared to work for Perot, but Jackson feared that a Clinton victory in the general election would freeze his group out of any governmental patronage in 1993. Any support for Perot's independent campaign would spell disaster for Jackson's future plans, which include one more campaign for the White House, possibly in the year 2000. Moreover, by early June, there were strong rumors that Perot's national campaign organization was in disarray. Jackson may have anticipated Perot's sudden withdrawal from the presidential race, after spending $10 million in the abortive effort.

Third, and most importantly, Jackson was forced to embrace a white, Southern politician whom he strongly despised, because of the internal weaknesses and contradictory character of his own formation, the Rainbow Coalition. Back in 1988, Jackson had briefly had the people, resources and organizational capacity to launch a major independent campaign to challenge both capitalist parties. Most of America's organized left, including the Democratic Socialists of America and the US Communist Party, played supportive roles in the mobilization of Jackson's campaign. But in 1989 Jackson dismantled the activist branches of the Rainbow at the state level by insisting upon a new, autocratic command structure. Workers, activists and young people by the thousands left in disgust. Rainbow organizers in the leadership were replaced because of Jackson's reservations about having strong, assertive people around him. Jackson's refusal to launch an independent group which could contest elections with both parties created the political space which permitted the DLC and Clinton to seize the offensive.

The only positive impact of the DLC–Clinton "political coup" is that the ideological and organizational "space" for a left alternative to both major parties has grown dramatically in the past year. A conservative Democratic administration would be only marginally better than the Reagan–Bush regime, with social grievances and political unrest from the poor, working people and racial minorities reaching boiling point. Los Angeles was only a harbinger of the widespread social upheavals on America's political horizon. But to be prepared for these events, black activists and the American left must be willing to go beyond the ideological limitations of "liberal integrationism."

FOUR

RACE AND CLASS IN THE US
PRESIDENTIAL ELECTION OF 1992

E very four years the American people engage in a public spectacle called a "presidential election." It is a ritualized contest which has as many cultural implications as practical political consequences. On the first Tuesday of November of every leap year, two representatives of the various factions of the ruling classes are lifted into the ring of public opinion to slug it out until the final bell is rung. The complicated aspect of this electoral sport is in the scoring. The popular vote does not actually select the winner. Rather, each state is allocated a certain number of "electoral votes," determined by the total number of a state's elected members in the House of Representatives and the Senate.

In nearly all cases, the majority or plurality winner of a state's popular votes is awarded the entire electoral vote of a particular state. In effect, slim majorities for a candidate in a small number of heavily populated states (such as California, New York, Texas, Florida or Illinois) could produce victory in the electoral college, even if such a candidate lost the overall popular vote nationally. This has happened several times in American history: the victor of the popular election was denied the presidency because of his inability to gain a majority in the electoral college. And if no one reaches an absolute majority of votes in the electoral college, the House of Representatives chooses the president. Even the scoring system in boxing matches, notoriously corrupt as it is, is considerably less complicated than the archaic American presidential process.

Despite the idiosyncrasies of this political system, which is designed to cement consensus among the governed, certain long-term patterns can be identified in American political culture and the presidency. There are two governing rules to keep in mind. Rule one: American presidents who run for re-election usually win, unless there is an economic recession or some unusual political calamity. In the twentieth century, with the exception of the 1912 presidential contest, no incumbent president has ever received less than 39.6 per cent of the popular vote. Even the last Democratic presidential incumbent, the unpopular former Georgia governor Jimmy Carter, who was humiliated by the Iranian hostage crisis, massively high domestic unemployment rates and high interest rates, still received 41 per cent of the popular vote in a three-way race. On average, with the exception of the 1912 election, presidential incumbents have received 53.6 per cent of the popular vote.[1]

Rule two: since the outbreak of the Cold War nearly half a century ago, the majority of white Americans have consistently chosen Republicans over Democratic presidential candidates. In over forty years, a majority of white voters have voted for a Democratic candidate only once – Lyndon Johnson in 1964. Two-thirds of all white voters backed Ronald Reagan in 1984, and 60 per cent of all whites supported George Bush against Massachusetts governor Michael Dukakis four years ago. In the South, with its history of racial hatred and religious fundamentalism, overall white support for Republican presidential candidates has been 70 per cent, and among white evangelical Christians, 80 per cent. Since the election of Ronald Reagan in 1980, in presidential contests the Republican Party operates almost like a white united front, dominated by the most racist, reactionary sectors of corporate and finance capital, and the most backward cultural and religious movements.[2]

Before the event, the 1992 presidential campaign was predicted by nearly every observer to be a coronation of Bush, and a crushing victory for Republicans in the House and Senate races. The decennial redistricting of congressional seats in 1992 greatly favored Republicans, because many new House districts were created in conservative areas like southern California, Texas and Florida. Congressional scandals over recent years, including the passing of salary increases for themselves in the middle of the night, created a widespread hostility and anger aimed at the predominantly Democratic Congress. Fresh from his murderous military triumph over Iraq, Bush basked in the warm glow of public-approval polls, which for a time stood above 80 per cent. The Democratic Party's primary public spokespersons, such as New York governor Mario Cuomo, Jesse Jackson and New Jersey senator Bill Bradley, refused to run. Even worse, the Democrat who finally emerged from the long and bloody nomination process, Arkansas governor Bill Clinton, had been seriously tarnished by charges of marital infidelity, marijuana smoking and dodging the military draft during the Vietnam War. Surely Bush would be re-elected in a landslide, like Reagan in 1984.

The victory of Clinton in the 1992 presidential election represented not simply a reversal from the conservative Reagan–Bush regime of the previous twelve years, but an almost unprecedented repudiation of an American leader. Bush received 38 million popular votes, only 37.5 per cent of the overall electorate. This was the lowest percentage of the popular vote recorded by any incumbent president seeking re-election in eighty years. Bush received 168 electoral votes to Clinton's 370; Clinton carried reliably Republican states which a Democrat had not carried in a generation, such as New Hampshire, New Jersey, and New Mexico. The anti-Bush vote was divided between Clinton and Perot. Perot's 18.8 per cent of the total popular vote (19.2 million votes) was the second highest vote total of any independent candidate seeking the presidency in the twentieth century. Clinton received more than 43.7 million popular votes, which was 43 per cent of the overall electorate.[3]

A closer analysis of Clinton's core constituency reveals that it was essentially composed of racial and ethnic minorities, working-class and poor people, and people who depended heavily on governmental programs, such as welfare, student educational loans, social-security payments and other social services. According to voters' exit-polling data, 82 per cent of all African-Americans who voted selected Clinton, the highest level of support that the Democratic candidate received from any group. Clinton also received substantial support from Jewish voters (78 per cent) and from Latinos (62 per cent). Blue-collar workers and the poor overwhelmingly backed Clinton as well. Of the people earning less than $15,000 per year, 59 per cent went for the Arkansas Democrat. Others in this group included trade-union members and members of households (55 per cent), the unemployed (56 per cent) and women without a high-school diploma (58 per cent). A relative majority of Americans over the age of 60 (50 per cent), full-time students (50 per cent) and first-time voters (49 per cent) endorsed Clinton over Bush and Perot. The only upper-income group which clearly aligned itself with Clinton was Americans with postgraduate university education or degrees (49 per cent). Bush's core supporters were strikingly different: overwhelmingly white, economically privileged, and culturally conservative.

Bush scored best among "born-again Christian" evangelicals (61 per cent), Southern white males (48 per cent), the small and relatively affluent Asian-American community (62 per cent), ideological conservatives (65 per cent) and people earning more than $75,000 annually (48 per cent). If African-Americans and Latinos had stayed home from the polls, Bush would have received a narrow electoral-college and popular-vote victory. A relative majority of all white voters went for Bush (41 per cent) over Clinton (39 per cent) and Perot (20 per cent). The overwhelming backing of blacks, for example, meant that Clinton was able to carry a number of states in which the majority of white voters favored Bush. For example, Clinton's narrow victories over Bush in Georgia (44 as against 43 per cent), Louisiana (46 as against 42 per cent), Tennessee (47 as against 43 per cent), New Jersey (43 as against 41 per cent) and Ohio (40 as against 39 per cent) were attributable to strong support by the African-American electorate. Latinos in New Mexico (38 per cent of the state's voters), California (26 per cent Latino) and Colorado (13 per cent) gave Clinton crucial support, helping him to win these states.[4]

There are several key issues or questions which illuminate the larger political significance of the electoral events of November 1992. How and why was Bush defeated? How did Bill Clinton overcome long odds and achieve his life-long ambition of winning the presidency, and what is the meaning of the Democratic Party's ideological and policy shift to the right during the campaign? And what was the role of race and racism?

Why Bush Lost

Bill Clinton did not really win the presidency; George Bush lost it. There are many reasons why George Bush became a one-term president, to be remembered chiefly for his narrowness of political vision, an absence of personal ethics, and afflicted with a sheep-like devotion to the whims and interests of corporate capitalism.

Every American election from 1948 until 1988 had occurred in the context of the Cold War and the international conflict between the United States and the Soviet Union. In selecting a leader, many American voters thought of the qualities necessary for leadership against what Reagan termed the "evil empire." Expertise in international affairs, some intimate knowledge of America's military arsenal, and even personal experience in the armed forces were considered essential. The domestic impact of the Cold War was to push the entire axis of American politics to the right. Reagan's rise to power in 1980 was the triumph of a whole history of growing economic reaction, racism and class warfare against working people. And George Bush was a logical product of that repressive history: a decorated veteran of the Second World War, the son of a wealthy Republican senator, two-term congressman from Texas, former head of the Central Intelligence Agency, and vice president to Reagan. Whenever Bush's personal beliefs conflicted with his drive for power, he eagerly sacrificed his principles. In the

1988 Republican primaries, Bush challenged Reagan by denouncing his economic plans as "voodoo economics"; twelve years later, he had become voodoo's high priest.

But, with the collapse of the Berlin Wall, the dismantling of the Soviet bloc in Europe and, finally, the termination of the USSR, everything changed. Both the United States and the Soviet Union actually lost the Cold War. The real costs to the American people should be weighed by the hundreds of billions of dollars annually wasted on nuclear and conventional weaponry, the lack of investment in upgrading factories and in new technologies, the deterioration of highways and bridges, and the lack of adequate federal-government support for schools, health care, housing and other basic human needs. No amount of anti-communist rhetoric could hide the millions of lost jobs, the decline in real incomes for millions of workers, and the rise in poverty rates. Somehow, Bush never understood this. He had never felt the pain of hunger, discrimination or poverty in his lifetime. He could not comprehend the heartache of being without a job, or the fear of not being able to buy warm winter clothes for his children, as the winter months approached. Nor could he feel the deep anxieties of middle-class families, the fear of losing their homes. "Anxiety" for President Bush was not knowing which fork to use at a formal dinner.

Millions of white Americans, who had never been personally touched by the agony of joblessness and economic despair, were plunged into chaos. According to the Census Bureau, median income levels when adjusted for the rate of inflation shrank in twenty-four of the fifty states in the 1980s. Overall household incomes increased by an average of only 6.5 per cent, far below the rate of other costs; in the same years, for example, housing jumped 27 per cent in cost. A majority of the Americans who are poor, or who live in federally subsidized housing, or who receive welfare payments, are not Latino or black – they are white.

During the summer of 1992, the Bush administration negotiated the North American Free Trade Agreement with Canada and Mexico, which proposed the elimination of almost all restrictions on exports, imports and corporate investment between these nations. Despite Bush's enthusiastic endorsement for the accord, critics pointed out that hundreds of thousands of mostly lower-paying jobs in the USA would be destroyed. The real incomes of workers without a college education had dropped 20 per cent since 1979. And without a massive, federally funded educational and vocational retraining program to prepare blue-collar workers for the new technologies, unemployment would become even worse. Bush failed to speak to any of these economic fears. By the end of October 1992, among Americans who had an opinion about the North American trade pact, it was opposed by nearly two to one. The general impression that Bush cared little about workers' and poor people's jobs was widely accepted.

The economic recession which Bush boasted of having ended more than a year ago continued to depress wages and increase unemployment lines. In the twelve months prior to the election, over 20 per cent of all American families had experience of someone who had lost a job during that time. Of those jobless Americans who had obtained new employment, more than half had experienced a loss in wages in their new jobs. But the Bush campaign virtually ignored this entire class of American working people.

However, Bush's most crucial electoral mistake was in underestimating Clinton's political strengths, and the capacity of the national Democratic Party to mount a serious campaign. If political clout is calculated by the number of ballots one receives, Clinton had emerged from the Democratic primaries as the strongest candidate in decades. Clinton had received a higher percentage of the national primary vote, 52 per cent, than any Democrat seeking the presidency in twenty years. He won 10.5 million primary votes, more than any Democrat or Republican in the history of presidential primary elections. And by mid July nearly all of the major leaders of the Democratic Party, including Jesse Jackson, had come together to endorse his nomination. For several critical months in the spring and early summer of 1992, Bush's campaign strategists assumed mistakenly that their chief electoral rival was H. Ross Perot, not Clinton; consequently, they aimed their rhetorical fire largely against the Texas billionaire. This was a serious strategic error, and although Bush closed much of the gap between himself and Clinton during the campaign's final weeks, his mistakes in political judgment cost him the presidency. In the end, Americans desperately wanted "change." Most people who voted for Clinton weren't endorsing the Democratic nominee. They were voting against George Bush.[5]

Race and the Election

The shadow of race is always present in American politics, and the recent contest was no exception. Yet the curious reality is that, in the political aftermath of the racial uprisings in Los Angeles in April–May 1992 – the most costly and violent social explosion in American history – none of the major candidates really addressed the fundamental racial crisis in this country. As political critic Alan Ehrenhalt observed: "In every Presidential election since 1968, the middle-class concerns of race and crime have been at the center of campaign debate. This year, they have scarcely been discussed."[6]

George Bush's public record on race relations is filled with ambiguity and cynical opportunism. As a student at Yale University nearly five decades ago, he led the fund-raising drive for the United Negro College Fund, providing much-needed support for historically black colleges. As a local Republican leader in Texas, he placed party funds in a black-owned bank. He personally opposed racial discrimination in housing, explaining to conservative whites that "it seems fundamental that a man should not have a door slammed in his face because he is a Negro." But Bush could also readily jettison any commitments to black equality, depending upon the circumstances. In 1964, he vigorously opposed the Civil Rights Act which outlawed racial segregation in public accommodations, condemning the measure as "bad legislation." In the 1988 presidential campaign, Bush benefited from the manipulations of ugly racist sentiments against his Democratic challenger, Michael Dukakis of Massachusetts. Pro-Bush advertisements depicted the case of Willie Horton, a black convict who had raped and beaten a white woman while on Dukakis's prison furlough program. The political commercials were used to illustrate Dukakis's "softness" on violent crime and his "permissive" attitude towards African-Americans. As president, Bush vetoed the 1990 Civil Rights Act, demagogically smearing the measure as fostering strict "racial quotas." Bush's manipulation of the political "race card" contributed directly to the emergence of even more racist spokesmen on the far right, such as journalist Patrick Buchanan and David Duke, unsuccessful Republican gubernatorial candidate in Louisiana in 1991.[7]

Ross Perot received some surprisingly strong support from blacks at the beginning of his independent candidacy. For months, Jesse Jackson openly flirted with Perot, and his Rainbow Coalition nearly endorsed him. In June, a national survey of African-American voters aged eighteen to thirty-four found that 21 per cent favored Perot. But a negative reaction against Perot developed when it was learned that the Texas billionaire opposed affirmative action. When the Electronic Data Systems corporation was under Perot's ownership, the company had barely 1 per cent black and Latino managers and administrators. Perot inflicted irreparable damage upon himself as far as African-Americans were concerned when he delivered a dreadfully paternalistic speech before the national convention of the NAACP (National Association for the Advancement of Colored People). Perot referred to blacks as "you people" – a phrase reflecting both his personal and political distance from the real problems of African-Americans.[8]

Clinton's relationship with the black community was far more complicated. Growing up in a rural, impoverished family with an abusive, alcoholic stepfather, Clinton's personal experiences gave him some insight into the inherent unfairness of class and racial oppression. As an idealistic college student at Georgetown University, he assisted poor, rural African-Americans participating in a civil-rights protest in Washington DC, led by the Reverend Ralph David Abernathy. As governor of a small southern state, he cultivated cordial links with African-American constituents, appointing more blacks to governmental positions than all previous Arkansas governors combined.

Clinton could speak with compassion and power in his denunciations of racism and economic inequality, something completely alien to both Perot and Bush. In the aftermath of the Los Angeles racial revolt of April-May 1992, for instance, the Democratic candidate declared:

> The Republicans, when they needed to prove Michael Dukakis was soft on crime, brought out Willie Horton. The Republicans, when they needed to cover up for their senseless economic strategy that is driving income down for most American families while they work harder, blame it on quotas so there can be racial resentment instead of honest analysis of our economic falsehoods.... We have made a great deal of progress for those of us who live in the mainstream of America. But what has happened beneath that? Beneath that, there are those who are not part of our community, where values have been shredded by the hard knife of experience, where there is the disintegration of family and neighborhood and jobs and the rise of drugs and guns and gangs.[9]

But Clinton's advisers, painfully aware that no Democratic presidential candidate had received a majority of the white vote in nearly thirty years, sharply advised Clinton to distance himself from the problems of lower-income blacks in general, and from Jesse Jackson in particular. This was the reason for Clinton's calculated public break with Jackson over the "Sister Souljah" controversy. Clinton also embraced changes in welfare laws which would deny increased payments to poor mothers who had additional children while on welfare. Throughout the campaign, Clinton deliberately distanced himself from Jackson, even avoiding being photographed with him.[10]

None of this seemed to matter to most African-American mayors, legislators and civil-rights leaders, who are nearly all Democrats. On the day following the election, they were already preaching the gospel of "Let's give Clinton a chance" among their working-class and poor constituents. Deliberately ignored was the fact that Arkansas under Clinton was only one of two states which never passed a civil-rights law; that Arkansas blacks have one of the highest poverty rates in the nation – 43 per cent, compared to only 14.5 per cent for Arkansas whites, and 30 per cent for African-Americans nationwide. None of the black Democrats praising Clinton's victory discussed the president-elect's frequent golfing excursions at all-white private country clubs.

The reason that Clinton could treat Jackson with public contempt while successfully maintaining backing among African-Americans was his conscious appeal to only part of the black community – the middle class. According to the US Census Bureau, since 1967 the number of African-American families classified as "middle class" has increased by 400 per cent. Hundreds of thousands of these families have moved out of the ghetto into the suburbs; and middle-class, professional neighborhoods which are largely black have grown inside many cities. By 1990, about 15 per cent of all black households were earning above $50,000 annually, and the average income among the top 20 per cent of all African-American families was $61,213. Upper-income, college-educated blacks vote at rates comparable to white middle-class voters. For example, about 75 per cent of all blacks earning more than $50,000 voted in the presidential election, while barely 30 per cent of impoverished blacks voted. By appealing to the black petty bourgeoisie, emphasizing the role of capitalism as a positive force for African-American development, Clinton attempted to construct a "post-civil-rights" constituency among blacks.

Clinton's model for this "middle-class black" electoral strategy owes much to African-American Democratic leader Douglas Wilder. Elected governor of Virginia in 1990, Wilder based his campaign on a conservative approach to economic development. He called for increased police expenditures, the death penalty and cuts in welfare programs. Wilder also pushed away Jesse Jackson to arm's length, symbolically telling the white electorate that he was unsympathetic to the Rainbow Coalition's social-democratic agenda.

Clinton is reaching for a new set of black advisers who, like Wilder, are economic "pragmatists" and who are also more conservative on social and international issues than Jackson. Some of these new black political accommodationists include former Texas congresswoman Barbara Jordan, congressman Mike Espy of Mississippi, mayor Norm Rice of Seattle, and former Urban League director Vernon Jordan. They have been political outsiders for so long, with conservative Republicans controlling the White House, the courts and federal bureaucracy for twenty out of the past twenty-four years, that they seem willing to go along with nearly anything Clinton says or does. As representative John Lewis, the veteran civil-rights activist, declared: "In 1992, we don't need a candidate singing 'We shall overcome', or carrying a sign."[11]

Some astute Republicans also followed Clinton's lead in exploiting the growing class divisions among African-Americans. In the closely contested senatorial race in New York, conservative Republican incumbent Alfonse D'Amato sought to split the traditionally Democratic black vote. Spending $10 million overall in his campaign, he saturated black and Hispanic radio stations in New York City, attacking his Democratic challenger Robert Abrams. On the eve of the election, D'Amato held a surprise press conference, announcing his endorsement by several prominent black ministers and by the nation's best-known African-American newspaper, *The Amsterdam News*. Given D'Amato's filthy record – he strongly opposes affirmative action, had voted against the Civil Rights Act of 1990, and had even channeled financing from the Department of Housing and Urban Development away from poor black neighborhoods towards white companies – the actions of these middle-class black leaders were, at best, perplexing. In its apologetic endorsement, The *Amsterdam News* explained that D'Amato was perhaps "the lesser of two evils." Black voters were warned to reject the white liberal Democratic candidate in favor of the conservative Republican, but were told to "keep both eyes open all night." *The Amsterdam News* editorial persuaded thousands of African-Americans to take a chance on D'Amato. According to exit polling data, 16 per cent of all black voters backed D'Amato. That was the margin which permitted the racist Republican D'Amato to achieve victory (with 51 per cent of the vote).[12] D'Amato's last-minute triumph indicates that slavery is perhaps not yet dead in America: some blacks can still be purchased by the highest bidder.

Notes

1. See Mark Helprin, "Why Bush Will Win," *Wall Street Journal* (27 October 1992).
2. See Jeffrey H. Birnbaum, "Republicans' Dream of Big Gains in House May End as Just That," *Wall Street Journal* (27 October 1992).
3. "Strongest Third Party Finishes" and "Portrait of the Electorate," *New York Times* (5 November 1992).
4. "Portrait of the Electorate"; James M. Perry, "Hispanic Voters Confound the GOP, Turn in Droves to Support Democrats," *Wall Street Journal* (27 October 1992).
5. Sources on George Bush in the 1992 presidential election include George Bush "Policies That Will Help Rebuild America's Cities," *Los Angeles Times* (14 May 1992), Peter Applebome, "Religious Right Intensifies Campaign for Bush," *New York Times* (31 October 1992); and Maureen Dowd, "Bush:

As the Loss Sinks In, Some Begin Pointing Fingers," *New York Times* (5 November 1992).

6. Alan Ehrenhalt, "An Era Ends. Silently," *New York Times* (1 November 1992).

7. Steven A. Holmes, "When the Subject is Civil Rights, There Are Two George Bushes," *New York Times* (9 June 1991).

8. On Ross Perot's relations with the black community, see Steven A. Holmes, "Perot Brings Mixed Record to His First Black Audience," *New York Times* (11 July 1992); "Excerpts from Perot's Nashville talk" *New York Times* (12 July 1992); Steven A. Holmes, "Perot Makes Plea for Racial Harmony," *New York Times* (19 July 1992); and Debbie Howlett, "Perot Trips on Tactics, Remarks," *USA Today* (13 July 1992). Perot blurted out before his NAACP audience: "Financially at least it's going to be a long hot summer, right? I don't have to tell you who gets hurt first when this sort of thing happens, do I? You, your people do. Your people do. I know that and you know that."

9. Gwen Ifill, "Clinton Blames Bush and Republicans for Racial Turmoil," *New York Times* (3 May 1992).

10. See Gwen Ifill, "Clinton Deftly Navigates Shoals of Racial Issues," *New York Times* (17 June 1992); Gwen Ifill, "Clinton Backs New Jersey's Changes in Welfare System," *New York Times* (23 May 1992); and Michael Tomasky, "Clinton's Death Dance," *Village Voice*, vol. 37, no. 25, 23 June 1992.

11. On the political currents within black America during the 1992 election, see Colbert L. King, "The Dilemma of Black Republicans," *Washington Post National Weekly Edition* (28 September–4 October 1992), p. 29; Dorothy J. Gaiter, "Many Black Voters Broaden Their Agenda Beyond Civil Rights," *Wall Street Journal* (13 October 1992); Felicity Barringer, "Rich–Poor Gulf Widens among Blacks," *New York Times* (25 September 1992); and Sam Roberts, "When Race is an Issue in Politics," *New York Times* (12 October 1992).

12. Catherine S. Manegold, "In New York Senate Race, a Wooing of Black Voters," *New York Times* (30 October 1992).

FIVE

POLITICS, PERSONALITY AND PROTEST IN HARLEM: THE RANGEL–POWELL CONGRESSIONAL RACE

In Harlem, things are rarely actually what they may seem. Consider the current Democratic congressional primary race in the Fifteenth District, pitting a powerhouse against the son of a legend: incumbent Charles B. Rangel vs. insurgent Adam Clayton Powell, IV. The media has neatly characterized the contest under the "politics of personality" category. A quarter of a century ago, on 24 June 1970, an idealistic, relatively inexperienced Rangel won a tiny 150-vote victory over Harlem's most charismatic and controversial elected official, Adam Clayton Powell, Jr. The entire white political establishment in the Democratic Party had waged an unrelenting campaign for years to oust Harlem's unpredictable legislator from his congressional seat of power. Rangel, a New York State assemblyman for barely four years, with a brief and undistinguished record as assistant US attorney, managed by only the slenderest of means to defeat the man who arguably had been, overall, the most influential politician in African-American history.

Today, the political cycle has supposedly returned full circle. Rangel, now the established political veteran, is confronted by the boyish, energetic son of the man he had defeated. Rangel, worried and defensive, takes no chances: he hires political guru Bill Lynch as his campaign manager and places top congressional lieutenant Frank Jasmine into the mobilization effort. Under the slogan, "Keep the Power," Rangel attempts to remind constituents how generously they have benefited from federal government programs through his access to power in Washington. Powell is criticized as an ineffective neophyte. Conversely, Powell's basic campaign slogan can be summed up simplistically in one word: "angry." His campaign literature attacks "politicians who *claim* to have power, but only keep what little they have to themselves and their cronies," without specifically naming Rangel. Powell insists that he "is angry when our small businesses are being pushed aside for large corporations that don't hire people in our neighborhood." Thus, potential voters are cajoled: "If you're as *Angry* as Adam, do something." By voting for Powell, you too can be *"Angry For Change."*

This is the abysmal level of political discourse to which we have been reduced: anger, power, my father's loss, and revenge. This campaign should be part of a television soap opera, rather than a contest which might shed illumination and analysis, describing the depths of human tragedy and pain which are an organic part of daily life in Harlem. One might even be reminded in this campaign of the *Eighteenth Brumaire* and Marx's admonition that history repeats itself: "the first time as tragedy and the second time as farce." Or as the *New York Times* summed up the Harlem contest: "It's tough to run against a boulevard." The only way to understand the meaning of the Rangel–Powell contest is to step back from the personalities, separating rhetoric from reality. To discern the deeper significance of this Democratic primary race, you'll need to know something about the history of black politics in Harlem, throughout this city and across the country.

Although African-Americans have been present in this city for centuries, their social presence was at best secondary and their political clout nonexistent prior to World War I. Blacks comprised only 2 per cent of the city's total population in 1900, and 3 per cent in the 1920 census. During the twentieth century, however, as the size and social weight of the black community began to expand in New York, three fundamental political traditions emerged as strategies for group empowerment. In general, the strategies can be termed "accommodation," "reform from below," and "reform from above." Each of these strategies developed its own unique style: a set of white coalition partners; a specific public rhetoric and social discourse; an approach toward the utilization of governmental resources for the public welfare; and a structural link to core constituencies, institutions and neighborhood organizations which provide cadre and supporters on the streets to realize their goals.

"Accommodation" was the first method used by black elites to gain some measure of local power and privilege. As the first massive waves of African-American migrants from the Deep South came into Harlem, the dominant political power citywide was Tammany Hall, the Democratic Party machine. Tammany was the gatekeeper for thousands of municipal jobs, exercising control over vast resources. At the national level, African-American educator Booker T. Washington had already advanced a strategy of conservative coalition-building with white Republicans. Washington had acquiesced to legal racial segregation in order to gain patronage jobs for a limited number of black professionals, and to be permitted to develop black-owned businesses, real estate and homes within the confines of the ghetto. As the architect of "black capitalism," Washington favored alliances with the wealthy white propertied classes, and vigorously opposed labor unions and coalitions between black and white workers. The political language of accommodation was characterized by phrases like "mutual responsibilities," "gradualism," "protection of private property," "hard work" and "thrift."

Similarly at the local level in New York, the strategy of accommodation linked this first generation of black politicians to the conservative, authoritarian structure of power, Tammany Hall. Black members of the Democratic Party found themselves in segregated clubs, under the label "United Colored Democracy." In 1915, Tammany boss Charles F. Murphy selected Ferdinand Q. Morton to direct his growing black sub-organization in Harlem. For his allegiance, Morton was named assistant district attorney that same year, and was subsequently appointed to the Municipal Civil Service Commission. Morton's allies and lieutenants in Harlem received similar benefits, as the black population of the city grew. In parallel fashion, black Republicans developed their own clientage relationship with powerful whites, under the leadership of Charles Anderson. But in both cases, white conservatives ruthlessly dominated the resources of the black community, and severely restricted the access of African-American leaders to the actual levers of power. One indication of this is that it was not until 1930 that Harlem's black Republicans took over their own district leaderships in the Nineteenth and Twenty-First Assembly Districts. In Brooklyn, the situation for blacks was even worse. When black attorney Lewis Flagg ran for the Seventeenth Assembly District in 1932 on a black nationalist-oriented program, he received only 1 per cent of the district's vote.

"Accommodation" broke down as an effective social and political strategy for managing dissent within the black community for three basic reasons: population, poverty and protest. By the 1930s, Harlem had become the capital of black America, the most famous and influential urban environment of the black experience. Manhattan had nearly a quarter of a million black residents, with another 69,000 blacks living in Brooklyn in the 1930 census. The Great Depression was most severely felt within New York's growing black community. Black nationalist leader Marcus Garvey had already successfully mobilized tens of thousands of Harlem's poorest and most oppressed blacks behind his charismatic rhetoric and ambitious Back-to-Africa program. Now, thousands more began to clamor for democratic changes. Spontaneous rent strikes, street protests and demonstrations against job discrimination proliferated, frequently sparked and led by Harlem's Communist Party activists. The levels of mass discontent culminated in the race riots of 1935 and 1943. In the later riot, five people were killed, more than three hundred were injured, with $5 million worth of property destroyed.

"Reform from below" was now on the agenda. It was characterized by a political rhetoric of contempt for the powerful and privileged, a charismatic leadership style to appeal to the grassroots and working poor, the mobilization of protest campaigns around a series of real social grievances. The greatest representatives of reform from below in Harlem history during the Depression and World War II were Adam Clayton Powell, Jr. and Benjamin Davis, Harlem's premier Communist spokesperson and New York City Council member from 1943 to 1949. Utilizing his base at the powerful Abyssinian Baptist Church, Powell used the language and tactics of radical reform from below for more than a decade before being elected to Congress in 1944. Powell eventually earned the political respect of activists such as Malcolm X, who once exclaimed that if black Americans had as many as ten representatives who possessed the acumen and wide array of skills as the charismatic congressman from Harlem, then he could "retire." At his pinnacle of power in 1961, Powell assumed the chair of the House Committee on Education and Labor, producing sixty major pieces of reform legislation on civil rights in five years. He influenced public policies on federal aid to education, opening up access to college training to hundreds of thousands of African-Americans.

Simultaneously, Powell cultivated as many enemies as he made allies and supporters. He was notoriously lavish in his personal habits, and eventually came to ignore his own working-class and impoverished constituency beyond rhetorical flourishes and charismatic public posturing. In national politics, Powell was equally unreliable, flirting periodically with the Republican administration of Dwight Eisenhower while expressing solidarity with Afro-Asian revolutionaries across the Third World. After a series of legal problems, the national Democratic Party decided once and for all to eliminate this powerful maverick – an uncontrollable but always potentially dangerous force – from their ranks. In 1967 the House of Representatives voted to exclude him from Congress. When the Supreme Court ruled that this action was blatantly unconstitutional, Powell was summarily stripped of his seniority and chairmanship. He was forced into exile on the Caribbean island of Bimini, yet for several years still had the clout to get re-elected to Congress from Harlem. In short, Powell's greatness as an advocate of the reform-from-below tradition can be measured directly by the level of social-protest mobilization and political organization in Harlem's streets.

When the level of militancy and activism died out during the Cold War period of the 1950s, as the Communist Party was buried beneath McCarthyism and state repression, Powell became disconnected from the masses. No progressive organization representing the grievances and aspirations of the poor, the homeless, the working people could effectively guide or check his behavior. This more than anything else was the principal factor in his tragic downfall.

Even Powell's sharpest critics concede that Harlem's tribune for civil rights, at his best, effectively articulated a vision for democratic reform and the empowerment of black people. Rangel recently recalled: "There is no question that Adam Powell was one of the most effective legislators who ever served in the Congress. He was the only idol we had in Harlem. He was audacious power and all of us thought, when we entered politics, that we wanted to be like Adam." The problem for the Democratic Party was that the accommodationist model was no longer viable. Powell's genuine success in national politics and his quarter-century grip on Harlem's congressional seat had proved this. Thus, in the post-World War II era, a third model for black empowerment was born: "reform from above." Black middle-class representatives would now be permitted to share access to resources and power, but in an explicit partnership with white liberal elites, foundations and corporations. The state sector thus becomes the chief avenue for expanding opportunities for a growing African-American professional class. In effect, "reform from above" represents a cultural, political and economic philosophy of "inclusion" – let us please have a share of the pie, a part of the power structure. The problem is, of course, that partial ownership and access to an inherently inegalitarian and racist social order only fosters the illusion of democratic change. Inclusionary reform from above certainly benefited the black middle class via public-policy concessions like affirmative action, but did little to address the deep structural problems of the working class and the poor.

With the outbreak of the Second Reconstruction, the modern civil-rights movement, white liberalism desperately needed to support and promote the rise of a new leadership class in the urban black community: a professional/managerial elite which was genuinely committed to democratic reforms for urban renewal, yet a leadership that instinctively knew how far to press the limits, the boundaries of pragmatic reform. The new elite should be astute in the noisy discourse of the streets, but comfortable in the quiet confines of corporate headquarters and Wall Street. This creative blend of entrepreneurial, polemical and pragmatic tendencies sets the "reformer from above" apart from Adam Clayton Powell, Jr. in fundamental ways.

Probably the single outstanding representative of the reformer-from-above model in Harlem is attorney/entrepreneur Percy Sutton. In earlier days, Sutton was close to street radicals and activists within the Communist Party. In the mid-1960s, he served briefly as Malcolm X's attorney, and earned a reputation as an intelligent, insightful voice within black urban affairs nationally. But he also astutely worked the other side of the street, managing to win friends within the national Democratic Party in corporate headquarters downtown.

At the congressional level, Rangel has played a parallel role to Sutton. At strategic points, he has astutely caught the political mood of urban black America around a host of public policy issues. In 1984, he was one of the few nationally prominent black Democrats to put muscle behind the Rainbow Coalition presidential campaign of Jesse Jackson. Rangel has been the Democratic Party's key congressional leader on the "war on drugs" for over a decade. And, to his credit, on economic policy he has actually moved more to the left in recent years, with the formulation of an urban Empowerment Zone for Manhattan and the Bronx.

Rangel's central dilemma, unfortunately, is that the strategy of pragmatic "reform from above" can only work well within an environment of white political liberalism and Keynesian economics. Social change can only be managed from above by carving out limited resources for those at the bottom. If the pie shrinks, or if the welfare state becomes Hobbesian, or if the white electorate becomes racist and nasty toward black folks, the whole strategy falls apart.

And in slow motion, over a twenty-year period, that is actually what has happened. At the local level, the retreat from reform began in earnest in 1977, with the election of Ed Koch as mayor. Probably the kindest thing one can say about Koch is that he was essentially urban America's George Wallace – a bitter, petty demagogue who deliberately manipulated ethnic prejudices and social bigotry for the explicit purpose of suppressing the black community. A former liberal, Koch seized power by constructing what was in effect an anti-black united front, aimed at consolidating white ethnic power citywide. When it became apparent that white hegemony couldn't work as an explicit program for reaction, Koch carefully cultivated conservative Latinos and Asian Americans to splinter the possibility of a progressive, multicultural democratic movement. Koch's opportunistic switch to social conservatism, such as his support for the death penalty and opposition to affirmative action, also appealed to the neo-conservative trend within New York's traditionally Jewish community. At the national level, the political retreat of Koch from liberal reform to social intolerance was also reflected in the political and ideological triumph of Reaganism in the 1980s, and in the failure of the Clinton administration to advance meaningful urban policies in the 1990s.

The collapse of white liberalism, the death of the welfare state, and the rise of white ethnic racism closed the historical door to the option of reform from above, just as the Great Depression destroyed the effectiveness of the old accommodationist model of black clientage leadership three generations ago. But in politics, historical categories for interpreting reality usually lag behind the creation of new social forces which actually operate in the here and now. We still use phrases like the "black–Jewish alliance," for example, although it has functionally ceased to exist. In the campaign, Rangel's forces manipulate phrases like "Keep the Power," which seem oddly anarchistic at best, at least to his most impoverished constituents. And Powell's "angry" exhortations seem almost surreal, devoid as they are of a coherent public-policy agenda which actually identifies Harlem's real problems and suggests democratic alternatives to the bankruptcy of liberal social engineering.

From a personal standpoint, Powell also appears to be burdened by the same inconsistencies of behavior as his father. On the City Council, he voted against the Dinkins administration budget, to the outrage of Speaker Peter F. Vallone. He has been widely criticized for poor attendance at important committee meetings, and he introduced only two bills during his first year in office. Chris Meyer, lobbyist for the New York Public Interest Research Group, has observed Powell in action on the Council. For the *New York Times*, Meyer applauded Powell's willingness "to buck the leadership" and commended him for his "populist" style, but noted that he has not been "a legislative force." That is a record which Republican councilman Charles Millard describes as "very unpredictable, and sometimes that's been good." Sometimes, however, unpredictability can be very bad. When Powell recently decided to accept a $5,000 campaign contribution from members of a rightist, anti-Castro Cuban group based in Miami, he effectively repudiated his father's generally progressive political posture on Third World issues.

Rangel should easily win this election. But there is another race which will be far more difficult for him to win. Despite the successful efforts to spark economic revitalization in Harlem, including the expansion of businesses along the 125th Street corridor and the promise of greater development under the new Empowerment Zone, there is a deep sense of social alienation and anger within Harlem's black population. Real unemployment rates for adults are over 20 per cent. Harlem currently has more than one-third of the estimated 33,000 abandoned apartment units in the city. On some streets, city service agencies have essentially given up any intervention activities or programs, overwhelmed by rat infestation, drugs, random violence and decaying housing. In terms of health care, the situation for low-income and poor Harlem residents is nothing short of a crisis. Harlem Hospital leads the city in TB cases, with twenty-four times the national average. Several years ago, the *New England Journal of Medicine* reported that males in Bangladesh, one of the most impoverished Third World nations, have statistically higher life expectancy rates than Harlem's male population. Only 40 per cent of Harlem males live to the age of sixty-five, compared to nearly 80 per cent of white American males. Death rates in Harlem for cancer are 50 per cent higher today then when Rangel was first elected. The list of devastating socioeconomic statistics pertaining to Harlem goes on and on.

So it is not surprising that Rangel is running a little scared. The social space for a rebirth of militancy already exists. The wild card in Harlem's political future, however, is its growing Latino community. As early as 1930, 45,000 Puerto Ricans lived in East Harlem. In recent decades, West Harlem has become increasingly Latino. Washington Heights is overwhelmingly Dominican. If a new multicultural, radical reform-from-below movement emerges, it must speak Spanish as well as black English; it must capture the cultural specificity of what is distinctive between Puerto Ricans, Dominicans and Central American people, who are central to Harlem's future. If such a protest erupts, it will not easily be confined to the boundaries of political liberalism and the Democratic Party. Powell will fail because what Harlem needs most is not a return to the past, however charismatic or nostalgic. What is desperately required is a breakthrough of political imagination, of a social vision of democratic empowerment liberating the energies, talents and abilities of the most oppressed and alienated members of society. The Rangel–Powell race is only the latest act of that old historical drama, the struggle to define the role of race in urban public policy and within the structures of power and ownership in America. But it foreshadows a social storm which may sweep away the older strategies and models of black empowerment.

SIX

AFFIRMATIVE ACTION
AND THE POLITICS OF RACE

The triumph of "Newtonian Republicanism" is not a temporary aberration: it is the culmination of a thirty-year ideological and political war against the logic of the reforms of the 1960s. Advocates of civil rights, affirmative action, and other policies reflecting left-of-center political values must recognize how and why the context for progressive reform has fundamentally changed. And, instead of pleasant-sounding but simplistic defenses of "affirmative action as it is," we need to do some hard thinking about the reasons why several significant constituencies which have greatly benefited from affirmative action have done relatively little to defend it. We need to recognize what the critical theoretical and strategic differences are which separate liberals and progressives on how to achieve a nonracist society. And we urgently need to reframe the context of the political debate, taking the initiative away from the right.

The first difficulty in developing a more effective progressive model for affirmative action goes back to the concept's complex definition, history and political evolution. "Affirmative action" *per se* was never a law, or even a coherently developed set of governmental policies designed to attack institutional racism and societal discrimination. It was instead a series of presidential executive orders, civil-rights laws and governmental programs regarding the awarding of federal contracts, fair employment practices and licenses, with the goal of uprooting bigotry. Historically, at its origins, it was designed to provide some degree of compensatory justice to the victims of slavery, Jim Crow segregation and institutional racism. This was at the heart of the Civil Rights Act of 1866, which stated that "all persons within the jurisdiction of the United States shall have the same right in every State and Territory, to make and enforce contracts, to sue, be parties, give evidence, and to the full and equal benefit of all laws and proceedings for the security of persons and property as is enjoyed by white citizens."

During the Great Depression, the role of the federal government in protecting the equal rights of black Americans was expanded again through the direct militancy and agitation of black people. In 1941, socialist and trade-union leader A. Philip Randolph mobilized thousands of black workers to participate in the "Negro March on Washington Movement," calling upon the administration of Franklin D. Roosevelt to carry out a series of reforms favorable to civil rights. To halt this mobilization, Roosevelt agreed to sign Executive Order 8802, which outlawed segregationist hiring policies by defense-related industries that held federal contracts. This executive order not only greatly increased the number of African-Americans who were employed in wartime industries, but also expanded the political idea that government could not take a passive role in the dismantling of institutional racism.

This position was reaffirmed in 1953, by President Harry S. Truman's Committee on Government Contract Compliance, which urged the Bureau of Employment Security "to act positively and affirmatively to implement the policy of nondiscrimination in its functions of placement counseling, occupational analysis and industrial services, labor market information, and community participation in employment services." Thus, despite the fact that the actual phrase, "affirmative action" was not used by a chief executive until President John F. Kennedy's Executive Order 11246 in 1961, the fundamental idea of taking proactive steps to dismantle prejudice has been around for more than a century.

What complicates the current discussion of affirmative action is that historically liberals and progressives were at odds over the guiding social and cultural philosophy which should inform the implementation of policies on racial discrimination. Progressives like W.E.B. Du Bois were convinced that the way to achieve a nonracist society was through the development of strong black institutions, and the preservation of African-American cultural identity. The strategy of Du Bois was reflected in his concept of "double consciousness," that black American identity was simultaneously African and American, and that dismantling racism should not require the aesthetic and cultural assimilation of blackness into white values and social norms. The alternative to the Du Boisian position was expressed by integrationist leaders and intellectuals like Walter White, Roy Wilkins, Bayard Rustin and Kenneth Clark. They, too, fought to destroy Jim Crow. But their cultural philosophy for the Negro rested on "inclusion" rather than pluralism. They deeply believed that the long-term existence of separate all-black institutions was counterproductive to the goal of a "color-blind" society, in which racial categories would become socially insignificant or even irrelevant to the relations of power. Rustin, for instance, personally looked forward to the day when Harlem would cease to exist as a segregated, identifiably black neighborhood. Blacks should be assimilated or culturally incorporated into the mainstream.

My central criticism of the desegregationist strategy of the "inclusion-ists" (Rustin, White, Wilkins, et al.) is that they consistently confused "culture" with "race," underestimating the importance of fostering black cultural identity as an essential component of the critique of white supremacy. The existence of separate black institutions or a self-defined, all-black community was not necessarily an impediment to interracial cooperation and multicultural dialogue. Nevertheless, both desegregationist positions from the 1930s onward were expressed by the organizations and leadership of the civil-rights movement. These divisions were usually obscured by a common language of reform, and a common social vision which embraced color-blindness as an ultimate goal. For example, both positions are reflected in the main thrust of the language in the Civil Rights Act of 1964, which declared that workplace discrimination on the basis of "race, color, religion, sex or national origin" should be outlawed. However, the inclusionist orientation of Wilkins, Rustin and company is also apparent in the 1964 Act's assertion that it should not be interpreted as having to require any employers "to grant preferential treatment to any individual or to any group."

Five years later, after Richard Nixon's narrow victory for the presi-dency, it was the Republicans' turn to interpret and implement civil-rights policy. The strategy of Nixon had a profound impact upon the political culture of America, and continues to have direct consequences within the debates about affirmative action today. Through the counterintelligence program of the FBI, the Nixon administration vigorously suppressed the radical wing of the black movement. Second, it appealed to the racial anxieties and grievances of George Wallace voters, recruiting segregationists like Jesse Helms and Strom Thurmond into the ranks of the Republican Party. On affirmative action and issues of equal opportunity, however, Nixon's goal was to utilize a liberal reform for conservative objectives, the expansion of the African-American middle class, which might benefit the Republican Party. Under Nixon in 1969, the federal government authorized what became known as the "Philadelphia Plan." This program required federal contractors to set specific goals for minority hiring. As a result, the number of racial minorities in the construction industry increased from 1 to 12 per cent. The Nixon administration supported provisions for minority set-asides to promote black and Hispanic entrepreneurship; it placed Federal Reserve funds in black-owned banks. Nixon himself publicly praised the concept of "Black Power," carefully interpreting it as "black capitalism."

It was under the moderate conservative aegis of the Nixon–Ford administrations of 1969–1977 that the set of policies which we identify with "affirmative action" were implemented nationally in both the public and private sectors. Even after the 1978 Bakke decision, in which the Supreme Court overturned the admission policy of the University of California at Davis, which had set aside 16 out of 100 medical-school openings for racial minorities, the political impetus for racial reform was not destroyed. What did occur, even before the triumph of reaction under Reagan in the early 1980s, was that political conservatives deliberately usurped the "color-blind" discourse of many liberals from the desegregation movement. Conservatives retreated from the Nixonian strategy of utilizing affirmative-action tools to achieve conservative political goals, and began to appeal to the latent racist sentiments within the white population. They cultivated the racist mythology that affirmative action was nothing less than a rigid system of inflexible quotas which rewarded the incompetent and the unqualified (who happened to be nonwhite) at the expense of hard-working, tax-paying Americans (who happened to be white). White conservatives were able to define "merit" in a manner that would reinforce white male privilege, but in an inverted language which would make the real victims of discrimination appear to be the "racists." It was, in retrospect, a brilliant political maneuver. And the liberals were at a loss in fighting back effectively precisely because they lacked a consensus internally about the means and goals for achieving genuine equality. Traditional "liberals," like Morris Dees of the Southern Poverty Law Center, who favored an inclusionist "color-blind" ideology of reform often ended up inside the camp of racial reactionaries, who cynically learned to manipulate the discourse of fairness.

The consequences of these shifts and realignments within American political culture by the 1990s on how to achieve greater fairness and equality for those who have experienced discrimination were profound. In general, most white Americans have made a clear break from the overtly racist Jim Crow segregationist policies of a generation ago. They want to be perceived as being "fair" toward racial minorities and women, and they acknowledge that policies like affirmative action are necessary to foster a more socially just society. According to the 17–19 March 1995 *USA Today*/CNN/Gallup poll, when asked, "Do you favor or oppose affirmative action programs," 53 per cent of whites polled expressed support, compared to only 36 per cent who opposed. Not surprisingly, African-Americans expressed much stronger support: 72

per cent for affirmative-action programs to only 21 per cent against. Despite widespread rhetoric that the vast majority of white males have supposedly lost jobs and opportunities due to affirmative-action policies, the poll indicated that only 15 per cent of all white males believe that "they've lost a job because of affirmative-action policies."

However, there is a severe erosion of white support for affirmative action when the focus is more narrowly on specific steps or remedies addressing discrimination. For example, the *USA Today*/CNN/Gallup poll indicates that only 30 per cent of whites favor the establishment of gender and racial "quotas" in businesses, with 68 per cent opposed. Conversely, two-thirds of all African-Americans expressed support for "quotas" in business employment, with only 30 per cent opposed. When asked whether quotas should be created "that require schools to admit a certain number of minorities and women," 61 per cent of whites were opposed, with 35 per cent in favor. Nearly two-thirds of all whites would also reject policies which "require private businesses to set up specific goals and timetables for hiring women and minorities if there were not government programs that included hiring quotas." On the issue of implementing government-supported initiatives for social equality, most black and white Americans still live in two distinct racial universes.

It is not surprising that "angry white men" form the core of those who are against affirmative action. What is striking, however, is the general orientation of white American women on this issue. White women have been overwhelmingly the primary beneficiaries of affirmative action. Millions of white women have gained access to educational and employment opportunities through the implementation and enforcement of such policies. But most of them clearly do not share the political perspectives of African-Americans and Hispanics on this issue, nor do they perceive their own principal interests to be at risk if affirmative-action programs were to be abandoned by the federal government or outlawed in the courts. For example, in the same *USA Today*/CNN/Gallup poll, only 8 per cent of all white women stated that their "colleagues at work or school privately questioned" their qualifications due to affirmative action, compared to 19 per cent of black women and 28 per cent of black men. Fewer than one in five white women polled defined workplace discrimination as a "major problem," compared to 41 per cent of blacks and 38 per cent of Latinos. Some 40 per cent of the white women polled described job discrimination as "not being a problem" at all. These survey results may help to explain why middle-class-oriented liberal feminist leaders and constituencies have been relatively less vocal than African-Americans in the mobilization to defend affirmative action.

A quarter of a century of affirmative-action programs, goals and timetables has clearly been effective in transforming the status of white women in the labor force. It is certainly true that white males still dominate the upper ranks of senior management: while constituting 47 per cent of the nation's total workforce, white males constitute 95 per cent of all senior managerial positions at the rank of vice president or above. However, women of all races now constitute about 40 per cent of the total workforce overall. As of the 1990 census, white women held nearly 40 per cent of all middle-management positions. While their median incomes lag behind those of white males, over the past twenty years white women have gained far greater ground in terms of real earnings than black or Hispanic males in the labor force. In this context, civil-rights advocates and traditional defenders of affirmative action must ask themselves whether the majority of white American women actually perceive their material interests to be tied to the battles for income equity and affirmative action that most blacks and Latinos, women and men alike, continue to fight for.

We should also recognize that, although all people of color suffer in varying degrees from the stigmatization of racism and economic disadvantage within American society, they do not have the same material interests or identify themselves with the same politics as the vast majority of African-Americans. For example, according to the 1990 census, the mean on-the-job earnings for all Americans adults totaled $15,105. Blacks' mean on-the-job annual earnings came to $10,912; Native Americans', $11,949; Hispanics', $11,219. But it is crucial to disaggregate social categories like "Hispanics" and "Asian Americans" to gain a true picture of the real material and social experiences within significant populations of color.

About half of all Hispanics, according to the Bureau of the Census, term themselves "white," regardless of their actual physical appearance. Puerto Ricans in New York City have lower median incomes than African-Americans, while Argentines, a Hispanic group which claims benefits from affirmative-action programs, have mean on-the-job incomes of $15,956 per year. The Hmong, immigrants from Southeast Asia, have mean on-the-job incomes of $3,194; in striking contrast, the Japanese have annual incomes higher than those of whites. None of these statistics negates the reality of racial domination and discrimination in terms of social relations, access to employment opportunities or job advancement. But they do tell us part of the reason why no broad coalition of people of color has coalesced behind the political demand for affirmative action; various groups interpret their interests narrowly in divergent ways, looking out primarily for themselves rather than addressing the structural inequalities within the social fabric of the society as a whole.

So where do progressives and liberals go from here, given that the right has seized the political initiative in dismantling affirmative action, minority economic set-asides and the entire spectrum of civil-rights reforms? We must return to the theoretical perspectives of Du Bois, with some honest dialogue about why race relations have soured so profoundly in recent years. Affirmative action was largely responsible for a significant increase in the size of the black middle class; it opened many professional and managerial positions to blacks, Latinos and women for the first time. But in many other respects, affirmative action can and should be criticized from the left, not because it was "too liberal" in its pursuit and implementation of measures to achieve equality, but because it was "too conservative." It sought to increase representative numbers of minorities and women within the existing structure and arrangements of power, rather than challenging or redefining the institutions of authority and privilege. As implemented under a series of presidential administrations, liberal and conservative alike, affirmative action was always more concerned with advancing remedial remedies for unequal racial outcomes than with uprooting racism as a system of white power.

Rethinking progressive and liberal strategies on affirmative action would require sympathetic whites to acknowledge that much of the anti-affirmative-action rhetoric among Democrats is really a retreat from a meaningful engagement on issues of race, and that the vast majority of Americans who have benefited materially from affirmative action have not been black at all. A Du Boisian strategy on affirmative action would argue that, despite the death of legal segregation a generation ago, we have not yet reached the point where a color-blind society is possible, especially in terms of the actual organization and structure of white power and privilege. Institutional racism is real, and the central focus of affirmative action must deal with the continuing burden of racial inequality and discrimination in American life.

There are many ways to measure the powerful reality of contemporary racism. For example, a 1994 study of the Office of Personnel Management found that African-American federal employees are more than twice as likely to be dismissed as their white counterparts. Blacks are likely to be fired at much higher rates than whites in jobs where they constitute a significant share of the labor force: for example, black clerk typists are 4.7 times more likely to be dismissed than whites, and black custodians 4.1 times more likely to be fired. Discrimination is also rampant in capital markets. Banks continue policies of "red lining," denying loans in neighborhoods which are largely black and Hispanic. And even after years of affirmative-action programs, blacks and Latinos remain grossly underrepresented in a wide number of professions. For example, African-Americans and Hispanics represent 12.4 per cent and 9.5 per cent respectively of the US adult population. But of all American physicians, blacks account for barely 4.2 per cent, and Latinos 5.2 per cent. Among engineers, blacks represent 3.7 per cent, Latinos 3.3 per cent; among lawyers, blacks account for 3.3 per cent, Latinos 3.1 per cent; and for all university and college professors, blacks made up 5 per cent, Latinos 2.9 per cent. As Jesse Jackson observed in a speech before the National Press Club, while native-born white males constitute only one-third of the US population, they constitute 80 per cent of all tenured professors, 92 per cent of the Forbes 400 chief executive officers, and 97 per cent of all school superintendents.

If affirmative action is to be criticized, it should be on the grounds that it has not gone far enough in transforming the actual power relations between black and white within US society. More evidence for this is addressed in a new book by sociologists Melvin Oliver and Thomas Shapiro, *Black Wealth/White Wealth*. They point out that "the typical black family has eleven cents of wealth for every dollar owned by the typical white family." Even middle-class African-Americans – people who often benefited from affirmative action – are significantly poorer than whites who earn identical incomes. If housing and vehicles owned are included in the definition of "net wealth," the median middle-class African-American family has only $8,300 in total assets, to $56,000 for the comparable white family. Why are blacks at all income levels much poorer than whites in terms of wealth? African-American families not only inherit much less wealth, they are affected daily by institutional inequality and discrimination. For years they were denied life-insurance policies by white firms. They are still denied home mortgages at twice the rate of similarly qualified white applicants. African-Americans are less likely to receive government-backed home loans.

Given the statistical profile of racial inequality, liberals must reject the economistic temptation to move away from "race-conscious remedies" to "race-neutral" reforms defined by income or class criteria. Affirmative action has always had a distinct and separate function from antipoverty programs. Income and social class inequality affect millions of whites, Asian Americans, Latinos and blacks alike, and programs which expand employment, educational access and social-service benefits based on narrowly defined economic criteria are absolutely essential. The impetus for racism is not narrowly "economic" in origin. Racial prejudice is still a destructive force in the lives of upper-middle-class, college-educated

African-Americans, as well as poor blacks, and programs designed to address the discrimination they feel and experience collectively every day must be grounded in the context of race. However, affirmative action is legitimately related to class questions, but in a different way. A truly integrated workplace, where people of divergent racial backgrounds, languages and cultural identities learn to interact and respect each other, is an essential precondition for building a broadly pluralistic movement for radical democracy. The expanded implementation of affirmative action, despite its liberal limitations, would assist in creating the social conditions essential for pluralistic coalitions for full employment and more progressive social policies.

What is required among progressives is not a reflective, uncritical defense of affirmative action, but a recognition of its contradictory evolution and conceptual limitations, as well as its benefits and strengths. We need a thoughtful and innovative approach in challenging discrimination which, like that of Du Bois, reaffirms the centrality of the struggle against racism within the development of affirmative-action measures. We must build upon the American majority's continued support for affirmative action, linking the general public's commitment to social fairness with creative measures that actually target the real patterns and processes of discrimination which millions of Latinos and blacks experience every day. And we must not be pressured by false debate to choose between race or class in the development and framing of public policies to address discrimination. A movement toward the long-term goal of a "color-blind" society, the deconstruction of racism, does not mean that we become "neutral" about the continuing significance of race in American life.

As the national debate concerning the possible elimination of affirmative action defines the 1996 presidential campaign, black and progressive Americans must re-evaluate their strategies for reform. In recent years we have tended to rely on elections, the legislative process, and the courts to achieve racial equality. We should remember how the struggle to dismantle Jim Crow segregation was won. We engaged in economic boycotts, civil disobedience, teach-ins, freedom schools, "freedom rides," community-based coalitions and united fronts. There is a direct relationship between our ability to mobilize people in communities to protest and the pressure we can exert on elected officials to protect and enforce civil rights. Voting is absolutely essential, but it isn't enough. We must channel the profound discontent, the alienation and the anger which presently exist in the black community toward constructive, progressive forms of political intervention and resistance. As we fight for affirmative action, let us understand that we are fighting for a larger ideal: the ultimate elimination of race and gender inequality, the uprooting of prejudice and discrimination, and the realization of a truly democratic America.

PART II

AFRICAN-AMERICAN LEADERSHIP: SOCIETY, EDUCATION AND POLITICAL CHANGE

SEVEN

CLARENCE THOMAS AND THE CRISIS
OF BLACK POLITICAL CULTURE

The controversy surrounding Clarence Thomas's nomination and confirmation as an associate justice of the Supreme Court represents the first decisive national debate in the post-civil-rights era. The Second Reconstruction, the great historical epoch characterized by the democratic upsurge of African-Americans against the structures of racial discrimination and social inequality, effectively ended with the Reagan administration. Although much of the commentary on Thomas focused largely on the sexual harassment charges made against him by former aide Anita Hill, the case must be seen against even larger political currents that symbolize the contemporary crisis within the African-American political culture. This crisis is represented by the overlapping contradictions of gender, race, and the flawed ideology of liberalism. Each of these elements simultaneously illuminates and obscures the actual character of American politics and the status of African-Americans within the apparatus of state power. Beyond the dimensions of personality, they alone explain how and why Clarence Thomas succeeded in being appointed to the Supreme Court and why the majority of African-Americans were persuaded to support his nomination.

Clarence Thomas's climb to power is directly related to his abandonment of the principles of the black freedom struggle. A quarter of a century ago, as a college student in the late 1960s, Thomas proclaimed himself a devoted disciple of Malcolm X. Thomas wore the black beret of the Black Panther Party and signed his letters "Power to the People." He secured a position at Yale Law School due to its aggressive affirmative-action program, which had set aside roughly 10 per cent of all places in each class to racial minorities. Yet, less than a decade later Thomas would condemn affirmative action as being destructive to blacks' interests. When initially appointed head of the Equal Employment Opportunity Commission, Thomas embraced for a time the use of numerical hiring goals and timetables as a means to increase the employment of blacks. However, following Reagan's landslide victory in 1984, he reversed his position and strongly attacked affirmative-action goals and timetables. Two years later, when seeking reappointment to the EEOC from a Democratic-controlled Congress, Thomas solemnly promised that he would reinstate affirmative-action measures inside his office.

In dozens of published articles and in more than one hundred public speeches, Thomas repeatedly attacked the entire civil-rights agenda as hopelessly anachronistic and irrelevant to the more conservative political environment of the 1980s. Thomas denounced welfare and other liberal reforms of the Great Society as a form of government-sponsored paternalism that reinforced dependency and undermined self-help and practical initiative within the black community. Thomas even went so far as to criticize the famous 1954 Supreme Court decision *Brown* v. *Board of Education of Topeka, Kansas,* which abolished racially segregated schools, as being based on "dubious social science" evidence. Thomas's subsequent appointment to a federal judgeship in Washington DC was due less to his reputation as a legal scholar and for judicial temperament, which was nonexistent, than for his noteworthy service as a partisan ideologue for conservative Republicanism.

Moreover, Thomas was one of the few people of color elevated by both former President Reagan and President Bush to federal judgeships. During Bush's first two years as president, he appointed seventy federal judges, nearly all of whom were white, affluent males. Less than 12 per cent of Bush's federal judges were women; only 6.5 per cent were from racial minority groups. Virtually all of his selections were deeply hostile to civil rights, affirmative-action enforcement, civil liberties for those charged with criminal offenses, environmental-protection laws, and the freedom of choice for women on the issue of abortion. Thus, the reality of Thomas's racial identity, and any personal or political connections he might have had with the African-American community, were secondary to his role as legal apologist for reactionary politics. Indeed, during these years Thomas attempted to "transcend" his blackness and condemned those who argued that his race necessarily imposed an obligation to conform to certain progressive political attitudes or policies.

From the moment of Bush's nomination of Thomas to replace liberal Associate Justice Thurgood Marshall on the Supreme Court, the president's justification and defense of the black conservative were essentially a series of unambiguous lies. No one in Congress or the legal profession seriously believed Bush's assertion that Thomas was nominated because he was "the best-qualified" jurist in the nation. No one was convinced by Bush's initial claims that Thomas's race had "nothing" to do with the decision to advance his candidacy. At best, Thomas's published writings revealed the workings of a mediocre mind. If Bush had genuinely desired to nominate a black Republican judge with outstanding legal credentials, he would have ignored Thomas entirely and selected Amalya Kearse, an African-American currently serving on the federal appeals court in New York. But Kearse's legal reputation as a moderate, despite her Republican Party affiliation, made her unacceptable to the extreme right wing. Bush's objective in selecting Thomas was, in part, to gain political capital at the expense of the core constituencies within the Democratic Party, astutely pitting feminists against civil-rights activists.

By contrast, other Republican presidents when considering Supreme Court appointments have frequently chosen quality over narrow partisanship. Dwight Eisenhower appointed two of the most liberal Supreme Court justices in American history: Chief Justice Earl Warren and Associate Justice William Brennan. Gerald Ford appointed to the court Justice John Paul Stevens, who is viewed today as a moderate. Even Reagan nominated Sandra Day O'Connor, who is essentially a moderate conservative. Bush's goal clearly was not judicial excellence. He wanted a nominee who was opposed to a woman's freedom of choice on abortion, an ideologue with slim intellectual qualifications who would attack the liberal political agenda from the protected confines of the court for the next thirty years. Even before Professor Anita Hill's charges of sexual misconduct began to circulate, thoughtful observers noted in Thomas's record a disturbing characteristic of contempt for African-American women. This perception was not directly linked to his divorce from his first wife, an African-American, and his remarriage in 1987 to Virginia Bess Lamp, a white Republican attorney. Thomas had first come to the attention of white conservatives nationally at a San Francisco conference sponsored by black Reaganites in the late 1980s. In his remarks before the conference, Thomas attacked the welfare programs for perpetuating dependent behavior among blacks by focusing his negative remarks on his own sister, Emma Mae Martin. "She gets mad when the mailman is late with her welfare check," Thomas announced, as other black conservatives laughed aloud. "That's how dependent she is," Thomas affirmed.

Years later, journalists investigated Thomas's statements and discovered that they were false, because his sister was not on welfare at the time of his speech. Thomas didn't mention that his sister had received none of the educational advantages and affirmative-action benefits that he had taken for granted. It was also Thomas's sister who had assumed the responsibility of caring for their mother, and had taken two part-time jobs to get off welfare. As economist Julianne Malveaux critically observed: "For providing that kind of support in her family, Emma Mae Martin earned her brother's public scorn. What can the rest of us women expect from Supreme Court Justice Clarence Thomas as issues of pay equity and family policy come before this court?"

As Hill's charges of sexual harassment by Thomas reached the headlines, other disturbing evidence surfaced. Classmates of Thomas during his years at Yale Law School had already informed members of the Senate Judiciary Committee that he had displayed a strong "interest in pornographic films" at that time. Most damaging was Hill's testimony before the committee, which was detailed, credible and persuasive. Witnesses also corroborated her testimony. Hill's charges of sexual misconduct echoed sharply across the country and transcended the specific case of Thomas, largely because the experience of sexual harassment was so common to millions of working women, regardless of their race, ethnicity, education, or class background. According to an October 1991 *New York Times*/CBS News poll, about four out of ten women across the country have been the "object of sexual advances, propositions, or unwanted sexual discussions from men" in supervisory positions at their places of employment. Only one out of eight women who had been sexually harassed actually reported the incident. Like Hill, they knew that without hard evidence their assertions were unlikely to be believed. Their professional careers would suffer. Interestingly, even half of all men polled admitted that they have "said or done something which could have been construed by a female colleague as harassment."

The Senate and the Bush administration were first inclined to ignore the gravity of Hill's charges, which had originally been made in private, and to rush a confirmation vote on Thomas. But the public outcry, particularly from women's groups, was so profound that the leaders of both parties were forced to retreat. Part of the dilemma for the White House was the collapse of its basic strategy, which had avoided any analysis of Thomas's meager record as a legal scholar or federal judge, and had concentrated totally on his Horatio Alger, "Up from Slavery" saga. Now it was exactly Thomas's personality, character, and private morals that were seriously open to question.

But as the Senate committee was forced to reopen the hearings to evaluate Hill's testimony, the scales were tipped decisively in Thomas's favor. First, both the White House and the Senate were determined to keep the hearings from becoming, as Bush lieutenants put it, a "referendum on sexual harassment." Thomas should not be the "victim of two thousand years of male dominance." None of the senators had any familiarity with the legal requirements for sexual harassment, and had no knowledge of the massive body of scholarship and legal decisions on the issue. Second, a strategic error was committed by Senate Judiciary Committee chairman Joseph Biden. Biden perceived Hill's accusations in the context of a criminal trial, with the presumption of innocence resting with Thomas. But this was completely erroneous; no one had filed criminal charges against Thomas. The process should not have been seen as a trial, with the issue of establishing witness credibility, but as a political hearing to determine the qualifications and fitness of Thomas to serve on the Supreme Court. The point should have been made repeatedly that even if Hill did not exist, or even if grave doubts could be established concerning her testimony, there was already more than sufficient evidence to reject Thomas's nomination to the court.

Thomas helped his own case by taking the offensive. "If someone wanted to block me from the Supreme Court of the United States because of my views on the Constitution, that's fine," he declared before the committee. "But to destroy me? ... I would have preferred an assassin's bullet to this kind of living hell that they have put me and my family through." Thomas proclaimed himself the martyr of an elaborate smear campaign inspired by racism. Without even listening to Hill's testimony or specific charges, Thomas declared that he was the victim of a "high-tech lynching." This was, of course, the most supreme irony: the black conservative who had done so much to destroy affirmative-action and civil-rights programs designed to attack racial discrimination now sought refuge on the grounds of racism. As Janelle Boyd, a lawyer with the NAACP Legal Defense Fund, observed: "Thomas has run from his blackness, and now that he is backed into a corner, all of a sudden, Judge Thomas is black. He had used race in the most manipulative way." Nevertheless, Thomas's strategy was effective. The white liberal Democratic senators did not wish to be accused of racism, and they deliberately permitted Thomas to dictate the terms of the discourse. They were so effectively cowed that they neglected even to ask Thomas about the evidence of his long-time interest in pornographic films.

As the Democrats equivocated, the Reaganite Republicans smelled blood and circled for the political kill. The Senate's leading demagogue, Alan Simpson of Wyoming, vowed that Hill would be "destroyed, belittled, hounded, and harassed." With sinister innuendoes, he claimed to have faxes and letters attacking Hill's credibility "hanging out of my pockets," which warned him to "watch out for this woman." Senator

Strom Thurmond of South Carolina declared Hill's allegations to be "totally without merit," even before listening to her testimony!

In a racist, sexist society, it is relatively easy for white men with power to discredit and to dismiss a black woman. The media contributed to the political assassination of Hill by projecting the controversy as part soap opera, part public trial, and by accepting the interpretation that Thomas merited the presumption of innocence. In this context it was not terribly surprising that the majority of Americans witnessing the spectacle concluded that Thomas was telling the truth and that Hill was lying. But in response to those who smeared Anita Hill for possessing the courage and dignity to step forward, one should ask: Why would she lie? What did she actually gain from her actions? Politically a conservative and identified with her tenure in the Reagan administration, she clearly was not a liberal. Conservative politicians, ideologues, and sexists may attack her personal integrity and professionalism for decades to come. Her probable goal of one day becoming a federal judge is lost forever. As University of Maryland law professor Tanya Banks observed, Hill certainly "would not have taken this step without full consideration of consequences."

But at the moment of truth the liberals lacked the courage of their convictions. They sacrificed their principles before the volatile politics of gender and race. They physically recoiled when Thomas, in a moment of desperation, cynically charged "racism." They refused to acknowledge the reality that Anita Hill, not Thomas, was the real victim of "lynching" – not once, but twice: the first time a decade ago, when she was sexually humiliated and harassed in private, and the second time on Capitol Hill before the eyes of the world.

From the vantage point of African-American politics, the most crucial factor that contributed to Thomas's narrow confirmation by the Senate was the obvious support he had received from the majority of blacks. In several polls, about 60 per cent of all African-Americans expressed support for Thomas's confirmation, even after Hill's charges were widely circulated. The Southern Christian Leadership Conference, established in 1957 by Martin Luther King, Jr., announced its endorsement of Thomas. The National Urban League took no official position against Thomas's nomination. The reality of black support for Thomas was a major reason that several southern Democrats who faced re-election in 1992 gave their votes to the black nominee. These senators included Wyche Fowler, Jr. of Georgia; Richard Shelby of Alabama; and John B. Breaux of Louisiana. Several other southern Democrats who had voted against Robert Bork's nomination to the Supreme Court four years before, including Senators J. Bennett Johnston of Louisiana and

Sam Nunn of Georgia, also cast their votes for Thomas. Black southern votes were absolutely essential for these white Democrats to survive politically.

When Bush first selected Thomas to replace Marshall, most African-American leaders and national organizations expressed strong opposition. The Congressional Black Caucus, with few exceptions, condemned Thomas as unfit to serve in Marshall's place. After some initial hesitancy, the NAACP came out against the black Reaganite on the grounds of his bitter hostility to civil rights and affirmative action. Many powerful black religious and trade-union leaders also issued similar condemnations of Thomas's nomination.

But the initial opinion polls of African-Americans clearly indicated a willingness to support Thomas's appointment. There were at least three reasons for this curious response. The first factor was due to the growth of black "neo-accommodation." Since the rise of Reaganism within national politics more than a decade ago, white conservatives have made an effort to establish a base of political support within the African-American community. One primary reason for this can be attributed to racial patterns in national presidential and congressional politics. Since 1948 the majority of white voters have given a democratic presidential candidate their support only once – Lyndon Johnson in 1964. Neither John F. Kennedy nor Jimmy Carter received a majority of whites' votes in their successful presidential elections. White middle-class voters, especially males, consistently support Republican candidates. Conversely, since 1964 an average of 88 per cent of all African-Americans have supported Democratic presidential candidates. Black support for Democratic senatorial candidates usually exceeds 90 per cent. Republicans recognize that they would only need to increase their electoral support among blacks to roughly 20 to 25 per cent – a realistic figure, given that Dwight Eisenhower received only 40 per cent of blacks' votes in 1956. With this increased black support, the Republicans would regain control over Congress, and would be virtually unbeatable in presidential contests, regardless of the Democratic candidate.

Thus, despite Reagan's vicious posturing and rhetoric against the civil-rights community and most black officials, the Republicans began to fashion a "black middle-class agenda": federal governmental support for black-owned banks and entrepreneurship, criticism of social-welfare programs, endorsement of all-black male public schools, embracing the discourse of "self-reliance" historically associated with Booker T. Washington and Elijah Muhammad. A series of neo-accommodationist conservative black spokespersons were promoted in the national media: economists Thomas Sowell and Walter Williams; journalist Tony Brown;

Glenn C. Loury, professor at Harvard University's Kennedy School of Government; Robert Woodson, president of the National Center for Neighborhood Enterprises; J.A.Y. Parker, president of the Lincoln Institute for Research and Education; and of course Thomas.

The collaboration between black Democrats and conservative Republicans began to grow in state-wide and congressional elections throughout the 1980s. In a half-million-dollar project, Benjamin L. Ginsberg, the chief counsel of the Republican National Committee, assisted civil-rights organizations in their legal challenges to redraft congressional district boundaries, which might increase the number of African-American and Latino representatives. Republicans frequently observed that about eighty white Democrats represented congressional districts that were at least 30 per cent black; for blacks to gain greater political power, they would have to do so at the expense of the Democratic Party's white establishment. Republicans began to provide Chicano and African-American groups free computer time, legal assistance, and political support. In several statewide races, blacks began to support "moderate" Republicans. In 1986, 60 per cent of all blacks voted for Republican incumbent Thomas Kean in New Jersey's gubernatorial race. In 1990, in Illinois, Republican gubernatorial candidate James Edgar received more than one-fifth of the black vote, and with this slender percentage was elected. Many black Chicagoans who had supported progressive mayor Harold Washington announced their support for Edgar.

Bush was well aware of these trends, and he sought to advance some public-policy positions that would appeal to the black middle class. One central example is provided by the Bush administration's inconsistent position on the desegregation of historically black state colleges. In July 1991, US Solicitor General Kenneth Starr was ordered to file an initial brief with the Supreme Court on a major school desegregation case, taking the position that states did not have to increase funds to black public colleges. The initial brief stated that there was no "independent obligation" for states "to correct disparities" between white and black public institutions. In protest, Bush's board of advisors on historically black colleges, chaired by former Howard University president James Cheek, demanded a meeting with the president. On 9 September 1991, Bush was told by his black advisors that Starr's brief had created a "crisis" among African-American educators. Partially due to the pressures of the Thomas nomination, Bush totally repudiated his earlier position, ordering Starr to issue a new brief stating that it was "incumbent" upon states to "eradicate discrimination" by implementing "equitable and fair funding to historically black institutions." Just in case the Supreme Court overlooked the significance of Bush's new position, the revised brief added: "Suggestions to the contrary in our opening brief no longer reflect the position of the United States."

The second factor contributing to black support for Thomas was the ideology of "liberal integrationism" that permeated the strategic and tactical vision of the entire black middle class. For nearly a century, since the founding of the NAACP, most middle-class blacks have espoused a political ideology of integrationism, a commitment to the eradication of racial barriers within government, business, and society. In its simplest terms, "liberal integrationism" argues that if individual African-Americans are advanced to positions of political, cultural, or corporate prominence, then the entire black community will benefit. This concept is essentially "symbolic representation": the conviction that the individual accomplishments of a Bill Cosby, Michael Jordan, Douglas Wilder, or Oprah Winfrey trickles down to empower millions of less fortunate African-Americans. In municipal politics, liberal integrationism's "symbolic representation" means that if the number of African-Americans appointed to the police department increases, or if a black professional becomes police commissioner, working-class black neighborhoods will eventually become safer, or police brutality will gradually be reduced. The 1989 mayoral victory of David Dinkins in New York, for example, is broadly interpreted in the black media as yet another "gain" for the entire race.

The fundamental contradiction inherent in the notion of integrationist "symbolic representation" is that it presumes that a degree of structural accountability and racial solidarity binds the black public figure with the larger masses of African-Americans. During the period of Jim Crow, the oppressive external constraints of legal discrimination imposed norms of racial conformity and solidarity. Whatever an individual's educational attainments, capital formation, or excellence on the athletic field, for example, he or she could never entirely escape the oppressive reality of segregation. The very definition of "race" was a social category defined by the presumed and very real hierarchies within the socioeconomic and political system, preserving and perpetuating black subordination. Black conservatives in an earlier era, such as George Schuyler, felt an obligation to their "race" that was imposed by the burden of exploitation, commonly experienced by all. But in the post-civil-rights period, in the absence of the legal structures of formal discrimination, the bonds of cultural kinship, social familiarity, and human responsibility that had once linked the most affluent and upwardly mobile African-Americans with their economically marginalized sisters and brothers were severely weakened. It is now possible for a member of the present-day Negro elite to live in the white suburbs, work in a white professional office, attend religious services in an all-white church or synagogue, belong to a white country club, and never come into intimate contact with the most oppressed segments of the black community. Moreover, for those privileged blacks within the expanding elite, the benefits of betraying the liberal politics and social-democratic assumptions deeply entrenched within the black working class are greater than ever. So the argument that, regardless of individual personal histories, class affinities, and cultural identities, the professional successes of individuals within the African-American elite benefit the entire black community is no longer valid.

But old beliefs die hard. A number of black liberal intellectuals, whose world-views and political perceptions were hardened by the turmoil of the 1960s and the heroic struggles against legal segregation, implicitly accept the notion of symbolic representation, and the totality of the ideological baggage of liberal integration. Noted author Maya Angelou expressed her support for Thomas in a *New York Times* editorial. Stephen Carter of Yale University, author of the controversial book *Reflections of an Affirmative Action Baby*, termed many of the charges leveled against Thomas by blacks irrelevant and "ridiculous." Carter declared that he "admire[d] much of what [Thomas] stands for," and insisted that the black conservative, who in fact had done so much to undermine the black struggle for equality, nevertheless represented "an important voice in the black community and in national affairs. His ostracism as a traitor, an enemy, and Uncle Tom, reflects no credit on those who have sought to cast him out." Carter's effort to salvage a degree of credibility from Thomas's shabby and shameful record was based on a faulty set of political assumptions. Carter never questioned the belief that a Thomas victory in the Senate would translate into a type of political advancement for other African-Americans.

Other liberal integrationists in the media admitted having second thoughts about Thomas, but gradually voiced approval for his nomination to the Supreme Court. Columnist William Raspberry expressed his willingness to accommodate to the dominant conservative realities of the Reagan–Bush era. "I never thought of Thomas as some sort of judicial Tonto, willing to betray his people for his own selfish interests," Raspberry observed. Raspberry's principal "disappointment" with Bush's selection was not ideological; it was based on the grounds that Thomas was "too inexperienced and untested for so important a post." However, with the startling revelations of Hill, Raspberry's hostility shifted easily from right to left. The idea that such a gentle-man as Thomas might actually engage in vulgar sexist intimidation was inconceivable. Without a shred of evidence, Raspberry declared that the "sexual harassment allegations" were nothing less than "cheap shots, eleventh hour flimflammery and character assassination." He also condemned the Congressional Black Caucus's opposition to Thomas, which was deplored for having been determined "with no debate" and with "no witnesses." Raspberry's stuffy rhetoric might have made sense if Thomas had not had a decade-long track record as an opponent of civil rights and affirmative action, or if Hill's politics had been identified with feminism or the left. But within its immediate context Raspberry's argument represented a restatement of old dogmas and tired integrationist formulas, a faith in the bourgeois respectability of the Negro elite.

Liberal journalist Juan Williams, author of the documentary history of the civil-rights movement, *Eyes on the Prize*, also rushed to Thomas's defense. The liberals' criticism of Thomas, Williams worried, had gone too far. "[Thomas] has been conveniently transformed into a monster about whom it is fair to say anything," Williams charged. "In pursuit of abuses by a conservative president, the liberals have become the abusive monsters." Williams's assertions helped to justify Thomas's hypocritical claim that he was the victim of a political "lynching" because of his racial identity. By equating Hill's plausible charges with the bloody record of terror by the Klan, Thomas was able to swing millions of undecided blacks behind his cynical campaign to obtain a lifetime appointment.

However, the most articulate defense of Thomas from liberal black quarters was offered by Harvard sociologist Orlando Patterson. Thomas was probably guilty of violating the cultural norms of "his white, upper-middle-class work world," Patterson suggested. But he had only offered sexual advances "to an aloof woman who is esthetically and socially very similar to himself, who had made no secret of her own deep admiration for him." In short, Thomas was guilty of bad judgement and poor office manners. If anyone was to blame, it was Hill. Patterson argued:

> Raising the issue ten years later was unfair and disingenuous: unfair because, while she may well have been offended by his coarseness, there is no evidence that she suffered any emotional or career damage, and the punishment she belatedly sought was in no way commensurate with the offense; and disingenuous because she has lifted a verbal style that carries only minor sanction in one subcultural context and thrown it in the overheated cultural arena of mainstream, neo-Puritan America, where it incurs professional extinction.

The approach to redeem Thomas taken by Patterson is familiar to any African-American schooled in the cultural norms of their own people. How can any man be blamed for expressing his sexual interest in an available, attractive black woman? Doesn't the punishment for these sweet words uttered in the executive suite so many years ago far exceed the crime? Patterson goes so far as to defend Thomas's falsehoods given under oath because the black conservative's behavior did not merit censure: "Judge Thomas was justified in denying making the remarks, even if he had in fact made them," Patterson concluded, "not only because the deliberate displacement of his remarks made them something else but on the utilitarian moral grounds that any admission would have immediately incurred a self-destructive and grossly unfair punishment."

Patterson's thesis is grounded in several contradictory falsehoods. There is certainly a deep tradition of sexism within the black community, a pattern of denying human rights and leadership for women within our own institutions. In both black nationalist and integrationist formations, practices and policies of gender discrimination are apparent. But to dismiss the brutal language and offensive actions of Thomas by recalling similar behavior by other black men makes absolutely no sense. Should it not matter that when this incident occurred Thomas was the head of the Equal Employment Opportunity Commission, the agency responsible for outlawing sexual harassment in the workplace? Patterson's query concerning the number of years that had transpired between the alleged act of harassment and its public revelation blatantly ignores the legal evolution that has occurred in the past decade in such cases. The EEOC did not issue guidelines concerning sexual harassment, which was defined as any behavior that has the "purpose of unreasonably interfering with an individual's work performance or creating an intimidating or hostile or offensive environment," until 1980. It was not until 1986, in *Meritor Savings Bank* v. *Vinson*, that the Supreme Court actually ruled that sexual harassment in the workplace was a form of sex discrimination covered under Title VII of the 1964 Civil Rights Act. At the time of her harassment in the early 1980s, Hill would have had few legal avenues for redress. If she had filed a grievance, she would not have had a federal case because judges viewed sexist intimidation as merely "bad manners." Even as late as 1991, Hill would not have been able to recover damages from such a suit. Most professional women in this situation would have done what Hill did: stay with the position, hoping that her supervisor would change, or seek employment elsewhere without alienating her boss. But to claim as Patterson does that Thomas's obnoxious behavior was just a "down-home style of courting" is dishonest and disturbing.

A third factor that explains African-American support for Thomas can be attributed to the quasi-black-nationalist sentiment among millions of African-American working-class people and elements of the black middle class that were radicalized during the 1960s. A distinguishing feature of black nationalism is the belief that "race" is more important than other factors, such as gender or class, in determining social and political outcomes. Given the reality of Thomas's racial background, some black nationalists could support him on the grounds that Bush would simply appoint a white reactionary to the court if Thomas was rejected by the Senate. Some even argued that any black person, regardless of his or her public record as a reactionary, had nevertheless experienced daily life as a black person. The factor of race was inescapable, and certainly this meant that Thomas ought to be given the benefit of the doubt. With the security of a permanent judicial appointment, he might eventually come to embrace the progressive perspectives of other African-Americans.

The most articulate neo-accommodationist defense of Thomas from a "black-nationalist" perspective was offered by Dr. Niara Sudarkasa, noted anthropologist and president of Lincoln University in Pennsylvania. Sudarkasa has previously identified herself as a black nationalist, and has claimed that one of the most influential African-Americans in her own political development was Malcolm X. She has informed Lincoln University students and alumni that the "n" in the university's name stands for "nation-building," a phrase taken directly from the black-nationalist cultural upsurge of two decades ago. Nevertheless, Sudarkasa went before the Senate Judiciary Committee to praise Thomas's conservative credentials. She insisted that Thomas was "an open-minded and independent thinker" who should not be attacked for holding views in opposition to liberal integrationists in the civil-rights establishment. African-Americans "have been fortunate in having a long line of leaders who, in retrospect, seem right for their times," she argued. "These leaders did not always have the same ideology or agree on strategies, but they all agreed that the goal was to secure freedom and justice for our people.... Who can say that we are not better off for having the benefit of their separate and distinct voices?" Invoking black history, Sudarkasa perceived Thomas in the "nation-building" tradition of Frederick Douglass, Marcus Garvey, and Martin Luther King, Jr.

Sudarkasa's thesis is only partially true. Throughout African-American history the political ideology of black people has been characterized by a struggle for both human equality and political democracy. Different leaders have approached these goals with different strategies. Black nationalists such as Malcolm X and Marcus Garvey have sought to build strong, black-controlled economic, political, and social institutions that could empower the black community from within. They have linked our struggles for freedom with the larger currents of political protest in Africa and the Caribbean. Other black leaders, such as Frederick Douglass and Martin Luther King, Jr., have emphasized the necessity of achieving full integration and the eradication of all barriers to equality within the United States.

Sudarkasa's analysis presumes that Thomas and other upper-middle-class blacks who favor the repressive policies of the Reagan–Bush agenda are consciously working on behalf of other African-Americans as an oppressed national minority. Actually, they are working fundamentally to promote their own careers, manipulating the mantle of blackness to cloak political perfidy. No doubt Thomas feels some ambiguous connections with the historical achievements of previous African-American leaders, who made sacrifices to advance the boundaries of freedom for their people. The critical difference that separates him from this earlier leadership is a rupture between "race" and "ethnicity." Racially, Thomas remains "black": both by governmental definition and societal recognition, he belongs to a specific racial group characterized in part by physical appearance and political condition. Racial identity is essentially passive, a reality of being within a social formation stratified by the oppressive concept of race. Yet ethnically Thomas has ceased to be an African-American, in the context of political culture, social values and ideals, and commitment to collective interests. Thomas feels absolutely no active ideological or cultural obligations to the dispossessed, the hungry and the homeless who share the ethnic rituals, customs, and traditions of blackness. Thomas's accomplishment is a logical product not simply of personal cynicism but of the flawed perspective of liberal integrationism, which all too frequently made no distinction between race and ethnicity in black life. This is the reason that Louisiana racist politician and former neo-Nazi David Duke had little difficulty endorsing Thomas for appointment to the Supreme Court. Thomas was racially black, but in most other respects stood in bitter opposition to the resistance traditions in the culture of African-American people.

The great danger of Thomas's appointment will be measured in the political outlook and ideological attitudes of a new generation of African-Americans, who were born after the period of Jim Crow and have no personal memories or involvement in civil-rights demonstrations, protest marches, and Black Power activism. Like Thomas, they stand outside a period of history that binds them to a political culture of resistance and social transformation. Many seek not to challenge the established structures of power but to prepare themselves to assimilate within these systems. This tremendous sense of impending crisis for the future of young African-Americans was reinforced for me during a visit to Lincoln University, in the midst of the national debate over Thomas–Hill. One of Lincoln's most articulate young male students argued passionately, after I presented several critical comments on the Thomas nomination. The student did not deny that the evidence in the case weighed heavily against Thomas. Nevertheless, he insisted that African-Americans had no choice except to applaud this appointment to the Supreme Court. After all, Thomas claimed to be opposed to welfare and the white liberal policies of dependency; didn't this place Thomas in harmony with black activists such as Malcolm X and black nationalists like Elijah Muhammad, who advocated "self-help?" In brief, he forcefully presented Sudarkasa's thesis of neo-accommodationism. I was deeply impressed with the student's seriousness, and tried to raise every conceivable counter-argument. I argued just as passionately that Thomas's opposition to a woman's freedom of choice on abortion would mean that thousands of pregnant black women annually would be subjected to back-alley butchers. Thomas's hatred of affirmative action meant a monolithically conservative Supreme Court that would reduce blacks' opportunities in education and the job market.

The Lincoln University student replied: "That's the problem with black people today. We aren't willing to settle for half a loaf. Sometimes less than half a loaf is all we can expect, and we should be happy to get even that." This is not the political perspective of resistance, the enthusiastic defiance of youth that characterized the Student Nonviolent Coordinating Committee and the cadre of the Black Panther Party. This is not the aggressive posture of young people who oppose oppression and who are unwilling to accept anything less than freedom. The central tragedy of Thomas for black America is his powerful image as a negative role model for millions of young people who have never walked a picket line or occupied a public building in protest. Thomas's victory reinforces the tendencies toward compromise, accommodation, and pessimism. His elevation to the court illustrates to our next generation that any instincts toward the political culture of resistance must be forgotten, that the way forward is to accept the "less than half a loaf" offered to us by our oppressors.

The price of Thomas's personal advancement into the corridors of national power has thus been achieved at an unprecedented price. Our young people have witnessed an unprincipled individual with a deep hostility toward African-American women, and who possibly committed acts of sexual harassment, nevertheless rewarded and praised at the highest levels of government. Seldom has the black intelligentsia and political leadership been in such disarray, debating the merits of supporting an obvious opportunist. Seldom has the black middle class so confused its actual material interests with the symbolic satisfaction of seeing one of its own appointed to high judicial office. The Thomas case is one of the rare instances in which the majority of the African-American community has supported the wrong person for the wrong position for the wrong reasons. Unfortunately, given the profound level of confusion in both the strategic and ideological perspectives of the African-American middle class, its present inability to transcend the bankrupt politics of liberal integrationism, it is probable that we will witness more Clarence Thomases in the near future.

EIGHT

BLUEPRINT FOR

BLACK STUDIES

African-American Studies is at the edge of a second Renaissance, a new level of growth, institutionalization and theoretical advancement. A generation ago, as the black freedom movement collapsed the structures of legal segregation and led to the rise of Black Power, the first African-American Studies programs were initiated at white universities and colleges. More than three hundred departments, programs and research centers were initiated between 1964 and 1976. Most of these programs perceived themselves as operating in hostile intellectual and institutional terrain, with limited resources, uncertain faculty positions, and frequently ambiguous relations with administrators and academic colleagues. Black Studies endeavored to articulate its understanding of the collective experiences of the people of the African diaspora. This project was corrective of the dominant myths, stereotypes, and misinterpretations of the black experience which prevailed within the standard white curriculum. Simultaneously, Black Studies was also prescriptive in its efforts to suggest paths for the constructive resolution of problems which confronted African-American people.

Despite the elimination and reduction of many of these programs, the accomplishments of this first generation of Black Studies scholars in predominantly white institutions can now be measured and appreciated. A new generation of scholars trained in the social sciences and humanities has emerged with new insights, challenging established dogmas. New programs and centers are being developed, frequently in conjunction with university-wide efforts to restructure core curricula to reflect "multiculturalism," or greater ethnic and racial diversity. Foundations have taken a new interest in ethnic and Black Studies, partially due to changes within America's overall racial composition. By the middle of the twenty-first century, fully half of the total population of the United States will consist of people of color. Thus the demographic factor alone forces each white academic institution to rethink its approach towards the question of race in general, and African-American Studies specifically.

The future of African-American Studies will ultimately reside in its ability to address a number of theoretical, structural and political questions which confront this next generation of scholars and teachers. Black Studies must do more to address in a critical and comparative fashion the various theoretical paradigms and schools of interpretation within the African, Caribbean, and African-American experience. In the area of black literature there is a school of critics who analyze the creativity of such writers as Leopold Sedar Senghor and Aime Cesaire within the tradition of Negritude. A similar body of scholars in the United States focus their research on the Harlem Renaissance period of the 1920s, or the literature produced during the Black Arts Movement of the 1960s and early 1970s. However, in the social sciences we are only beginning to see research which explores the political and social experiences of black people in a Pan-Africanist context and perspective. This diasporal approach presumes subterranean connections between the politics and protest of people of African descent, whether in Johannesburg, Kingston, Brixton or Harlem. Are there systematic connections between the formation of intellectuals, the development of self-help economic institutions, and the construction of cultural and social groupings, which cut across the African diaspora; and if so, how can they be studied critically and analytically? Are there patterns of political and social leadership, or of social protest movements, which cut across the Caribbean, sub-Saharan Africa, and black America? The paradigm of pan-Africanism, or the construct of the African diaspora, should yield a wealth of critical scholarship.

In recent years, a critical discourse termed "Afrocentrism" has emerged within Black Studies. Its principal theoretician is Molefi Kete Asante, director of one of the most important African-American Studies departments in the United States, at Temple University. "Afrocentrism" – identification with the creative culture, values, traditions and rhetoric of people of African descent – is the philosophical foundation for the advance of the struggles of black people. Asante's *The Afrocentric Idea* and other works explore the black experience using this paradigm. Asante's criticism of Western cultural values parallels some of the work by other non-Western scholars, notably Samir Amin. Other promising work employing the Afrocentric paradigm is found in the psychological studies of Linda James Myers of Ohio

State University. Yet, this body of work has not been subjected to rigorous critique and examined for possible shortcomings. If we are to take our own intellectual currents and traditions seriously, then they must be debated and explored.

Black Studies must pursue the connections and contrasts between the African-American intellectual tradition and the Western European and American cultural tradition. Much black scholarship, literature and cultural criticism represents a meditation on the relationship between people of African descent and the "West." In essence, we are in the West but not of it; our status behind Du Bois's "veil" yields critical insights into another world which is not our own. We employ the language and technical tools of the West for the purpose of dismantling structures of inequality and domination which Europe deliberately imposed upon us. We find ourselves linked unwillingly to the leviathan, and that linkage leaves its mark in our scholarship and cultural production.

Professor Robert Hill of the University of California–Los Angeles has, for example, suggested striking parallels in the construction of W.E.B. Du Bois's *The Souls of Black Folk* and Goethe's *Faust*. In the Faust character, and later in Du Bois, one finds "two warring souls," the conflict of consciousness, and the relentless "striving" to achieve full wisdom and truth. The Faustian dilemma is mirrored in Du Bois's struggle of poverty and truth against "mammonism" and exploitation. An analysis of other central works featuring in African-American Studies yields similar parallels. A productive discussion could occur between scholars of Jean-Paul Sartre's *Anti-Semite and Jew* and black intellectuals influenced by Frantz Fanon's *Black Skin, White Masks*. An academic course on "Comparative Perspectives on Existentialism" could include Dostoevsky's *Notes from Underground*, Sartre's essay "The Wall," Albert Camus' *The Myth of Sisyphus*, and the writings of Richard Wright and Ralph Ellison. Shakespearean scholars of *The Tempest* would find new meanings in the characters of Prospero and Caliban from their utilization in George Lamming's *Of Age and Innocence*.

African-American Studies must do more to bring together scholars in the humanities, creative arts, and social sciences. In theory, Black Studies was initially advanced as an interdisciplinary mode of critical investigation, employing tools and resources from various disciplines. In practice, the curricula of most African-American Studies programs are taught in the same parochial manner as the traditional, discipline-based departments we have criticized. Let us conceive of an interdisciplinary course on the theme of "Resistance: Cultural, Social and Political." The central question in the course would be, "What is the correlation between African-American cultural and artistic creativity and the socioeconomic and political context that provides its birth and development?" Is it accidental that the classical tradition of the blues, the context for Leadbelly and Blind Lemon Jefferson, was the terror of the Jim Crow South, the annual lynching of over one hundred blacks, political disenfranchisement, sharecropping and convict leasing? What is the political economy of race and class represented in the blues? Or, we may turn to contemporary times, with the same questions framing our analysis of rap music and its emergence from the vernacular, folk tradition of resistance, survival and struggle in our inner cities. Is it accidental that rap has erupted precisely at the historical moment when African-American unemployment is massive, when crack has become a crippling epidemic, and as prisons and the criminal justice system have become a means for the institutional regulation of hundreds of thousands of young black people? Rap at its best represents a critique of the system of domination and exploitation, projecting into artistic form the political economy advanced by Malcolm X. By searching the contours of culture, we illuminate the essence of our political, economic and social environment.

To have any practical relevance to the actual conditions and problems experienced by African-American people, Black Studies must conceive itself as a type of *praxis*, a unity of theory and practical action. It is insufficient for black scholars to scale the pristine walls of the academic tower, looking down with calculated indifference on the ongoing struggles of black people. We must always remember that we are the product and beneficiaries of those struggles, and that our scholarship is without value unless it bears a message which nourishes the hope, dignity and resistance of our people. There are Black Studies programs at major universities which are conducting impressive research projects, producing monographs on various aspects of the black experience. Yet, much of this work is abstract and disconnected; it is framed in a discourse which is literally indecipherable except to a small body of scholars. It replicates the stilted, obtuse language that characterizes much of the Western intellectual tradition.

The knowledge base within our universities must be utilized to provide a framework for African-American development and awareness. In 1988, at Ohio State University, I initiated a course entitled "The Black Experience in Columbus, Ohio." With the assistance of several graduate students, I collected articles, books and sections from dissertations on various aspects of the African-American experience in Columbus and Central Ohio. A reader was constructed with materials on various themes: blacks in the public educational system; race and the criminal justice system; blacks within state and city government, and the electoral political process; residential segregation and the dynamics of the making of the black ghetto on Columbus's east side; poverty, joblessness and the homeless in the black community; health-care issues and the crack crisis; civil rights and the struggle against institutional racism in Columbus, and other topics. The course itself was sponsored by the university's Continuing Education Program, and offered in the Black Studies Department's community extension building, in the heart of Columbus's black neighborhood. Most of my students either lived in the black community or had some practical experience in one or more of the course's topics.

"The Black Experience in Columbus" was divided into two parts. The first hour of our class was organized around a lecture and discussion format, in which students reviewed the assigned readings in a particular topic. In the second hour, black and white representatives, community leaders and officials who were related to the evening's topic were invited into the class, and engaged in dynamic exchanges with students and community residents. The debates and discussions were videotaped, and later aired in a series of programs on public-access television. The curriculum was designed not merely to inform but to transform; the purpose of the course was to reconnect the black community with its own economic, social, cultural and political experience. The unity of theory and action within Black Studies serves to increase the capacity of African-Americans to perceive their own interests and to act in a conscious manner to empower themselves.

Black Studies must play a decisive role in the current debate across the academy concerning "multiculturalism." In theory, the debate about "multiculturalism" and the ancillary dispute concerning "political correctness" relates to the proper approach to the teaching of different cultures, ethnicity and gender issues, and their integration within core curricula. Critics of multiculturalism protest that they are not opposed to pluralism and diversity in themes and texts within universities, that they oppose "ethnocentrism" of any sort, and that they encourage the recruitment of minority students, faculty and administrators. But they charge that academic advocates of Black Studies, Chicano Studies, Feminist Studies and other inter-disciplinary-based programs generated on white, male-dominated campuses during the struggles of the 1960s are engaged in a "form of left-wing McCarthyism." Critics such as Diane Ravitch perceive Ethnic Studies courses as being "animated by a spirit of filiopietism and by fundamentalist notions of racial and ethnic purity." They contend that "innocent" professors are being dismissed or hounded into silence if they offer a text in their courses which is offensive to African-Americans, Hispanics, feminists or other activist constituencies. Ravitch asserts that this is a form of "particularism" which "says to members of the group that they have nothing in common with people who are of a different race, a different religion, a different culture. It breeds hatred and distrust."

What is most revealing about the intellectual bankruptcy of Ravitch and other conservative critics of Ethnic Studies is that their critique is silent on the actual power relationship between people of color and women and the dominant, upper-class elites which control American higher education. African-Americans represent less than 4 per cent of all university and college professors, and at most large research universities less than 2 per cent of all faculty and administrators. The majority of white campuses do not have a single course in African-American studies. At best, only a minority of universities have required that all students take one course in "non-Western" topics, which may include Black Studies, but rarely do these institutions earmark sufficient funds for the development of pluralistic themes and multicultural content in courses across the spectrum of the social sciences and humanities. All of this occurs at a historical conjuncture in which a conservative president vetoes a civil-rights bill, the Supreme Court undermines affirmative action, and the economic and social conditions of blacks and Latinos have deteriorated sharply. Therefore, to imply that minorities have the institutional means to intimidate thousands of white college teachers and administrators, to impose their multicultural imperatives on hapless white students, is at best grossly dishonest.

We must set the contours of the debate by advancing a clear framework for the institutionalization of multicultural values in higher education. What is the basis of multiculturalism? At heart, it is the recognition that the totality of American society within the United States is not expressed within one and only one cultural group, Western European, only one religion, Christianity, or only one language, English. Civilizations, cultures and language patterns from Africa, the Caribbean, Latin and Central America, Asia, the Pacific, and the Native American people, have also profoundly influenced the pluralistic American experience and the complex and contradictory identities of its people. Multiculturalism should approach each cultural tradition with an awareness of its own integrity, history, rituals and continuity. But, by definition, it must be critical and comparative in its approach, rather than myopic and parochial. Our scholarship and courses must examine the parallels, conflicts, and discontinuities between African-Americans – and by extension people of African descent across the globe – and other people of color as well as European cultures and societies. This implies an approach toward learning and education that rejects exclusivity and the elitism so deeply engrained in the West in favor of the richness, pluralism and diversity at the heart of the black intellectual tradition.

Moreover, multiculturalism and Black Studies must be articulated within a general theory of educational democracy. Inequality and systems of discrimination rooted in racial, gender and class differences within the larger social order are perpetuated and reinforced by the curricula and elites in American higher education. American universities largely reflect the sterile realities of "closed institutions": exclusionary, alienating, anti-democratic, disconnected from working-class and poor communities, administratively hierarchical. African-American Studies, and more generally the effort to create a more multicultural university, can only succeed if the university itself is fundamentally transformed. An "open institution," broadly based, flexible in its administrative structure, possessing a deep commitment to public responsibility and social obligations, and a commitment to the uprooting of racism, sexism and class inequality, must be the long-term goal. Because if Black Studies does not consciously seek to transform these elitist institutions, which are essentially designed to reproduce the daughters and sons of privileged social classes and racial groups, African-American Studies programs and departments will inevitably atrophy, becoming marginal appendages of the closed university system.

The expansion of the existing Black Studies programs will inevitably require the development of statewide and/or regional networks which can sponsor research projects, local and state conferences, journals, occasional-paper series, and other collective activities. African-American Studies departments located at larger, research-oriented universities must provide the leadership in extending resources and assistance to programs based at smaller institutions. Black Studies scholars and teachers must identify sources of financial support outside the regular college and university channels, such as the development of proposals for direct state funding for research projects, and joint programs with city, state and local agencies, community associations, civil rights organizations and local foundations. Collaborative efforts with local Black United Funds, and with social and cultural organizations, could provide not merely financial resources and support, but a network of potential political supporters which might generate an external constituency. We must never assume that the efforts to restructure university curricula, expand affirmative-action hiring policies, and increase the scope and size of African-American and Ethnic Studies departments and programs will occur without external pressure.

Finally, an essential element of the "adventure of blackness in Western culture," to paraphrase African-American critic George Kent, is the question of morals. A pivotal feature of the African-American Freedom Movement was the connection between black political objectives and ethical prerogatives. What was desired politically – the destruction of institutional racism – was simultaneously ethically and morally justified. This connection gave the rhetoric of Douglass, Du Bois, Robeson and King a moral grandeur and power vision which was simultaneously particular and universal. It spoke to the upliftment of the African-American, but its humanistic imperative reached to others in a moral context. African-American Studies must perceive itself in this tradition, as a critical enterprise which educates and transforms the larger society. The moral poverty in contemporary American society is found, in part, in the vast chasm which separates the conditions of material well-being, power and privilege of some from the others. The evil in our world is politically and socially engineered, and its products are poverty, home-lessness, illiteracy, political subservience, race and gender domination. The old problematic of the 1960s – whether we are part of the solution or part of the problem – is simultaneously moral, academic, and political. We cannot be disinterested observers, hiding behind the false mantle of "scholarly objectivity," as the physical and spiritual beings of millions of people of color and the poor are collectively crushed. As Robeson reminds us, we must take a stand if our endeavors are to have lasting meaning. Black Studies must project itself not just as an interpretation of reality, but as a projection of what should be and must become.

NINE

BLACK STUDIES, MULTICULTURALISM AND THE FUTURE OF AMERICAN EDUCATION

African-American Studies, broadly defined, is the systematic study of the black experience, framed by the socioeconomic, cultural and geographical boundaries of sub-Saharan Africa and the black diaspora of North America, the Caribbean, Brazil and Latin America, and increasingly Europe itself. At its core, it is also the black intellectual tradition as it has challenged and interacted with Western civilization and cultures. In the social sciences and the humanities, that intellectual tradition has assumed a complex burden over many generations, seeking to engage in a critical dialogue with white scholarship on a range of complex issues – most significantly, the definition and reality of race as a social construct, and the factors that explain the structures of inequality which greatly define the existence of black people across the globe. This definition was at the heart of W.E.B. Du Bois's assertion nearly a century ago that "the problem of the twentieth century is the problem of the color line."

From Du Bois's point of departure, we can assert that the problem of the twenty-first century is the challenge of "multicultural democracy": whether or not American political institutions and society can and will be radically restructured to recognize the genius and energy, the labor and aspirations of millions of people of color – Latinos, Asian Americans, American Indians, Arab Americans, African-Americans, and others.

I would like to explore three interrelated issues, which together provide a framework for discussing the study of the contemporary African-American experience, and questions of racial and ethnic diversity within a democratic society. The first is the debate over Black Studies and, more generally, what has been termed "multicultural-ism," especially in the context of higher education. The critics of both multiculturalism and Black Studies have linked the concepts with the concurrent controversy surrounding "political correctness" on campuses and in public-school curricula. However, to define "multiculturalism" properly we need to go beyond conservative rhetoric.

Second, what is the social context for a discussion of racial diversity and pluralism within American society as a whole? Because I am a social scientist of the African-American experience, my commentary will focus briefly on the disturbing trends away from equality within the national black community. These inequalities are leading us to two unequal Americas, divided not simply by racial identity but by sharply divergent levels of skills, learning and access to educational opportunities.

Finally, there is the larger issue of the future of race and ethnicity within American society itself. The question of difference within any society or culture is always conjunctural, ever-changing, and conditional. "Race" is not a permanent historical category, but an unequal relationship between social groups. We must rethink old categories and old ways of perceiving each other. We must define the issue of diversity as a dynamic, changing concept, leading us to explore problems of human relations and social equality in a manner which will expand the principles of fairness and opportunity to all members of society.

For any oppressed people, questions of culture and identity are linked to the structure of power and privilege within society. Culture is the textured pattern of collective memory, the critical consciousness and aspirations of a people. When culture is constructed in the context of oppression, it may become an act of resistance. This is why the national debate over "multiculturalism" assumes such critical significance within political discourse, as well as in the structure of the economy and society. With the demise of the Cold War, American conservatives have been denied the threat of communism as the ideological glue which could unify the voices of racism and reaction. Led by former Reagan secretary of education William Bennett and Republican presidential candidate Patrick Buchanan, conservatives have launched a "cultural war" against an unholy host of so-called new subversives, such as the proponents of "political correctness," affirmative action, Black Studies, gay and lesbian issues, feminism and, worst of all, "multiculturalism."

A working definition of "multiculturalism" begins with the recognition that our nation's cultural heritage does not begin and end with the intellectual and aesthetic products of Western Europe. Multiculturalism rejects the model of cultural assimilation and social conformity, which within the context of our schools has often relegated African-Americans, Latinos and other people of color to the cultural slums. The mythical "melting pot" in which a diverse number of ethnic antecedents were blended into a nonracist and thoroughly homogenized blend of cultures, never existed. Assimilation always assumed that the price for admission to America's cultural democracy for racial and ethnic minorities was the surrender of those things which truly made us unique: our languages and traditions, our foods and folkways, our religions, and even our names. The cultural foundations of the United States draw much of their creativity and originality from African, Latino, American Indian and Asian elements. Multiculturalism suggests that the cross-cultural literacy and awareness of these diverse groups is critical in understanding the essence of the American experience "from the bottom up."

Part of the general confusion about the concept of "multiculturalism" is that there are strikingly different and sometimes conflicting interpretations about its meaning. For example, in Western Europe, particularly in The Netherlands and the United Kingdom, a highly restrictive and regimented interpretation of multiculturalism exists. Different ethnic and racial minorities are, in effect, locked into their respective cultures, with an emphasis on the societal management of real or possible cultural, religious and social differences. "Tolerance" for diversity is the common denominator; all people are perceived as being equal, politically and socially – free to pursue their own unique rituals, collective traditions and creative arts without fear of discrimination or harassment. Within the parameters of this type of tolerance, there is an emphasis on the contours of difference, within the values, heritage and group behaviors of distinct cultural constituencies. Rarely is there any discussion linking culture to power, to a minority group's access to the resources, privileges and property which are concentrated within certain elites or classes. Institutional racism is hardly ever mentioned or even acknowledged.

Within the USA, there are at least four major interpretations of "multiculturalism," reflecting the widely diverse ethnic, racial and social-class composition of the nation. African-American Studies is an integral part of the multicultural debate. In very simplistic terms, these differing interpretations are "corporate multiculturalism," "liberal multiculturalism," "racial essentialism," and "radical democratic multiculturalism."

Corporate multiculturalism seeks to highlight the cultural and social diversity of America's population, making managers and corporate executives more sensitive to differences such as race, gender, age, language, physical ability, and sexual orientation in the labor force. A number of major corporations regularly sponsor special programs honoring Martin Luther King, Jr.'s Birthday, or the Mexican-American holiday "Cinco de Mayo." Others hold "multicultural audits" for their staff and personnel, workshops and training sessions emphasizing awareness and sensitivity to people of color, women and others.

The major reasons for this multicultural metamorphosis among hundreds of America's largest corporations can be summarized in two phrases: "minority markets" and "labor force demographics." The value of the African-American consumer market in the USA exceeds $300 billion annually; the Spanish-speaking consumer market is not far behind, at $240 billion annually. Since the early 1960s there has been substantial evidence from market researchers indicating that African-Americans and Latinos have strikingly different buying habits from whites. To reach this growing consumer market, white corporations are now forced to do much more than produce advertisements featuring black, Asian American and Hispanic actors displaying their products. Multicultural marketing utilizes elements of minority cultures in order to appeal directly to nonwhite consumers.

As the overall labor force becomes increasingly Asian, Latino, Caribbean and African-American, the pressure increases on corporations to hire greater numbers of nonwhite managers and executives, and to distribute their product through minority-owned firms. Of course, nowhere in the discourse of corporate multiculturalism is there the idea that "racism" is not an accidental element of corporate social relations. Instead, the basic concept is to "celebrate diversity" of all kinds and varieties, while criticizing no one. Troubling concepts like "exploitation," "racism," "sexism" and "homophobia" are rarely mentioned.

Liberal multiculturalism, by contrast, is explicitly anti-racist, and takes it for granted that educational institutions have a powerful social responsibility to deconstruct the ideology of human inequality. It is genuinely concerned with aesthetics, ideology, curriculum theory and cultural criticism. Liberal multiculturalism is broadly democratic as an intellectual approach for the deconstruction of the idea of race. But like corporate multiculturalism, it does not adequately or fully address the in-equalities of power, resources and privilege which separate most Latinos, African-Americans and many Asian Americans from the great majority of white upper- and middle-class Americans. It does not adequately conceive of itself as a praxis, a theory which seeks to transform the reality of unequal power relations. It deliberately emphasizes aesthetics over economics, art over politics. It attempts to articulate the perceived interests of minority groups to increase their influence within the existing mainstream. In short, liberal multiculturalism is "liberalism" within the framework of cultural diversity and pluralism. The most articulate and influential proponent of this perspective is Professor Henry Louis Gates, Harvard University's Director of African-American Studies.

The third model of multiculturalism is racial essentialism. Here, advocates of diversity praise the artefacts, rituals and histories of non-

Western people as "original," "unique," and even superior to those of Western Europe and white America. They juxtapose the destructive discrimination of "Eurocentrism" with the necessity to construct a counter-hegemonic ideological and cultural world-view. For many people of African descent, this has been translated into the cultural and educational movement called "Afrocentrism." First developed as a theoretical concept by Temple University scholar Molefi Asante, Afrocentrism has quickly inspired a virtual explosion of children's books; curriculum guides; cultural, historical, and educational textbooks; and literary works.

The strengths of the Afrocentric perspective and analysis are undeniable: the fostering of pride, group solidarity and self-respect among blacks themselves; a richer appreciation for African languages, art, music, ancient philosophies and cultural traditions; a commitment to unearth and describe the genius and creativity of blacks in the context of a racist and unforgiving America. As a paradigm for understanding and reinterpreting the contours of the African experience, Afrocentrism also advances an internationalist perspective, drawing correlations between black communities from Lagos to Los Angeles, from Brooklyn's Bedford-Stuyvesant to London's Brixton.

As many white Americans have retreated from an honest dialogue about the pervasiveness of racial inequality in American life, many black Americans are attracted to an Afrocentric perspective. In hundreds of communities where black parents are attempting to improve the quality of the education of their children, Afrocentrism has come to mean the demand to make curricula more culturally pluralistic. In dozens of social rituals of community life, from the kinte clothing used in weddings and ceremonial events, to the popularity of African art in private homes, Afrocentrism provides a coherent and logical oppositional framework to traditional Eurocentrism. In many ways, Afrocentrism has become broadly defined by many blacks outside the academy as simply the awareness of one's cultural heritage and recognition of the common destiny of all people of African descent. Afrocentrism draws upon the deep and very rich foundations of black nationalism within African-American civil society, which implicitly question the strategy and ideology of inclusion and assimilation. Because America's mainstream doesn't value or respect blackness, Afrocentrism provides the framework for an alternative world-view and oppositional consciousness.

The contradictions and weaknesses of Afrocentrism are just as striking. Although frequently discussed in the context of multiculturalism, in many respects Afrocentrism is theoretically and programmatically at odds with the larger trend toward pluralism and educational diversity.

Conceptually, many Afrocentrists have absolutely no desire to engage in a critical discourse with white America, at any level. They frequently retreat into a bipolar model of racial relations, which delineates the contours of the black experience from a photographic negative of whiteness. In effect, this "freezes" the meaning of culture, reducing the dynamics and multiple currents of interpersonal and group interaction to a rigid set of ahistorical categories.

From a practical standpoint, an Afrocentric perspective perceives Black Studies as a unified discipline – that is, a distinct body of knowledge informed by a coherent methodology and a distinct body of literature which helps to define the field. William M. King, for example, characterized the "Afrocentric perspective" in scholarship as the application of that "world view, normative assumptions, and frames of reference [which] grow out of the experiences and folk wisdom of black people." But this approach raised a host of questions. As Delores P. Aldridge, long-time coordinator of Black Studies at Emory University observed, "Many Black Studies departments, originating as a result of pressure and flawed liberal consciences, lacked an agreed upon body of knowledge, disciplined frames of reference or bases of knowledge – the very characteristics that defined every other standard academic discipline." To create the character of a "discipline," Afrocentrists utilized various tactics, both administrative and political. In the case of the African-American Studies Department at Temple University, chairperson Molefi Asante insisted that all faculty hired adhere to an "Afrocentric perspective" as their primary commitment toward scholarly research and teaching. Asante was sophisticated enough not to insist that this meant that whites were "unqualified" to teach in his field. On the contrary: Asante strongly denies that Afrocentrism is in any way "separatist" or a theory of racial essentialism. The subtle theoretical distinctions Asante utilizes, however, are frequently missing in the arguments and analysis of many of his followers, who perceive Afrocentrism in more fundamentalist terms. All too often, Afrocentrism has been translated into its lowest common racial denominator, black vs. white.

It is certainly true that in most instances, the argument that white people are unqualified by their racial classification and identity to teach courses in the African-American experience is usually made inside universities by white administrators and faculty, not by blacks. The hidden assumption at work here is that no one who was not born black would have any reason to cultivate a scholarly interest or the proper dedication for the study of black life and history. Setting aside the example of Herbert Aptheker, and the hundreds of gifted and dedicated white intellectuals who disprove this hypothesis, the great danger in this argument is that it assumes that knowledge is grounded in racial, biological or even genetic factors. But if race itself is a social construct, an unequal relationship between social groups characterized by concentrations of power, privilege and authority of one group over another, then anyone of any ethnic, class or social background should be able to learn the complex experiences of another group. Membership or identity within an oppressed racial group often yields unique personal insights, which may be translated into texts and utilized in classroom teaching. The harsh reality of racial oppression yields experiences and insights which are extremely valuable tools for cross-cultural education. But our imaginations do not have to be imprisoned by the boundaries of our different identities – whether defined by race, gender, religious upbringing, physical impairment, or sexual orientation.

The more separatist and racially essentialist variety of Afrocentrism rarely explores the profound cultural dynamics of creolization and multiple identities of nationalism and ethnicity found throughout the black world, from the Hispanicized blackness of the Dominicans, Puerto Ricans and Colombians, to the vast complexities of race in Cuba and Brazil, to the distinctions and tensions separating rural conservative Christian blacks in the Mississippi Delta and the cosmopolitan, urban, secular, hip-hop culture of young blacks in Watts, Harlem and Chicago's South Side. But the most serious weakness of Afrocentrism is its general failure to integrate the insights of cultural difference drawn from the perspectives of gender, sexual orientation, and class. It has no theory of power which goes beyond a racialized description of how whites, as a monolithic category, benefit materially, psychologically and politically from institutional racism. Thus, rather than seeking allies to transform the political economy of capitalism across the boundaries of race, gender and class, most Afrocentrists approach the world as the main character in Ralph Ellison's classic novel *Invisible Man*: enclosed inside a windowless room filled with thousands of glowing light bulbs – illumination without vision.

Finally, there is the insurgent movement toward "radical democratic multiculturalism," or what might be described more accurately as a transformationist cultural critique. These educators, artists, performers, writers and scholars are inspired by the legacy of W.E.B. Du Bois and Paul Robeson. They emphasize the parallels between the cultural experiences of America's minority groups with oppressed people throughout the world. Discussions of culture are always linked to the question of power, and the ways in which ideology and aesthetics are used to dominate or control oppressed people. The goal of the radical democratic multiculturalists is not the liberal inclusion of representative numbers of blacks, Latinos and others into the literary canon, media and cultural mainstream, but the radical democratic restructuring of the system of cultural and political power itself. It is to rethink the entire history of this country, redefining its heritage in order to lay claim to its future. It is to redefine "America" itself. Scholars in this current include Princeton University philosopher Cornel West; feminists bell hooks, Angela Davis and Patricia Hill Collins; legal scholars Patricia Williams and Lani Guinier; anthropologist Leith Mullings; political theorist James Jennings; historians Gerald Horne and Robin Kelley; and cultural critic Michael Eric Dyson.

The democratic multiculturalists approach Black Studies in a very different manner. They insist that African-American Studies is not a discipline, like physics or psychology, but a broad intellectual dialogue and exchange which incorporates divergent perspectives and concerns. Its intellectual anchor rests with a series of themes and questions which cut across individual disciplines. At the center of this exchange is the search for identity: who and what is the African-American – culturally, socially and in the oppressive context of racial domination and economic exploitation? How did the black community in America and elsewhere evolve over generations? What common cultural and social elements transcend geography and influence the construction of black reality in America, the Caribbean, Africa and elsewhere? By what strategies and means should we seek representation or empowerment? What is the future of African-American people within the context of a pluralistic democratic society which has yet to fulfill its promises of human equality and social justice? Such questions can be pursued through history, political science, religion, philosophy, sociology, anthropology, literature, economics, and a host of other disciplines.

This is not to say that the "radical democratic multiculturalists" agree with each other on all the essentials. Far from it. West is a powerful and articulate advocate of democratic socialism, and has expressed major reservations and criticisms about the term "multiculturalism." Hooks emphasizes the cultural dimensions of social change, and sharply dissents from a theoretical perspective which would place class as the singular or primary focus of her analysis of society. Guinier, the outstanding voice for challenging the problems inherent in "majority-rule democracy" of her generation, emphasizes the legal and policy dimensions of politics and empowerment, and is less concerned with cultural or ideological phenomena. Collins's analysis of black feminism is close conceptually to that of many Afrocentrists. Mullings and Davis, among others, approach social analysis from the vantage point of class relations, employing a Marxian methodology. One could argue that the differences between these public intellectuals of the multicultural left are just as significant as their similarities. Their "unity" is created to a great extent by the criticism of their opponents on the right, and by their common commitment to expand the definitions and boundaries of academic discourse and intellectual engagement to relate to the very real and practical problems of inequality which define urban America today.

The quest for a unified theoretical framework and approach to the study of race and diversity has been illusive. For nearly half a century, we have pursued the goal of "diversity" in higher education, with at best mixed and uneven results. In the 1950s and early 1960s, liberal educators declared proudly that they were committed to the goal of a "color-blind environment." I distinctly recall professors saying to me that they "could not remember" whether this or that student was "a Negro." They fully embraced the liberal perspective of Dr. Martin Luther King, Jr., that individuals should be judged "not by the color of their skin but the content of their character." At the same time, we should assert that "color blindness," the eradication of white privilege and superiority and the abolition of all hierarchies which perpetuate black inferiority, should be our ultimate goal. As the great reggae artist Bob Marley of Jamaica once observed: "Until the color of a man's skin is of no greater consequence that the color of his eyes, there will be war."

But the question should be, how do we get there? How can we "deconstruct" race? We cannot get there by pretending that "race" and "color" no longer matter, that they have magically declined in significance since the 1960s. In a racist society, color symbolizes the inequality of power relations, the ownership of property and resources, between various groups and classes. To end racial prejudice, we must restructure the power relations between people of color and upper- to middle-income whites. This means that we must pursue a "color-conscious" strategy to create the conditions where color is one day irrelevant to determining the positions of power, educational access, health care, and to other opportunities of daily life.

In the 1970s and 1980s, the ideal of color blindness gave way to what could be termed "symbolic representation." Liberal educators believed that the recipe for cultural diversity was to bring representatives of a new spectrum of interests into the academy – women, racial minorities, physically disabled people, lesbians and gays, and others. Programs were established to create new academic courses in Women's Studies, Black Studies, Chicano Studies, gay and lesbian studies, and Asian American Studies. Minorities and women were "symbolically represented" with their appointment as counselors and college recruiters. Multicultural student services centers were established to address perceived concerns of the students of color. These reforms should have represented the beginning, rather than the end, of a process of educational reconstruction on issues of social and cultural difference within the academy. Instead, somehow we have lost our way. And at many colleges and universities, we are actually moving backward. One reason is that women and racial minorities were usually hired and subsequently located in the bureaucratic margins of academic institutions, rather than within real centers of power. There were few deliberate programs which actually tried to identify scholars of color and/or female faculty with administrative abilities, to mentor and cultivate them, and to advance them. At some institutions, minority faculty occupied a revolving-door position, usually at the designated ranks of instructor or assistant professor, never to be tenured or reappointed.

In some institutions, a conspiracy of silence developed between white conservative administrators and those few black or other minority faculty who had been hired during the initial wave of affirmative action and minority recruitment. Many conservative white administrators employed the discourse of diversity, but privately never really believed in its validity. They never accepted the academic rationale of African-American Studies, yet they adopted these programs on their campuses largely out of political necessity. To quell student unrest, to reduce criticism from minority educators and elected officials, they created such programs and departments on a ghettoized basis. Such programs, white conservative (and liberal) educators were convinced, would appeal to minority students. Moreover, all-white departments with traditional curricula would not be forced to alter their way of teaching or their discriminatory hiring policies. History departments wouldn't have to offer African-American history to students if the Black Studies program were deemed responsible for it. Music departments could ignore Duke Ellington. Literature departments could skip Alice Walker, Langston Hughes, Toni Morrison and James Baldwin.

The conspiracy of silence on the part of some second-rate yet politically astute black educators, was expressed in the construction of academic ghettos. Some African-American Studies programs actively discouraged the cross-listing of courses with traditional departments, on the grounds that this would undermine the unit's academic autonomy and integrity. Students received the dangerous and erroneous impression that only individuals who happened to be of African descent had the cultural background and intellectual training necessary to teach all things black.

Active, dedicated younger African-American scholars hired by such programs were frequently discouraged from interacting with colleagues trained in the same disciplines but affiliated to different academic departments. One example of this process is represented by the Black Studies Department under Professor Len Jeffries at the City College of the City University of New York. The controversy surrounding Professor Jeffries over the past four years – his anti-Semitic speech in Albany, New York, in the summer of 1991; his subsequent, hasty dismissal as chairman of Black Studies at City College; and his successful legal suit to reclaim his position and damages of $400,000 – ignores the fundamental issue at stake. Jeffries had been reinstated as chair of Black Studies many times, going back over two decades, by the presidents of City College. His last reinstatement as chair had occurred barely one month prior to his controversial speech, which had sparked alumni and public criticism calling for his immediate ousting. Yet the CUNY central administration knew full well about the major academic shortcomings within the department – the assertions that some students received grades for submitting absolutely no written work, or that Jeffries often skipped classes, or that an atmosphere of intimidation and harassment existed for other black faculty who disapproved of Jeffries' version of vulgar Afrocentrism. They ignored a mountain of student and faculty complaints because of their own institutional racism – the vast majority of white, middle-class students at CUNY were unaffected.

We must be honest and rigorous in our criticisms of such programs. But we must also criticize the far more dangerous distortions of conservative intellectuals like Thomas Sowell, Shelby Steele, and William Bennett, who have concluded that multicultural studies have no relevance to higher education. On the contrary: the criteria for educational excellence must include a truly multicultural vision and definition. We must have African-American Studies programs and research institutes; Women's Studies and Ethnic Studies programs; academic programs reflecting the totality of the cultural and social diversity which is America. The challenge before us is to create such programs that are truly designed to impact the totality of the learning experience for all students. The challenge is to retrain our teachers and faculty so that they approach the art of instruction with a richer appreciation of the intricate factors of ethnicity and cultural diversity within their own disciplines. We must go beyond the traditional definitions of "diversity," the idea of cultural difference as a second-ary feature of higher education's periphery, to redefine the core or the mainstream of the academy's central mission for itself. We must assert, for example, that the serious study of the African-American experience is important not just to black students for reasons of ethnic and racial pride, but for everyone; that all students, regardless of their ethnic background or heritage, can become intellectually enriched by explorations into the African-American experience.

In practical terms, this means that Black Studies scholars must go beyond the mere development of new courses to engage in a general discussion about faculty and staff development, and the use of racial diversity criteria in the promotion and tenure of teachers and in the evaluation of classroom instruction. Courses in Black Studies must be included among the general requirements for all students, regardless of their ethnic backgrounds. We need to initiate collaborative projects that link our research to the development of issues which impact blacks and other people of color not only inside the US but across the globe. We must cultivate an internationalist perspective on education, recognizing that the solutions to the problems of learning in rapidly changing societies are not confined to any single country or culture.

Most importantly, Black Studies need to reassert the connections between academic excellence and social responsibility. The black community is faced with a series of economic, social and political problems, and scholarship must be the critical tool in analyzing the means for resolving and addressing contemporary issues. In the legacy of Du Bois and others, we must recognize that the struggle for liberation is linked to the best scholarly research. The next generation of Black Studies programs must recognize that "knowledge is power," and that the purpose of scholarly research is not merely to interpret but to change the world.

Compounding the challenges to the study of the black experience is the fact that the social composition of the African-American community has itself changed sharply since the 1960s. One cannot really speak about a "common racial experience" which parallels the universal opposition blacks felt when confronted by legal racial segregation. Moreover, the contemporary black experience can no longer be defined by a single set of socioeconomic, political and/or cultural characteristics. For roughly the upper third of the African-American population, the post-1960s era has represented real advancement in the quality of education, income, political representation and social status. Social scientists estimate that the size of the black middle class, for example, has increased by more than 400 per cent in the past three decades. One out of every seven black households, as of 1990, had an annual gross income exceeding $50,000. The recent experience of the middle third of the African-American population, in terms of income, has been a gradual deterioration in its material, educational and social conditions. For example, between 1974 and 1990, the median income of black Americans compared to that of white Americans declined from 63 per cent to 57 per cent. However, it is the bottom one-third of the black community which in this past quarter of a century has experienced the most devastating social consequences: the lack of health care, widespread unemployment, inadequate housing, and an absence of opportunity.

The triumph of white conservatism; changes in public policy towards black America and our central cities; and the resultant divisions within the black community – all have contributed to a profound social and economic crisis within black households and neighborhoods. For example, the infant mortality rate for black infants is twice that for whites. Blacks, who represent only 13 per cent of the total United States population, now account for approximately 80 per cent of all "premature deaths" of individuals aged fifteen to forty-four – those who die from preventable diseases and/or violence. There are currently more than 650,000 African-American men and women who are incarcerated, and at least half of these prisoners are under the age of twenty-nine. In many cities the dropout rate for nonwhite high-school students exceeds 40 per cent. The majority of urban homeless people are black and Latino, and, as of 1989, nearly half of all poor black families were spending at least 70 per cent of their income on shelter alone.

Black America also faces a crisis in leadership. In 1964 there were 104 black elected officials in the United States, with only five members of Congress and not one black mayor. Though small, this group of leaders were immediately and intimately connected with those they represented, because they had largely grown up in and continued to live and work within their constituent communities. By 1994 there were more than 8,200 black office-holders throughout the nation, including forty members of Congress and four hundred mayors. This growing number of African-American leaders, with a broad influence in federal, state and local governments, is largely composed of individuals who have their roots in the middle class – the upper third of the income earners within the African-American community. Black leaders frequently lack organic connections with working-class and low-income communities; although they frequently "speak" for the interests of the entire black community, they lack a scientific or critical method for assessing or articulating mass public opinion. Organizations such as the NAACP, for example, do not have any scientific or quantitative measure of their own members' opinions. National black leaders rarely, if ever, interact with key African-American social-science scholars or show familiarity with recent research on the socioeconomic state of the black community.

Black America stands at a challenging moment in its history: a time of massive social disruption, class stratification, political uncertainty, and ideological debate. The objectives for black politics in the age of

Jim Crow segregation were relatively simple: full social equality, voting rights, and the removal of "white" and "colored" signs from the doors of hotels and schools. Today's problems are fundamentally more complex in scope, character and intensity: the flight of capital investment from our central cities, with thousands of lost jobs; the deterioration of the urban tax base, with the decline of city services; black-on-black violence, homicide and crime; the decline in the quality of our public schools and the crisis of the community's values. To this familiar litany of problems one more must be added: the failure to identify, train and develop rising leaders within the African-American community who are informed by a critical and scientific understanding of the needs and perspectives of their own people.

This is the social-science challenge of Black Studies. In order to respond to this unique set of challenges, we must not only know the statistics; we must also acquire a concrete understanding of the views of black Americans. We must, furthermore, respond to the needs of African-Americans by encouraging the production of socially responsible scholarship and by nurturing the development of rising young leaders from within the black community. We need, with painful honesty and a clarity of vision, to engage in a dialogue concerning the real roots of the current economic, social, political and educational problems within African-American society. We must foster ideological and theoretical discussions which help to promote constructive discourse between and among Black Studies scholars. Equipped with this critical perspective, we may begin to implement long-term and comprehensive strategies for democratic empowerment and social change.

TEN

EDUCATION, FAITH AND THE PROMISE OF EQUALITY

Somewhere in our distant memory, black Americans collectively recall a time when it was forbidden to read and write. In a slave society, literacy was considered a subversive act. A slave unexpectedly caught with writing instruments and paper was certainly not to be trusted. Every master implicitly recognized that knowledge was power. So when the day of Jubilee dawned, hundreds of thousands of my people expressed their new-found freedom by constructing rough and unassuming schoolhouses. Frequently, the schoolhouse was built even before a teacher could be solicited to fill the position. Teenagers with a rudimentary knowledge of arithmetic, spelling and composition were often at the head of classes with sixty or more eager yet illiterate pupils. The classroom was the site of hope and aspiration for an entire race which was struggling to become free. It represented the possibility of acquiring the tools necessary to overcome ignorance and poverty, the chief pillars of the system of racial domination. The schoolhouse was a monument to the people's deep desire to become far more than others had expected they would be.

Education thus became the secular religion of the African-American community. In many households during the long night of Jim Crow, millions of parents told their children with absolute certainty that "education was the key" to a better life. "Even if the doors of opportunity and equality are now closed off to us," they counseled, "we have to be ready to accept the challenge, once it becomes available." Working late hours beside flickering electric lamps, those early generations of black students were taught religiously that "we have to be twice as good in order to be given the same chance" as our white counterparts. Everyone took this for granted. They knew from bitter experience that most whites never viewed us as equals, and would never accept us as competent unless we exhibited a degree of excellence which far surpassed the established standards.

My great-grandfather, Morris Marable, had been a slave until the age of twenty-one. Deprived of any formal education, he took great pride in the ability of other members of his community to exhibit their literacy. As a leader of the local black church, Morris cherished those moments when he was called upon to recite a special verse from the Bible. From his large suit pocket he lifted a well-worn copy of King James and would read slowly and carefully, as if each word were being weighed and measured. Few knew that Morris was completely illiterate. He had merely memorized each page and stanza of the Good Book, and knew by experience what each particular line said.

Morris's oldest son, Manning, was enrolled in a small local elementary school for four years, where he acquired the basics of reading, 'riting, and 'rithmetic. But in the early 1900s, particularly in rural areas dominated by sharecropping, knowledge was a function of agricultural production. Basic math was helpful when you took your crops to market, to avoid being cheated by the unscrupulous merchants and salesmen. A working knowledge of English grammar could be of assistance in reading the contracts with landlords. Geometry came in handy when measuring off the size of a field for ploughing and cultivation. Manning approached the question of education from the standpoint of economic development and security. He understood that business relations in the nearby commercial centers of Anniston and Roanoke rested on the tools of the classroom. He knew that a black family could not control its own property, or protect itself from harassment by local white authorities, unless it had some basic knowledge of the law. And so he encouraged his thirteen children to study, to attend the rural country school for colored children which was established during racial segregation. As he surveyed his growing family late at night, after walking in with the mules from the muddy fields, he probably prayed to himself that his children would have a better life than he had given them. With knowledge, all things were possible.

Seven hundred miles away, in the colored eastside neighborhood of Columbus, Ohio, my mother's father worked at the time in a large bookstore. At lunch time, he would take several cloth-bound copies of books from the most recent shipment, place them in his lunch box, and walk several blocks to the park. On a bench next to the flower garden, beneath the sunshine of midday, he would leisurely read a novel, or one of the latest books on world history or politics. Jack Morehead had completed high school in North Carolina. But his journey away from the prejudices and violence of the South had made him aware of his academic backwardness. Eagerly, he sought to remake himself, to be prepared for the opportunities that life in the North seemed to promise an educated, hard-working African-American. He devoured the daily newspapers, and kept current on relevant issues affecting blacks by reading the weekly *Pittsburgh Courier* or *Cleveland Call and Post*. He followed the arguments of race leaders such as W.E.B. Du Bois, and tried to interpret the meaning of public events to his friends and co-workers. Already with a wife and several children, Jack realized that college was beyond his grasp. Yet in his own way, the university curriculum within his own mind was structured to prepare him for some grander purpose in life.

After some uncertainty, Jack Morehead decided to join the clergy. Within several years, the former book clerk had become an ordained minister in the African-American Episcopal Church. It was at the beginning of the Great Depression that my grandfather began his career, which would continue for nearly five decades. My mother recalls the early days of his itinerancy. In an overstuffed Model T Ford, with several small children clinging to each other in the back seat, Jack and his young wife drove into the Ohio countryside. Beneath several hills would sit a small town, where a small church had been constructed for the community's colored population. From the moment the Model T drove up to the front door of the church, Jack Morehead would become transformed into the center of that community's attention. All of the ideas and skills he had acquired by reading were put into action. He was simultaneously the colored community's chief legal adviser, psychiatrist, social worker, political counselor and cultural critic.

The AME church was always much more than a house of prayer. It was the site for the colored community's cultural and social events. Plays, musical recitals and dramas were presented, in the hope that these would elevate the general educational and cultural level of the colored population. The artistic and cultural gifts of young children were cultivated, and the achievements of the teenagers were praised. The church was always there: to counsel the troubled of mind and spirit; to raise funds for the unemployed and to share the food supplies of the congregation to those less fortunate; to give Christmas gifts and food baskets during the holiday season; to keep track of those youngsters who had little or no family supervision or guidance, and to make sure that they kept to the straight and narrow. The church also served a broad political purpose. Northern segregation was always less severe than its Southern counterpart; nevertheless, the white society of rural Ohio was deeply prejudiced against Negroes, and rarely permitted them to occupy positions of authority or prominence. The church reinforced a positive self-conception among its members, and underscored their achievements. The house of faith was a place in which all human beings were seen as being equal.

But it was on Sundays that Jack Morehead's university of the mind found its highest expression. He would prepare for the Sunday sermon with meticulous care throughout the week, searching out from scholars' annotations the various interpretations of verses within the Bible. Jack would think through each passage of his argument, checking it for logical inconsistencies, with the technical skill of a philosopher preparing for a major address before his or her colleagues. He would sprinkle witty quotations from Shakespeare or John Donne into the text for the educational illumination of his flock. Or perhaps he would locate an event in the larger political and social world of the 1930s which would help to illustrate the issue explored within the Biblical text. The sermons were, to my grandfather, the primary method for bringing his two great passions, faith in God and love of learning, together within a single dramatic act.

My mother, June Morehead Marable, sat on the front pews of my grandfather's colored churches, and listened quietly to several thousand sermons and lectures as she grew up during the Depression. Like her father, she developed the values and skills which were at the foundation of the black community's educational faith: thrift, hard work, personal excellence, study and perseverance. She believed that racial prejudice rested on white ignorance and black inferiority; that to educate ourselves in all aspects of life would place Negroes potentially on an equal footing with their white counterparts. Although the family could not afford a typewriter during her high-school years, she traced the outline of the keys and their appropriate symbols on a sheet of paper. At night, at the family's kitchen table, she practiced hour after hour hitting the correct keys on the paper chart. When her father refused to pay the $3 necessary for her to enroll in a secretarial course, her mother gave June her donations which were meant to be dropped into the Sunday morning collection plate. After taking the course, upon completing high school my mother qualified for an appointment as a secretary at the Wright-Patterson Air Force base in Dayton, Ohio. The funds she saved from her meager salary during the wartime years were used for her tuition at Wilberforce College in central Ohio. Life in essence was a continuous learning experience, with education and technical training the ladder for personal and economic upward mobility.

For many decades, African-Americans stood outside the doors of opportunity, desperately searching for the appropriate keys to gain access. Education was the most reliable and widely recognized key, which promised to give black people the ability to achieve full equality. We taught our children and their children's children to be prepared, to be ready for the moment when that call was returned from the employment office, notifying us that we could begin our jobs that next Monday morning. In our pews at church, we prayed for the chance to show our skills, to be accepted for the quality of our minds, rather than be oppressed by the burden of racial inequality.

In the aftermath of the civil-rights movement, a majority of white Americans have grown tired of the demands for equality and opportunity which are issued from the representatives of the black and Latino ghettoes. They have grown weary of crime, of the thousands of homeless on the streets, sidewalks and alleys of the major cities. They have become accustomed to exposés on television documenting the problems of the inner-city schools, the gangs and drugs and fear. This majority has constructed walls of isolation and safety, to protect itself from the growing storms of human unrest and social destructiveness which sweep across the avenues of urban America.

Yet comfortable, well-fed middle class white America is itself constructed on a powerful fault line, the chasm of racial and class inequality which cuts across the entire social and economic order. By underfunding urban education – the reductions over the past decade in federally funded school-lunch programs, the cutbacks in federal support for computers in the classrooms, and the lack of full support for Head Start – our nation incrementally destroys that last hope which still resides within the ghetto, the secular faith of learning. Already, young black and Latino inner-city high-school graduates are increasingly faced with the stark alternative of working at "Mickey D's" (McDonald's) or not working at all. The deterioration of inner-city public transportation and the decline of industrial and commercial production in cities makes it difficult to tell young people that knowledge has an ultimate "payoff". To be well-prepared and knowledgeable enough for a position is not enough; for, when there are absolutely no prospects for decent employment, except by selling illegal drugs or through crime, an atmosphere of despair, cynicism and alienation is created.

But in the last analysis, no security alarms, barricades or private guards will keep the crisis of the central cities away from the comfortable enclaves of white suburbia. If the black community no longer believes in the secular tradition of its educational creed, if it has no hope that knowledge can be translated into a better life, then it has almost nothing left to lose. The fires of Los Angeles in April–May 1992, which stand astride the race and class urban fault-line like a warning, may easily be just the opening tremors of social unrest yet to come.

My own children – Malaika, Sojourner, and Joshua – were raised with the expectations of my parents, grandparents and great-grandparents. They were taught that knowledge was power, the primary key for mobility and advancement. They were given encyclopedias and taken to museums. Yet, like the children of the urban ghetto, that same cynicism and alienation influences their world-views and perceptions. They doubt that their own economic lives and professional careers will in any way be an improvement over their father's life. They question whether institutional racism and the yawning gap of inequality between blacks and whites will ever be narrowed. They challenge assertions that race is simply an attitude of unfairness and prejudice within any individual's mind – and sense that race will be the central variable in their lives for many years ahead.

So we stand perhaps at the end of that long secular tradition of learning and educational faith. Our challenge is to revive that ideal, by forging the conditions in our school systems and national educational policies to advance the promise of new levels of excellence. Until and unless we accomplish this, our entire country lurches toward an inevitable crisis, polarizing the difference between the affluent, educated "haves" and the undereducated, alienated "have nots." The choices we make over the next decade will largely determine the future of racial relations for the century ahead.

ELEVEN

MALCOLM AS MESSIAH: CULTURAL MYTH VERSUS HISTORICAL REALITY

In a racist society, the most profound question that can be raised by the oppressed is the issue of identity. "Who am I, and how can I act on behalf of myself?" It is this quest for critical self-consciousness which explains, in part, the continuing fascination by younger African-Americans with the charismatic and controversial figure of Malcolm X. According to a November 1992 *Newsweek* poll conducted by the Gallup organization, 57 per cent of all African-Americans polled agreed with the statement that Malcolm X should be considered "a hero for black Americans today." Malcolm X's greatest popularity was found among African-Americans between the ages of fifteen and twenty-four, with 84 per cent of those polled agreeing with the statement. When asked the reasons for Malcolm's popularity, blacks eschewed complex ideological explanations or theoretical excursions into the history of black nationalism. Some 84 per cent replied that Malcolm X stood for "blacks helping one another," 82 per cent responded that the black leader symbolized a "strong black male," with another 74 per cent indicating that he represented "black self-discipline." With the vast social destruction of our central cities today, with 23 per cent of all African-American males between the ages of twenty and twenty-nine currently in prison, on probation, parole, or awaiting a trial, Malcolm X personifies the ability of an individual to overcome the worst circumstances to achieve personal integrity and leadership.

It is in this larger social context that Spike Lee's magnificent yet profoundly flawed film *Malcolm X* must be understood. The massive political and financial controversies involved in making the film have been well documented. From the beginning, Lee planned a synthesis of recent black social history with the sweeping cinematic style of David

Lean's *Lawrence of Arabia*. Warner Brothers had agreed to finance a two-and-a-quarter hour film at a cost of $20 million. Lee wanted an epic-sized, three-hour-plus film at a cost exceeding $33 million. Going way over budget, the director appealed successfully to black celebrities such as Oprah Winfrey, Bill Cosby, and Michael Jordan to finance the shortfall. Throughout the filming, black critics such as prominent playwright/poet Amiri Baraka expressed the view that Lee was certainly the wrong person to be charged with the political responsibility for interpreting the life and times of a major black figure for a mass audience. Many black activists feared that Lee would focus too heavily on Malcolm X's pre-Nation of Islam career as "Detroit Red," street hustler and cocaine user, at the expense of a solid political analysis of Malcolm's ideological and personal evolution as a leader.

The final product of Lee's labors and shameless self-promotion, *Malcolm X*, is simultaneously a triumph of film-making, and a justification of Baraka's fears and frustrations. The film's major strengths begin with the truly outstanding performance of Denzel Washington as Malcolm X. Washington's detailed preparation for the role was quite remarkable – mimicking Malcolm's speaking style, even his tendency to place his right hand thoughtfully against his face, with two fingers extended. Malcolm's actual words are carefully woven into the dialogue. Washington gives us a very emotional and powerful depiction of a street hustler who goes through a series of moral and spiritual conversion experiences.

Al Freeman, Jr. and Angela Bassett are also excellent in portraying Malcolm's mentor, Elijah Muhammed, spiritual godfather of the Nation of Islam, and Malcolm's wife, Betty Shabazz, respectively. Freeman successfully conveys the autocratic style of the Black Muslim patriarch, illustrating his paternalistic compassion and his private hypocrisy. Bassett's role is decisive in providing the story with a central love interest which shows that a strong black woman was able to open Malcolm's innocent eyes to the truth that surrounded him. The film manages to demonstrate the enormous accomplishments of the black nationalist Nation of Islam in pulling thousands of drug dealers, prostitutes, and criminals off the streets; providing moral guidance and self-respect; and giving people denied an opportunity a belief in themselves as capable and productive members of society. The core ideology of the Nation – the "whites are devils" thesis – was always secondary to its constructive and positive contributions toward black working-class and low-income people.

But the film also falls far short in many significant ways. Lee would have us believe that the Federal Bureau of Investigation began to monitor Malcolm's political activities some time during his final, chaotic months of travel, reflection, and political struggle. Actually, the FBI began its systematic surveillance of Malcolm X more than ten years earlier, long before he had become a national figure. Malcolm's telephone was wiretapped illegally; his mail was monitored; his movements were carefully charted and followed. The New York City police placed double agents, including Malcolm's own bodyguard, inside the Nation of Islam. The FBI also attempted to recruit Malcolm himself to betray Elijah Muhammad's organization by the late 1950s, years prior to the eventual split. Scholars have known for years about all of this police-state-style surveillance and illegal disruption by authorities. Why does Lee treat this as a minor episode, leaving viewers with the distinct impression that the FBI was at best peripheral to Malcolm's assassination? The wiretapping scenes in the film's final minutes should have begun before the movie was halfway finished. Most of the assaults aimed against Malcolm X could have been planned by the FBI or other governmental authorities, and loyalists of Elijah Muhammad's Black Muslims could easily have been manipulated to act out the state's hatred and fear of the black nationalist leader.

Lee claims to have conducted extensive research in the construction of his screenplay; the film indicates otherwise. The storyline is essentially an adaptation of Alex Haley's classic text, *The Autobiography of Malcolm X*. The strengths of Haley's work are its powerful narrative, the moving descriptions of Malcolm's voice, his ambiguities, and intensely attractive human personality. Many of these elements are apparent in Lee's approach. But there are deep problems within *The Autobiography* which Lee failed to comprehend. The book is a narrative biography, related in piecemeal fashion from Malcolm to Alex Haley over a period of several years. Most of the interviews were given to Haley in the early 1960s, well *before* Malcolm X had become disillusioned with Elijah Muhammad and the Nation of Islam. Throughout this time, Malcolm was a bitter critic of Martin Luther King, Jr., his political philosophy of nonviolence, and the civil-rights establishment. Few interviews were incorporated into *The Autobiography* which reflected Malcolm's experiences after March 1964, when his entire political ideology had become radicalized.

The Autobiography and Lee's film, for example, suggest that it was Malcolm's 1964 *hajj* to Mecca which opened his eyes to the fundamental humanity of all people beyond the limitations of race, and that this final epiphany via the universalism of Islam had a profound impact upon his world-view and political behavior. But I would suggest that the ideological limitations of both Haley and Lee keep their interpretations of Malcolm located on safe, religious grounds rather than on the more dangerous terrain of race and class struggle. Haley was a longtime Republican, and a twenty-year veteran of the US Coast Guard. Lee is primarily a product of the post-civil-rights-era black middle class, who never directly participated in the massive black protest movements of the 1960s and 1970s. Both Lee and Haley ignore the long history of African-American nationalism in the USA, preferring to see Malcolm as a "reaction" to white racism and prejudice, rather than as the product of a long and rich protest tradition.

Lee also consulted Betty Shabazz and some of Malcolm's family members, friends, and former associates. But his approach to Malcolm was the construction of a mythic hero figure, not an actual political leader who made mistakes, assessed his errors, and went in new directions. The battle between Elijah Muhammad and Malcolm is shown as grounded in personalities, rather than in differences stemming from ideology and politics. Elijah Muhammad's sexual misadventures and Malcolm's "silencing" for his "Chickens Coming Home to Roost" remarks following the assassination of President John F. Kennedy are the principal reasons given for the rupture within the Nation of Islam.

To be sure, Malcolm was personally disillusioned with the private greed and public hypocrisy of the core leaders within the black nationalist formation, but he had been moving away from the Nation's focus on spiritual issues for many years. Throughout the years 1960–63, Malcolm X spoke at hundreds of public forums on public issues, the civil-rights movement and even foreign policy – something completely alien to Elijah Muhammad. Muhammad's brand of black nationalism sought solutions to the black community's problems from within, focusing largely on questions of business development, personal hygiene, and socially conservative behavior. Malcolm's vision was always fixed on the larger world. It was not sufficient to save souls if one could not challenge social injustice.

Another serious weakness in Lee's film is the perspective which asserts that Malcolm X and Martin Luther King, Jr. were inherently at odds over philosophies, strategies, and tactics in achieving freedom for African-Americans. Viewers obtain the distinct impression that King was an accommodating leader, seeking to reconcile black demands within the framework of white power and privilege. Nothing could be further from the truth. Such an approach ignores the fact that King broke with the Johnson administration over the Vietnam War, embraced a "Poor People's March" against poverty and hunger in Washington DC in 1968, and advocated a radical restructuring of America's economic system. Simply because Martin failed to match Malcolm X's fiery language and style, or refused to depart from nonviolence as a means of public protest and civil disobedience, doesn't make him an "Uncle Tom." In *Martin & Malcolm & America*, noted African-American theologian James Cone observed that these two gifted, charismatic figures were complementary:

> They were like two soldiers fighting their enemies from different angles of vision, each pointing out the others blind spots and correcting the other's errors. Each needed each other, for they represented – and continue to represent – the "yin and yang" deep in the soul of black America.

Lee's *Malcolm X* is an excellent introduction to this magnificent and articulate black spokesperson for liberation, but it is also seriously limited in terms of critical interpretation. The film-maker's goal was to create a cultural icon. But the black community does not need myths; it desperately requires practical solutions to its pressing problems. Malcolm's feet were always firmly planted on the ground, and he would have been the first to reject any notion that his legacy should be praised in a series of baseball caps, T-shirts, and wall posters. The creation of charismatic cultural Messiahs may be attractive to a middle-class artist like Lee, but it represents a political perspective grounded in conspiracy theories, social isolation, and theoretical confusion. If African-Americans conclude that only the genius of a Messiah can elevate the masses of oppressed people to the level of activism, no social protest is possible. If the mantle of leadership is elevated too far from the people, few will have the courage to reach toward that goal. Cone reminds us:

> [I]t is important to emphasize that Martin and Malcolm, despite the excessive adoration their followers often bestow upon them, were not messiahs. They show us what ordinary people can accomplish through intelligence and sincere commitment to the cause of justice and freedom. There is no need to look for messiahs to save the poor. Human beings can and must do it themselves.

To genuinely honor Malcolm X is to extend his political and ideological search into the struggles of inequality, racism, and economic oppression which define black liberation today. Black identity and personal dignity require something more than cultural manipulation of symbols without critical content.

TWELVE

MEMORY AND MILITANCY
IN TRANSITION: THE 1993
MARCH ON WASHINGTON

The national mobilization which culminated in the 28 August 1993 March on Washington represented a transitional moment in the history of black America. Perhaps 100,000 Americans made pilgrimage to the steps of the Lincoln Memorial under the protest banner of "Jobs, Justice and Peace." But the forces which gathered for this demonstration represented a wide variety of political and social interests, with conflicts in some instances simmering just below the surface. The genesis of this particular demonstration had occurred the previous winter, in a series of informal discussions between members of what could be termed the "civil-rights establishment" – Southern Christian Leadership Council (SCLC) president Joseph Lowery, former SCLC organizer and congressional delegate Walter E. Fauntroy, Urban League director John E. Jacob, and Coretta Scott King. As veteran leaders of any social movement approach the twilight of their public careers, there is a tendency to reflect nostalgically about one's contributions to the historical record, and the great events in which one participated. For this generation, the 28 August 1963 March on Washington was the seminal political event of their lives.

The 1963 march was actually grounded in the success of an even earlier protest mobilization, the 1941 Negro March on Washington Movement, led by the socialist trade-union leader A. Philip Randolph. The 1941 protest pressured President Franklin D. Roosevelt to sign Executive Order 8802, outlawing racial discrimination in defense factories which held federal contracts. Twenty-two years later, Randolph and his key lieutenant, Bayard Rustin, coordinated a new march which was designed to pressure Congress to ratify a comprehensive civil-rights act outlawing racial segregation in all public accommodations. Although the August

1963 march brought a quarter of a million nonviolent demonstrators to Washington DC – the largest peaceful protest in American history at that time – the demonstration was not without controversy.

The more conservative wing of the desegregation movement, represented by Roy Wilkins and the National Association for the Advancement of Colored People (NAACP), sharply opposed the march at first. Many feared that the demonstration would provoke unpredictable outbursts of violence in the streets between protesters and the police. Some Negro moderates privately opposed the selection of Rustin on the grounds of his homosexuality. On the left, members of the radical Student Nonviolent Coordinating Committee (SNCC) rejected the moderate demands of the demonstration, and openly called for massive civil disobedience against the government. The militant speech of SNCC chairman John L. Lewis was rewritten and censored by older leaders. At a distance, Malcolm X observed the behind-the-scenes discord and dubbed the event "the farce on Washington." But historical memory is always selective. Within the mainstream fabric of black political culture, what is remembered of that day is the powerful and unforgettable vision of democracy articulated by Martin Luther King, Jr., in his "I Have a Dream" speech.

Looking back, for traditional civil-rights leaders such as Lowery, King, Jacobs, Andrew Young and others, these were politically "good old days." Righteousness struggled openly against evil, and triumphed. I suspect that there remains a deep yearning for the simplicity of these innocent times within this group. Psychologically, the sojourn marking the thirtieth anniversary of the apex of the civil-rights movement was the political equivalent of searching for the "fountain of youth." But a public exercise in collective nostalgia would not justify such an endeavor. A second problem commanded the attention of the Negro elite: the utter failure to motivate and inspire millions of African-Americans under the age of thirty-five to participate in civil-rights organizations. Political apathy towards the older liberal integrationist leadership runs deep, and not only among the hip-hop generation, which turns to Public Enemy rather than to Jesse Jackson for its political analysis.

Thousands of black urban professionals – "buppies" – who, ironically, have achieved their successes in the job market precisely because of affirmative-action programs and the enforcement of civil-rights legislation, refused to join or donate funds to the NAACP, the SCLC, or Operation PUSH (People United to Serve Humanity). They feel that these traditional liberal formations really don't speak to their needs or their generational perspective. This becomes strikingly apparent when one considers that the newly-appointed secretary of the NAACP, 45-year-old Benjamin Chavis, is widely described as a "youth leader" by the older set of civil-rights bureaucrats. The veterans thus projected the 1993 march as a unique opportunity to "pass the torch" to the eager hands of a fresh generation of black activists. Yet, along the way, few appeared to ask whether the young organizers who were hand-selected actually represented the anger and frustration of inner-city youth and students, or whether they were ready to seize the political baton and move forward.

At least two other significant factors motivated the decisions of the civil-rights establishment. One was the bittersweet aftermath of the 1992 presidential election, and the subsequent disenchantment with the centrist policies of the Clinton administration. Clinton's inability to push through Congress a jobs bill in spring 1993 meant several hundred thousand additional unemployed young people in America's ghettoes. The president's refusal to endorse a comprehensive single-payer national health system like Canada's would mean that millions of blacks, Latinos and low-income people will not have access to equal health-care treatment. Clinton's retreat from the nomination of a series of African-American progressives from positions in his administration – notably the refusal to appoint Spelman College president Johnetta Cole as secretary of education and law professor Lani Guinier as US assistant attorney general for civil rights – outraged the black community.

Lowery complained sharply that he was deeply "disappointed" when the president "abandoned" Guinier, because it raised "questions about his commitment to the Voting Rights Act." Something had to be done to place the Clinton administration on notice that it could not simply take the black community for granted, ignoring its policy demands and urgent socioeconomic needs. Lowery favored some distancing between the civil-rights agenda and the Democratic Party: "We ought to have permanent political principles – not permanent political loyalties.... The [Democratic Party] often puts us on the expendable list, because we don't put them on the accountability list."[1] What was necessary was a sharp political reminder to Clinton that African-Americans had provided 15.3 per cent of his total electoral support in last year's election, and that their growing alienation would spell disaster for his administration.

But the central motivating factor for the liberal integrationist leadership was the widely recognized reality of its growing political marginalization and irrelevance, due largely to the rise of black elected officials. Three decades ago, there had been fewer than one hundred black elected and appointed officials nationwide. Effective political influence and power within the African-American community was wielded by ministers, labor leaders and community spokespersons. This leadership strata was reflected within the various formations of the civil-rights coalition: the NAACP, Urban League, SCLC and the Congress of Racial Equality. After the passage of the 1965 Voting Rights Act, the number of black elected officials soared: 1,100 by 1969; 3,600 in 1983; and roughly 8,000 in 1993. The Congressional Black Caucus, formed two decades ago, and the African-American mayors of the nation's largest cities exercised influence within the government and the national Democratic Party which transcended the public pressure-group model of the older civil-rights formations.

The new situation created tensions and jealousies between these two overlapping groups of middle-class elites. Washington DC congressional delegate Eleanor Holmes Norton, who in her youth had been a SNCC activist, observed: "The civil rights leaders are no longer as significantly national as they were before. The political leadership of the community … has replaced the civil-rights leadership as the driving force of black leadership."[2] Norton's analysis was essentially true, yet it stung many veterans of the desegregation campaigns in the South. Jesse Jackson, whose political education occurred within both CORE and as King's junior lieutenant in SCLC, strongly dissented: "The interests of vast numbers of people are left unprotected and unrepresented by the electoral system. Our politicians do one piece - they do legislative. But you really need lobbying, litigation, registration and independent political action. It takes all of that.… Legislative leadership is not enough."[3] For Lowery, the Reagan–Bush years were a period in which civil-rights leaders and organizations "let down our guard and reduced our vigilance. This [demonstration] is part of an effort to revive the [civil-rights] coalition, to spark a renaissance in social activism and pass the torch so the struggle will continue into the next century."[4]

What was at stake here were two very different strategies to achieve democratic reforms. Most African-American elected officials had reduced the concept of "politics" to electoral phenomena – running for office, voter registration, passing legislation. Strategically, electoralism basically meant loyalty and support for the Democratic Party. But the civil-rights veterans understood that electoralism was insufficient. Politics should also embrace economic boycotts, street demonstrations and pickets, lobbying, political education and civil disobedience. The two political elites were also largely divided by leadership styles. The civil-rights leaders tended to be closely connected with the church and traditional African-American social institutions. The most prominent among them employed a messianic, charismatic leadership style which cemented the loyalties of their followers to their own agendas. Jesse Jackson is, of course, the classic example of this type of charismatic style. The most prominent black elected officials and leaders within the Clinton administration – for example, secretary of commerce Ron Brown and former New York City mayor David Dinkins – could never be described as "charismatic" or "messianic" by anyone. Many were uncomfortable speaking to welfare mothers, unemployed workers and angry young people in the streets. But their familiar message of faith within the existing political process was rapidly running thin.

The civil-rights establishment sensed the deep pessimism and anger within the most oppressed sectors of the African-American community, and the breakdown of communications between racial groups. In August 1993 a *USA Today*/CNN/Gallup poll reflected this continuing burden of race within American society. While 51 per cent of all African-Americans polled stated that "the USA is moving toward two separate and unequal societies – one black, one white," only one-third of all whites concurred. While 70 per cent of all blacks favored "more laws to reduce discrimination," barely one-third of all whites agreed. Approximately half of all whites believed that "black civil rights groups ask for too much." And, when asked if African-Americans have as good a chance as whites to get jobs for which they are qualified, more than twice as many whites as blacks stated "yes."[5] In short, most of white middle-class America is uninterested in any realistic dialogue on racial inequality. As observed by prominent New York African-American Minister Calvin Butts, there is "an increasingly mean spirit growing in this nation, particularly against people of color."[6] The organizers of the 1993 March on Washington hoped to channel the anger and energy of the most oppressed segments of black America towards a renewed political activism.

Fauntroy, who had served as national coordinator of the highly successful twentieth-anniversary March on Washington in August 1983, was once again appointed national director. To ensure a strong turnout from organized labor, William Lucy, president of the Coalition of Black Trade Unionists and international secretary-treasurer of the American Federation of State, County and Municipal Employees (AFSCME), was selected as chair of the march's program committee. Coretta Scott King's cordial relations with AFL-CIO president Lane Kirkland were utilized, as the nation's largest labor federation endorsed the mobilization. Kirkland's public statement urged "all national and international unions and their members to support this event, to participate in the March, and to reaffirm the commitment of the trade union movement to the crusade for greater civil and economic rights." Individual unions were particularly active in their support for the march. About 5,000 members of the American Federation of Teachers, for example, led by conservative Democrat Albert Shanker, joined the demonstration. AFT bus caravans and delegations traveled from nearby east-coast cities, as well as from Ohio, Minnesota, Florida, Illinois and Kentucky.[7]

A significant role in the march was assumed by the National Organization of Women. NOW president Patricia Ireland acknowledged that "the modern wave of feminism is rooted in the civil rights movement as represented by the 1963 March on Washington." But this was more than historical nostalgia. Ireland observed:

> The march provides an opportunity for feminist activists to stand together with our sisters and brothers in the civil-rights and social justice movements – united against those who would oppress us based on our gender, our race, our sexual orientation or our economic status.... The themes of the 30th anniversary, Jobs, Justice and Peace, are particularly relevant to women. Many women – especially women of color – are still the last hired and first fired, trapped in dead-end minimum-wage jobs and continually victimized by an economic system that favors the white male.

NOW activists from some dozen chapters in the east, including Boston, New York, Baltimore, Philadelphia, Pittsburgh and Richmond, came as delegations. NOW organizers led feminist workshops in the educational activities during the day before the march, and served among the marshals for the march itself.[8]

The actual leadership structure for the march was divided into specific categories of co-chairpersons, labor co-chairs, honorary co-chairs, convenors and endorsers. The key co-chairs included King, Lowery, Chavis, Jacob, Ireland, Kirkland, former NAACP national secretary Benjamin Hooks, and the Reverend Jesse Jackson. Other co-chairs were selected to represent important constituencies: Rabbi David Saperstein of the Religious Action Center of Reform Judaism; Ms. Barbara Dudley of the environmentalist organization Greenpeace, USA, Inc.; Jose Velez, of the League of United Latin American Citizens (LULAC); Keith Geiger, of the National Educational Association; and James F. Zogby, head of the Arab American Institute. The convenors and endorsers represented as many as five hundred different interest groups and national organizations: for example, the National Congress of American Indians, the Office of Black Catholics, Asian Americans for Equality, the Arab American Anti-Discrimination Committee, the United Farm Workers of America, Friends of the Earth, the Gray Panthers, the National Association of Social Workers, Operation PUSH, the National Alliance Against Racist and Political Repression, the National Baptist Convention, and Chinese for Affirmative Action. This eclectic united front endorsed a specific legislative agenda, reflecting left-of-center priorities. At the top of the list for congressional implementation were a "jobs stimulus and investment appropriations" bill costed at $16.3 billion, which had originally been requested by President Clinton; the "Cesar Chavez workplace fairness" bill, which proposed to "ban the practice of permanently replacing striking workers when they demand better working conditions, better pay and benefits"; the "Violence Against Women Act of 1993," which would "combat violence and crimes against women"; the "Environmental Justice Act of 1992," originally proposed by congressman John Lewis, which would "establish a program to assure nondiscriminatory compliance with all environmental, health and safety laws" by corporations; the "Civil Rights Act of 1993," which would prohibit discrimination nationwide against lesbians, gay men and bisexuals; and the "Goals 2000: Educate America Act," proposed by Senator Edward Kennedy, which would "improve learning and teaching by providing a national framework for education reform."[9]

The central problem with the stated objectives of the mobilization, and the fundamental irony of the entire endeavor, was that this social movement was attempting to implement its legislative objectives without giving adequate or appropriate space to the individuals who could actually make this agenda happen – the members of Congress and, most specifically, the Congressional Black Caucus. Among the co-chairpersons, there were no voting members of Congress, and only three black elected officials – District of Columbia mayor Sharon Pratt Kelly, New York mayor David Dinkins, and Baltimore mayor Kurt Schmoke. John Lewis was given an honorific designation as "honorary co-chair," largely due to his historical role as leader of SNCC at the 1963 march. The honorary co-chairs actually listed more movie stars, recording artists and cultural figures (e.g., Stevie Wonder, Bill Cosby, Harry Belafonte, Ruby Dee, Jessye Norman) than black members of Congress (e.g., Kwesi Mfume, head of the Congressional Black Caucus, Missouri congressman Alan Wheat, and veteran congressman John Conyers.)[10] There was evidence that most African-American elected officials did little to promote or support the mobilization, as the publicity around the event circulated. In Washington DC, for instance, the bulk of the organizing was done in local churches, on university campuses, and by the local members of the NAACP chapter. Two weeks before the march, according to the *Washington Post*, "some District residents received calls from DC Council members asking them to march". Only days prior to 28 August "some received letters from Mayor Kelly urging them to march."[11]

But an even greater problem was an absence of coherent administrative organization within the march's internal hierarchy. Literature promoting the demonstration, which was scheduled for distribution early in the summer, never reached the community centers, labor-union halls, churches and mosques of black America. Relatively few press releases and advance feature articles appeared about the thirtieth anniversary March on Washington in the black newspapers. The African-American radio stations said little about the upcoming demonstration. Chavis decided that something had to be done urgently, and he convinced the NAACP board to release about twenty-five of its own staff members to assist in the planning and coordination of the march. Chavis's top assistant, Lewis Meyers, Jr., became the deputy for coordination of the march. NAACP board chair William Gibson assumed greater direct involvement in promoting the NAACP's role at the march.

Yet problems still erupted in unexpected places. On 13 August Rabbi David Saperstein issued a "confidential and personal" fax to the top leaders of the mobilization: King, Fauntroy, Lucy, Jackson, Gibson, Chavis and Lane Kirkland. Saperstein observed that hundreds of Jewish organizations and synagogues throughout the northeast states were going to be contacted, "urging them to send delegations to the march." Unfortunately, he commented, two "major problems have arisen" which might culminate in the withdrawal of "all of the Jewish groups." He had been informed that "a tentative decision was made yesterday to invite Rev. Louis Farrakhan. I don't need to tell you," he noted, "what a devastating blow this would be to the solidarity of the coalition supporting the march." Saperstein also opposed the decision "to extend invitations to representatives of the Palestinian and Israeli peace delegation to speak." This would be a "tactical error," because the entire issue of the Arab–Israeli conflict should be kept "out of the march." Although NAACP officials and other leaders refused to comment directly on the Saperstein memo, some kind of discussion occurred between the principals over the potential controversy. A decision was reached not to permit Louis Farrakhan to speak. Even activists who were critical of the Nation of Islam's brand of conservative racial separatism and male chauvinism were amazed and saddened by the march organizers' decision to exclude Farrakhan. Only ten years before, at the twentieth-anniversary march, Farrakhan had delivered "an articulate message of multiracial political unity" to an audience which was at least one-third white.[12]

In the citadels of power, others also watched the march mobilization with questionable enthusiasm. The Clinton administration had no problems with the march leaders' tendency toward nostalgia. Clinton himself described King's "I Have A Dream" address as "the greatest speech by an American in my lifetime."[13] But never quite forgotten were the radical implications of civil-rights activism, which were most decisively represented by Martin Luther King himself during his last two years of public life. Key march leaders, especially with organized labor, sharply opposed the Clinton administration's support for the North American Free Trade Agreement with Canada and Mexico, which promised to destroy thousands of lower- to moderate-income jobs inside the USA. One week before the mobilization was scheduled, march leaders officially informed Clinton that they wanted to meet directly with him.

The Clinton administration's response was a polite embrace, but at arm's length. Attorney general Janet Reno and housing secretary Henry Cisneros were selected to represent the President at the gathering. On the day of the march, Clinton devoted his regular weekly radio message to the Washington march. He mouthed, essentially, a string of political platitudes: "We've come a long way, but clearly we've got a long way to go.... We owe it to [Dr. King] to rededicate ourselves today to the causes of civil rights, civic responsibility and economic opportunity for every American. In the last seven months, we've made some great strides on that road."[14] It was true that Clinton's apathy and lack of interest in urban affairs was scarcely equivalent to the overtly racist and reactionary agenda of the former Reagan administration. Yet, for the millions of African-Americans who had provided his critical margin of victory the previous November, Clinton's cool posture towards the black freedom movement was, at best, disappointing. For Clinton's more realistic critics, the administration's attitude only confirmed what they already knew too well: the Democratic Party had little use for African-Americans except on election day.

The sun towering above the crowd that late August day was brutal. By noon, the temperature reached the nineties, and a dull haze obscured the long view from the steps of the Lincoln Memorial back towards the towering Washington Monument. Tens of thousands of marchers clustered in hundreds of different groups, carrying posters, colorful banners and signs of all kinds. Veterans from the previous marches of 1963 and 1983 embraced each other and recalled the triumphs and tragedies of their political past. Although there was spontaneous singing and chanting in unison, the noise from the crowd was muted by the high humidity and overwhelming heat. The United States Park Police estimated at 3:30 p.m. that the crowd numbered some 75,000 people; Chavis placed the size of the demonstration at 200,000. As I stood at the foot of the podium, looking back upon the waves of people, I roughly judged the gathering at 100,000, at least. But, regardless of the specific numbers, the crowd was one of the largest public political demonstrations led by African-Americans in the twentieth century. People had come to bear witness to memory, and to find the road back towards a new militancy.

One sign of this occurred at the very beginning of the public addresses. As Eleanor Holmes Norton was speaking, the security perimeter which separated the large crowd from the speakers' tent and the media was breached. Over 1,000 marchers tumbled forward on to the small seating area near the platform, at the base of the Lincoln Memorial steps. Symbolically at least, the vast distance between the "leaders" and "followers" was at one accidental stroke eliminated.

The program of the 1963 March on Washington had contained only thirteen speakers, which included the top leadership of all the civil-rights organizations. By contrast, thirty years later over sixty people were scheduled to take the podium. The spectrum of speakers crossed racial, ethnic, ideological and cultural boundaries: actresses Eartha Kitt and Halle Berry; John Sweeney, president of the Service Employees' International Union; Marian Wright Edelman, president of the Children's Defense Fund; Phil Wilson, director of public policy of the National Gay and Lesbian Task Force; William Gray, president of the United Negro College Fund; Cardinal James Hickey of the US Catholic Conference on Justice; Jose Velez, president of the League of United Latin American Citizens; Senator Ben Nighthorse Campbell of Colorado, a Native American; Norman Hill of the A. Philip Randolph Institute; John Jacob of the National Urban League; Jose Serrano, chairman of the Congressional Hispanic Caucus; and Kwesi Mfume, chairman of the Congressional Black Caucus.

Coretta Scott King, one of the principal speakers, who was introduced as "the first lady of our movement," seemed gratified by the massive crowd and the optimistic spirit of the hour. "Dr. King's spirit is here with us," she declared. "When Martin Luther King, Jr. stood on these steps thirty years ago today, he challenged good people across the nation to rise up and fulfill his dream.... There is still too much racism, there is still too much poverty, there is still too much hunger and there is still too much homelessness." Thousands of union members, wearing red, blue, yellow and green tee-shirts with union designations and carrying placards opposing Clinton's North American Free Trade Agreement, applauded the speech of AFL-CIO leader Lane Kirkland. "Today we return in unity to raise one voice against hate, against greed and persecution," Kirkland proclaimed. "We want a trade policy that will uplift human standards rather than destroy them."[15]

The speeches of Chavis and Lowery were lively and well-delivered, but essentially covered familiar ground. The Clinton administration was mildly rebuked for its failure to deliver on promises to the black community. "The president chose to stay in Martha's Vineyard," declared Lowery, reminding his audience that Clinton was then vacationing in Massachusetts in a resort area. "When you come home, Bill, from Martha's Vineyard, the Lord's vineyard will still be here. You've got to plow the soil and put in the fertilizer of jobs ... of justice, of economic opportunity."[16] But, despite the unbearable heat, virtually all of the crowd were waiting through the mediocre presentations for what promised to be the rhetorical highlight of the afternoon, the scheduled message by Jesse Jackson. At 4.00 p.m., as gray thunderclouds began to form across the Potomac River south towards Virginia, Jackson walked deliberately to the speakers' platform.

Jackson did not disappoint his audience, delivering one of the best political presentations in his long public career. He first evoked the memory of the collective struggles of the past. "We gather today – ardent messengers of an urgent petition, crying out with our very bodies for jobs, for justice, for equal opportunity and equal protection," the Reverend addressed the crowd. "Many despair. The day is hot. The road is long. The mountain too steep. The people too tired. The powerful too distant. But do not despair. We have come a long way." The poetry in the language and the power of his argument had deep roots within black America, reminding some veterans of Martin's celebrated "How Long, Not Long" address of 1965, culminating the Selma-to-Montgomery Alabama protest march.[17]

Jackson reminded the marchers of the historical context for the 1963 march. At that time, King had come to Washington DC seeking to "redeem a check that had bounced ... marked 'insufficient funds'." But in the midst of a Cold War against communism, neither a "conservative Congress" nor a "young president" could help. But Martin was not dismayed or disillusioned. With "a passion for justice and a will to suffer and sacrifice for an authentic new world order," democratic reforms were achieved by young Americans. Three decades later, King's dream had not yet been achieved. Drawing on the obvious historical parallels between the Kennedy and Clinton administrations, Jackson continued:

> Once again, the check has bounced. Insufficient funds they say. The deficit must be addressed. The military must police the world. A conservative Congress will not help. A young President cannot deliver. So, just as thirty years ago – the march was a beginning, not an end, so this march is a beginning, too. We cannot sit on our hands when so many of our brothers and sisters are forced to their knees. And so we march.[18]

Jackson quickly catalogued the immediate legislative, economic and social reforms which were essential to rebuild urban America: full employment, an end to police brutality and prejudicial treatment within the criminal justice system for racial minorities, a "single payer national health care plan that makes health care a right for everyone," and the enforcement of civil-rights laws. He explicitly denounced Clinton's North American Free Trade Agreement as a treaty "that will drag our workers down, and drain our jobs south." But, more powerfully, he tried to inspire those who had experienced the greatest oppression – the despair of poverty, unemployment and social alimentation:

> Though the plant gates are closing and jobs are shifting to cheap labor markets subsidized by our own government. Though the White House and the Congress offer a crime bill to contain the people rather than an economic stimulus plan to develop the people. Don't let them break your spirit. *Keep Hope Alive!* ... Let's go forward back to our towns and hamlets to build new structures for freedom, new vehicles for hope in our quest to redeem the soul of America and to make our world more secure. From Angola to Alabama, New York to Niagara, Birmingham to Brazil, let the world know that we will stand fast and never surrender.[19]

Although Jesse's rhetoric soared and captured the praises and applause of the large crowd, the greatest contribution to the entire gathering and the most significant gains achieved were by the NAACP. More than any other force, the NAACP had been responsible for bringing thousands of its members and supporters to Washington DC. In New York City alone, the NAACP worked with unions to reserve buses to carry 5,000 people. Fifty-five buses were coordinated by the NAACP from the northeastern states.[20] As the crowd began to thin out late in the afternoon sun, I had the opportunity to speak directly with both Chavis and Gibson, the NAACP's top leaders. In the interview, Chavis dismissed public speculation concerning the ideological differences between himself and the more conservative members of the NAACP's national board. He argued that the civil-rights movement during the twentieth century had experienced three basic phases: first, the struggle against Jim Crow segregation; then the battle for political representation and equal rights; and now the struggle for economic and social democracy, the material prerequisites to a decent life necessary for all citizens. Knowing Chavis's background – a celebrated political prisoner of the "Wilmington Ten" case from North Carolina in the 1970s, who had spent over four years in prison – it was crystal clear where he intended to lead the NAACP. When I mentioned the connections between "economic democracy" and the radical viewpoints of the NAACP's founder, W.E.B. Du Bois, neither Chavis nor Gibson backed away from this identification. What we intend to do by this march and other activities is to "revive the spirit of Du Bois," Chavis explained.

Can the NAACP "revive the spirit of Du Bois?" In 1948 Du Bois was fired from the national office of the NAACP, a casualty of the Cold War. For years afterwards, the Association had been in the moderate-to-conservative wing of the black freedom movement, advocating a strategic alliance with the Democratic Party and liberal corporate capitalism. Now, with the collapse of the Cold War and the demise of international communism, it was no longer as easy to "red bait" domestic radicals, or to isolate them from mainstream, reformist organizations. The urban crisis and the destruction of the African-American community has become so overwhelming that even black "moderates" are listening seriously to policy initiatives and arguments from erstwhile "radicals" about the reasons for the pervasiveness of poverty, violence and un-employment. What is urgently needed is a national black formation of the entire people, from the unemployed to the homeless, to blue-collar and service workers, to the affluent suburbs of the black middle-class professionals. Such an organization should be dedicated to a social program of "economic democracy," a redefinition of the social contact between the people and state, which would mandate national health care, a job as a human right, decent housing, and the abolition of drugs and violence in urban communities. To "revive the spirit of Du Bois," the NAACP would have to move deliberately in this direction. But its central political strategy for empowerment would have to go far beyond simplistic electoralism, and its reliance on the Democratic Party.

The bitter experience of the Rainbow Coalition for black progressives, culminating in Jackson's refusal to establish an independent political base for a left social-democratic agenda, should caution us about great expectations. Yet the irony of black history is that the NAACP – the great bastion of moderation – may evolve into a bulwark for a new militancy, embracing the mass democratic demands and protests of millions of African-Americans. As the African National Congress evolved in another racist environment during the 1950s from moderation to militancy under the impetus of Nelson Mandela, the NAACP could, conceivably, be poised to make a similar leap of political development. The masses of African-American people are more than ready for a renaissance of activism, informed by a radical economic and social analysis. With its current membership of over 500,000, the NAACP is actually the only organization which could accomplish this. It is also instructive that key black radicals such as former communist Angela Davis have already reached similar conclusions, and have recently joined the NAACP. Under Chavis's leadership, and with the proper economic and political strategy, the Association could make a qualitative advance and create the conditions for a new movement. The 1993 March on

Washington DC began by looking back; but it might mark the beginnings of a reconfiguration of the entire protest map of black America.

Notes

1. Interview with Dr. Joseph Lowery, *People's Weekly World* (28 August 1993).
2. Lynne Duke, "A New Challenge Faces an Evolving Black Leadership," *Washington Post* (28 August 1993).
3. Ibid.
4. Interview with Dr. Joseph Lowery.
5. Patricia Edmonds, "Poll: Two Separate Societies Evolving" and "Poll: Race Relations in the '90s," *USA Today* (27 August 1993).
6. Blair Boardman and Ludmilla Lelis, "Past, Present Activists' Views on Fulfilling King's Dream," *USA Today* (27 August 1993).
7. See press release, "March on Washington Draws Thousands of AFT Members," American Federation of Teachers (28 August 1993); press release by Gerald W. McEntee, international president, American Federation of State, County and Municipal Employees, AFL-CIO (28 August 1993); and Lane Kirkland, "Trade Unions Reaffirm Commitment," *30th Anniversary March on Washington Mobilization National Action Alert* (August 1993).
8. Press release, "NOW President, Activists Support 30th Anniversary March on Washington," National Organization for Women (27 August 1993); and Patricia Ireland, "A Perspective from the National Organization of Women (NOW)," *30th Anniversary March on Washington Mobilization National Action Alert*.
9. List of co-chairpersons, labor co-chairs, honorary co-chairs, convenors and endorsers; and "Legislative demands," *30th Anniversary March on Washington Mobilization National Action Alert*.
10. Ibid.
11. DeNeen L. Brown, "Without Fire of '63, March Aims Modestly," *Washington Post* (26 August 1993).
12. Although their leader had been barred from the speakers' platform, a delegation of Nation of Islam members did attend the march – but distributed xeroxed copies of the Saperstein memo, along with a flyer declaring "Farrakhan's Absence Proof of Jews' Power and Domination over Black Leadership!!" (Rabbi David Saperstein to Coretta Scott King, Walter Fauntroy, Bill Lucy, Jesse Jackson, William Gibson, Ben Chavis and Lane Kirkland, fax communication dated 13 August 1993; flyer distributed by the Nation of Islam at the March on Washington DC, 28 August 1993; and Manning Marable, *Black American Politics* [London, 1985], p. 120.)
13. DeNeen L. Brown, "Thousands March to Mark a Dream: Mall Gathering Hails Progress," *Washington Post* (29 August 1993).
14. Robin Toner, "King's Speech Commemorated by Thousands," *New York Times* (29 August 1993).

15. Brown, "Thousands March to Mark a Dream."
16. Ibid.
17. Reverend Jesse Jackson, "Why We Must March Today, 28 August 1993," text of speech, National Rainbow Coalition. See also William Robert Miller, *Martin Luther King, Jr.: His Life, Martyrdom and Meaning for the World* (New York, 1968), pp. 228, 231.
18. Ibid.
19. Ibid.
20. Greg Wade, "Thousands Are Expected for March on Washington," *New York Amsterdam News* (28 August 1993).

THIRTEEN

BENJAMIN CHAVIS AND THE
CRISIS OF BLACK LEADERSHIP

The 1994 controversy over the tenure of Benjamin Chavis as executive director of the NAACP, which resulted in his firing, was the culmination of a campaign of vilification that had lasted for nearly nine months. In August 1994 the NAACP's board voted overwhelmingly to dismiss Chavis, stating that he had failed adequately to explain the use of the organization's funds to settle a threatened lawsuit by former employee Mary E. Stansel. Abandoned by his principal supporter, NAACP president William Gibson, Chavis felt bitterly betrayed. Within days, he filed a lawsuit in the District of Columbia Superior Court, demanding his reinstatement as executive director. To the media, Chavis angrily blamed outside forces for manipulating the board's vote, and described his ousting as a "crucifixion." Earl Shinhoster, the Association's field secretary, was selected by the board to replace Chavis temporarily. Within less than a year, Gibson himself was narrowly defeated for the NAACP presidency by Myrlie Evers-Williams, the widow of martyred activist Medgar Evers.

Chavis and his closest associates referred to his involuntary departure from the NAACP leadership as a "lynching." But in truth, the ousting of Chavis as head of the oldest civil-rights organization in America had little to do with Mary Stansel, or the fact that Chavis was no wizard at financial management. One of the central questions at the heart of the controversy was whether African-American people have the right to select their own leaders and make them accountable to our concerns and demands. Who speaks for black people in this country? And do we have the right to develop strategies which address our own concerns and advocate programs which advance our interests? Is it possible to develop a political process and framework that brings together black organizations and institutions which reflect a wide variety of perspectives, yet work in concert toward constructive goals and objectives? The debate over Chavis represents a greater dilemma, the crisis of black leadership in America, in the aftermath of the civil-rights movement of a generation ago.

Following the desegregation campaigns and legislative reforms of the 1960s, the NAACP and the civil-rights movement were confronted with four basic challenges, which they never fully understood or overcame. First, the economic crisis of America's inner cities created profound problems for black leadership. Jobs disappeared in the ghetto, as thousands of plants and factories relocated to the suburbs and the sunbelt. Second, the fiscal crisis of federal, state and local governments reduced funds for social programs. Reaganism represented a war against the cities, and African-Americans and Latinos were the chief victims of that war. Civil-rights organizations were challenged to shift their energies from cooperating with the federal government to obtain legal and political reforms, to pressuring Congress and the White House to reverse regressive and repressive social programs. As Republican administrations increasingly relied on expansion of the prison system as the primary means of social control over the black community, the NAACP and other organizations were pushed by blacks from all social classes to become more militant and aggressive. Yet under the leadership of NAACP executive director Benjamin Hooks, the organization drifted, lacking a clear political or ideological compass.

The third major challenge was the growth of class divisions within the African-American community itself. Since the late 1960s, the size of the black middle class has increased by over 400 per cent. Millions of African-Americans moved from the inner cities to the suburbs. Those who were trapped in the worst neighborhoods of the urban ghettoes tended to be the poor, the unemployed, the homeless, young women and children. In the 1980s, there was an explosion of gang violence connected with the economics of illegal drugs in urban black communities. The NAACP made few efforts to understand or address the growing social crisis being experienced by the most oppressed African-Americans.

Fourth, there was the political and social impact of Reaganism within the black community. True, more than 90 per cent of all African-Americans voted against Reagan; nevertheless, like other Americans, they were affected by the administration's agenda in many more subtle ways. In the 1960s, blacks believed overwhelmingly that government was "on their side." The federal government was a bulwark against racial segregation, at least in the Johnson administration. But Reaganism undercut blacks' attitudes toward the role of the federal government, and also eroded the belief in multiracial coalitions. Considering that two-thirds of all whites voted for Reagan in 1984 – and that in the New York mayoral election 78 per cent of white New Yorkers cast ballots for Rudolph Giuliani – it became difficult to argue that multiracial coalitions were possible.

As white Americans moved right, the political culture of black America became fertile terrain for the reactionary agenda of conservative black nationalism and the resurgence of Louis Farrakhan. Black support for Farrakhan has less to do with his odious anti-Semitism or narrow and dogmatic sexism, than his unique ability to express the rage and frustration of broad sectors of the urban underclass. Thus African-Americans may reject the bigotry of the Nation of Islam, but nevertheless feel that Farrakhan expresses some important ideas reflecting the mood of the community.

Ben Chavis implicitly understood all of this. Chavis had been a political prisoner in North Carolina for nearly five years in the 1970s. I became friends with Ben when we were both leaders of the National Black Independent Political Party in the early 1980s. He had been an early critic of what became known as "environmental racism," and won praise as the director of the Commission of Racial Justice of the United Church of Christ. Chavis was an astute observer and participant in social-protest politics. He understood that organizations like the NAACP had radically to redefine their mission in order to capture the support of the post-civil-rights generation. This was the fundamental reason that Chavis inevitably came under attack by the white political establishment.

In the months following Ben Chavis's appointment as NAACP executive director, he moved quickly to establish a new direction for the organization. He reached out to the hip-hop generation, talking directly with gang leaders and rap artists. He pushed a more aggressive economic program favored by William Gibson, NAACP board president, which included pressuring corporations such as Denny's to sign agreements addressing employment and discrimination issues. Chavis explored the development of an international agenda, reviving the vision of W.E.B. Du Bois by proposing the establishment of a permanent Association office in post-apartheid South Africa. But Chavis's greatest strength was his youthful energy and creative determination that the NAACP should re-establish its position as the central force building black solidarity in America. Chavis felt that no black leaders, however controversial, should be excluded from the process of dialogue. After the Congressional Black Caucus weekend conference in September 1993, Chavis agreed to host a national summit of black leadership.

This is not to say that Chavis made no errors of political judgement. The Clinton administration was deeply hostile to Jesse Jackson, and when Chavis emerged as the leader of the NAACP in 1993, there was profound relief that Jackson had been denied the position. Reliable sources indicate that vice president Al Gore even phoned Chavis, offering his congratulations for the defeat of Jackson. Months later, during the administration's efforts to pass the North American Free Trade Agreement (NAFTA), Chavis was summoned to the White House and asked to support their position. Although the NAACP had officially taken a position against NAFTA, Chavis consented to use his influence to swing several members of Congress behind NAFTA. Chavis's role in this severely strained his relations with black leaders in organized labor, who were strongly opposed to NAFTA. Furthermore, Chavis did not make sufficient effort, even from his earliest days as national secretary, to engage in constructive dialogue with powerful leaders of local NAACP branches who had originally opposed him. Nor did he take sufficient steps to neutralize his potential critics within the civil-rights establishment, notably Joseph Lowery, leader of the Southern Christian Leadership Conference (SCLC), and Jackson.

Perhaps Chavis's greatest mistake at this point was in not articulating a coherent social vision; one which broke with the NAACP's past. Chavis's politics rested on two strategic assumptions. First, he was convinced that a broad united front of black organizations and political constituencies had to be constructed which transcended personalities and petty disagreements. The purpose of this grand coalition would be to build black institutions, providing resources and services directly to black people, and promoting the networking of experience and ideas nationwide. Second, the civil-rights movement should fight aggressively against the national conservative agenda, articulating a program of progressive, democratic reforms aimed at increasing the social programs which provided resources directly to the most disadvantaged members of society. Those of us who knew Chavis well understood that he was clearly committed to these strategic objectives. At times, he could deliver a powerful expression of these ideas; on other occasions, however, despite all of his activities, it was unclear where he was going.

Meanwhile, gradually, a coalition of interests began to emerge in opposition to Chavis's "new directions." Some opponents came from the Baltimore office of the NAACP national headquarters. Chavis's selection of attorney Lew Myers as deputy director and Don Rojas – who had been the press secretary for the late Maurice Bishop, prime minister of Grenada – as communications director generated fears that he was incorporating black nationalist and leftist elements in the leadership of the Association. Opponents in local branches began to pressure Gibson and Chavis to remove Rojas, in an attempt to deny Chavis his own staff. Corporations which had provided support for the NAACP in the past began to question Chavis's new initiatives. But the chief critics were probably the traditional, white "liberals" who had a long-standing relationship with the integrationist posture and program of the NAACP, and ideological conservatives who strongly opposed any progressive realignment of the African-American freedom movement.

Many of these white conservatives were connected with *Commentary* magazine, *The New Republic,* and the *Forward Newspaper.* Intellectually, they made absolutely no distinction between "integration" and "equality." They never comprehended the desire of African-American people to be permitted the political and social space to discuss their own problems occasionally behind closed doors. They could not tolerate any organization which engaged in political dialogue with anti-Semites like Farrakhan. But, most importantly, they feared being isolated from a new NAACP which was actively building a broad-based, black united front around an aggressive, post-civil-rights agenda. This had profound implications for the entire American liberal-left community. As one prominent white publisher explained to me, "We would rather have a black leadership which *goes nowhere,* than a black progressive leadership which talks to Farrakhan."

Everything Chavis represented rang loud alarm bells within the white conservative establishment. The opening salvo in the assault against Chavis was a polemic in the *New Republic* in January 1994 by Arch Puddington, an aide to the late integrationist leader Bayard Rustin. The article, ominously entitled "The NAACP Turns Left," warned that Chavis was a leader "consciously identified with the Left," who "has not been above issuing a gratuitous attack on 'Zionism'." Puddington observed that Chavis had "begun to fill the NAACP staff with individuals who share his leftist political orientation." In short, Chavis was a dangerous presence within the civil-rights community, an uncompromising radical who "championed Leninist political movements" and who had "adopted a relentlessly anti-Israel stance during the 1980s." A similar diatribe was written, also in January 1994, by the *New York Times* columnist A.M. Rosenthal, entitled "On Black Anti-Semitism." Rosenthal charged that Chavis and the NAACP, as well as other black leaders such as Jesse Jackson, were "willing to ally themselves with the salesmen for a new Holocaust."

Other criticisms against Chavis gradually began to surface. Chavis was attacked for his efforts to reach the hip-hop generation, including engaging in dialogue with gang members. His endorsement of NAFTA remained a point of alienation for many leaders of black organized labor. But the simmering criticisms reached boiling point when Don Rojas, Chavis's communications director, coordinated a special "invitation only" meeting with prominent black nationalists and pan-Africanists in Detroit. The private session, held in early 1994, which was coordinated by the Detroit branch of the NAACP, was convened to create "a deliberate mechanism for communications" between black activists and the Association. A controversy subsequently erupted over whether Gibson and other members of the board had been informed about this "private" meeting in advance. In the late spring, conservative critics on the board demanded Rojas's resignation and a vote of "no confidence" in Chavis. This effort failed, but it created real tensions and an atmosphere of uncertainty within the Association's national headquarters in Baltimore and among many branches across the country.

When it became obvious that Chavis intended to move the NAACP beyond the ideological boundaries of liberal integrationism, an orchestrated political attack emerged both from within and outside the organization. One key black opposition figure was Michael Meyers. Meyers heads a paper organization, the New York Civil Rights Coalition, and previously served as an NAACP assistant director. Despite the lack of any genuine support or recognition by the black community in New York City or anywhere else, Meyers was repeatedly featured on national television and on the op-ed pages of the *New York Times*. Meyers's main criticism was that Chavis's quest for black solidarity directly contradicted the central purpose of the Association. Meyers asserted: "The NAACP has never purported to be an all-black 'big tent' organization dedicated to racial unity." Although Meyers was isolated from virtually every major black organization and leader with the exception of Kenneth Clark, his criticisms of Chavis became the dominant perspective reflected in white institutions and throughout the national media. From the vantage point of most black scholars and legitimate representatives, Meyers's voice carried absolutely no weight or consequence. But the fact that the media had usurped his arguments and attacks against Chavis placed the new NAACP leadership increasingly at a political disadvantage.

The June 1994 Summit of African-American Leadership accelerated the political assault against Chavis. The majority of the African-American elected officials, trade-union leaders and "traditional" civil-rights leaders such as Lowery of the SCLC, Mary Frances Berry of the US Commission on Civil Rights, and Coretta Scott King, refused to show up. By contrast, about one hundred black leaders representing organizations totaling millions of people did attend the historic gathering. The social composition of the meeting reflected the areas where Chavis had established constituencies and strong bases of support. There were a number of representatives from black fraternal organizations, activist-oriented local institutions and black religious denominations. The most striking moment for me was to sit at a large table between Louis Farrakhan and Betty Shabazz, who seemed to personify two very different perspectives and histories. It was also significant that several of the key discussion documents for the summit were prepared by scholars identified with the left, including Julianne Malveaux, Cornel West, and myself. As West observed, "this summit generated remarkable energy ... around the crucial issues of economic development, youth and community empowerment, and moral and spiritual renewal." Farrakhan was in attendance with his full entourage, but represented only one of many different constituencies and organizations with a range of ideologies and political perspectives. Nevertheless, the showdown to determine the future of black leadership became inevitable.

The July 1994 convention of the NAACP appeared to most observers to be an overwhelming vindication of Chavis's leadership as executive director. Three thousand convention delegates expressed general support for the executive director and the Association's aggressive new orientation. Popular congresswoman Maxine Waters praised Chavis and NAACP president William Gibson at the convention for "doing a wonderful job." She admonished the delegates, "don't let anybody pull you apart." A proposal to establish a permanent office in South Africa at a projected cost of $750,000 was approved. With great confidence, Gibson declared to the media that Chavis had his unqualified support. "If we had to do it again today, we would have the votes to re-elect him," Gibson affirmed.

Despite Chavis's renewed mandate from the convention, the chorus of critics still mounted. Despite the growth in its national membership, the NAACP recorded a decline in membership dues of $100,000 in 1993. Association officials explained that young people, who paid as little as $3 annually to join, represented two-thirds of all new members. Chavis's growing constituency was actually bringing in little new money. Critics continued to complain about Chavis's pattern of wasteful spending – such as $125,000 spent in April, 1994 for Gibson and thirteen NAACP board and staff members to observe Nelson Mandela's electoral campaign in South Africa.

The shocking revelations that Chavis had used Association funds to sidestep a possible lawsuit involving sex discrimination and sexual-harassment charges by former assistant Mary Stansel quickly intensified the campaign to oust him. Within days, Chavis's shaky support virtually disintegrated within many constituencies. On 3 August the Ford Foundation froze $250,000 in support to the Association. Prominent branch leaders began to call for a general reassessment of Chavis's tenure. Even many progressives became more critical of his record. Julianne Malveaux, for example, observed, "If Stansel is telling the truth, Chavis's actions are morally indefensible and he needs to step aside."

At the emergency board meeting in Baltimore, in an emotional eight-hour session, Chavis was finally relieved of his position by an overwhelmingly one-sided vote. Chavis's key assistants, Lew Myers and Don Rojas, were promptly placed on administrative leave. In the days before the meeting, board president William Gibson abandoned Chavis, telling his allies to "vote with their own conscience." Defiantly, Chavis explained to the media that he had been the victim of an orchestrated "lynching." He reached out again to Minister Farrakhan and other African-American leaders who had gathered the following day for the second caucus of the national black summit. Immediately there was speculation that Chavis would take his fight to NAACP rank-and-file members, or perhaps even launch a new protest organization.

On balance, the NAACP solved one problem but created many more by the firing of Ben Chavis. Nearly fifty years ago, the NAACP also fired W.E.B. Du Bois for holding progressive but unpopular views. The Association compromised itself by permitting Du Bois and prominent artist-activist Paul Robeson to be destroyed during the Cold War. As the Association became more irrelevant to the needs of the black masses, new leaders such as Dr. Martin Luther King, Jr., and new organizations such as SCLC and SNCC, arose. The great danger presented by Chavis's ousting is that the NAACP may make the identical mistake again. It may interpret the public criticism against Chavis as an excuse for retreating from the former executive director's visionary and dynamic agenda. The vast majority of black people desperately want and need a leadership which addresses the current social crisis. We can not afford to permit anyone to dictate who our leaders should be, and who we should talk with inside our own community.

This is not to suggest that Chavis was lacking in blame for his demise. Chavis is a good man, and my personal friend. But he committed serious errors of judgement, both administrative and political. His handling of the Stansel affair illustrated a general failure to address actively concerns which black women have about sexism within African-American institutions. Tactically, Chavis needed to solidify his own political base within the Association's ranks, and needed to understand better the internal political culture of the organization. He underestimated the deep resentment and fear which any sort of change at the top of the Association would generate throughout the entire structure. In retrospect, Chavis needed to wait several years for the planning of a national summit, and should have first consolidated his programmatic agenda and leadership inside the NAACP. Too frequently he would schedule visits to cities and communities with substantial NAACP membership, but failed to give adequate notice to local leaders.

Another major error was the manner in which Chavis related to Farrakhan. At the Baltimore summit, after the initial session on Sunday afternoon, Chavis walked lock-step, arm-in-arm with Farrakhan before representatives of the national media. Chavis emphasized that Farrakhan was a legitimate national leader whose constituency had to play a role at any national political gathering reflecting the full spectrum of black opinion. This was a correct position to take, but Chavis did not adequately or forcefully indicate his distinct differences from the leader of the Nation of Islam. Farrakhan merited a place at the table; but critical disagreement should have been expressed on a number of issues, including anti-Semitism and abortion rights. As long as the central issue being debated by the media was Farrakhan's participation in a national gathering of black leaders, then Chavis was placed in a no-win situation. Chavis should have done more to create a genuine perception of collective leadership and real dialogue rather than turn the focus solely on Farrakhan's involvement.

Chavis frequently made public commitments to major public activities, such as the national leadership summit, without sufficient planning, resources or staff consultation. But perhaps Chavis's most critical error was the failure to reach out sufficiently to the liberal-left, progressive leadership in the black community, his logical base and constituency. At the June summit, for example, out of one hundred black representatives, the only participants who could be described as "democratic leftists" were philosopher Cornel West, activist Damu Smith and myself. No trade-union leaders were present, and feminists, gays and lesbians and other radical voices within the African-American community were not heard. There was much good will toward Chavis among black gays and lesbians, community activists with personal histories in the organized left, and other more radical constituencies. But Chavis did little to cultivate this political grouping. He should have recognized that a strong constituency on his left was absolutely essential in pushing the NAACP toward a political position favorable to democratic social transformation.

In the year after his expulsion from the NAACP's leadership, Chavis drew even closer to Farrakhan and his conservative black nationalist followers. Chavis agreed to become a national spokesperson for an ambitious project promoted by Farrakhan, a massive demonstration of

African-American males which was scheduled to be held in October 1995 in Washington DC. The "Million Man March" attracted the support of a range of middle-class black leaders in social organizations, electoral politics and business, and greatly enhanced Farrakhan's influence within mainstream currents of the black community. Once again, Chavis appeared to embrace Farrakhan's interests uncritically. He endorsed the march's call for black women not to be active participants, which implied that they should stay at home, pray and look after the children. Chavis publicly accepted the march's central theme that African-American men should come to the nation's capital for spiritual "atonement," rather than to challenge the Republican-controlled Congress and its reactionary political program. The mobilization lacked a progressive or even liberal public policy agenda, and found few supporters among black labor leaders and African-American feminists. In his eagerness to rehabilitate himself within black America, Chavis failed to articulate his own agenda in his own words.

Nevertheless, Chavis's brief tenure as head of the NAACP defined the preliminary boundaries of a progressive agenda for the post-civil-rights era. Chavis expressed the desire to move beyond the liberal integrationism and incremental reformism of the traditional NAACP. His departure represented a real setback for the progressive, left-of-center perspective within the African-American freedom movement. It was a lost opportunity which in some respects was actually greater than the disastrous demise of the Rainbow Coalition following the 1988 presidential election. As Jesse Jackson deliberately demobilized his own political group, and a progressive alternative to mainstream Democratic Party politics collapsed, black activists found themselves in a political wilderness. Similarly, Chavis' abortive strategy to move the NAACP from inclusion to transformation demoralized and frustrated many people who hoped for a more progressive alternative to traditional civil-rights politics. The question now being asked is whether the NAACP can ever become an organization that is hospitable to a new progressive black generation, searching for genuine social change in an era of reaction.

FOURTEEN

BLACK INTELLECTUALS
IN CONFLICT

African-American and white liberal academic circles are still buzzing
about Adolph Reed's controversial essay in the 11 April 1995 issue
of the *Village Voice* on "The Current Crisis of the Black Intellectual."
The Northwestern University black political scientist launched a major
polemical broadside against some of America's best-known and most
publicized black scholars. Although Reed's title echoed the classic
critique of an earlier generation of black scholars published in 1967
by Harold Cruse, *The Crisis of the Negro Intellectual*, Reed's fundamental
criticism was aimed at only two individuals, who are both professors
of African-American Studies at Harvard University: Cornel West, the
author of *Race Matters* and other works; and African-American Studies
chairperson and literary scholar Henry Louis Gates. Other black scholars
whom Reed criticized were black feminist bell hooks, a professor of
literature at the City University of New York; cultural critic Michael
Eric Dyson, professor of communications and African-American Studies
at the University of North Carolina; and New York University history
professor Robin Kelley.

Reed's basic argument was that these scholars presented themselves
as "authentically black" spokespersons, yet actually lacked viable constituencies or any genuine accountability within the African-American
community. In stark contrast to the black intellectual tradition, which
engaged in a serious and lively conversation on "such questions as the
definition, status, and functions of black literature, the foundations
of black identity, [and] topical critiques of ideological programs and
tendencies in social affairs," Reed claims that the new breed "exhibit
little sense of debate or controversy among themselves." He charges that
this group's "absence of controversy betrays a lack of critical content and

purpose." Reed equates the new intellectuals with the Tuskegee Institute founder Booker T. Washington, a conservative black Republican and chief architect of black capitalism a century ago. To Reed, Washington was simply a "purely freelance race spokesman; his status depended on designation by white elites rather than by any black electorate or social movement." Similarly, the politics and statements of these black "public intellectuals ... exude *pro forma* moralism, not passion," and are supposedly disconnected from the masses of black folk.

If Reed had left matters there, perhaps there would be the basis for the political engagement or dialogue which theoretically he claims to be seeking. But for good measure, Reed found it necessary to add a series of mean-spirited criticisms against those characterized as "the children of Booker T. Washington." Gates was defined as "the voice" of a "black, self-consciously petit bourgeois centrism." West was nothing less than "a freelance race relations consultant and Moral Voice for white elites." Kelley was charged with "spinning narratives that ultimately demean political action by claiming to find it everywhere." And hooks and Dyson were slurred as simply "hustlers, blending bombast, clichés, psychobabble, and lame guilt tripping in service to the 'pay me' principle."

If an informal poll were conducted among most black intellectuals today, many might agree with part of Reed's analysis. There is a growing sense that a significant number of black scholars speak primarily to white elites, rather than addressing the specific problems of the African-American community. But the two major factors for this are: (1) the growth of class stratification and social fragmentation within black civil society, in which large institutions like the black Church, civic associations and civil-rights organizations have lost much of their influence; and (2) the decline of the black freedom movement, and, more generally, the deterioration of progressive and liberal political coalitions, of which blacks were a significant element. Black intellectuals during the era of racial segregation were forced to maintain contacts with all-black organizations, professionally and socially. With the legal integration of civil society and the assimilation of black students and faculty within formerly all-white academic institutions, the linkages which kept black intellectuals in the orbit of African-American political culture and society were largely ruptured. Few black intellectuals today maintain an authentic, organic relationship with multi-class, black formations which have significant constituencies among working-class and poor people.

Political clout among black intellectuals these days is all too often measured by one's ability to leverage policy within powerful white circles, rather than inside social-protest formations. For example, probably the most influential social scientist in America today is University of Chicago's sociologist William Julius Wilson. The author of the controversial *The Declining Significance of Race*, Wilson's ties with the Clinton administration and his criticisms of affirmative action carry much greater weight in public-policy circles than any of the intellectuals Reed cites. On the right, the work of conservative scholars like economist Thomas Sowell, the apologist for Reaganism, has been devastating to blacks' collective interests. Sowell, Walter Williams, Alan Keyes, Clarence Thomas, Glen Loury and other black conservatives proudly proclaim their distance and lack of accountability to the African-American community. Reed certainly has the right, and even the responsibility, to critique any political tendency within the black community. But to single out black scholars who are to the left of center in a manner which is abusive and nearly intolerant in tone comes close, given this context, to confusing our friends with our enemies.

The greatest degree of antagonism expressed today against any single liberal intellectual within the African-American community is probably reserved for Gates, who has been described publicly and privately as something of a "modern Booker T. Washington" in the realm of cultural studies and literary criticism over the past five years. Like the "Wizard of Tuskegee," Gates sees himself as something of an entrepreneur; he has extensive influence within foundation circles and inside the white media.

Gates broke into the public sphere with a controversial op-ed essay in the *New York Times* which condemned anti-Semitism within the black community. The essay provoked deep anger and outrage among many blacks, who felt it pandered to elements within the Jewish community which had become alienated from black issues and interests. In the context of national politics, Gates is unambiguously a liberal; he implicitly embraces a social philosophy of inclusionist integration, appealing to the most liberal wing of white corporate and political power. But simultaneously, he has a strong grasp of currents within black popular culture, and has the political imagination to build personal and political bridges with leaders and intellectuals who are ideologically to his left. Gates is a thoughtful and gifted writer, who has no aspirations to play the role of a contemporary "race leader" of the masses.

Although frequently associated with Gates, West has a very different political history. West developed a distinct constituency among blacks by first working in progressive and black-nationalist-oriented religious and political circles fifteen years ago. He became associated with the white moderate left in his capacity as nominal leader of the Democratic Socialists of America, following the death of socialist writer Michael

Harrington. West also became closely linked with writer Michael Lerner, and the liberal Jewish publication *Tikkun*. Criticism of West within some black circles began several years later, as he spoke out against the sentiments of "nihilism" and social alienation found within contemporary urban culture. But when he accepted an academic appointment at Harvard in late 1993 in the African-American Studies program directed by "Skip" Gates, West increased the general perception that he had become part of Gates's entourage. After the publication of *Race Matters*, black academicians who had never taken part in a protest action or walked a picket line in their lives, began to attack West's politics. As in the case of Gates, some of this criticism was jealousy, pure and simple. Part of it was the distrust West generated among some blacks by his efforts to reach out to liberal whites and Jews with his message of coalition-building and radical democracy. But part of the trouble was that West's more recent work, especially in *Race Matters*, tended to be framed in a language and style which was more at home with traditional liberalism than with the left. Some radicals such as Stephen Steinberg felt that West was prepared to sacrifice the importance of race on the high altar of class. In an essay for *New Politics* in the summer of 1994, Steinberg accused West of shifting "the focus of analysis and of blame away from the structures of racial oppression," and of engaging in "a tortuous reasoning that subverts the whole logic behind affirmative action."

Reed's analysis captures some of these details, but misses the mark by lumping together scholars with widely divergent interests, styles of communication, and political orientations. For example, bell hooks established her reputation as a feminist critic and social commentator with the publication of her book *Ain't I A Woman* in 1982. A series of books have followed, increasingly moving toward themes which focus on gender and social relations, cultural behavior and issues of representation within black contemporary life. It is true that the real impact of her books and essays is less evident within the traditional academy than among hundreds of thousands of black women, who find inspiration in her ideas and commentary. Hooks has never in her work treated class with the sharpness of focus that other feminist scholars, such as Angela Davis, have done. But it seems that Reed is hostile and impatient with hooks because she doesn't engage in the kind of quantitative research or detailed political analysis that he values. However, he should recognize that political intervention can and often does take a variety of forms. Challenging sexism and forms of patriarchy within the black community, the central concern of hooks, makes a fundamental political contribution.

Reed's criticisms of Dyson and Kelley seemed especially petty. Dyson has produced a collection of social essays and a book assessing the cultural and social impact of the Malcolm X phenomenon of the 1990s; Kelley has written several books, including an invaluable study of black rural protest from the Great Depression, *Hammer and Hoe*. Both younger scholars are thoughtful and have a special awareness of the centrality of popular cultural forms, such as hip-hop, to the construction of a political consciousness of resistance and group empowerment. They represent a vanguard of the post-civil-rights generation of new scholarship on black identity, cultural and social history.

Reed fails to capture the diversity among this group of scholars. But the greatest errors within his analysis are essentially historical and conjunctural. First, Reed's characterization of Washington and the politics of the Tuskegee Machine is grossly inaccurate. Washington was certainly a black Republican, an opponent of labor unions, and publicly an apologist for Jim Crow segregation; but, without question, he had a strong following among a segment of the black community. Washington was actively promoted by white capitalists and conservatives, but he also constructed his own effective constituency by establishing the National Negro Business League. He was deeply interested in pan-Africanism, encouraged students from Africa to attend Tuskegee, and inspired an entire generation of early African nationalists, including the founder of the African National Congress, John Langalibalele Dube. He was an astute politician who fought secretly against segregation, hiring lobbyists to oppose Jim Crow laws. These aspects of Washington's program explain why black nationalists such as Marcus Garvey praised and respected him. Reed is a serious scholar of black political history. He surely understands the profound significance of the black capitalist and accommodationist tradition within black political history, and its intimate connections with conservative black nationalism. In the final analysis, Du Bois was right: Washington's accommodationist approach toward white power was profoundly flawed, and at times even criminal, in that it gave legitimacy to the lynching and disfranchisement of black people. However, that doesn't make him an "Uncle Tom." Washington's primary role was to articulate the interests of the entrepreneurial, conservative wing of the emerging black middle class to the representatives of corporate and political power in the white world.

The new black public intellectuals of a century later are engaged in a totally different political enterprise. They are not building educational institutions like Tuskegee Institute, or political machines which negotiate for influence within the white establishment. They utilize the power of words to impact the contours of political culture and public discourse.

Unlike Washington, their commitment is to theoretical and cultural engagement, analyzing the meaning of race, gender and class issues in the context of a post-civil-rights reality of unrelenting attacks against affirmative action, welfare and multicultural education. To be sure, many of them are sadly disconnected from the social forces and struggles of working-class and poor peoples' communities. And as a result, their political discourse is frequently obscure, and they lack any intimate or textured awareness of the efforts for empowerment and social change being waged by most African-Americans today. Reed understands this. But by wielding a polemical sledgehammer against West, hooks, and others, Reed ignores a far greater danger to the possibilities for progressive black politics.

Since the early 1990s, the far right has waged an ideological war against the politics of liberal democratic social change. With the declining strength of the organized labor movement, the deterioration of the liberal wing of the Democratic Party, and the disarray of the civil-rights movement, one of the few sectors of growing left-of-center influence in national political culture is the black intelligentsia. The black population overall is significantly to the left of the general society on socioeconomic issues; this permits many progressive, anti-corporate capitalist intellectuals like Angela Davis to exercise significant influence.

White conservatives made a strategic decision to delegitimate the liberal-left black intelligentsia several years ago. After Clinton's election to the presidency, for example, conservatives attacked prominent black anthropologist Johnetta Cole, the president of Spelman College, to deny her possible nomination as secretary of education. In 1994, legal scholar Lani Guinier was publicly smeared as the "Quota Queen" by the far right, after being nominated as the assistant attorney general for civil rights. Clinton's retreat from Guinier's nomination signaled a victory for conservatives which led directly to today's assault against affirmative action, minority economic set-asides and an entire range of civil-rights initiatives.

In the *New Republic* in March 1995, Cornel West was viciously attacked in a vitriolic polemic by Leon Wieseltier. Accurately described by Michael Lerner as the "errand boy and hatchet man" for Martin Peretz, the publisher of the *New Republic*, Wieseltier denounced West's writings as "almost completely worthless." Reed backhandedly defends Wieseltier's thesis as being "right-for-the-wrong-reasons." This position is not only irresponsible, but directly feeds into the retreat from an anti-racist politics among white liberals and so-called radicals who are among the *Village Voice* readers. To join the chorus of the far right, to deplore and denounce the works of an entire group of black intellectuals espousing progressive ideas, is alien to the best traditions of black scholarship. Many black activists suspect that the real motivation behind Wieseltier's article was West's principled decision to participate in the National African American Leadership Summit, called by former NAACP national secretary Benjamin Chavis in the summer of 1994. West strongly defended the political initiatives taken by Chavis to revitalize the NAACP, and vigorously opposed Chavis's ousting. His well-publicized defense of the need to engage in direct dialogue with Nation of Islam leader Louis Farrakhan, and his endorsement of the senatorial campaign of Al Sharpton in New York in the fall of 1994, may have triggered the polemical attack in the *New Republic*.

Growing up in a Midwestern industrial town in the 1960s, I witnessed hundreds of petty quarrels between representatives of our small black community which were animated by jealousy and a desire for influence within the white elite. Among ourselves, we used to complain that middle-class Negroes frequently responded to each others' successes like "crabs in a barrel" – pulling each other down. Reed identifies himself with the radical left, but all too often seems to behave in the same manner. In many ways, the sharply confrontational style of Reed is reminiscent of other voices of independent black radicalism, such as William Monroe Trotter. Reed is often unfairly dismissed, like Trotter, as something of a loner, so ideologically "left" that his criticism carries little weight among most black activists. His scathing book on the 1984 presidential campaign of the Rainbow Coalition was so hostile to Jesse Jackson that most blacks concluded erroneously that Reed was a "black conservative" like Sowell, Loury and Thomas. But the supposed virtue of being further to the left than anyone else may mean that one is indeed outside the real experiences of one's people.

Reed's essay does make an important contribution by presenting a sociological critique of black intellectuals. Unlike W.E.B. Du Bois, C.L.R. James and E. Franklin Frazier, many of today's black middle-class scholars are not organically connected to the problems and struggles of the African-American community. However, Reed should also recognize that West, Gates and company should not be the primary objects of his political scorn and contempt. At a time when we need to construct a new left-of-center paradigm as an alternative to mass conservatism, we need to engage in a thoughtful, civil dialogue among ourselves – not a public mugging of black intellectuals who share democratic, progressive values.

PART III

BEYOND BLACK AND WHITE

FIFTEEN

AFRICAN-AMERICAN EMPOWERMENT IN THE FACE OF RACISM: THE POLITICAL AFTERMATH OF THE BATTLE OF LOS ANGELES

The racial violence which erupted across Los Angeles in 1992 represented the most profound urban unrest in the United States since the turbulent sixties. Yet the fires which torched thousands of buildings had not even cooled before white politicians and the media attempted to attribute the rebellion to various sociological problems within the African-American community. Vice President Dan Quayle pointed to the factors of sexual permissiveness, welfare, and the breakdown of the nuclear family as contributing to the racial unrest among African-Americans. Others in the media criticized African-American political leaders, especially congresswoman Maxine Waters, for characterizing the "riot" as a "rebellion," and for failing to uphold law and order in the ghetto. Lost in all the accusations was any serious effort to comprehend the social significance of this cathartic event.

An understanding of the racial "Battle of Los Angeles" requires consideration of at least three pivotal issues. We must first identify the root causes of the racial uprising. The disgraceful verdict of the Rodney King trial, which vindicated the brutal actions of four white police officers, was only the immediate catalyst for the social explosion. Second, how did the uprising affect sectors of the African-American community specifically, and various racial and ethnic groups generally? What was the special significance of the Rodney King trial, for example, to upper-middle-class African-Americans who lived miles away from south-central Los Angeles? What is the significance of the assaults aimed at Asian-American-owned property by young African-Americans? How did white Americans perceive this unanticipated revolt?

Third, and most significantly, is the burning issue of violence in a racist society. We cannot begin to analyze Los Angeles without exploring the essential nexus between coercion or violence and the historical and contemporary status of African-Americans as an oppressed people. Racism is, in essence, institutionalized violence aimed against African-American people – in economics, education, employment, political affairs, and all aspects of daily life. When African-Americans resort to violence against that system of social control, are they simply "rioting" or do their collective actions have a more profound meaning? And, given the history of racist coercion, what are the prospects of more serious African-American acts of violence against the system in the near future?

For generations, California has been known for its San Andreas fault, the geological fracture beneath the earth's crust. The periodic eruptions along the fault line have been responsible for massive destruction and hundreds of deaths. Yet, far more devastating than the San Andreas fault is America's "race/class fault line," the jagged division of color and income, education and privilege which slashes across the soul of this nation. In California, the race/class fault line rudely separates the posh affluence of Hollywood and Beverly Hills from the crime, fear, and hunger of south-central Los Angeles. That same race and class division runs down Detroit's Eight Mile Road, separating the poor, unemployed, and homeless from comfortable suburban white enclaves. It sets apart Harlem and Bedford-Stuyvesant from the multimillion-dollar estates in Connecticut's posh suburbs. The Los Angeles race uprising can be understood only from the vantage point of the race/class fault line, because the violence unleashed by Rodney King's court case was just a tremor along that division.

On different sides of the race/class fault, each group tends to perceive issues in radically different ways. The vast majority of all Americans – African-American, Latino, Asian American and white – believed that the "innocent" verdict in the King case was wrong. But according to a poll in *USA Today*, 81 per cent of all African-Americans stated that the criminal justice system was clearly "biased against Black people." Some 60 per cent of all African-Americans agreed that there was "very much" police brutality against people of color, and another 33 per cent believed that such violence was "considerable." Conversely, only 36 per cent of all whites who responded believed that the justice system was racially biased. Only 17 per cent of whites were convinced that there was "excessive police brutality" against minorities.

The white public's racist attitudes were reinforced by the rhetoric and contempt for African-Americans displayed by the nation's white elected officials. For example, in a shameful display of political cowardice, President George Bush's initial instinct was to attribute blame for the

Los Angles race revolt on the liberal "Great Society" programs of Lyndon Johnson, a quarter of a century ago. But when pressed for specific programs which had contributed to the racial crisis of today, White House press secretary Marlin Fitzwater could only mumble, "I don't have a list with me."

Did Bush mean the 1964 Civil Rights Act, which had outlawed racial discrimination in public accommodations? Was the president blaming the National Housing Act of 1968, which established the National Housing Partnership to promote the construction of houses for low- to middle-income people? Or maybe the reason people rioted was the 1965 Voting Rights Act, which had established the principle of "one person, one vote" a century after the abolition of slavery. Bush's pathetic effort to rewrite racial history, to blame the victim, was yet another example of his "Willie Horton" racial politics. The current agony of our inner cities is a direct and deliberate consequence of Reagan–Bush policies, and no amount of historical distortion can erase that fact.

On the white side of the race/class fault line, the response of most middle- and upper-class white Americans to the Los Angeles unrest was profoundly mixed. Opinion polls showed a new appreciation of the ghetto's socioeconomic problems, and greater sympathy for the racism experienced by African-Americans within the legal system. But middle-class whites in southern California also took immediate steps to protect themselves, fearing that the police would be unable to check the unrest. In the first eleven days of May, California residents purchased 20,578 guns, a 50 per cent increase over last year's rate. Frightened corporate personnel and professionals who had never owned firearms now stood in line, demanding shotguns and semi-automatic weapons. The National Rifle Association, with 2.8 million members, added one thousand new members each day in the month after the racial explosion. Newspapers even reported instances where suburban whites fled in panic when confronted by anyone with a black face – delivery boys, mail carriers, and sanitation workers. Motivated by racism, guilt, anger, and fear, many whites tried to isolate themselves from the social chaos. In downtown Los Angeles at the peak of the unrest, dozens of whites drove the wrong way down one way streets, speeding through red lights. Barricades were erected in Westwood, and a swanky shopping mall in Beverly Hills was closed.

But the race/class fault line which trembled and shook across impoverished south-central Los Angeles also runs directly beneath the affluent white suburbs. This time, African-American and Latino young rebels weren't content to destroy the symbols of ghetto economic exploitation. Violence and arson unexpectedly struck against white-owned property across Los Angeles County. The Bloods and Crips street gangs established a fragile peace pact, announcing to the media that the current street violence was "a slave rebellion, like other slave rebellions in Black history." One local Samoan rap group declared that the rebellion was "great," but that the violence against property should have been directed not against the Korean stores but at "the rich people in Beverly Hills."

Much of the violence was in fact directed against the Asian American community. Over 1,800 Korean-owned stores were destroyed or vandalized, with property damage estimated at $300 million. Yet, as deplorable as this violence was, it represented a dual tragedy for both Asian Americans and African-Americans. Young African-Americans need to understand that it is not the Korean American small merchant who denies capital for investment in the African-American community, or controls the banks and financial institutions. It is not the Korean American community which commits police brutality against Latino and African-American citizens, or controls governmental policies, or dominates the political parties. Aggression against people of color is misplaced and misdirected. This doesn't negate the legitimate grievances or differences of opinion which separate Korean Americans from Latinos and African-Americans. But it makes a unified response to race and class oppression virtually impossible.

The unanticipated eruption of rage stripped away the façade of African-American progress in the central cities, to show them boiling with the problems of poverty, drugs, gang violence, unemployment, poor schools, and deteriorating public housing. The white media tried desperately to turn attention away from these issues, in part by arguing that the Los Angeles uprising was merely a "riot" which was opposed by most African-Americans. This ignores the historical evidence about the dynamics of all civil unrest. After the Watts racial rebellion of 1965, for example, sociologists later determined that only about 15 per cent of all African-American ghetto residents had actually participated in the arson and violence. However, between one-third and half of all residents later expressed support for those who had destroyed white-owned property and attacked symbols of white authority. About two-thirds later agreed that "the targets of the rebellion got what they deserved." So, although the majority of African-Americans in south-central Los Angeles didn't take to the streets, that doesn't mean that they aren't alienated and outraged by race and class oppression.

A critical distinction must be made, therefore, between the notion of a "riot" and other forms of collective resistance – "insurrections," "revolts," "rebellions," and "strikes." The term "riot" connotes widespread criminal behavior disconnected from political objectives. An individualistic desire to loot and burn can be interpreted as just anti-social behavior, linked to Daniel Patrick Moynihan's "Black Matriarchy Thesis" and the absence of strong parental role models – at least according to Quayle. But any analysis based on what young African-Americans are actually saying and feeling in the streets should lead to an opposite conclusion. Los Angles was an "insurrection" or a "rebellion" precisely because people acted collectively rather than as individuals. There was clearly a political motivation for hurling rocks at police squad cars, which symbolized the vehicles of an oppressive, occupying army in the African-American community. No one, except perhaps the Israelis, would denigrate the "Intifada" as just a "riot" against political authorities in the occupied West Bank. Similarly, African-Americans engaged in violence against white-owned property are motivated by the same political alienation which we see in the faces of young, militant Palestinians.

For African-American middle-class professionals, many of whom had come to believe the mythology about racial progress in the Reagan–Bush era, the King verdict was like a "firebell in the night." They were jolted into the realization that they, like Rodney King, could be halted by the police, brutalized, kicked, and possibly killed, and that their assailants in police uniforms would probably walk away free. They were awakened by the haunting fear that their college-bound sons and daughters could be stopped for minor traffic violations, and later be found dead or dying in the city streets. This is what Representative Floyd Flake of Queens meant when he explained why the hopes of millions of African-Americans in the inherent fairness of the legal system were shattered: "When Rodney King was on the ground getting beat, we were all on the ground getting beat."

But if we listen carefully to young African-Americans in the streets, this generation is expressing more than just its dissatisfaction with the King verdict. The violence was not directly generated by reactions to courtroom decisions. What our young people painfully realize is that the entire "system" – the government and its politicians, the courts and the police, the corporations and the media – has written them off. They recognize that Bush had virtually no coherent policies addressing urban problems until he was confronted by massive street violence. They feel instinctively that American businesses have no intention of hiring them at real "living wages," that the courts refuse to treat them as human beings, and that the politicians take their votes and ignore their needs. By taking to the streets, they are crying out to society: "We will be heard! We will not be ignored, and we will not go away quietly. And if the system, and society, refuse to listen to us, we intend to burn it to the ground."

White America wonders whether the Los Angeles "riot" represents just the beginning of a new wave of social unrest and violence throughout urban America. But the young people who challenged police cars and public authorities in the streets earlier this year were not responsible for introducing the question of violence into the context of American race relations. The essential definition of "racism" throughout American history has been the systematic discrimination and exploitation of a people defined as a subordinate and inferior "racial group." And the force which perpetuated inequality of material conditions between African-Americans and whites, the absence of full voting and legal rights, the substandard pay at places of employment, was violence. During the period of slavery, from 1619 until 1865, few whites ever questioned whether African-Americans were not inherently inferior to whites. Slaves were the constant victims of all types of violence, from the forced separation of families to systematic rape and whippings.

Violence against African-Americans was endemic to the Jim Crow segregated South. Between 1884 and 1917 more than 3,600 African-Americans were lynched across the South. The terror was a deliberate part of a social order designed to maintain the permanent inferiority of African-Americans. The violence also preserved whites as a group with a privileged status, giving them access to higher wages, better schools and homes than any African-Americans could ever hope to attain.

When World War I broke out, African-Americans overwhelmingly supported the popular effort to defeat Germany. They purchased over $250 million in war bonds, hoping that their patriotism would help shield them from racist violence, and permit them to secure greater democratic rights. Yet immediately following the conflict, in the "Red Summer of 1919," over seventy African-Americans were lynched and eleven were burned alive – some still in uniform.

When African-Americans mobilized in nonviolent demonstrations to overthrow the Jim Crow system a generation ago, they were again confronted by white violence. African-American churches and homes were bombed, civil-rights leaders and community organizers by the thousand were beaten and arrested, and dozens of key leaders were assassinated, most prominently Dr. Martin Luther King, Jr. and Medgar Evers.

The eruption of inner-city violence in the 1960s was the first significant demonstration of illegal force by thousands of African-Americans, aimed against the symbols of white civil authority and private property. The urban "riots" of 1964–72 led to 250 deaths, 10,000 serious injuries, and 60,000 arrests. In Detroit's 1967 civil unrest, 43 residents were killed, about 2,000 were injured, and over 2,700 white-owned businesses were torched and vandalized – half completely gutted by fire. Although the media described these acts of collective violence as "riots," this obscures both the political element which motivated thousands of young African-Americans to take to the streets, and the degree of concurrence with these actions by African-Americans who stood on the sidelines. People committed arson, theft, and assaults not because they were "law-breakers" or "criminals"; they acted in the belief that the established civil authorities and the standard rules of society were structured in a way to preserve white power and domination over African-American lives. Thus African-Americans acted in violence against a system and its symbols which, in turn, represented violence and inequalities in their daily lives.

Violence by whites against African-Americans also continues to permeate African-American life, although it manifests itself no longer in the traditional forms of lynching or terrorism against African-American leaders. High rates of unemployment, the closure of businesses in African-American areas, the proliferation of drugs, and the failure by government to provide decent housing and health care for the poor are perceived as forms of institutional "violence."

Although virtually all civil-rights leaders and African-American elected officials are firmly committed to legal forms of protest and oppose violent acts of disruption against civil authority or vandalism of property, the Los Angeles uprising may easily trigger a series of massive urban conflagrations over the next decade. For the young men who have been socialized in a world of urban street gangs, drugs, and black-on-black murder feel within them a nearly ungovernable rage against all forms of power and privilege. That rage may express itself in collective acts of violence and selective terror similar to those identified with the Irish Republican Army in the United Kingdom, or by several radical Palestinian groups. If people feel that all avenues of realistic, effective change within the established order are blocked, they may move to a new level of violence, which could be targeted at officials, prominent executives, and the police. The next stage of racial violence could become more sophisticated and terrifying for the authorities.

If violence descends into terror, the historical figure who might provide the greatest insights for this generation of young African-Americans may not be Malcolm X but George Jackson. Sentenced at the age of eighteen to a term of "one year to life" for the theft of $70, Jackson spent his entire adult life in a California prison. Yet such was his radical influence within the black liberation movement that he was appointed national "field marshall" of the Black Panther Party while imprisoned. Before his execution in San Quentin prison in August 1971, Jackson authored two texts on the uses of "revolutionary violence," *Soledad Brother* and *Blood in*

My Eye. For Jackson, the struggle against racism and class exploitation had to transcend the nonviolent policies of Martin Luther King, Jr. and the civil-rights movement.

"Any claims that nonviolent, purely nonviolent political agitation has served to force back the legions of capitalist expansion are false," Jackson wrote in *Soledad Brother*. "There is no case of successful liberation without violence. How could you neutralize an army without violence?" Jackson believed that only through armed struggle could African-Americans finally achieve full human rights and self-determination. And if the government attempted to eliminate prominent African-American leaders and street organizers, the only appropriate response was political assassinations, bombings, and other methods of violence. "If terror is going to be a choice of weapons," Jackson warned, "there must be funerals on both sides."

The "Battle of Los Angeles" raises the fundamental question of whether white mainstream America will accept the missions of inner-city African-Americans and Latinos on the basis of full human equality without thousands of office buildings, businesses, and police stations being assaulted and burned to the ground. If George Jackson is right, then retaliatory violence by African-Americans and the widespread use of terror may be necessary. There will indeed be "funerals on both sides" so long as the legitimate grievances of African-Americans go unanswered. But ultimately, the choice of "violence or nonviolence" is not ours, but white America's. Those who make peaceful change and democratic advancement impossible make violent revolution inevitable.

SIXTEEN

BEYOND RACIAL IDENTITY POLITICS: TOWARD A LIBERATION THEORY FOR MULTICULTURAL DEMOCRACY

Americans are arguably the most "race-conscious" people on earth. Even in South Africa, the masters of apartheid recognized the necessity to distinguish between "Coloureds" and "black Africans." Under the bizarre regulations of apartheid, a visiting delegation of Japanese corporate executives, or the diplomatic corps of a client African regime such as Malawi, could be classified as "honorary whites." But in the USA, "nationality" has been closely linked historically to the categories and hierarchy of national racial identity. Despite the orthodox cultural ideology of the so-called "melting pot," power, privilege and the ownership of productive resources and property have always been unequally allocated in a social hierarchy stratified by class, gender and race. Those who benefit directly from these institutional arrangements have historically been defined as "white," overwhelmingly upper class and male. And it is precisely here within this structure of power and privilege that "national identity" in the context of mass political culture is located. To be an "all-American" is by definition *not* to be an Asian American, Pacific American, American Indian, Latino, Arab American or African-American. Or viewed another way, the hegemonic ideology of "whiteness" is absolutely central in rationalizing and justifying the gross inequalities of race, gender and class, experienced by millions of Americans relegated to the politically peripheral status of "Others." As Marxist cultural critic E. San Juan has observed, "whenever the question of the national identity is at stake, boundaries in space and time are drawn.... A decision is made to represent the Others – people of color – as missing, absent, or supplement." "Whiteness" becomes the very "center" of the dominant criteria for national prestige, decision-making, authority and intellectual leadership.

Ironically, because of the centrality of "whiteness" within the dominant national identity, Americans generally make few distinctions between "ethnicity" and "race," and the two concepts are usually used interchangeably. Both the oppressors and those who are oppressed are therefore imprisoned by the closed dialectic of race. "Black" and "white" are usually viewed as fixed, permanent and often antagonistic social categories. Yet, in reality, "race" should be understood not as an entity within the histories of all human societies, or grounded in some inescapable or permanent biological or genetic difference between human beings. "Race" is first and foremost an unequal relationship between social aggregates, characterized by dominant and subordinate forms of social interaction, and reinforced by the intricate patterns of public discourse, power, ownership and privilege within the economic, social and political institutions of society.

Race only becomes "real" as a social force when individuals or groups behave toward each other in ways which either reflect or perpetuate the hegemonic ideology of subordination and the patterns of inequality in daily life. These are, in turn, justified and explained by assumed differences in physical and biological characteristics, or in theories of cultural deprivation or intellectual inferiority. Thus, far from being static or fixed, race as an oppressive concept within social relations is fluid and ever-changing. An oppressed "racial group" changes over time, geographical space and historical conjuncture. That which is termed "black," "Hispanic" or "Oriental" by those in power to describe one human being's "racial background" in a particular setting can have little historical or practical meaning within another social formation which is also racially stratified, but in a different manner.

Since so many Americans view the world through the prism of permanent racial categories, it is difficult to convey the idea that radically different ethnic groups may have roughly the same "racial identity" imposed on them. For example, although native-born African-Americans, Trinidadians, Haitians, Nigerians and Afro-Brazilians would all be termed "black" on the streets of New York City, they have remarkably little in common in terms of language, culture, ethnic traditions, rituals, and religious affiliations. Yet they are all "black" racially, in the sense that they will share many of the pitfalls and prejudices built into the in-stitutional arrangements of the established social order for those defined as "black." Similarly, an even wider spectrum of divergent ethnic groups – from Japanese Americans, Chinese Americans, Filipino Americans, and Korean Americans to Hawaiians, Pakistanis, Vietnamese, Arabs and Uzbekis – are described and defined by the dominant society as "Asians" or, worse still, as "Orientals." In the rigid, racially stratified

American social order, the specific nationality, ethnicity and culture of a person of color has traditionally been secondary to an individual's "racial category," a label of inequality which is imposed from without rather than constructed by the group from within. Yet as Michael Omi, Asian American Studies professor at the University of California at Berkeley has observed, we are also "in a period in which our conception of racial categories is being radically transformed." The waves of recent immigrants create new concepts of what the older ethnic communities have been. The observations and generalizations we imparted "to racial identities" in the past no longer make that much sense.

In the United States, "race" for the oppressed has also come to mean an identity of survival, victimization and opposition to those racial groups or elites which exercise power and privilege. What we are looking at here is *not* an *ethnic* identification or culture, but an awareness of shared experience, suffering and struggles against the barriers of racial division. These collective experiences, survival tales and grievances form the basis of a historical consciousness – a group's recognition of what it has witnessed and what it can anticipate in the near future. This second distinct sense of racial identity is imposed on the oppressed and yet represents a reconstructed critical memory of the character of the group's collective ordeals. Both definitions of "race" and "racial identity" give character and substance to the movements for power and influence among people of color.

In the African-American experience, the politics of racial identity have been expressed by two great traditions of racial ideology and social protest: integrationism and black nationalism. The integrationist tradition was initiated in the antebellum political activism of the free Negro community of the North, articulated by the great abolitionist orator Frederick Douglass. The black nationalist tradition was a product of the same social classes, but influenced by the pessimism generated by the Compromise of 1850, the Fugitive Slave Act, the Dred Scott decision, and the failure of the slave uprisings and revolts such as Nat Turner's to end the tyranny and inhumanity of the slave regime. The integrationist perspective was anchored in a firm belief in American democracy, and in the struggle to outlaw all legal barriers which restricted equal access and opportunities to racial minorities. It was linked to the politics of building coalitions with sympathetic white constituencies, aimed at achieving reforms within the context of the system. The integrationist version of racial politics sought the deracial-ization of the hierarchies of power within society and the economic system. By contrast, the black nationalist approach to racial politics was profoundly skeptical of America's ability to live up to its democratic ideals. It assumed that "racial categories" were real and fundamentally significant, and that efforts to accumulate power had to be structured along the boundaries of race for centuries to come. The nationalist tradition emphasized the cultural kinship of black Americans to Africa, and emphasized the need to establish all-black-owned institutions to provide goods and services to the African-American community.

Although the integrationists and nationalists seemed to hold radically divergent points of view, there was a subterranean symmetry between the two ideologies. Both were based on the idea that the essential dilemma or problem confronting black people was the omnipresent reality of race. The integrationists sought power to dismantle the barriers of race, to outlaw legal restrictions on blacks' access to the institutions of authority and ownership, and to assimilate into the cultural "mainstream" without regard to race. The black nationalists favored a separatist path toward empowerment, believing that even the most liberal-minded whites could not be trusted to destroy the elaborate network of privileges from which they benefited, called "white supremacy." But along the assimilationist-separatist axis of racial-identity politics is the common perception that "race," however it is defined, is the most critical organizing variable within society. Race mattered so much more than other factors or variables that, to a considerable degree, the concept of race was perpetuated by the types of political interventions and tactical assumptions by activists and leaders on both sides of the assimilationist/separatist axis.

Both schools of racial identity espoused what can be termed the politics of "symbolic representation." Both the nationalists and integrationists believed that they were speaking to "white power brokers" on behalf of their "constituents" – that is, black Americans. They believed that the real measure of racial power a group wielded within any society could be calibrated according to the institutions it dominated or the numbers of positions it controlled which influenced others. For the integrationists, it was a relatively simple matter of counting noses. If the number of African-Americans in elective offices nationwide increased from 103 in 1964 to over 8,000 in 1993, for example, one could argue that African-Americans as a *group* had increased their political power. Any increase in the number of blacks as mayors, members of federal courts, and on boards of education, was championed as a victory for *all* black people. The black nationalists tended to be far more skeptical about the promise or viability of an electoral route to group empowerment. However, they often shared the same notions of symbolic representation when it came to the construction of social and economic institutions based on private-ownership models. The development of a black-owned shopping plaza, supermarket or private school was widely interpreted as black social and economic empowerment for the group as a whole.

The problem with "symbolic representation" is that it presumes structures of accountability and allegiance between those blacks who are elevated into powerful positions of authority in the capitalist state and the millions of African-Americans clinging to the margins of economic and social existence. The unifying discourse of race obscures the growing class stratification within the African-American community. According to the Census Bureau, for example, back in 1967 about 85 per cent of all African-American families earned between $5,000 and $50,000 annually, measured in inflation-adjusted 1990 dollars. Some 41 per cent earned between $10,000 and $25,000. In short, the number of extremely poor and destitute families was relatively small. The Census Bureau's statistics on African-American households as of 1990 were strikingly different. The size of the black working class and the number of moderate-income people had declined significantly, and the two extremes of poverty and affluence had grown sharply. By 1990, about 12 per cent of all black households earned less than $5,000 annually. One-third of all blacks lived below the federal government's poverty level.

Conversely, a strong African-American petty bourgeoisie, representing the growth of thousands of white-collar professionals, executives and managers created by affirmative-action requirements, has been established. The average median income of African-American families in which both the wife and husband were employed rose from about $28,700 in 1967 to over $40,000 in 1990, an increase of 40 per cent. More than 15 per cent of all African-American households earn above $50,000 annually, and thousands of black professional families have incomes exceeding $100,000 annually. Many of these newly affluent blacks have moved far from the problems of the main cities into the comfortable white enclaves of suburbia. Nevertheless, many of the strongest advocates of racial-identity politics since the demise of Black Power and the black freedom movement come from the most privileged, elitist sectors of the black upper middle class. The dogmatic idea that "race" alone explains virtually everything that occurs within society has a special appeal to some African-American suburban elites who have little personal connection with the vast human crisis of ghetto unemployment, black-on-black crime, a rampant drugs trade, gang violence, and deteriorating schools. Moreover, for black entrepreneurs, traditional race categories could be employed as a tool to promote petty capital accumulation, by urging black consumers to "buy black." Racial-identity politics in this context is contradictory and conceptually limited in other critical respects. As noted, it tends to minimize greatly any awareness or analysis of class stratification and concentrations of poverty or affluence among the members of the defined "racial minority group."

Issues of poverty, hunger, unemployment and homelessness are viewed and interpreted within a narrowly racial context – that is, as a by-product of the large racist contradiction within the society as a whole. Conversely, concentrations of wealth or social privilege within sectors of the racial group are projected as "success stories" – see, for example, issue after issue of *Ebony*, *Black Enterprise* and *Jet*. In the context of racial-identity politics, the idea of "social change" is usually expressed in utilitarian and pragmatic terms, if change is expressed at all. The integrationists generally favor working within the established structures of authority, influencing those in power to dole out new favors or additional privileges to minorities. Their argument is that "democracy" works best when it is truly pluralistic and inclusive, with the viewpoints of all "racial groups" taken into account. But such a strategy rarely if ever gets to the root of the real problem of the persuasiveness of racism – social inequality. It articulates an eclectic, opportunistic approach to change, rather than a comprehensive or systemic critique, informed by social theory. In the case of the racial separatists, the general belief that "race" is a relatively permanent social category in all multiethnic societies, and that virtually all whites are immutably racist, either for genetic, biological or psychological reasons, compromises the very concept of meaningful social change. If allies are nonexistent or at best untrustworthy, or if dialogues with progressive whites must await the construction of broad-based unity among virtually all blacks, then even tactical alliances with social forces outside the black community become difficult to sustain.

But perhaps the greatest single weakness in the politics of racial identity is that it is rooted implicitly in a competitive model of group empowerment. If the purpose of politics is the realization of a group or constituency's specific objective interest, then racial-identity politics utilizes racial consciousness or the group's collective memory and experiences as the essential framework for interpreting the actions and interests of all other social groups. This approach is not unlike a model of political competition based on a "zero-sum" game such as poker, in which a player can be a "winner" only if one or more other players are "losers." The prism of a group's racial experiences tends to diffuse the parallels, continuities and common interests which might exist between oppressed racial groups; this serves to highlight and emphasize areas of dissension and antagonism.

The black-nationalist-oriented intelligentsia, tied to elements of the new African-American upper middle class by income, social position, and cultural outlook, began to search for ways of expressing itself through the "permanent" prism of race, while rationalizing its relatively privileged class position. One expression of this search for a social theory was found in the writings of Afrocentric theorist Molefi Asante. Born Arthur Lee Smith in 1942, Asante emerged as the founding editor of the *Journal of Black Studies* in 1969. Asante became a leading force in the National Council of Black Studies, the African Heritage Studies Association, and, after 1980, occupied the chair of the African-American Studies Department at Temple University. Asante's basic thesis, the cultural philosophy of "Afrocentrism," began with the insight that people of European descent or cultures have a radically different understanding of the human condition from people of African and/or non-Western cultures and societies. "Human beings tend to recognize three fundamental existential postures one can take with respect to the human condition: feeling, knowing, and acting," Asante observed in 1983. Europeans utilize these concepts separately in order to understand them objectively. Thus "Eurocentrists" tend to understand their subjects "apart from the emotions, attitudes, and cultural definitions of a given context." Scholars with a "Eurocentric" perspective – those who view the entire history of human development from the vantage point of European civilization – are also primarily concerned with a "subject/object duality" which exists in a linear environment. European cultures and people are viewed as the central subjects of history, the creative forces which dominate and transform the world over time. Asante states that this "Euro-linear" viewpoint helps to explain the construction of institutional racism, apartheid and imperialism across the nonwhite world.

By contrast, the Afrocentric framework for comprehending society and human development is radically different, according to Asante. Afrocentrism "understands that the interrelationship of knowledge with cosmology, society, religion, medicine, and traditions stands alongside the interactive metaphors of discourse as principle means of achieving a measure of knowledge about experience." Unlike a linear view of the world, the Afrocentric approach is a "circular view" of human interaction which "seeks to interpret and understand." In theoretical terms, this means that the study of African and African-American phenomena should be within their original cultural contexts, and not within the paradigmatic frameworks of Eurocentrism. Drawing upon African cultural themes, values and concepts, Afrocentrism seeks therefore the creation of a harmonious environment in which all divergent cultures could coexist and learn from each other. Rather than seeking the illusion of the melting pot, Asante calls for the construction of "parallel frames of reference" within the context of a multicultural, pluralistic environment. "Universality," Asante warns, "can only be dreamed about when we have slept on truth based on specific cultural experience."

The practical impact of the theory of Afrocentrism was found among black educators. After all, if people of African descent had a radically different cultural heritage, cosmology and philosophy of being than whites, it made sense to devise an alternate curriculum which was "Afrocentric." Such an alternative approach to education would be completely comprehensive, Asante insisted, expressing the necessity for "every topic, economics, law communication, science, religion, history, literature, and sociology to be reviewed through Afrocentric eyes." No African-American child should "attend classes as they are currently being taught or read books as they are currently being written without raising questions about our capability as a people.... All children must be centered in a historical place, or their self-esteem suffers." By 1991, approximately 350 "Afrocentric academies" and private schools were educating more than 50,000 African-American students throughout the country. Many large public-school districts adopted Afrocentric supplementary and required textbooks, or brought in Afrocentric-oriented educators for curriculum-development workshops. Several public-school systems, notably in Detroit, Baltimore, and Milwaukee, established entire "Afrocentric schools" for hundreds of school-aged children, transforming all aspects of their learning experience. On college campuses, many Black Studies programs began to restructure their courses to reflect Asante's Afrocentric philosophy.

There is no doubt that Afrocentrism established a vital and coherent cultural philosophy which encouraged African-Americans to react favorably towards black nationalism. Some Afrocentric scholars in the area of psychology, notably Linda James Myers, established innovative and effective measures for promoting the development of positive self-conception among African-Americans. Asante used his position at Temple to create a scholastic tradition which represented a sharp critique and challenge to Eurocentrism. The difficulty was that this scholarly version of Afrocentrism tended to be far more sophisticated than the more popular version of the philosophy embraced by elements of the dogmatically separatist, culturally nationalist community. One such Afrocentric popularizer was Professor Len Jeffries, the chair of the Black Studies program at the City College of New York. Jeffries claimed that white Americans were "ice people" due to environmental, psychological and cultural factors inherent in their evolution in Europe; African-Americans by contrast were defined as "sun people," characteristically warm, open, and charitable. At the level of popular history, the vulgar Afrocentrists glorified in an oversimplistic manner the African heritage of black Americans. In their writings, they rarely related the actual complexities of the local cultures, divergence of languages, religions, and political institutions, and tended to homogenize the sharply different social structures found within the African diaspora. They pointed with pride to the dynasties of Egypt as the classical foundation of African civilization, without also examining with equal vigor or detail Egypt's slave structure. At times, the racial separatists of vulgar Afrocentrism embraced elements of a black chauvinism and intolerance towards others, and espoused public positions which were blatantly anti-Semitic. Jeffries' public statements attacking Jews, and the counter-charge that he espoused anti-Semitic viewpoints, made it easier for white conservatives to denigrate all African-American Studies, and to undermine efforts to require multicultural curricula within public schools.

Scholarly Afrocentrism coexisted uneasily with its populist variety. When Jeffries was deposed as chair of City College's Black Studies Department in the controversy following his anti-Semitic remarks, Asante wisely stayed outside the debate. Nevertheless, there remained theoretical problems inherent in the more scholarly paradigm. Afro-centric intellectuals gave eloquent lip service to the insights of black scholars such as W.E.B. Du Bois as "pillars" of their own perspective, without also acknowledging that Du Bois's philosophy of culture and history conflicted sharply with their own. Du Bois's major cultural and philosophical observation, expressed nearly a century ago in *The Souls of Black Folk,* claimed that the African-American expresses a "double consciousness." The black American was "an American, a Negro; two souls, two thoughts, two unreconciled strivings; two warring ideals in one dark body, whose dogged strength alone keeps it from being torn asunder." Africa in effect represents only half of the dialectical consciousness of African-American people. Blacks are also legitimately Americans, and by our suffering, struggle and culture we have a destiny within this geographical and political space equal to or stronger than any white American. This realization that the essence of the inner spirit of African-American people was reflected in this core duality was fundamentally ignored by the Afrocentrists.

Vulgar Afrocentrists deliberately ignored or obscured the historical reality of social class stratification within the African diaspora. They essentially argued that the interests of all black people – from Joint Chiefs of Staff chairman General Colin Powell to conservative Supreme Court Associate Justice Clarence Thomas, to the black unemployed, homeless, and hungry of America's decaying urban ghettoes – were philosophically, culturally and racially the same. Even the scholarly Afrocentric approach elevated a neo-Kantian idealism above even a dialectical idealist analysis, much less speaking to historical materialism except to attack it as such. Populist Afrocentrism was the perfect social theory for the upwardly mobile black petty bourgeoisie. It gave them a vague sense of ethnic superiority and cultural originality, without requiring the hard, critical study of historical realities. It provided a philosophical blueprint to avoid concrete struggle within the real world, since potential white "allies" certainly were nonexistent and all cultural change began from within. It was, in short, only the latest theoretical construct of a politics of racial identity, a world-view designed to discuss the world but never really to change it.

How do we transcend the theoretical limitations and social con-tradictions of the politics of racial identity? The challenge begins by constructing new cultural and political "identities," based on the realities of America's changing multicultural, democratic milieu. The task of constructing a tradition of unity between various groups of color in America is a far more complex and contradictory process than progressive activists or scholars have admitted, precisely because of divergent cultural traditions, languages and conflicting politics of racial identity – on the part of Latinos, African-Americans, Asian Americans, Pacific Island Americans, Arab Americans, American Indians and others. Highlighting the current dilemma in the 1990s, is the collapsing myth of "brown–black solidarity."

Back in the 1960s and early 1970s, with the explosion of the civil-rights and black power movements in the African-American community, activist formations with similar objectives also emerged among Latinos. The Black Panther Party and the League of Revolutionary Black Workers, for example, found their counterparts among Chicano militants in La Raza Unida Party in Texas, and the Crusade for Justice in Colorado. The Council of La Raza and the Mexican American Legal Defense Fund began to push for civil-rights reforms within government, and for expanding influence for Latinos within the Democratic Party, paralleling the same strategies of Jesse Jackson's Operation PUSH and the NAACP Legal Defense Fund.

With the growth of a more class-conscious black and Latino petty bourgeoisie – ironically, a social product of affirmative action and civil-rights gains – tensions between these two large communities of people of color began to deteriorate. The representatives of the African-American middle class consolidated their electoral control of the city councils and mayoral posts of major cities throughout the country. Black entrepreneurship increased, as the black American consumer market reached a gross sales figure of $270 billion by 1991, an amount equal to the gross domestic product of the fourteenth wealthiest nation on earth. The really important "symbolic triumphs" of this privileged strata of the African-American community were not the dynamic 1984 and 1988 presidential campaigns of Jesse Jackson; they were instead the electoral victory of Democratic "moderate" Doug Wilder as Virginia governor in 1990, and the appointment of former-Jackson-lieutenant-turned-moderate Ron Brown as head of the Democratic National Committee. Despite the defeats represented by Reaganism and the absence of affirmative-action enforcement, there was a sense that the strategy of "symbolic representation" had cemented this stratum's hegemony over the bulk of the black population. Black politicians like Doug Wilder and television celebrity journalists such as black-nationalist-turned-Republican Tony Brown weren't interested in pursuing coalitions between blacks and other people of color. Multiracial, multi-class alliances raised too many questions about the absence of political accountability between middle-class "leaders" and their working-class and low-income "followers." Even Jesse Jackson shied away from addressing a black–Latino alliance except in the most superficial terms.

By the late 1980s and early 1990s, however, the long-delayed brown–black dialogue at the national level began crystallizing into tensions around at least four critical issues. First, after the census of 1990, scores of congressional districts were reapportioned with African-American or Latino pluralities or majorities, guaranteeing greater minority-group representation in Congress. However, in cities and districts where Latinos and blacks were roughly divided, and especially in those districts which blacks had controlled in previous years but in which Latinos were now in the majority, disagreements often led to fractious ethnic conflicts. Latinos claimed that they were grossly underrepresented within the political process. African-American middle-class leaders argued that "Latinos" actually represented four distinct groups with little to no shared history or common culture: Mexican Americans, concentrated overwhelmingly in the southwestern states; Hispanics from the Caribbean, chiefly Puerto Ricans and Dominicans, most of whom had migrated to New York City and the northeast since 1945; Cuban Americans, mostly middle- to upper-class exiles of Castro's Cuba, and who voted heavily Republican; and the most recent Spanish-speaking emigrants from Central and South America. Blacks insisted that Cuban Americans were definitely not an "underprivileged minority," and as such did not merit minority set-aside economic programs, affirmative-action and equal-opportunity programs. The cultural politics of Afrocentrism made it difficult for

many African-Americans to recognize that they might share any
common interest with Latinos.

Second, immigration issues are also at the center of recent
Latino–black conflicts. Over one-third of the Latino population of more
that 24 million in the USA consists of undocumented workers. Some
middle-class African-American leaders have taken the politically conservative viewpoint that undocumented Latino workers deprive poor blacks
of jobs within the low-wage sectors of the economy. Third, bilingual
education and efforts to impose linguistic and cultural conformity upon
all sectors of society (such as "English-only" referenda) have also been
issues of contention. Finally, the key element that drives these topics of
debate is the rapid transformation of America's nonwhite demography.
Because of relatively higher birth rates than the general population
and substantial immigration, within less than two decades Latinos as a
group will outnumber African-Americans as the largest minority group
in the USA. Even by 1990, about one out of nine US households spoke
a non-English language at home, predominately Spanish.

Black middle-class leaders who were accustomed to advocating the
interests of their constituents in simplistic racial terms were increasingly
confronted by Latinos who felt alienated from the system and largely
ignored and underrepresented by the political process. Thus in May 1991,
Latinos took to the streets in Washington DC, hurling bottles and rocks
and looting over a dozen stores, in response to the shooting by the local
police of a Salvadorian man whom they claimed had wielded a knife.
African-American mayor Sharon Pratt Dixon ordered over one thousand
police officers to patrol the city's Latino neighborhoods, and used tear
gas to quell the public disturbances. In effect, a black administration
in Washington DC used the power of the police and courts to suppress
the grievances of Latinos – just as the white administration had done
against black protesters during the urban uprisings of 1968.

The tragedy here is that too little is done by either African-American
or Latino "mainstream" leaders, who practice racial-identity politics to
transcend their parochialism and to redefine their agendas on common
ground. Latinos and blacks alike can agree on an overwhelming list of
issues – such as the inclusion of multicultural curricula in public schools,
improvements in public health care, job training initiative, the expansion
of public transportation and housing for low- to moderate-income people;
and greater fairness and legal rights within the criminal justice system.
Despite the image that Latinos as a group are more "economically
privileged" than African-Americans, Mexican American families earn
only slightly more than black households, and Puerto Rican families
earn less than black Americans on average. Economically, Latinos and

African-Americans have both experienced the greatest declines in real incomes and some of the greatest increases in poverty rates within the USA. From 1973 to 1990, for example, the incomes for families headed by a parent under thirty years of age declined by 28 per cent for Latino families and by 48 per cent for African-American families. The poverty rates for young families in these same years rose 44 per cent for Latinos and 58 per cent for blacks.

There is also substantial evidence that Latinos continue to experience discrimination in elementary, secondary and higher education which is in many respects more severe than that experienced by African-Americans. Although high-school graduation rates for the entire population have steadily improved, the rates for Latinos have declined consistently since the mid 1980s. In 1989, for instance, 76 per cent of all African-Americans and 82 per cent of all whites aged between eighteen and twenty-four had graduated from high school. By contrast, the graduation rate for Latinos in 1989 was 56 per cent. By 1992, the high-school completion rate for Latino males dropped to its lowest level, 47.8 per cent, since 1972 – the year such figures began to be compiled by the American Council on Education. In colleges and universities, the pattern of Latino inequality was the same. In 1991, 34 per cent of all whites and 24 per cent of all African-Americans aged between eighteen and twenty-four were enrolled in college. Latino college enrollment for the same age group was barely 18 per cent. As of 1992, approximately 22 per cent of the non-Latino adult population in the USA possessed at least a four-year college degree. College graduation rates for Latino adults were just 10 per cent. Thus, on a series of public policy issues – access to quality education, economic opportunity, the availability of human services, and civil rights – Latinos and African-Americans share a core set of common concerns and long-term interests. What is missing is the dynamic vision and political leadership necessary to build something more permanent than temporary electoral coalitions between these groups.

A parallel situation exists between Asian Americans, Pacific Americans and the black American community. Two generations ago, the Asian American population was comparatively small, except in states such as California, Washington, and New York. With the end of discriminatory immigration restrictions on Asians in 1965, however, the Asian American population began to soar dramatically, changing the ethnic and racial character of urban America. For example, in the years 1970 to 1990 the Korean population increased from 70,000 to 820,000. Since 1980, about 33,000 Koreans have entered the USA each year, a rate of immigration exceeded only by Latinos and Filipinos. According to the

1990 census, the Asian American and Pacific Islander population in the USA exceeds 7.3 million.

Some of the newer Asian immigrants in the 1970s and 1980s were of middle-class origin with backgrounds in entrepreneurship, small manufacturing and the white-collar professions. Thousands of Asian American small-scale, family-owned businesses began to develop in black and Latino neighborhoods, in many instances taking the place of the Jewish merchants in the ghettoes a generation before. It did not take long before Latino and black petty hostilities and grievances against this new ethnic entrepreneurial group crystallized into deep racial hatred. When African-American rapper Ice Cube expressed his anger against Los Angeles's Korean American business community in the 1991 song "Black Korea," he was also voicing the popular sentiments of many younger blacks:

> So don't follow me up and down your market, or your little chop-suey ass will be a target of the nationwide boycott. Choose with the people, that's what the boy got. So pay respect to the black fist, or we'll burn down your store, right down to a crisp, and then we'll see you, 'cause you can't turn the ghetto into Black Korea.

Simmering ethnic tensions boiled into open outrage in Los Angeles when a black teenage girl was killed by Korean American merchant Soon Ja Du. Although convicted of voluntary manslaughter, Du was sentenced to probation and community service only. Similarly, in the early 1990s African-Americans launched economic boycotts of, and political confrontations with, Korean American small merchants in New York. Thus, in the aftermath of the blatant miscarriage of justice in Los Angeles last year – the acquittal of four white police officers for the violent beating of Rodney King – the anger and outrage within the African-American community was channeled not against the state and the corporations, but against small Korean American merchants. Throughout Los Angeles, over 1,500 Korean-American-owned stores were destroyed, burned or looted. Following the urban uprising, a fiercely anti-Asian sentiment continued to permeate sections of Los Angeles. In 1992–93 there have been a series of incidents of Asian Americans being harassed or beaten in southern California. After the rail-system contract was awarded to a Japanese company, a chauvinistic movement was launched to "buy American." Asian Americans are still popularly projected to other nonwhites as America's successful "model minorities," fostering resentment, misunderstandings and hostilities among people of color. Yet black leaders have consistently failed to explain to African-Americans that Asian-Americans as a group do not own the major corporations or banks which control access to capital. They do not own massive amounts of real estate, control the courts or city governments, have ownership of the mainstream media, dominate police forces, or set urban policies.

While African-Americans, Latinos and Asian-Americans scramble over which group should control the mom-and-pop grocery store in their neighborhood, almost no one questions the racist "redlining" policies of large banks which restrict access to capital to nearly all people of color. Black and Latino working people usually are not told by their race-conscious leaders and middle-class "symbolic representatives" that institutional racism has also frequently targeted Asian Americans throughout US history – from the recruitment and exploitation of Asian laborers, to a series of lynchings and violent assaults culminating in the mass incarceration of Japanese Americans during World War II, to the slaying of Vincent Chin in Detroit and the violence and harassment of other Asian Americans. A central ideological pillar of "whiteness" is the consistent scapegoating of the "oriental menace." As legal scholar Mari Matsuda observes:

> There is an unbroken line of poor and working Americans turning their anger and frustration into hatred of Asian Americans. Every time this happens, the real villains – the corporations and politicians who put profits before human needs – are allowed to go about their business free from public scrutiny, and the anger that could go to organizing for positive social change goes instead to Asian-bashing.

What is required is a radical break from the narrow, race-based politics of the past, which characterized the core assumptions about black empowerment since the mid nineteenth century. We need to recognize that the two perspectives of racial-identity politics that are frequently juxtaposed, integration/assimilation and nationalist/separatism, are actually two sides of the same ideological and strategic axis. To move into the future will require that we bury the racial barriers of the past, for good. The essential point of departure is the deconstruction of the idea of "whiteness," the ideology of white power, privilege and elitism which remains heavily embedded within the dominant culture, social institutions and economic arrangements of the society. But we must do more than critique the white pillars of race, gender and class domination. We must rethink and restructure the central social categories of collective struggle by which we conceive and understand our own political reality. We must redefine "blackness" and other traditional racial categories to be more inclusive of contemporary ethnic realities.

To be truly liberating, a social theory must reflect the actual problems of a historical conjuncture with a commitment to rigor and scholastic truth. "Afrocentrism" fails on all counts to provide that clarity of insight into the contemporary African-American urban experience. It looks to a romantic, mythical reconstruction of yesterday to find some understanding of the cultural basis of today's racial and class challenges. Yet that critical understanding of reality cannot begin with an examination of the lives of Egyptian Pharaohs. It must begin by critiquing the vast structure of power and privilege which characterizes the political economy of post-industrial capitalist America. According to the Center on Budget and Policy Priorities, during the Reagan–Bush era of the 1980s the poorest one-fifth of all Americans earned about $7,725 annually, and experienced a decline in before-tax household incomes of 3.8 per cent over the decade. The middle fifth of all US households earned about $31,000 annually, with an income gain of 3.1 per cent during the 1980s. Yet the top fifth of household incomes reached over $105,200 annually by 1990, with before-tax incomes growing by 29.8 per cent over the 1980s. The richest 5 per cent of all American households exceeded $206,000 annually, improving their incomes by 44.9 per cent under Reagan and Bush. The wealthiest 1 per cent of all US households reached nearly $550,000 per year, with average before-tax incomes increasing by 75.3 per cent. In effect, since 1980 the income gap between America's wealthiest 1 per cent and the middle class *nearly doubled.* As the Center on Budget and Policy Priorities relates, the wealthiest 1 per cent of all Americans – roughly 2.5 million people – receive "nearly as much income after taxes as the bottom 40 per cent, about 100 million people. While wealthy households are taking a larger share of the national income, the tax burden has been shifted down the income pyramid." A social theory of a reconstructed, multicultural democracy must advance the reorganization and ownership of capital resources, the expansion of production in minority areas, and provision of guarantees for social welfare – such as a single-payer, national health-care system.

The factor of "race" by itself does not and cannot explain the massive transformation of the structure of capitalism in its post-industrial phase, or the destructive redefinition of "work" itself, as we enter the twenty-first century. Increasingly in Western Europe and America, the new division between "haves" and "have nots" is characterized by a new segmentation of the labor force. The division is between those workers who have maintained basic economic security and benefits – such as full health insurance, term life insurance, pensions, educational stipends or subsidies for the employee's children, paid vacations, and so forth – and those marginal workers who are either unemployed, or part-time employees, or who labor but have few if any benefits. Since 1982, "temporary employment" or part-time hirings without benefits have increased 250 per cent across the USA, while all employment has grown by less that 20 per cent. Today, the largest private employer in the USA is Manpower, Inc., the world's largest temporary employment agency, with 560,000 workers. By the year 2000, half of all American workers will be classified as part-time employees, or, as they are termed within IBM, "the peripherals." The reason for this massive restructuring of labor relations is capital's search for surplus value or profits.

Increasingly, disproportionately high percentages of Latino and African-American workers will be trapped within this second-tier of the labor market. Black, Latino, Asian-American, and low-income white workers all share a stake in fighting for a new social contract relating to work and social benefits: the right to a good job should be guaranteed in the same way as the human right to vote; the right to free high-quality health care should be as secure as the freedom of speech. The radical changes within the domestic economy require that black leadership reaches out to other oppressed sectors of the society, creating a common program for economic and social justice. Vulgar Afrocentrism looks inward; the new black liberation of the twenty-first century must look outward, embracing those people of color and oppressed people of divergent ethnic backgrounds who share our democratic vision.

The multicultural democratic critique must consider the changing demographic, cultural and class realities of modern post-industrial America. By the year 2000, one-third of the total US population will consist of people of color. Within seventy years, roughly half of America's entire population will be Latino, American Indian, Pacific American, Arab American and African-American. The ability to create a framework for multicultural democracy, inter-group dialogue, and interaction within and between the most progressive leaders, grassroots activists, intellectuals and working people of these communities will determine the future of American society itself. Our ability to transcend racial chauvinism and inter-ethnic hatred and the old definitions of "race," to recognize the class commonalities and joint social-justice interests of all groups in the restructuring of this nation's economy and social order, will be the key to constructing a nonracist democracy, transcending ancient walls of white violence, corporate power and class privilege. By dismantling the narrow politics of racial identity and selective self-interest, by going beyond "black" and "white," we may construct new values, new institutions and new visions of an America beyond traditional racial categories and racial oppression.

SEVENTEEN

THE DIVIDED MIND OF BLACK AMERICA: RACE, IDEOLOGY AND POLITICS IN THE POST-CIVIL-RIGHTS ERA

Coauthored with Leith Mullings

I

It is nearly one hundred years since the death of Frederick Douglass and the emergence of Booker T. Washington as the national spokesperson and leader of the African-American community. As historian August Meier observed, the "Atlanta Compromise" address of September 1895 by Washington expressed "in a phraseology acceptable to the dominant elements of the New South – the shift in Negro thought from political to economic action, from immediate integration and protest to self-help, and from rights to duties."[1] The new contours of racial ideology at the end of the last century were prefigured by the collapse of the First Reconstruction, civil rights and representative democracy across the South, the institutionalization of the totalitarian repression and violence of Jim Crow, and the confident expansion of capitalism and industrial development across the continent.

In the context of urban America a century later, history repeats itself. Capitalism is once again triumphant, with the destruction of the Soviet model of socialism and the consolidation of the world's economic order on the basis of private markets. The Second Reconstruction, ending with the triumph of the reactionary administration of Ronald Reagan in 1980, culminates in our version of conservative Democrat Grover Cleveland – Bill Clinton. Once again, both political parties have turned against the civil-rights agenda. And once again, as the race searches to find itself, it turns inward, as the voices of both separatism and accommodation grow stronger. How does "race" express itself in the contemporary urban site, in the current political conjuncture? And how does the transformation of the political economy express itself in the realignment of racial ideologies?

The generation since the civil-rights movement has witnessed many real examples of African-American upward mobility and individual achievement, and the growth of a large and increasingly influential African-American middle class. For example, the median income of African-American families in which both the wife and the husband were employed rose from about $28,700 in 1967 (in 1990 inflation-adjusted dollars) to over $40,000 in 1990, a real increase of 40 per cent. More than one in seven black families currently earns above $50,000 annually, and thousands of black households now earn over $100,000 annually. Many of these African-American households have moved outside of the major cities into the suburbs, which are predominantly white. Consequently many of the social, economic and cultural linkages, which previously connected various social classes and organizations, began to erode.

By contrast, since the late 1970s general conditions for most of the African-American community have become worse. For example, the percentage of black high-school graduates between the ages of eighteen and twenty-six who go on to college have declined since 1975. The real incomes of younger black workers have fallen sharply during that same period. Standards in health care for millions within the African-American community have fallen, with the black male life expectancy declining to only 64.7 years in 1993. By 1990 about 12 per cent of all black families were earning less than $5,000 annually. One-third of all African-American families now live below the federal government's poverty level, and 46 per cent of all black families are headed by single women. Within the criminal justice system, more than 40 per cent of the 1.4 million prisoners currently incarcerated in federal penitentiaries, prisons and municipal jails of all types, are African-Americans. By 1992, 23 per cent of all young African-American men between the ages of twenty and twenty-nine were in prison, on probation, parole, or awaiting trial. In New York City alone, the percentage of young black men within the penal and criminal justice system was 31 per cent.

The two key elements which explain the socioeconomic crisis being faced by millions of African-American families are: (1) the deep structural crisis of the economies in major American cities, in which thousands of businesses and corporations have divested and relocated either to the suburbs or outside the country; and (2) the fiscal crisis of the federal, state and local governments, in which the resources to fund social programs have been significantly reduced. Throughout the 1980s, black communities across the country have experienced massive increases in homelessness and unemployment, a proliferation in instances of deadly violence, and a deterioration in the quality of public education, public health-care facilities, and public transportation.

It is within this difficult context that the current generation of African-American leaders must be judged. Thirty years ago, during the height of Jim Crow segregation, the number of elected black officials nationwide was barely one hundred; the number of African-Americans in Congress was five; and the number of blacks serving as mayors of US cities and towns of all sizes was zero. Today, forty African-Americans sit in the US Congress; more than forty African-Americans are mayors; and over eight thousand blacks have been elected to government positions. Yet, these major increases in the number of black representatives have not been matched by an increase in leverage or clout within the political system.

There are several reasons for this disparity. First, despite the massive increase in black representation, African-Americans today still account for only 2 per cent of all elected and appointed officials throughout the nation. In dozens of counties with substantial black constituencies, there are few or no African-American elected officials. Blacks still remain underrepresented within the electoral structure of power and decision-making.

Second, in many instances African-American elected officials have what might be termed "responsibility without authority." Many black mayors, for instance, exercise relatively little control or authority over local governmental bureaucracies. They have their hands on few levers of power by means of which they might distribute goods, services or positions of influence to their supporters. In some cases, this has contributed to a sense of political disillusionment among sectors of the African-American electorate and a decline in voter registration and political participation rates.

Elsewhere, the question of black leadership is challenged by the recent emergence of what could be termed "post-black politics" – that is, the rise of African-American political candidates who have relatively few connections with organic black social and political formations and institutions, and consciously minimize their identity as "minority" or "black." The background of "post-black politics" was created by another dimension of US political behavior: the regrettable yet unavoidable fact that the vast majority of white voters will generally not cast ballots for a black, first-time candidate for public office, regardless of her or his party label, ideology, or history of civic involvement. Until 1989, no first-time African-American mayoral candidate had earned more than 30 per cent of the white vote – in effect, a "racial ceiling" blacks have failed to overcome. The refusal of whites to support black candidates has been particularly apparent in urban areas, and in cities where blacks or other racial minorities represent substantial shares of the overall electorate.

By contrast, blacks as a group continued to exhibit "nonracial" electoral behavior – that is, voting overwhelmingly for white candidates whose views on public policy they support over black candidates who embraced conservative or Republican positions. For instance, in the recent mayoral election in New York City, 95 per cent of all black voters supported incumbent candidate David Dinkins, and gave over 90 per cent of their vote to the mayor's white Democratic running mates for citywide offices. Such a constituency was nowhere present among the city's white Democratic voters, who rejected Dinkins by a margin of nearly four to one.

Some black elected officials who encountered this inevitable "race ceiling" in politics began, by the late 1980s, to minimize or downplay their racial identity or affiliations with institutions within the African-American community. Candidates began to run for public office who "happened to be black," or who refused to be identified as "black politicians." Some of the more successful politicians representing this "deracialized politics" included Mayor Michael White of Cleveland, Mayor Norm Rice of Seattle, and Virginia's governor Douglas Wilder. To be sure, the development of a deracialized current of black politics represents a successful culmination of the racial philosophy of integration. After all, it was Dr. Martin Luther King, Jr. who articulated the hope that African-Americans would be judged "not by the color of [their] skin, but by the content of [their] character." The irony of racial inequality in the 1990s is that while this statement certainly expresses a long-term aspiration of the black freedom movement, it cannot grasp or address the tragic spirit of class inequality, poverty, unemployment, violence and social destruction that is manifestly represented in *racial* terms. Race and institutional racism have not yet declined in significance.

Compounding this sense of social-class and vocational division within the black community is yet another growing schism: a deepening division of culture, values and social relations. To a real extent, the cultural clash is intergenerational, symbolized by the radical differences in discourse, political experiences, and social expectations between those African-Americans born before 1964 and those who were born after the great legislative victories of the civil-rights movement. Simplistically, one might describe this great division as being between the "We Shall Overcome" generation and the "hip-hop" generation. The former lived through the most dynamic and icon-shattering decade of the twentieth century, the 1960s. This earlier generation witnessed the collapse of Jim Crow, the growth of a vast black middle class and professional/political elite, the rise and fall of Black Power, the leadership of Malcolm and Martin, and the eruption of social revolutions across Africa and the Caribbean. This turbulent history left indelible marks on the political culture and group psychology of this earlier generation. For those who stood in the streets defiantly facing Alabama state troopers at the Edmund Pettus bridge in Selma in 1965; or who seized student union buildings and dormitories at dozens of white college campuses to force recalcitrant administrations to initiate Black Studies departments; or who registered hundreds of thousands of new voters, from the Mississippi Delta to Chicago's sprawling South Side, the possibilities in politics were only limited by the boundaries of our imaginations. Everything seemed possible for a brief, shining moment. Real incomes for black families had increased dramatically from 1945 to 1975; the number of African-Americans enrolled in colleges and post-secondary schools had soared from 40,000 to nearly 700,000 in only thirty years. Tomorrow would always be better than yesterday.

The "hip-hop" generation's primary experience in politics can be characterized in one word: defeat. The generation's most dominating and influential national political figure was President Ronald Reagan. The generation which produced the dynamic cultural expression of rap music came to maturity in a context of rising black-on-black violence, symbolized by the Crips vs. the Bloods in south-central Los Angeles. During the next five years, more black people will be killed in our major cities than the total number of American troops killed during the Vietnam War. Hip-hop emerged in the context of widespread unemployment, homelessness, and the omnipresence of fear and social alienation. For many of our young people there is no sense or expectation that a future is worth living for, or that it even exists. One lives for today, because tomorrow might never come.

We live in New York City, and the full dimensions of the crisis of race and class for this current generation of African-Americans throughout urban America are apparent to everyone. In New York City, between 1980 and 1992, 87,000 private-sector jobs were lost. During the same years, the number of African-Americans living below the poverty level increased from 520,000 to 664,000 people. The average black family in New York City now earns $24,000 annually, compared to over $40,000 per year for whites. Black adult male unemployment rates are officially 13 per cent; but actual labor-force participation rates among adults in Harlem and Bedford-Stuyvesant, within the formal sector of the economy, are actually below 60 per cent.

The criminal justice system has become the chief means for regulating the vast supply of unemployed, undereducated, young black workers. In central Harlem alone, 2,500 young people were arrested in 1992. Some 95 per cent of those in jail in New York City are African-Americans and Latinos. What is the profile of this prison population? A full 90 per cent lack a high-school diploma; more than half have lower than a sixth-grade level of educational ability. Two-thirds of all young black people who are in jail are awaiting trial, at an average cost of $150 each per day. The average pre-trial detention in New York City is fifty days; costing $7,900 per prisoner. Tens of millions of dollars are wasted on warehousing unemployed labor. Nationwide, our prison population is expected to double within the next six years. One recent estimate predicted that, at current growth rates, by the year 2053 there will be more Americans of all races *inside* prison than on the *outside*.

The most tragic casualties of the race/class crisis in our cities today, however, are the children. In the area of health care, six out of ten pre-school children in New York City are not immunized. There are currently only ninety-six nurses for the six hundred elementary schools throughout the city. Every day in New York, 70,500 children use drugs. Thirty-five babies are born daily with low birth weights. More than 160,000 children, mostly African-American and Latino, have no health insurance. And today, AIDS is the leading cause of death in New York City for children under the age of five. In the area of housing and homelessness, New York currently has about 90,000 homeless people, 90 per cent of whom are black and Hispanic. Every night, some 24,000 people, including nearly 10,000 children, will sleep in city-run homeless shelters. During the next five years, one out of every twelve black children in New York City will sleep in a homeless shelter.

II

We are, in effect, in a new historical period; it is marked by intensification of race and class inequalities in our cities, social-class polarization within the African-American community, fragmentation and confusion among black leadership, quiet contempt for black interests expressed by both major parties. The increasing withdrawal of millions of black people from the electoral political process reflects a growing disillusionment with the possibilities for social equality and democratic empowerment through the existing system. How have black intellectuals responded to the new period and, more specifically, what is the social responsibility of the African-American intelligentsia?

In a study in progress on the theme of "Race, Inequality and Power," we are attempting to chart the shifting currents of contemporary racial ideology within America. Within the African-American community, since the middle of the nineteenth century, essentially three overlapping, strategic visions have been expressed by various leaders, institutions and social-protest organizations about the nature of the political economy, the meaning of "race," and what practical steps should be taken to improve the material conditions of black people. These three strategic visions may be termed "inclusion" or "pragmatic integration," "black nationalism" or "racial separatism," and "transformation" or "radical multicultural democracy." Each of these currents has evolved from long historical memory and the deep ideological and cultural traditions within the African-American experience. Let us discuss the contemporary and historical examples of each; their assumptions, goals and ideological perspectives; their respective social bases or core constituencies; and the conditions under which they exert influence and authority within the African-American population.

This model of racial ideology suggests overlapping spheres of political culture, ideology and social forces, not distinctly separate parties or tendencies. The very reality of oppression forces upon black people the simple recognition that no clear or unambiguous theory or political orientation by itself will be sufficient to create the context for group development and collective mobilization around matters of mutual concern. Blacks have long recognized that they can ill afford to maintain political stances isolated from each other, simply for the sake of being more correct than their ideological critics. And by themselves, such theoretical models are always inherently limited. They explain some things and not others. The great majority of African-American people find themselves located at the conjunctural center of these three great visions; they may favor "nationalism," "integration" or the demands of "radical democracy" to varying degrees at different times, depending upon the racial attitudes of the white majority, the state of the economy, and other factors. The major point to be made here is that the cultural and material content of black political traditions and the collective experience acquired through the struggle for power have created several different approaches and strategic understandings for mobilization, resistance and the development of leadership.

The "inclusionist" vision incorporates the traditional integrationist perspective of the earlier twentieth century, but also neo-liberal and pragmatic currents of the post-civil-rights period. The inclusionists' vision implicitly assumes that African-Americans are basically "Americans who happen to be black"; it calls for the eradication of all sites of racial particularity and social isolation; it seeks affirmation and legitimacy within the state and civil society of American capitalism; and it works within established institutions to influence public policy. The historical roots of the inclusionist position are found in the aspirations of the free Negro communities of the North before the Civil War; in the politics of Walter White, Roy Wilkins, the younger Du Bois and the older A. Philip Randolph. Its social base is found within the black middle class, the professional and managerial elite, public-sector employees, and elements of the stable blue-collar working class in the cities. The inclusionist vision is expressed ideologically as pragmatic liberalism; although, with the expansion of a class-conscious black elite in the 1970s and 1980s, theorists such as Shelby Steele and economist Thomas Sowell have emerged, who reflect the growing opportunism and materialism within this stratum. Pragmatic liberalism as an ideology is best expressed in the social-science literature by William Julius Wilson; in the humanities, its most prominent representative is our colleague in African-American Studies, Henry Louis Gates. In the *New York Times* recently, Gates denounced racial separatists such as Khalid Abdul Muhammad as "calculating demagogues," criticizing narrowly based "identity politics," and calling for "a liberalism of heart and spine."[2] The inclusionist position gains strength when the state and white civil society create opportunities for the articulation and expression of blacks' grievances, and when there is a sense of political optimism pervasive within the African-American community. The chief difficulty for the inclusionist vision is that despite concrete victories in the legal and political sphere for blacks and the growth of a professional managerial elite, the actual material conditions for the majority of black people have grown clearly worse in the last fifteen years. The overwhelming crisis of race and class in our cities, and the retreat by white liberals from their previous advocacy of blacks' interests, undermines the legitimacy of inclusionist politics.

In reverse, yet mirror-like, opposition to inclusionism are the black nationalist and racial-separatist visions of race relations. The complex reality of African-American nationalism includes a number of political subcategories, such as emigrationism – the social impulse to create alternative, all-black communities. The separatist current of black nationalism is probably the most profound and influential of these. The orientation of black nationalism assumes that "race" is a historically fixed category, which will not magically decline in significance over time; it suggests that blacks must define themselves within their own autonomous cultural context; and it is deeply pessimistic about the ability or willingness of white civil society to transform itself democratically to include the demands of people of color. Culturally, it suggests that

African-Americans are African people who happen to speak English and live in America. Or, as Malcolm X once declared: "Just because a cat has kittens in an oven, you don't call the kittens biscuits." There is a subterranean link between inclusionist and black-nationalist visions: one usually advances in influence within black political culture when the other retreats.

The historical roots of the black-nationalist and separatist perspective can be traced to the maroon impulse of runaway slaves, in their creation of all-black towns such as Mound Bayou, Mississippi in 1887, or to the back-to-Africa ideas of Martin Delany. In the early twentieth century, black nationalism was best expressed in a mass movement by the Universal Negro Improvement Association of Marcus Garvey, and subsequently within the Nation of Islam of Elijah Muhammad. The separatist explosion of the 1960s gave us numerous tendencies within black nationalism: the revolutionary nationalism of the League of Revolutionary Black Workers in Detroit and the Black Panther Party in Oakland; the neo-Booker T. Washington, black-capitalist nationalism of Roy Innis and Floyd McKissick of the Congress of Racial Equality; the cultural nationalism of Maulana Karenga and Amiri Baraka, the establishment of rituals such as Kwanzaa; and the political nationalism manifested in the Gary Black Convention of 1972 and the National Black Political Assembly. The primary social base for nationalism today comes from the hip-hop generation, the marginalized African-American working class, and a strong segment of the entrepreneurial black elite. On 125th Street in Harlem, for example, one can observe the nationalism of the marketplace, or "vendor nationalism"; racial solidarity and "buy black" sentiment is utilized for capital formation.

Among the many black-nationalist and separatist currents of today, the most scholarly and influential is Afrocentrism; its chief representatives would include Temple University African-American Studies head Molefi Asante, City College Black Studies chair Len Jeffries, and Lincoln University president Niara Sudarkasa. Unlike the inclusionists, the nationalists have always understood the absolutely essential connections between *culture, identity and politics*: one's sense of history, the practicing of rituals, the structure of family, and physical appearance (such as hair, kente cloth, etc.), transform individuals' behavior and critical consciousness of self and community. But many black nationalists frequently reify culture, thinking of it as "fixed" rather than dynamic and dialectical. They embrace an "essentialist" racial identity. The black-nationalist perspective among the masses of African-American people usually gains popularity with the conjuncture of several factors: when there is a general expansion within the capitalist economy, but with blacks lagging behind; when both major white political parties repudiate measures to address racial inequalities; when there is a rise of racist violence against black people, be it vigilante violence (e.g. lynchings in the 1890s–1900s) or institutional violence, such as today's massive incarcerations and imprisonment of hundreds of thousands of young blacks; when the traditional black leadership is either unwilling or unable to articulate the grievances of the disaffected, such as marginalized young people, the homeless and unemployed workers; and when the dominant discourse justifies the unequal division of power and resources in terms of black biological or cultural inferiority (e.g. the "culture of poverty" and "underclass" theses). All of these conditions occurred in the 1920s, and the result was the Garvey movement; parallel conditions arose in the 1960s, and the result was Black Power; and today, once more, the black nationalist perspective has become a significant influence on college campuses and inner-city communities.

The third vision among African-American people is the transformative perspective, or the politics of radical democracy. It differs from inclusionist and black-nationalist perspectives, in that its chief objective is the dismantling or destruction of all forms of inequality. It seeks to challenge the institutions of power and privilege, and the ownership patterns, of the dominant society. Racism is perceived not in biological or genetic terms, as a fixed reality of life, but as an unequal relationship between social aggregates, based on power and violence. Often, black people have begun with the objective of abolishing racism, but in the process of struggle have come to realize that wider power relationships must also be transformed to achieve full human equality – such as the inequalities and oppression rooted in gender and sexual orientation.

The transformative vision, unlike inclusionism and black nationalism, was always far more fragmentary in its social expression and institutional development. It was expressed in the militancy of a Nat Turner or Harriet Tubman, who sought to destroy slavery; in the uncompromising militancy of Ida B. Wells; in the radicalism of W.E.B. Du Bois for much of his life after 1934; in the young A. Philip Randolph, called "the most dangerous Negro in America" by Woodrow Wilson; in the long list of African-Americans who identified themselves with the Communist Party, such as Cyril V. Briggs, Benjamin Davis, Henry Winston, Angela Y. Davis, Charlene Mitchell, Jarvis Tyner, and Kendra Alexander; and in the activities of black radicals within the labor movement, the Southern Youth Congress of the 1940s, the Student Nonviolent Coordinating Committee of the 1960s, and the Black Workers Congress of the 1970s. The cultural politics of the transformative vision have been grounded in anti-imperialism and internationalism. The assumption here is that colonialism abroad is inextricably connected with capitalism at home, and that race as a social category cannot be deconstructed by relying on liberal solutions.

The transformationist vision is embedded in a wide variety of writings by prominent black intellectuals: the critical race theory of Patricia Williams, Lani Guinier and Kimberle Crenshaw; the feminist thought of Angela Y. Davis, bell hooks, Michelle Wallace and Patricia Hill Collins; the historical works of Gerald Horne and Robin D.G. Kelley; the political analysis of Clarence Lusane and James Jennings; the cultural work of Dennis Brutus, Jan Carew, and Melba Joyce Boyd; and the essays and criticism of Cornel West. Yet, at this historical moment, the transformationist current's organizational and institutional base is weaker than it has been since the depths of the Cold War, when Robeson and Du Bois were silenced and thousands of radicals were purged or imprisoned. However, elements of the transformationist perspective have notably been expressed in recent political movements, such as the Harold Washington mayoral campaigns in Chicago in 1983 and 1987; the left wing of Jesse Jackson's Rainbow Coalition; and the radical tendency of the anti-apartheid movement in the 1980s. The social base for transformationist politics is located in the radicalized elements of the black intelligentsia; the more progressive elements of the black working class and middle class; and also, to some degree, among the marginalized youth. Its chief limitation, however, is the powerful reality of the demise of the Cold War, the destruction of both social-democratic and Marxist-Leninist models of social change across the globe, and the domestic demise of the trade-union movement. It is exceedingly difficult to advocate radical ideas for democratic social transformation when there are few, if any, actual models which express one's hopes and aspirations.

So – to paraphrase Martin Luther King's final query – where do we go from here? We are in the midst of a major ideological realignment within black America with the demarcation of potentially antagonistic and confrontational formations and groups that will battle for the future of our people. Increasingly, the ideological disputes between inclusionist intellectuals such as Gates and Afrocentric scholars like Asante have fostered barriers of mistrust and misunderstanding. We must not make the mistake of claiming some privileged truth at the expense of seeking broader theoretical and programmatic unity transcending boundaries within our community. However, we also should not approach questions of difference within the black community with the assumption that there will inevitably be consensus and group harmony. Class, gender, and social divisions within the black community are real, not only in the United States but throughout the black diaspora. The extreme reactionary wing of black racial fundamentalism, reflected in the recent remarks of Khalid Muhammad, is essentially our version of Hamas in the Middle East, or the Zulu reactionary nationalism of Buthelezi, which confronts the ANC and collaborates with white racists. Black nationalism can be progressive, but it can also be reactionary, sexist, homophobic, and pro-corporate capitalist. At the present time, we must build strong black institutions which address the material and social needs of the African-American community; to do so, transformationists must engage in a constructive dialogue with many different elements within black nationalism. But we must engage in an honest dialogue, clearly separating their vision of politics from our own.

Those of us who stand in the transformationist tradition, in the tradition of Fannie Lou Hamer and Paul Robeson, in the tradition of C.L.R. James, Walter Rodney, and Amilcar Cabral, have work to do. In the aftermath of the Cold War, and with the collapse of Eastern European Communism, there is no coherent alternative to Western capitalism. Our task at the level of theory is to develop a comprehensive social analysis which critiques the irrationality and social destructiveness of capitalism as a social system, and redefines the social contract between the people and the state in our societies. The new progressive paradigm must grasp the common sense of our people, their recognition of the inequalities in daily life which exist under a racist and capitalist social order, and create the possibilities for new resistance movements.

Politically, this requires the social theorists of transformation to link their work to the actual social forces within the black community – including religious, labor, community-based, women's and youth organizations. Within groups such as the National Association for the Advancement of Colored People, for example, this could mean helping to develop leadership-training schools which would identify young women and men from dozens of communities across the nation engaged in civil-rights struggles, and present a curriculum of economics, social and political analysis allowing for discussion and mutual exchange from a transformationist perspective. We must challenge contemporary black leadership to understand that an inclusionist strategy of seeking incremental reforms within the existing social system will never create the conditions for black equality. To deconstruct the concept of race, we must restructure the power relationship between ourselves, the white capitalist ruling class, and the state. That can only be achieved through a return of mass democratic resistance movements; but these can only succeed if they are informed by democratic, anti-racist social theory.

In the era of globalized capitalism, it is more important than ever to understand both the limitations and power of the idea of race. We are fighting to achieve the conditions where race is immaterial to the allocation of resources and power within society. Yet to accomplish this, we must simultaneously mobilize on the basis of racial oppression, building institutions and social protest movements which empower black people. Such struggles against racial domination will become increasingly global, given the vast movements of labor and capital across the world. The political and ideological struggles to deconstruct race are being waged from western Europe to southern Africa, from Latin America to North America's urban ghetto. Pessimism and a tendency to retreat into the illusions of both liberal inclusionism and identity politics will never permit us effectively to "fight the power."

Although we disagree with his politics, the reflections of T.S. Eliot are highly relevant to our own struggles today:

> Because I do not hope to know again
> The infirm glory of the positive hour...
> Because I know that time is always time
> And place is always and only place
> And what is actual is actual only for one time
> And only for one place
> I rejoice that things are as they are...
> Because I cannot hope to turn again
> Consequently I rejoice, having to construct something
> Upon which to rejoice.
>
> *Ash Wednesday*

Through a renewed commitment to struggle, let our rejoicing begin. Through a vision of human equality and social justice, let the fight for democracy take place. We must combine our scholarship, the search for a transformationist theoretical paradigm for the twenty-first century, with practical struggle; our theoretical work must have the passion to challenge the sharp inequalities which exist at every level of life and society.

Notes

1. August Meier, *Negro Thought in America, 1880–1915* (Ann Arbor 1965), p. 25.
2. *New York Times* (27 March 1994).

EIGHTEEN

HISTORY AND BLACK CONSCIOUSNESS: THE POLITICAL CULTURE OF BLACK AMERICA

The central theme of black American history has been the constant struggle to overcome the barriers of race and the reality of unequal racial identities between black and white. This racial bifurcation has created parallel realities or racial universes, in which blacks and whites may interact closely with one another but perceive social reality in dramatically different ways. These collective experiences of discrimination, and this memory of resistance and oppression, have given rise to several overlapping group strategies or critical perspectives within the African-American community, which have as their objective the ultimate empowerment of black people. In this sense, the contours of struggle for black people have given rise to a very specific consciousness: a sense of our community, its needs and aspirations for itself. The major ideological debates which map the dimensions of the political mind of black America have always been about the orientation and objectives of black political culture and consciousness. The great historical battles between Booker T. Washington, the architect of the "Atlanta Compromise" of 1895, and W.E.B. Du Bois, the founder of the NAACP, and the conflicts between Du Bois and black nationalist leader Marcus Garvey, were fought largely over the manner in which the black community would define for itself the political and economic tools necessary for its empowerment and future development. Sometimes the battle lines in these struggles for black leadership and for shaping the consciousness of the African-American community were defined by class divisions. More generally, the lines of separation had less to do with class than with the internalized definitions of what "race" meant to African-Americans themselves in the context of black political culture.

Ironically, the historical meaning and reality of race was always fundamentally a product of class domination. Race, in the last analysis, is neither biologically nor genetically derived. It is a structure rooted in white supremacy, economic exploitation and social privilege. It evolved in the process of slavery and the transatlantic slave trade. Racism has power only as a set of institutional arrangements and social outcomes which perpetuate the exploitation of black labor and the subordination of the black community's social and cultural life. But all of this is masked by institutional racism to those who experience the weight of its oppression. The oppressed perceive domination through the language and appearance of racial forms, although such policies and practices always served a larger class objective. As a result, the political culture of black America is organized around racial themes, either an effort to overcome or escape the manifestations of institutional racism, or to build alternative institutions which empower black people within environments of whiteness. The approach of political empowerment is distinctly racial, rather than class-oriented.

Most historians characterized the central divisions within black political culture as the 150-year struggle between "integration" and "separation." In 1925, this division was perceived as separating Du Bois and the NAACP from the Garveyites. In 1995, the division is used to distinguish such pragmatic multicultural liberals as Henry Louis Gates, director of Harvard University's Afro-American Studies department, from the architect of Afrocentrism, Temple University Professor Molefi Asante. However, this theoretical model has serious limitations. The simple fact is that the vast majority of African-American people usually would not define themselves as either Roy Wilkins-style integrationists or black separatists like City University of New York Black Studies director Leonard Jeffries. Most blacks have perceived integration or black nationalism as alternative strategies which might serve the larger purpose of empowering their community and assisting in the deconstruction of institutions perpetuating racial inequality. As anthropologist Leith Mullings and I have argued (Chapter 17 above), a more accurate description of black political culture would identify three strategic visions; these can be termed "inclusion" or integration, "black nationalism," and "transformation."

Since the rise of the free Negro community in the North during the antebellum era, inclusion has been the central impulse for reform among black Americans. The inclusionists have sought to minimize or even eradicate the worst effects and manifestations of racism within the African-American community. They have mobilized resources to alter or abolish legal restrictions on the activities of blacks, and have agitated to achieve acceptance of racial diversity by the white majority. Essentially, the inclusionists have operated philosophically and ideologically as "liberals": they usually believe that the state is inherently a "neutral apparatus," open to the pressure and persuasion of competing interest groups. They have attempted to influence public opinion and mass behavior on issues of race by changing public policies, and educational and cultural activity. But the theoretical guiding star of the inclusionists has been what I term "symbolic representation." They firmly believe that the elevation and advancement of select numbers of well-educated, affluent and/or powerful blacks into positions of authority helps to dismantle the patterns and structures of racial discrimination. The theory is that if blacks are well represented inside government, businesses and social institutions, then this will go a long way toward combatting the traditional practices of inequality and patterns of discrimination. Black representatives within the system of power would use their leverage to carry out policies that benefited the entire African-American population.

Embedded deeply within the logic of inclusionism were two additional ideas. First, the intellectual foundations of inclusionism drew a strong parallel between the pursuit of freedom and the acquisition of private property. To unshackle oneself from the bonds of inequality was, in part, to achieve the material resources necessary to improve one's life and the lives of those in one's family. This meant that freedom was defined by one's ability to gain access to resources and to the prerequisites of power. Implicitly, the orientation of inclusionism reinforced the logic and legitimacy of America's economic system and class structure, seeking to assimilate blacks within them. Second, inclusionists usually had a cultural philosophy of integration within the aesthetic norms and civil society created by the white majority. Inclusionists sought to transcend racism by acting in ways which whites would not find objectionable or repulsive. The more one behaved in a manner which emulated whites, the less likely one might encounter the negative impact and effects of Jim Crow. By assimilating the culture of whites and by minimizing the cultural originality and creativity of African-Americans, one might find the basis for a "universalist" dialogue that transcends the ancient barriers of color. Historically, the inclusionists can be traced to those groups of former slaves in colonial America who assimilated themselves into majority white societies, who forgot African languages and traditions and tried to participate fully in the social institutions that whites had built for themselves. In the nineteenth century, the inclusionists' outstanding leader was Frederick Douglass. Today, the inclusionists include most of the traditional leadership of the civil-rights organizations such as the National Association for the Advancement of Colored People and the National Urban League, the bulk of the Congressional Black Caucus and most African-American elected officials, and the majority of the older and more influential black middle class, professionals and managerial elites.

On balance, the inclusionists' strategy sought to transcend race by creating a context wherein individuals could be judged on the basis of what they accomplished rather than on the color of their skin. This approach minimized the extensive interconnectedness between color and inequality; it tended to conceive racism as a kind of social disease rather than the logical and coherent consequence of institutional arrangements, private property and power relations, reinforced by systemic violence. The inclusionists seriously underestimated the capacity and willingness of white authorities to utilize coercion to preserve and defend white privilege and property. Integration, in short, was a strategy to avoid the worst manifestations of racism, without upsetting the deep structures of inequality which set into motion the core dynamics of white oppression and domination.

Although the inclusionist perspective dominates the literature that interprets black history, it never consolidated itself as a consensus framework for the politics of the entire black community. A sizable component of the African-American population always rejected integration as a means of transcending institutional racism. This alternative vision was black nationalism. Black nationalism sought to overturn racial discrimination by building institutions controlled and owned by blacks, providing resources and services to the community. The nationalists distrusted the capacity of whites as a group to overcome the debilitating effects of white privilege, and questioned the inclusionists' simple-minded faith in the power of legal reforms. Nationalists rejected the culture and aesthetics of white Euro-America in favor of what today would be termed an Afrocentric identity. Historically, the initial nationalist impulse for black group autonomous development really began with those slaves who ran away from the plantations and farms of whites, and who established "maroons," frontier enclaves or villages of defiant African-Americans, or who mounted slave rebellions. Malcolm X and Marcus Garvey, among others, are within this cultural, intellectual and political tradition. However, like the inclusionists, the nationalists often tended to reify race, perceiving racial categories as static and ahistorical, rather than fluid and constantly subject to renegotiation and reconfiguration. They struggled to uproot race, but were frequently imprisoned themselves by the language and logic of inverted racial thinking. They utilized racial categories to mobilize their core constituencies without fully appreciating their own internal contradictions.

The black nationalist tradition within black political culture was, and remains, tremendously complex, rich and varied. At root, its existential foundations were the national consciousness and collective identity of people of African descent, as they struggled against racism and class exploitation. But, as in any form of nationalism, this tradition of resistance and group consciousness expressed itself politically around many different coordinates and tendencies. Within black nationalism is the separatist current, which tends to perceive the entire white community as racially monolithic and articulates racial politics with starkly confrontational and antagonistic overtones. Today, one could point to educator Len Jeffries' controversial descriptions of European Americans as "ice people" – cold, calculating, materialistic – and African-Americans as "sun people" – warm, generous, humanistic – as a separatist-oriented, conservative social theory within the nationalist tradition. The Nation of Islam's theory of Yacub, first advanced under the leadership of Elijah Muhammad, projected an image of whites as "devils," incapable of positive change. At the other end of the nationalist spectrum were radicals like Hubert H. Harrison, Cyril V. Briggs and Huey P. Newton, and militant groups such as the League of Revolutionary Black Workers from the late 1960s, who incorporated a class analysis and the demand for socialism within their politics. To this radical tendency, black nationalism had to rely on the collaboration of other oppressed people regardless of the color of their skin, languages or nationalities. Between these two tendencies is the black nationalism of the rising black petty bourgeoisie, which utilizes racial segregation as a barrier to facilitate capital accumulation from the mostly working-class, black consumer market. Nationalist rhetoric such as "buy black" becomes part of the appeal employed by black entrepreneurs to generate profits. All of these contradictory currents are part of the complex historical terrain of black nationalism.

The basic problem confronting both inclusionism and black nationalism is that the distinct social structure, political economy and ethnic demography which created both strategic visions for black advancement has been radically transformed, especially in the past quarter of a century. Segregation imposed a kind of social uniformity on the vast majority of black people, regardless of their class affiliation, education or social condition. The stark brutality of legal Jim Crow, combined with the unforgiving and vicious character of the repression that was essential to such a system, could only generate two major reactions: a struggle to be acknowledged and accepted despite one's racial designation, or a struggle to create an alternative set of cultural, political and social axioms which could sustain a distinctly different group identity against "whiteness." But as the social definition of what it means to be "different" in the USA has changed, the whole basis for both of these traditional racial outlooks within African-American society becomes far more contentious and problematic.

Many people from divergent ethnic backgrounds, speaking various languages and possessing different cultures, now share a common experience of inequality in the USA – poor housing, homelessness, inadequate health care, underrepresentation within government, lagging incomes and high rates of unemployment, discrimination in capital markets, and police brutality on the streets. Yet there is an absence of unity between these constituencies, in part because their leaders are imprisoned ideologically and theoretically by the assumptions and realities of the past. The rhetoric of racial solidarity, for instance, can be used to mask class contradictions and divisions within the black, Latino and Asian American communities. Symbolic representation can be manipulated to promote the narrow interest of minority elected officials who may have little commitment to advancing the material concerns of the most oppressed sectors of multicultural America.

What is also missing is a common language of resistance. Race as a social construction generates its own internal logic and social expressions of pain, anger and alienation within various communities. These are often barriers to an understanding of the larger social and economic forces at work which undermine our common humanity. From the cultural threads of our own experiences, we must find parallel patterns and symbols of struggle which permit us to draw connections between various groups within society. This requires the construction of a new lexicon of activism, a language which transcends the narrow boundaries of singular ethnic identity and embraces a vision of democratic pluralism.

The immediate factors involved in a general strategic rethinking of the paradigms for black American struggle are also international. A generation ago, black Americans with an internationalist perspective might see themselves as part of the diverse nonaligned movement of Third World nations, strategically distanced between capitalist America and Communist Russia. Like legal racial segregation, the system of Soviet Communism and the Soviet Union itself no longer exist. Apartheid as a system of white privilege and political totalitarianism no longer exists, as the liberation forces of Nelson Mandela and the African National Congress struggle to construct a multiracial democracy. The Sandinistas of Nicaragua lost power, as their model of a pluralistic, socialist-oriented society was overturned, at least for the time being. Throughout the rest of the Third World, from Ghana to Vietnam, socialists moved rapidly to learn the language of markets and foreign investment, and were forced to curtail egalitarian programs and accommodate themselves to the ideological requirements of the "New World Order" and the demands of transnational capital. Millions of people of color were on the move, one of the largest migrations in human history. Rural and agricultural populations migrated to cities in search of work and food; millions traveled from the Third World periphery to the metropolitan cores of Western Europe and North America to occupy the lowest levels of labor. In many instances, these new groups were socially stigmatized and economically dominated, in part by the older categories of "race" and the social divisions of "difference" which separated the newest immigrants from the white "mainstream."

Nevertheless, within this changing demographic/ethnic mix which increasingly characterizes the urban environments of Western Europe and North America, the older racial identities and categories have begun in many instances to break down, with new identities and group symbols being formulated by various "minorities." In the United Kingdom by the 1970s, immigrants – of radically divergent ethnic backgrounds and languages – from the Caribbean, Asia and Africa began to term themselves "black" as a political entity. In the US, the search for both disaggregation and rearticulation of group identity and consciousness among people of color is also occurring, although along different lines due to distinct historical experiences and backgrounds. In the Hawaiian islands, for example, many of the quarter of a million native Hawaiians support the movement for political sovereignty and self-determination. But do native Hawaiians have more in common culturally and politically with American Indians or Pacific islanders? What are the parallels and distinctions between the discrimination experienced by Mexican Americans in the US Southwest, and African-Americans under slavery and Jim Crow segregation? Do the more than five million Americans of Arab, Kurdish, Turkish and Iranian nationality and descent have a socioeconomic experience in the USA which puts them in conflict with native-born African-Americans, or is there sufficient commonality of interest and social affinity to provide the potential framework for principled activism and unity?

Similar questions about social distinctions rooted in mixed ethnic heritages and backgrounds could be raised within the black community itself. At least three out of four native-born Americans of African descent in the USA have to some extent a racial heritage which is also American Indian, European, Asian and/or Hispanic. Throughout much of the Americas, racial categories were varied and complex, reflecting a range of social perceptions based on physical appearance, color, hair texture, class, social status and other considerations. In the USA prior to the civil-rights movement, with a few exceptions, the overwhelmingly dominant categorization was "black" and "white." In the late 1970s, the federal government adopted a model for collecting census data based on four "races" – black, Asian, American Indian and white – and two ethnic groups, Hispanic and non-Hispanic, which could be of whatever "racial" identity. Today, all of these categories are being contested and questioned. Some of the hundreds of thousands of African-Americans and whites who intermarry have begun to call for a special category for their children – "multiracial." By 1994, three states required a "multiracial" designation on public-school forms, and Georgia has established the "multiracial" category on its mandatory state paperwork. The "multiracial" designation, if popularized and structured into the state bureaucracy, could have the dangerous effect of siphoning off a segment of what had been the "black community" into a distinct and potentially privileged elite, protected from the normal vicissitudes and ordeals experienced by black folk under institutional racism. It could become a kind of "passing" for the twenty-first century, standing apart from the definition of blackness. Conversely, as more immigrants from the African continent and the Caribbean intermarry with native-born black Americans, notions of what it means to be "black" become culturally and ethnically far more pluralistic and international. The category of "blackness" becomes less parochial and more expansive, incorporating the diverse languages, histories, rituals and aesthetic textures of new populations and societies.

Inside the United States, other political and social factors have contributed to the reframing of debates on race and our understanding of the social character of the black community. In just the past five years, we have experienced the decline and near-disappearance of Jesse Jackson's Rainbow Coalition and efforts to liberalize and reform the Democratic Party from within; the explosive growth of a current of conservative black nationalism and extreme racial separatism within significant sections of the African-American community; the vast social uprising of the Los Angeles rebellion in April and May 1992, triggered by a Not Guilty verdict on police officers who had viciously beaten a black man; and the political triumph of mass conservatism in the 1994 congressional elections, due primarily to an overwhelmingly Republican vote by millions of angry white males. Behind these trends and events, from the perspective of racial history, was an even larger dilemma: the failure of the modern black American freedom movement to address or even to listen to the perspectives and political insights of the "hip-hop" generation, those African-Americans born and/or socialized after the March on Washington of 1963 and the passage of the Civil Rights Act a year later. The hip-hop generation was largely pessimistic about the quality and character of black leadership, and questioned the legitimacy and relevancy of organizations like the NAACP. Although the hip-hop movement incorporated elements of black nationalism into its wide array of music and art, notably through its iconization of Malcolm X in 1990–93, it nevertheless failed to articulate a coherent program or approach to social change which addressed the complex diversities of black civil society. Both inclusionism and black nationalism had come to represent fragmented social visions and archaic agendas, which drew eclectically from racial memory. Both ideologies failed to appreciate how radically different the future might be for black people, especially in the context of a post-Cold War, postmodern, post-industrial future. The sad and sorry debacle surrounding the public vilification and firing of NAACP former national secretary Benjamin Chavis, for example, illustrated both the lack of internal democracy and accountability of black political institutions, as well as the absence of any coherent program which could speak meaningfully to the new social, political and cultural realities.

The urgent need to redefine the discourse and strategic orientation of the black movement is more abundantly clear in the mid 1990s than ever before. Proposition 187 in California, which denied medical, educational, and social services to undocumented immigrants, as well as the current national debates about affirmative action and welfare, all have one thing in common: the cynical and deliberate manipulation of racial and ethnic stereotypes by the far right. White conservatives understand the power of "race." They have made a strategic decision to employ code-words and symbols which evoke the deepest fears and anxieties of white middle-class and working-class Americans with regard to African-American issues and interests.

The reasons for this strategy are not difficult to discern. Since the emergence of Reaganism in the United States, corporate capitalism has attempted to restrict the redistributive authority and social-program agenda of the state. Many of the reform programs, from the legal desegregation of society in the 1960s to the Johnson administration's "War on Poverty," were created through pressure from below. The initiation of affirmative-action programs for women and minorities and the expansion of the welfare state contributed to some extent to a more humane and democratic society. The prerogatives of capital were not abolished by any means, but the democratic rights of minorities, women and working people were expanded. As capitalist investment and production became more global, the demand for cheap labor increased dramatically. Capital aggressively pressured Third World countries to suppress or outlaw unions, reduce wage levels, and eliminate the voices of left opposition. Simultaneously, millions of workers were forced to move from rural environments into cities in the desperate search for work. The "Latinization" of cities, from Los Angeles to New York, is a product of this destructive, massive economic process.

In the United States since the early 1980s, corporate capital has pushed aggressively for lower taxes, deregulation, a relaxation of affirmative action and environmental protection laws, and generally more favorable social and political conditions for corporate profits. Over the past twenty years, this has meant that real incomes of working people in the United States, adjusted for inflation, have fallen significantly. Between 1947 and 1973, the average hourly and weekly earnings of US production and nonsupervisory workers increased dramatically – from $6.75 per hour to $12.06 per hour (in 1993 inflation-adjusted dollars). But after 1973, production workers lost ground – from $12.06 per hour in 1979 to $11.26 per hour in 1989 to only $10.83 per hour in 1993. According to the research of the Children's Defense Fund, the greatest losses occurred among families with children under the age of eighteen where the household head was also younger than the age of thirty. The inflation-adjusted income of white households in this category fell 22 per cent between 1973 and 1990. For young Latino families with children, the decline during these years was 27.9 per cent. For young black families, the drop was a devastating 48.3 per cent.

During the Reagan administration, the United States witnessed a massive redistribution of wealth upward, unequaled in our history. In 1989, the top 1 per cent of all US households received 16.4 per cent of all US incomes in salaries and wages; it possessed 48.1 per cent of the total financial wealth of the country. In other words, the top 1 per cent of all households controlled a significantly greater amount of wealth than the bottom 95 per cent of all US households (which controlled only 27.7 per cent). These trends produced a degree of economic uncertainty and fear for millions of households unparalleled since the Great Depression. White working-class families found themselves working harder, yet falling further behind. "Race" in this uncertain political environment easily became a vehicle for orienting politics toward the right. If a white worker cannot afford a modest home in the suburbs such as his or her parents could have purchased thirty years ago, the fault is attributed not to falling wages but to affirmative action. If the cost of public education spirals skyward, white teenagers and their parents often conclude that the fault is not due to budget cuts but to the fact that "undeserving" blacks and Hispanics have taken the places of "qualified" white students.

As significant policy debates focus on the continuing burden of race within society, the black movement is challenged to rethink its past and to restructure radically the character of its political culture. Race is all too often a barrier to understanding the central role of class in shaping personal and collective outcomes within a capitalist society. Black social theory must transcend the theoretical limitations and programmatic contradictions of the old assimilationist/integrationist paradigm on the one hand, and of separatist black nationalism on the other. We have to replace the bipolar categories, rigid racial discourses and assumptions of the segregationist past with an approach toward politics and social dialogue which is pluralistic, multicultural, and nonexclusionary. In short, we must go beyond black and white, seeking power in a world which is increasingly characterized by broad diversity in ethnic and social groupings, but structured hierarchically in terms of privilege and social inequality. We must go beyond black and white, but never at the price of forgetting the bitter lessons of our collective struggles and history, never failing to appreciate our unique cultural and aesthetic gifts or lacking an awareness of our common destiny with others of African descent. We must find a language that clearly identifies the role of class as central to the theoretical and programmatic critique of contemporary society. And we must do this in a manner which reaches out to the newer voices and colors of US society – Latinos, Asian Americans, Pacific Island Americans, Middle East Americans, American Indians, and others.

We have entered a period in which our traditional definitions of what it has meant to be "black" must be transformed. The old racial bifurcation of white versus black no longer accurately or adequately describes the social composition and ethnic character of the United States. Harlem, the cultural capital of black America, is now more than 40 per cent Spanish-speaking. Blackness as an identity now embraces a spectrum of nationalities, languages, and ethnicities, from the Jamaican and Trinidadian cultures of the West Indies to the Hispanicized blackness of Panama and the Dominican Republic. More than ever before, we must recognize the limitations and inherent weaknesses of a model of politics which is grounded solely or fundamentally in racial categories. The diversity of ethnicities which constitute the urban United States today should help us to recognize the basic common dynamics of class undergirding the economic and social environment of struggle for everyone.

Historically, there is an alternative approach to the politics and social analysis of black empowerment which is neither inclusionist nor nationalist. This third strategy can be called "transformationist." Essentially, transformationists within the racial history of America have sought to deconstruct or destroy the ideological foundations, social categories and institutional power of race. Transformationists have sought neither incorporation nor assimilation into a white mainstream, nor the static isolation of racial separation; instead they have advocated a restructuring of power relations and authority between groups and classes, in such a manner as to make race potentially irrelevant as a social force. This critical approach to social change begins with a radical understanding of culture. The transformationist sees culture not as a set of artefacts or formal rituals, but as the human content and product of history itself. Culture is both the result of and the consequences of struggle; it is dynamic and ever-changing, yet structured around collective memories and traditions. The cultural history of black Americans is, in part, the struggle to maintain their own group's sense of identity, social cohesion and integrity, in the face of policies which have been designed to deny both their common humanity and particularity. To transform race in American life, therefore, demands a dialectical approach toward culture which must simultaneously preserve and destroy. We must create the conditions for a vital and creative black cultural identity – in the arts and literature, in music and film – which also has the internal confidence and grace of being to draw parallels and assume lines of convergence with other ethnic traditions. But we must destroy and uproot the language and logic of inferiority and racial inequality, which sees blackness as a permanent caste and whiteness as the eternal symbol of purity, power and privilege.

The transformationist tradition is also grounded in a radical approach to politics and the state. Unlike the integrationists, who seek "representation" within the system as it is, or the nationalists, who generally favor the construction of parallel racial institutions controlled by blacks, the transformationists basically seek the redistribution of resources and the democratization of state power along more egalitarian lines. A transformationist approach to politics begins with the formulation of a new social contract between people and the state which asks: "What do people have a right to expect from their government in terms of basic human needs which all share in common?" Should all citizens have a right to vote, but have no right to employment? Should Americans have a right to freedom of speech and unfettered expression, but no right to universal public health care? These are some of the questions that should be at the heart of the social policy agenda of a new movement for radical multicultural democracy.

The transformationist tradition in black political history embraces the radical abolitionists of the nineteenth century, the rich intellectual legacy of W.E.B. Du Bois, and the activism of militants from Paul Robeson to Fannie Lou Hamer. But it is also crucial to emphasize that these three perspectives – inclusion, black nationalism, and transformation – are not mutually exclusive or isolated from one another. Many integrationists have struggled to achieve racial equality through the policies of liberal desegregation, and have moved toward more radical means as they became disenchanted with the pace of social change. The best example of integrationist transformationism is provided by the final two years of Martin Luther King, Jr.'s public life: anti-Vietnam War activism; advocacy of a "Poor People's March" on Washington DC; the mobilization of black sanitation workers in Memphis, Tennessee; and support for economic democracy. Similarly, many other black activists began their careers as black nationalists, and gradually came to the realization that racial inequality cannot be abolished until and unless the basic power structure and ownership patterns of society are transformed. This requires at some level the establishment of principled coalitions between black people and others who experience oppression or social inequality. The best example of a black nationalist who acquired a transformationist perspective is, of course, Malcolm X, who left the Nation of Islam in March 1964 and created the Organization of Afro-American Unity several months later. In the African diaspora, a transformationist perspective in politics and social theory is best expressed in the writings of Amilcar Cabral, C.L.R. James and Walter Rodney.

In the wake of the "failure" of world socialism, the triumph of mass conservatism in politics, and the ideological hegemony of the values of markets, private enterprise and individual self-interest, black politics has to a great extent retreated from the transformationist perspective in recent years. It is difficult, if not impossible, to talk seriously about group economic development, collective interests and the radical restructuring of resources along democratic lines. Yet I am convinced that the road toward black empowerment in the multinational corporate and political environment of the post-Cold War would require a radical leap in social imagination, rather than a retreat to the discourse and logic of the racial past.

Our greatest challenge in rethinking race as ideology is to recognize how we unconsciously participate in its recreation and legitimization. Despite the legal desegregation of American civil society a generation ago, the destructive power and perverse logic of race still continues.

Most Americans continue to perceive social reality in a manner which grossly underestimates the role of social class, and legitimates the categories of race as central to the ways in which privilege and authority are organized. We must provide the basis for a progressive alternative to the interpretation of race relations, moving the political culture of black America from a racialized discourse and analysis to a critique of inequality which has the capacity and potential to speak to the majority of American people. This leap in theory and social analysis must be made, if black America has any hope of transcending its current impasse of powerlessness and systemic inequality. As C.L.R. James astutely observed: "The race question is subsidiary to the class question in politics, and to think of imperialism in terms of race is disastrous. But to neglect the racial factor as merely incidental is an error only less grave than to make it fundamental."

NINETEEN

HARLEM AND THE RACIAL IMAGINATION: REFLECTIONS ON THE MILLION YOUTH MARCH

"Harlem" has multiple meanings: It is at once a geographical space; a neighborhood of constantly changing ethnicities, nationalities, and languages; the birthplace of a famous cultural and artistic movement; an economic environment where poverty and affluence exist on the same streets; a site of black resistance and history. For many years, it has not been the largest black community in the country or even in New York City. At the height of the Harlem Renaissance in 1927, complained that stereotypes all too frequently distorted the image of this community. "It is not chiefly cabarets, it is chiefly homes; it is not all color, song and dance, it is work, thrift and sacrifice," Du Bois stated. If Harlem is to be "bribed and bought by white wastrels, distorted by unfair novelists and lied about by sensationalists, it will lose sight of its own soul and wander bewildered in a scoffing world."[1] Yet Harlem continues to be the foremost home of the racial imagination of black urban America.

In October 1995, the largest mass mobilization of African-Americans in US history took place: the Million Man March. Conceived by conservative black nationalist Louis Farrakhan, head of the Nation of Islam, the event was billed as a "Day of Atonement." Curiously, the march organizers said little about the Republican-controlled Congress's assault against affirmative action, civil-rights enforcement, and social welfare policies then well underway. Instead, a program of racial self-help, spirituality, and patriarchy was emphasized. The Million Man March was followed subsequently by the Million Woman March, which brought several hundred thousand African-American women to Philadelphia and was also oriented around a culturally conservative program. Both marches generated broad-based enthusiasm and support within the national black community, although a significant number of black feminists, gay and lesbian activists, and other political radicals voiced their strong opposition to Farrakhan's leadership. What had given impetus to these public mobilizations was a widespread sense of crisis inside the national black community. Federal and state governments were abandoning public programs and social policies that directly benefitted many black Americans. The mainstream African-American leadership seemed ineffectual in turning the situation around. Farrakhan subsequently attempted to construct a political formation, the African-American Leadership Council, to take advantage of the social momentum following these marches. The group quickly fell apart behind Farrakhan's controversial and separatist politics. Nevertheless, it was probably inevitable that other black activists would soon propose the call for a Million Youth March. The object of this new mass mobilization would be to highlight the highly problematic status of African-American children and young adults throughout the United States.

African-American elected officials and civil-rights leaders who had been outflanked by Farrakhan's Million Man March decided not to stay on the sidelines this time around. In Atlanta, when African-American youth activists began plans to hold a Labor Day weekend rally, mainstream organizations quickly backed the effort. A broad-based coalition emerged, including representatives from National Association for the Advancement of Colored People (NAACP) youth chapters, the Urban League, the National Council of Negro Women, the Nation of Islam, Jesse Jackson's Rainbow Coalition, and many black churches. Rally organizers informed the press the event would "center on political empowerment through voter registration and participation."[2] However, a closer examination of the actual program of Atlanta's Million Youth Movement reveals an emphasis not on politics but on religion. The Million Youth Movement's announced platform called for a great "spiritual awakening" among African-American young people: "It is our goal to strengthen or re-establish our relationship with the Creator and allow spiritual enterprise must "make an Atonement to all those whom we have injured and in doing so, we can once again be at one with our Creator." Economically, the movement's objectives included "instill[ing] the principles of collective work and ownership, harness[ing] our dollars into responsible spending and investment" and "entrepreneurship."[3] Many of these priorities could have been comfortably accommodated in the program of the Christian Coalition, the Promise Keepers, or other mass evangelical, conservative formations. Few observers were subsequently surprised when barely 1,000 African-American young people came to the Atlanta rally. The mobilization's emphasis was too "mainstream" and clearly out of step with a generation defined by the militancy of hip-hop popular culture.

Yet when other more militant black activists announced plans to hold a similar mobilization of African-American young people in New York City on the same weekend, expectations rose dramatically for an event as well attended as the rallies in Washington, D.C., and Philadelphia. With 2.4 million people of African descent living in the city's boundaries, black New York had long played a central role in the racial imagination of black America. A protest march championing the rights of young African-Americans, built around a militant program of empowerment, could potentially inspire new movements throughout the entire country. And nowhere in New York City or the nation were black youth more "at risk" than in the neighborhood of Central Harlem, which was ultimately selected as the venue for the march.

Saying both "Harlem" and "black," for most African-Americans, is being redundant. Central Harlem today is still overwhelmingly a non-Hispanic black urban center, with only a 12.5 per cent nonblack population as of 1990. In the past three decades, however, the community has undergone major changes in its social and economic characteristics. In 1970, Central Harlem's population stood at 159,300; ten years later, it was 105,600, a one-third decline. By 1990, Central Harlem's population had dropped just below 100,000, but since that time, it has grown to just over 108,000. Although in recent years a number of black professionals, artists, and corporate executives have purchased and renovated a number of Harlem's gorgeous brownstones, most working-class and low-income residents have little in common with this affluence or privileged lifestyle. As of 1990, 30,600 residents lived on public assistance, such as Aid to Families with Dependent Children; another 8,900 depended on Supplemental Security Income.[4]

Another major problem in Central Harlem is housing. Beginning in 1984, the city government began to place indigent families living in the city's hotel shelter system in Harlem. By the early 1990s, more than 4,500 homeless families had been relocated into Central Harlem. Simultaneously, the city failed to provide the necessary social services to support these families.[5] In 1993, Central Harlem had an estimated 40,500 households, of which the overwhelming number (39,300) were renters. Nearly 20 per cent of all families lived in public housing. The median income for Central Harlemites living in rental housing was just $10,200.[6]

As in other major American cities in the past two decades, deindustrialization and the decline of jobs and social services had a devastating impact on black and brown children and young adults. According to the Children's Defense Fund, in 1987, the poverty rate for black children in New York City (52 per cent) was more than double that for white children. By 1994, 62.1 per cent of all African-American children and 75 per cent of Latino children in New York City were born into poverty. Most children and adolescents growing up in low-income black households have only limited access to health-care services. About 20 per cent of New York City's black and Latino population have no health insurance. Sixty-one per cent of the uninsured children and young adults in this group are black.[7]

Major health indicators also clearly illustrate the social consequences of poverty, unemployment, and government neglect in Central Harlem. In 1991, infant mortality rates in the neighborhood were 15.3 per 1,000 live births, well above the citywide average (11.2). One out of seven infants was classified as a low birth-weight baby, nearly twice the citywide figure. The annual number of tuberculosis cases in the community per 100,000 (165.0) was over three times the city's rate. The annual number of AIDS cases diagnosed in Central Harlem per 100,000 (352.0) was double that for the city.[8]

A similar situation exists in economic life. Official unemployment rates for adults in Harlem is consistently estimated by officials at 20 to 25 per cent. However, real labor force participation rates are below 60 per cent. This means that roughly 45 per cent of all Harlem residents are outside of the paid labor force. Most Harlem businesses are not owned by blacks, and many still adhere to policies of employment discrimination. With immigrants from Korea and the Dominican Republic purchasing Harlem-based businesses during the past twenty years, large numbers of jobs have begun to disappear for young black women and men. In a survey of Korean merchants in Harlem and other black neighborhoods in New York City, sociologist Pyong Gap Min found that only 5 per cent of all employees of Korean-owned businesses in the city are black. In Harlem, less than one-third of all employees at Korean owned stores are black, whereas over 90 per cent of their sales are to black consumers. The standard complaint is that "blacks don't want to work." In reality, there is fierce competition for low-wage employment in Harlem. At the McDonald's restaurant on 125th Street, about 300 people apply every month for jobs that pay $4.25 per hour. Overall, there are about fourteen job applicants for every low-wage job in Harlem's fast-food establishments.[9]

Nevertheless, these depressing statistics should not obscure the considerable strengths and resources within the Harlem community. There is an elaborate network of neighborhood-based social institutions: churches and mosques, social clubs, fraternities and sororities, business associations, tenants' groups, parents' organizations, small collectives of artists, writers and musicians. There is also a long and very rich history of political and social protest that is well known to community residents. Thus, when prominent black nationalist Khallid Abdul Muhammad announced plans for a national Million Youth March to be held in Harlem sometime in September 1998, many Harlemites initially agreed that a carefully planned and well-organized protest should find significant support in their neighborhood.

To describe Khallid Muhammad as a controversial public figure would be a considerable understatement. Born Harold Moore Jr., in Houston, Texas, for two decades he worked his way up the hierarchy of the Nation of Islam, eventually becoming Louis Farrakhan's national spokesman. In February 1988, he was sentenced to three years in federal prison for using false information, including doctored tax returns, to obtain a home mortgage in Atlanta. Emerging from prison just as Farrakhan was attempting to become more mainstream, Muhammad's constant references to Jews as "bloodsuckers" who "deserved Hitler" were an embarrassment. Despite being demoted from the Nation of Islam's hierarchy, Muhammad continued to profit from his career of offensive hate speech, receiving as much as $10,000 per public engagement. Typical of Muhammad's public polemics was a 1997 speech to college students in California, where he declared the Holocaust to be a hoax and smeared Jews as "hooked-nose, bagel-eating, lox-eating, perpetrating-a-fraud, so-called Jews who just crawled out of the ghettoes of Europe."[10]

Other notable characteristics of Khallid Muhammad, beyond his outrageous anti-Semitism, are his boundless egotism and shameless self-promotion. Muhammad's official biography, posted on the Million Youth March website, declared that "the most distinct trait of this handsome black man, this lexical pyrotech, is that he speaks for the liberation and salvation of the black nation, the downtrodden and the oppressed." He applauded himself for possessing "a sense of humor that can have the audience bouncing in their seats with laughter" yet having the ability to "bring tears to the eyes of the toughest of his listeners." Muhammad listed among his many "accomplishments" serving as associate director of the Urban Crisis Center, a race relations consulting firm whose clients included US Steel, Federal Express, IBM, AT&T, police agencies, and the federal government.[11] In his biographical profile, Muhammad also characterized his notorious speech at Kean College in New Jersey in November 1993 as one that "shook the racist Zionist, imperialist white supremacist foundation of the world." This hate speech is curious for a self-described corporate and government consultant on race relations. More recently, Muhammad made national headlines in June 1998 by leading armed members of two militant groups, the new Black Panthers and the New Black Muslim Movement, into Jasper, Texas, to protest the white supremacist murder of a black man. Local residents and the victim's family denounced Muhammad for "exploiting their tragedy."[12]

Many Harlemites who had heard of Muhammad knew he had recently purchased a magnificent nineteenth-century brownstone on Harlem's famous Strivers' Row, with an estimated market value of $1 million. With no office, Muhammad frequently conducts his business, according to *New York* magazine "out of the trunk of his $140,000 ocean-blue Rolls-Royce."[13]

When Khallid Muhammad began preparations to hold his Million Youth March in Harlem, he largely ignored the community's middle-class community and local political leaders. He probably assumed that the socioeconomic conditions within the Harlem community were so severe that a natural constituency of grassroots supporters would quickly emerge. Bill Perkins, Harlem's City Councilman, complained to the press that rally organizers had refused to consult anyone within his constituency. "Not me, not the clergy, not our youth leaders – nobody!" he emphasized. "It's like somebody coming into your house and just telling you he's taking over and throwing himself a party."[14] Many local black leaders came out against the mobilization because of Muhammad's central role in it. "Yon can't build something off a person like Khallid Muhammad," stated New York Urban League president Dennis Wolcott. "I can't separate the march from the messenger." Others such as Harlem congressman Charles Rangel denounced Muhammad but encouraged participation, urging "church choirs to participate and Boy Scouts to show up in uniform, so that they might … take the hate that's been associated with this assembly and substitute it with love and concern."[15] Even Louis Farrakhan, concerned about the negative repercussions that would occur if the Harlem rally degenerated into violence, sternly cautioned his former protégé against any behavior that might provoke the police. Farrakhan undoubtedly recalled the events of 1964, when a protest march against police brutality in Harlem erupted into violence between police and demonstrators. After several days of unrest, one person had been killed, 141 seriously injured, and over 500 people had been arrested, with property damage exceeding tens of thousands of dollars.[16]

It was at this moment that New York mayor Rudolph Giuliani came to Khallid Muhammad's rescue. The conservative Republican was first elected in 1993, defeating black liberal Democratic incumbent David

Dinkins. During his tenure as the city's chief executive, a cold war had developed between the mayor's administration and the vast majority of the African-American community. It is fair to say that Giuliani was as widely despised among most blacks as he was praised and admired by the majority of the city's white electorate. The city administration curtly refused to grant a permit for the event in Harlem, and Giuliani repeatedly denounced the event as a "hate march." City officials would only allow the rally to take place on Randall's Island or in Van Cortlandt Park in the Bronx. Taking the city to court, US District Court judge Lewis Kaplan ruled in favor of the march organizers, declaring that city officials had violated their constitutional rights to free speech and due process. A subsequent decision by a federal appeals court, however, restricted the rally to a six-block area on Malcolm X Boulevard and for a duration of four hours.[17] Giuliani's opposition immediately generated unmerited yet widespread support throughout Harlem for Muhammad's efforts. Triumphant, Muhammad declared to his supporters that Giuliani was nothing but "an ordinary cracker" who had simply chosen "to ignore the law."[18]

However, with only days to go before the demonstration, local activists loudly complained that Muhammad's people had still done next to nothing to prepare for a mass public audience. No one had assembled the basic elements essential for a major rally, such as a stage, portable toilets, a sound system, and insurance bond. Regional coordinators of the 1995 Million Man March such as Sadiki Kammon, head of the Black Community Information Center in Boston, had not even been contacted by organizers of the New York event. NAACP youth leaders in Philadelphia, Washington, D.C., and other major cities declared to the press that they had "nothing to do with the event." Few plans had been made to coordinate buses to bring people to the rally site. Veteran Harlem politicians and activists began to suspect that Muhammad and his coterie of followers had no intention of mobilizing black youth around social issues. City Councilman Perkins complained: "I've seen block parties that were better organized and planned. This has been the Khallid Muhammad show. It has nothing to do with the legitimate concerns and aspirations of young people."[19] Nevertheless, in mid-August, lawyers for Muhammad maintained that the march was expected to draw 175,000 people. One reporter for the *Financial Times* (London) predicted on the eve of the march that it "is still expected to draw many tens of thousands of young people from as far away as Ohio and California."[20]

On the morning of 5 September, it was immediately apparent that the New York Police Department, not the marchers, was eager for a show of force. Over 3,000 police officers were assigned to the Harlem demonstration – a number easily large enough to handle 250,000 people. Barricades had been erected in the center of Malcolm X Boulevard, and dozens of surrounding streets were blocked off. The subway stations in Central Harlem were closed, with police using the underground sites for command posts. Police observers were stationed on the roofs of buildings overlooking the crowd. Police deliberately halted or diverted many people trying to cross intersections. Shoppers were kept from local stores; patients released from Harlem Hospital were denied permission to cross the barricaded street. Most of the people who were inconvenienced by these excessive police tactics were Harlem residents who had nothing to do with the march. It was like waking up and living in a military occupation zone.

The rally itself was something of an anti-climax. Only 10,000 people attended the peaceful, four-hour rally. Police estimated the crowd to number only 6,000. Nearly all who came were not motivated by anti-Semitism, racism, or any sort of bigotry. This largely working-class and poor people's audience wanted to make a public statement concerning the challenges facing young African-Americans across the nation and especially in Harlem. Virtually no national figures were featured on the platform. Local Afrocentric educator Leonard Jeffries presented a demand for African-American reparations, and Al Sharpton delivered a political and entertaining speech. Unfortunately, there were no significant proposals about how to address the real problems confronting young adults and children within the black community.

At five minutes before 4 pm, just before the rally was supposed to end, Khallid Muhammad finally took the stage and began to harangue the police officers surrounding the crowd, many now dressed in helmets and riot gear. Suddenly a police helicopter swooped less than 200 feet above the crowd. As officers rushed the stage, Muhammad responded with irresponsible and inflammatory rhetoric: "If anyone attacks you … beat the hell out of them…. If they attack you, take their guns away, and use their guns in self-defense."[21]

There was confusion, shock, and outrage in the unarmed crowd as a phalanx of police attempted to clear the stage and the streets. Activists tried to shield and protect smaller children in the crowd. Some of the crowd began throwing bottles at the police, and the cops responded by swinging their batons indiscriminately. Several people yelled, "This is South Africa!" Fortunately, only the remarkable restraint shown by the vast majority of those who had come to the rally defused the situation. Within an hour, most of the crowd had been dispersed. Outraged Harlem political and religious leaders demanded to see Giuliani to

BEYOND BLACK AND WHITE

protest the use of excessive police force in their community. Typically, Giuliani refused even to consider meeting with them. Attorney Dorothea Caldwell-Brown spoke for most black New Yorkers by observing that the mayor's actions "feed these young people to Khallid. He stands up and says, 'Look at how they treat you,' and here they come rushing in doing exactly what he says. Giuliani and Khallid are in concert ... They need one another."[22]

In Harlem folklore, the events of 5 September 1998 will probably be remembered as the "Million Cop March," where the integrity and civil liberties of an entire community were violated. Yet beyond the irresponsible misleadership of both Muhammad and Giuliani, the difficult challenges facing Harlem and the rest of black urban America still remain. But the history of our racial imagination provides real hope that new democratic movements for fundamental change may still be created.

Notes

1. W.E.B. Du Bois, "Harlem," *Crisis* 34: 7 (September 1927), p. 240.
2. Larry Bivens, "Black Youth Marches Play Down Differences," *USA Today* (31 August 1998).
3. "Million Youth Movement Ten Year Action Plan-Agenda," website, www. millionyouthmovement.com (August 1998).
4. Manhattan Community Board No. 10, *Statement of District Needs*, published by the City of New York, 1996.
5. Ibid.
6. City of New York, *Rent Stabilized Manhattan: An Apartment Building Income and Expense Profile*, compiled by Ted Fields, City of New York Rent Guideline Board (January 1997).
7. Phyllis Y. Harris, "Impact of Social Factors on Health," in the June Jackson Christmas, ed., *Growing Up ... Against the Odds: The Health of Black Children and Adolescents in New York City* (New York 1997), pp. 15–18.
8. Phyllis Y. Harris and June Jackson Christmas, "Profiles of Three Black Communities," in Christmas, ed., *Growing Up ... Against the Odds*, pp. 19–26.
9. Jonathan Kaufman, "Help Unwanted: Immigrants in US Refuse to Hire Blacks in Inner City," *Asian Wall Street Journal* (7 June 1995).
10. Henry Goldman, "Judge: Can't Bar Million Youth March Permit," *Philadelphia Inquirer* (27 August 1998).
11. "Dr. Khallid Abdul Muhammad Biography," website, available: www. millionyouthmarch.com.
12. David M. Halbfinger, "Behind Hate Speech, an Enigma," *New York Times* (31 August 1998).
13. Peter Noel, "Blood Brother," *New York* 31: 34 (7 September 1998) p. 25.

14. Goldman, "Judge: Can't Bar Million Youth March Permit."

15. Henry Goldman, "N.Y. Youth March Is On, But Are Organizers Ready?" *Philadelphia Inquirer* (2 September 1998).

16. Basil Wilson and Charles Green, *The Struggle for Black Empowerment* (New York 1992), p. 20.

17. Patricia Hurtado, "Marching Order/Court Places Restrictions of Six Blocks and Four Hours," *Newsday* (2 September 1998).

18. Abby Goodnough, "Youth March Organizer, Celebrating Ruling, Taunts Giuliani," *New York Times* (28 August 1998).

19. Raymond Hernandez and Monte Williams, "Days Before Harlem Youth Rally, Little Effort to Draw Big Turnout," *New York Times* (3 September 1998).

20. John Labate, "Confrontation Flares Over Million Youth Solidarity March," *Financial Times* (London), (4 September 1998).

21. Dan Barry, "Rally in Harlem Ends in Clashes with the Police," *New York Times* (6 September 1998).

22. Somini Sengupta, "Voicing Anger at a Day Turned Upside Down," and Mike Allen, "Some Experts Say the Rules on Rallies Were Ignored," *New York Times* (7 September 1998).

TWENTY

THE POLITICAL AND THEORETICAL CONTEXTS OF THE CHANGING RACIAL TERRAIN

At the first Pan-African Conference held in London in August 1900, the great African-American scholar, W.E.B. Du Bois, predicted that "the problem of the twentieth century is the problem of the color line – the relation of the darker to the lighter races of men in Asia and Africa, in America and the islands of the sea." Today, with the tragic and triumphant racial experiences of the twentieth century behind us, we may say from the vantage point of universal culture that the problem of the twenty-first century is the problem of "global apartheid," the construction of new racialized ethnic hierarchies, discourses, and processes of domination and subordination in the context of economic globalization and neoliberal public policies. Within the narrower context of the United States, the fundamental problem of the twenty-first century is the problem of "structural racism": the deeply entrenched patterns of socioeconomic and political inequality and accumulated disadvantage that are coded by race and color and are consistently justified in public and private discourses by racist stereotypes, white indifference, and the prison industrial complex.

African political scientist and anthropologist Mahmood Mamdani has observed that, beginning with the imposition of European colonial rule in Africa, "race was the central organizing principle of the development of the modern state." This also holds true for the US. In the United States, racial identities were, more than anything else, politically constructed. That is, racial identities were legally sanctioned categories, supported by the weight of the courts, political institutions, organized religion, and custom, and they were reinforced by deliberate and random acts of violence. Thus, the African-American became the permanent reference point for the racialized *other* within political and civil society.

To be black was to be excluded from the social contract that linked white citizens to the state through sets of rights and responsibilities.

After more than a century of black civic and political exclusion, the early American colonies, even before the American Revolution against the British and the consolidation of the new federal system of a United States in 1787, were structured such that the centrality of race was the main organizing principle of power. Marxist sociologist Nicos Poulantzas first used the phrase *the relative autonomy of the state* to describe the indirect and interactive dynamics between political institutions and the economic structures of private ownership and production within liberal democratic societies. That is, for Poulantzas, the modern state was not, as some traditional Marxists once interpreted it, simply the dictatorship of a capitalist ruling class. Poulantzas suggested that the capitalist state itself was the site of extensive contestation, group negotiation, and conflict reflecting a disconnection between average citizens and the modes and relations of production. But I suggest that we must go further than Poulantzas; I argue that the power dynamics of all modern states are organized around the central principle of race.

Structural racism creates its own distinctive political materiality, its hierarchies and patterns and relations of power. Thus, the modern racist state may be organized around many different types of economies, including those defined by private markets as well as those of state collectivism. We should interrogate state power as an organizing principle on its own. For nearly four hundred years, two very different political narratives have evolved to explain the nature of US democracy, how the American nation-state was founded, and the character of the social contract between the American people and the state. For most white Americans, US democracy is best represented by values such as personal liberty, individualism, and the ownership of private property. For most African-Americans, the central goals of the black freedom movement have always been equality and self-determination: the eradication of all structural barriers to full citizenship and full participation in economic relations and other aspects of public life, and the ability to decide, on their own collective terms, what their future as a community with a unique history and culture might be. For black Americans, freedom was always perceived in collective terms, as something achievable by group action and capacity building. Equality meant the elimination of all social deficits between blacks and whites as well as the eradication of cultural and social stereotypes and patterns of social isolation and group exclusion generated by white structural racism over several centuries. The current debate regarding black reparations reflects this central conflict over the nature of US democracy and whether a deeply racialized and class-stratified society can be transformed. Many who support black reparations believe that racial peace can be achieved only through social justice – coming to terms with the ways America and, broadly, even Western civilizations have related to people of African descent. As Marcus Garvey scholar Robert Hill of UCLA observed recently, the campaign for black reparations is "the final chapter in the five-hundred-year struggle to suppress the transatlantic slave trade, slavery, and the consequences of its effects."

Structural Racism: History and Evolution

Historically, the United States has witnessed two great struggles to achieve a truly multicultural democracy, struggles that have centered on the status of African-Americans. The First Reconstruction (1865–1877) ended slavery and briefly gave black men voting rights, but failed to provide meaningful compensation for two centuries of unpaid labor. The promise of "forty acres and a mule" was, for most blacks, a dream deferred. The Second Reconstruction (1954–1968), or the modern civil-rights movement, outlawed legal segregation in public accommodations and achieved major legislative victories such as voting rights. But these successes paradoxically obscure the tremendous human costs of historically accumulated disadvantage that remain central to black Americans' lives. The disproportionate wealth that most white Americans enjoy today was first constructed from centuries of unpaid black labor. Many white institutions, including Ivy League universities, insurance companies, and banks, profited from slavery. This pattern of white privilege and black inequality continues today, decades after legal segregation was ended. For example, so-called "equity inequity" – the absence of black capital formation – is a direct historical consequence of America's structural racism. One in three black households actually has a negative net wealth. In 1998, the typical black family's net wealth was $16,400 – less than one-fifth that of white families. Black families are denied home loans at twice the rate of whites. Blacks are frequently forced to turn to predatory lenders who charge outrageously high home mortgage rates. In the labor force, blacks remain the last hired and first fired during recessions. For example, during the 1990–1991 recession, African-Americans suffered disproportionally. At the Coca Cola Company, 42 per cent of employees who lost their jobs were black; at Sears, Roebuck & Co., the number was 54 per cent. black workers usually have less job seniority and fewer informal networks of friends and relatives who could aid hiring and job retention. In regard to health, blacks have significantly shorter life expectancies, partly because of racism in the health establishment. Blacks are statistically less likely than whites to be referred for kidney transplants or early-stage cancer surgery. Blacks are about twice as likely as whites to lack health insurance. In criminal justice, African-Americans constitute only about 14 per cent of all drug users, yet are the subject of 35 per cent of all drug arrests, 55 per cent of drug convictions, and 75 per cent of prison admissions for drug offenses. Among juveniles arrested and charged with a crime, black youths are six times more likely than whites to be sentenced to prison.

Resistance Strategies

How have African-Americans responded to the evolving domains of this structural racism? In terms of racial counter-hegemonic approaches, the black American community over the course of 150 years has developed three overlapping protest strategies: integration or racial assimilation, black nationalism or black separatism, and what feminist anthropologist Leith Mullings and I have termed *transformation*. Integrationist movements sought full democratic rights and interracial assimilation within the existing institutions of society. Integration called for the desegregation of public accommodation, schools, and residential patterns, as well as more equitable black representation throughout the class structure. black nationalism was premised on the pessimistic (or realistic) notion that most white Americans' prejudices were relatively fixed, that meaningful racial reforms were impossible in the long run. What was required was the construction of strong black-owned institutions, businesses, and schools, an emphasis on black cultural awareness and group consciousness, and frequently a strong identification with Africa. Transformationalism, or black radicalism, focused on the link between racial oppression and class exploitation, calling on a redistribution of wealth as being key in dismantling racism. Transformationists attempted to construct strategic coalitions across racial boundaries, focusing on issues of socioeconomic inequality and the day-to-day violence perpetuated by poverty.

Each of these three strategies had strengths and weaknesses. Integrationists placed too much faith in the American capitalist class's commitment to liberal democracy, as well as social fairness, and tended to believe that racism was rooted in ignorance, rather than cold, deliberate exploitation. black nationalists perhaps underestimated how "American" black Americans really are – how African-Americans as a people share many of the same economic values, political aspirations, and cultural practices as white Americans. Strategies of black entrepreneurial capitalism along segregated racialized markets cannot work, particularly in a period that has seen the rise of global markets and transnational corporations. Transformationists may have unduly emphasized class conflict as the driving force in social history and underestimated the psychological and cultural factors that justified and perpetuated white power and privilege.

As UCLA legal scholar Cheryl Harris observed over a decade ago, in a racialized social hierarchy, whiteness is essentially a form of private property. The state is organized around the processes of what can be termed *racial accumulation*. Such accumulation of racial benefits occurs with whites' higher salaries, superior working conditions, lower rates of unemployment, higher rates of home ownership, greater access to professional and managerial positions, and average life expectancies that are seven years longer than those of black Americans. White Americans have benefited from nearly four hundred years of accumulated white privilege, which is reflected in vast disparities in material resources and property between racial groups.

The challenges of the current political situation in the US differ in several significant respects from those that gave rise to the mass movement against Jim Crow segregation. In our political system, both major parties have, to varying degrees, moved significantly to the ideological right. Reaganite Republicans and so-called New Democrats alike now adhere to neo-liberal, pro-corporate policies. The extreme right has waged a twenty-year war against all public sector institutions, pushing for the privatization of public schools, health care services, public transportation, public housing, and other government-funded programs. Closely related to this privatization campaign are the concerted efforts to bust labor unions. Today's Democrats look and sound similar in many respects. In terms of criminal justice, the nation's prison population grew by seven hundred thousand during President Bill Clinton's administration and now exceeds two million. On any given day, the US now has approximately 5.4 million individuals under criminal jurisdiction – either in prisons or jails, on probation, parole or awaiting trial. More than 4.3 million Americans, of whom 1.7 million are black, have permanently lost the right to vote because of prior felony convictions. In 1994, government funding for Pell grants that assisted prisoners seeking college training was eliminated.

In the context of racial policy, the retreat from the civil-rights agenda continues to accelerate – in our courts, state legislatures and in Congress. Affirmative action programs such as minority-economic set-asides and race-based academic scholarships, which were endorsed by many Republicans thirty years ago, are now routinely described in our media as examples of "racial quotas." Within the African-American community, however, there is some uncertainty about what steps should be taken to respond to this conservative political assault. A number of black religious leaders endorsed the Bush administration's faith-based initiatives, a push to encourage churches, mosques, and synagogues to provide social services – a trend that actually threatens to undermine publicly funded social services for the vast majority of poor and working people. Even local leaders of the NAACP and some black elected officials have endorsed school vouchers and other proposals to reallocate scarce public funds to private educational corporations. We must acknowledge that there exist growing divisions within black America, which is fragmented by social class and income, age, political affiliations, and other divisions.

In this time of global apartheid, Western democratic states increasingly construct authoritarian and elitist barriers to popular participation and decision making. Privatization in such societies organized around racial hierarchies becomes nothing less than a new racialization. In the United States, more than 30 per cent of all African-Americans are employed by the public sector. Any significant decline in government employment will have disproportionately been imposed on the growing but still fragile black middle class.

The ultimate goal of the anti-racist movement should be the delegitimization and destruction of the idea of *race* itself. Social scientists now agree that race is socially constructed, that it has no biological or genetic validity. This does not mean racial consequences aren't starkly real: embedded in the way race functions in society are the concepts of hierarchy and oppression. The social processes of racialization involve the realities of domination and subordination, which inevitably culminate in social conflict. Or as reggae artist Bob Marley once sang, "Until the color of a man's skin is of no more significance than the color of his eyes, me say war." The difficult challenge, of course, is how do we get there?

Marginalized and Exploited: Black–Asian Bonds

First, scholars who study ethnicity and race, especially as they relate to modes of state power, should contribute to a richer theoretical and historically grounded understanding of diversity. Instead of just celebrating diversity, we must theorize and interrogate it and actively seek the parallels and connections between peoples of various communities. Instead of merely talking about race, we should popularize the public's understanding of the social processes of racialization – that is, how certain groups in US society have been relegated to an oppressed status, by the weight of law, social policy, and economic exploitation.

This oppression has never occurred solely within a black–white paradigm. Although slavery and Jim Crow segregation were decisive in framing the US social hierarchy, with whiteness defined at the top, and blackness at the bottom, people of African descent have never experienced racialization by themselves. As historian Gary Okihiro has observed, the 1790 Naturalization Act defined citizenship only for immigrants who were "free white persons." Asian immigrants who were born outside the US were largely excluded from citizenship until 1952. US courts constantly redefined the rules determining who was white and who was not. For example, as Okihiro observes, Armenians were originally classed as Asians and thus were nonwhite, but legally became whites by a 1909 court decision. Syrians were white in court decisions in 1909 and 1910; they became nonwhite in 1913 and became white again in 1915. Asian Indians were legally white in 1910, but nonwhite after 1923. Historians such as David Roediger and Noel Ignatiev illustrate how a series of ethnic minorities, such as the Irish and Jews, experienced racialization, but scaled the hierarchy of whiteness.

Let me provide an example of the richness of a comparative approach to the study of racialized ethnicity. Any critical study of the complex, multilayered relationship between Asians and blacks in the United States must begin with the historical background of Asia's extensive interactions with Africa and its people. Historians have long established the links of economic trade between China and eastern Africa bordering the Indian Ocean. Islam created a transnational faith community that extended from what is today Senegal to Indonesia. The political, economic, and cultural interactions between Arabs and Africans are represented, for example, by both the Kiswahili language, and the oppressive east African slave trade, developed over many centuries, on the other. One also finds parallels and connections between Asians and Africans in the development of the Americas and Caribbean societies. About 15 million Africans were involuntarily transported as chattel slaves to the western hemisphere between the years 1550 and 1870. People of African descent, working in sugar cane fields from Bahia, northeast Brazil, to the South Carolina and Georgia coasts, constructed cultures, traditions, and societies that drew from their African past and reflected their new material conditions and social realities. Similarly, European colonialism and imperialism were responsible for the derogatorily labeled "coolie trade," the coerced migrations of Chinese and Indians into Africa, the Caribbean, and the Americas. As ethnic studies scholar Lisa Yun observes, sometimes the same ships that were used to transport enslaved Africans across the notorious Middle Passage of the Atlantic were later utilized to bring these Asian workers across the Pacific. For the slave, coerced Asian laborer, and non-European indentured worker, the physical conditions of exploitation were often indistinguishable.

The construction of Asian diasporas created new societies: those of the the Cape Malays of the Western Cape Colony, South Africa; the Indian communities of Natal, South Africa; the Indians of Uganda, Kenya and Tanzania; the Indian communities of Trinidad and Guyana; the Chinese laborers who built the railroads from the Pacific across the mountains in the western US in the mid-nineteenth century; and the Japanese agricultural workers of Hawaii. Asian and African peoples share common histories of slavery and indentured servitude, of physical exploitation, political disfranchisement, social exclusion and cultural marginalization. Despite the obvious differences between these groups in their cultures and languages of origin, the Asian and African diasporas broadly overlap with each other, with complex and often remarkable patterns of assimilation and shared struggles for freedom.

W.E.B. Du Bois's famous 1915 essay, "The African Roots of the War," documenting European colonial expansion as the driving force behind World War I, is echoed in the revolutionary writings of Sun Yat-sen and Ho Chi Minh. Mohandas Gandhi brought nonviolent civil disobedience and the philosophy of satyagraha, *soul force*, to the struggle against racism in South Africa, and Martin Luther King Jr., adopting Gandhi's model to the conditions of the US South, helped launch the Montgomery bus boycott in 1955. The political project of Third World nonalignment in the aftermath of World War II was essentially an Asian–African collaboration, uniting Sukarno of Indonesia, India's Nehru, Kwame Nkrumah of Ghana, and Gamal Abdel Nasser of Egypt. Both Malcolm X and later Muhammad Ali, in different ways, became heroes in the Afro-Asian and Islamic worlds. The struggles by non-European peoples against French colonialism link Vietnam with Algeria and both with the Haitian revolution of Toussaint L'Ouverture. Hip-hop and reggae are as integral within the popular youth cultures of Seoul and Tokyo as they are in Kingston, Brixton, South Central Los Angeles and Harlem. So when we discuss multicultural study with an emphasis on Asians and blacks, it is essential to start first with our profound interactions and parallel developments from a historical and comparative approach, and then consider areas of group conflict and possible divergence within that historical framework.

Reproducing Categories of Difference

Historically, oppressed groups frequently – and often unconsciously – defined themselves by the identity boundaries that were superimposed by dominant groups. Jean-Paul Sartre once referred to this social dynamic as "overdetermination." Oppressed people living at the bottom of any social hierarchy are constantly encouraged to see themselves as the other, as individuals who dwell outside of society's social contract, and as subordinated categories of marginalized, fixed so-called minorities. Frequently, oppressed people have utilized these categories and even terms of insult and stigmatization, such as *nigger* or *queer*, as a site of resistance and counterhegemonic struggle.

This kind of oppositional politics tends to anchor individuals to narrowly defined, one-dimensional identities that essentially are invented by others. For example, how did African people become known as *black*, or in Spanish, *negro*? Europeans launching the slave trade across the Atlantic four hundred years ago created the terminology as a way of lumping together in one category the peoples of an entire continent – one with tremendous variations in language, religion, ethnicity, kinship patterns and cultural traditions. Blackness, or the state of being black, was completely artificial; *no people* in Africa call themselves *black*. Blackness exists only as a social construct in relation to something else, something it is not. That "something else" became known as *whiteness*. Thus, blackness became a totalizing category relegating other identities – ethnicity, sexual orientation, gender, class affiliation, religious traditions, kinship affiliations – to secondary or even nonexistent status.

In other words, those who control or dominate hierarchies, whether through their ownership of the means of production or through their domination of the state, have a vested interest in manufacturing and reproducing categories of difference. An excellent recent example of this occurred in the United States in 1971, when the US Census Bureau invented the *Hispanic* category. At that time, the category was imposed on a population of nearly twenty million people who represented widely divergent and often contradictory nationalities, racialized ethnic identities, cultural traditions, and political affinities: Spanish-speaking black Panamanians of Jamaican or Trinidadian descent; Argentines of Italian or German descent; anti-Castro, white upper-class Cubans in Miami's Dade County; impoverished Mexican American farm workers in California's Central Valley; and black Dominican working-class people in New York City's Washington Heights. Despite this enormous range of humanity, the state had named them as one category of other. That act of naming created its own materiality for these groups, as it does for oppressed groups in general. Government resources, economic empowerment zones, and affirmative action scholarships are in part determined by who is classified as *Hispanic* and who is not. Identities may be situational, but when the power and resources of the state are used to categorize groups under a "one-size-fits-all" designation, the life chances of individuals who are defined within these categories are largely set and determined by others.

Revitalizing Protest

Scholars who are involved in social change projects must also focus on capacity building: How do we begin to rebuild resistance organizations and their protest capacity within black, Latino, Asian Pacific Island, and other racialized and immigrant communities? Part of this effort must be frankly defensive, the construction of racialized minority-based institutions to provide goods and services, educational and childcare resources, and health clinics that must be able to flourish with little or no government funding.

Nongovernmental organizations such as neighborhood associations and comprehensive community initiatives potentially enhance the ability of disadvantaged groups to realize their specific, objective interests. We need new approaches to combat what Angela Davis describes as "civic death," the legal marginalization and civic disempowerment that has become so widespread that it threatens to negate not only the Voting Rights Act of 1965, but also threatens, in effect, to void the Fifteenth Amendment of the US Constitution, which granted black males the right to vote.

To revitalize the African-American social-protest movement, we must also break with the idea that the electoral arena is the only place where politics takes place. Voter registration and mobilization are, of course, crucial tools in the struggle for black empowerment. But electoral politics, by itself, cannot transform the actual power relations between racialized, oppressed minorities and the white majority. New tactical protest approaches that use creative political confrontations by mass constituencies of African-Americans must be initiated. black political history, moreover, provides several successful models of mass collective mobilizations around issues of public policy.

One excellent example is A. Philip Randolph's Negro March on Washington Movement of 1941. This mobilization, the first of its kind, was established outside the formal organizational structures of such civil rights groups as the NAACP. Like Garvey's Universal Negro Improvement Association, it was largely if not exclusively an all-black movement. It advanced a specific set of public policy objectives that pointed toward the ultimate elimination of legal Jim Crow segregation. The Negro March on Washington focused its energies not on persuading white liberals to support racial reforms. Instead, it emphasized action by the black masses through town hall-style meetings and protest demonstrations. It linked the issues of the most oppressed sectors of the black community to the organized efforts of black unions and more progressive black middle-class organizations.

Randolph's intervention forced President Franklin Roosevelt to issue Executive Order 8802, declaring that "there shall be no discrimination in the employment of workers in defense industries or government because of race, creed, color or national origin." Roosevelt also established the Fair Employment Practices Committee. Because of Executive Order 8802, more than a quarter million African-Americans were hired in the defense industries during World War II. The Negro March on Washington created a new political environment of black militancy that directly contributed to the creation of the Congress of Racial Equality in 1941 and to the unprecedented growth of the NAACP, increasing its membership from fifty thousand in 1940 to over two hundred thousand by 1945.

The demand for black reparations may have the same potential for transforming the national public-policy discourse on race relations as the Negro March on Washington Movement did sixty years ago. Randolph's 1941 movement brought together young leftist intellectuals such as Ralph Bunche with black trade unionists, constructing a multiclass, black-identified coalition that espoused both a long-term vision – the complete dismantling of Jim Crow segregation and the democratic access of negroes to all levels of American society and public life – and short-term objectives, such as the end of racial exclusion in hiring at wartime industries and the outlawing of racially segregated units in the US military. The reparations campaign must approach the challenge of breaking apart the leviathan of American structural racism in a similar way. We must clearly set out the long-term objective: the realization of a truly multicultural, pluralistic democracy without the barriers of race, class, and gender. At the same time, we must focus specifically on immediate, realizable reforms that are necessary to achieve as first steps in a broad counter-hegemonic democratic movement.

Poor and Female: Stark Patterns

We must also consider the intersections of race with gender, sexuality, and class. For decades, black feminists have made the effective theoretical observation that institutional racism does not exist in a gender vacuum, that structures of domination and social hierarchy reinforce each other across the boundaries of identity. In practical political terms, from day-to-day experiences working with multiethnic communities, we can observe how gender, sexuality, and class intersect with structural racism.

For example, Andrea Smith, a Native American pacifist and activist, wrote in the Winter 2000 edition of *Color Lines* that in the 1970s, as many as 30 per cent of all Puerto Rican women, and 25–40 per cent of American Indian women were sterilized without their consent. Smith also cited statistics showing that "women of color are 64 per cent of the [US] female prison population and serve longer sentences for the same crime[s] as do white women or men of color." The Women of Color Center in Berkeley, California, issued a remarkable report, *Working Hard, Staying Poor: Women and Children in the Wake of Welfare Reform*, that graphically illustrates the intersectionalities of oppression. As of 1998, African-Americans, who represent 12.5 per cent of the US population, comprise 26.4 per cent of all poor people. Latinos comprise 23.4 per cent of those below the federal government's poverty line. Although only 8.2 per cent of all non-Hispanic whites are poor, 12.5 per cent of all Asians and Pacific Islanders are below the poverty line.

Immigrants are 50 per cent more likely to be poor than the native-born. In female-headed households with children, the statistics are much worse: 21 per cent of all non-Hispanic white female-headed households were poor in 1998, compared to 46 per cent of African-Americans and 48 per cent of Latinas. Within two years of the 1998 abolition of Aid to Families with Dependent Children, 50 per cent of Mexican American former welfare recipients in Santa Clara, California, reported food shortages, as had 26 per cent of all Vietnamese women in the city. In Wisconsin, one out of three Hmong women recipients had run out of food at some point during a six-month period. A 1998 study in San Francisco of immigrant households whose food stamps had been cut found that 33 per cent of all immigrant children were experiencing moderate to severe hunger. Anti-racist politics that do not acknowledge the profound connections of gender, sexuality, and class with race cannot develop a language that speaks to the vast majority of the world's oppressed people.

Crossing Borders: Common Struggles

The future politics of racialized ethnicity must also address transnational contexts. The black freedom movement in the US must reorient itself in a period of globalization and transnational corporations toward the anti-racist struggles being waged internationally. White supremacy in the US has always tried to reinforce political parochialism among the African-American people, encouraging blacks to perceive themselves in isolation from the rest of the racialized nonwhite world. Those black revolutionary activists and progressive social reformers who advocated internationalist perspectives on black liberation – Du Bois, Paul Robeson, King, Angela Y. Davis and Malcolm X, among others – were invariably perceived to be the most subversive and threatening to the established order. Yet in the age of globalization, there can be no *national* solution to the problem of structural racism. As the power of nation-states declines relative to the growth of transnational capital, individual counter-hegemonic political projects confined to one narrow geographic area will lack the theoretical and organizational tools to transform their societies.

More than fifty years ago, representatives of the non-European world met at Bandung, Indonesia, to initiate the nonaligned movement, articulating an agenda independent of the capitalist West and the Communist states. As theorist Samir Amin suggested last year in Durban, South Africa, the central task before us is the renaissance of an "Afro-Asian [and Latino] front," capable of challenging the global apartheid supported by international bodies like the International Monetary Fund (IMF), World Trade Organization (WTO), and the World Bank.

The twenty-first century truly began – politically, socially, and psychologically – with two epochal events: the World Conference Against Racism held in Durban, South Africa, last summer and the terrorist attacks of 11 September 2001, which destroyed the World Trade Center towers and part of the Pentagon. These events were directly linked to the political economy of global apartheid, to the crystallization of new transnational hierarchies of racialized otherness, and to new expressions of power and powerlessness.

At Durban, the Third World, led primarily by African-Americans and African people, attempted through diplomacy to renegotiate their historically unequal and subordinate relationships with Western imperialism and globalized capitalism. Reparations were seen by black delegates at Durban as a necessary precondition for the socioeconomic development of the black community in the US, as well as in African and Caribbean nation states. September 11 was another type of renegotiation – but this was one of terror, a violent statement by fundamentalist Muslims demanding an end to the economic and political subordination of Arab peoples by American imperialism. Both events challenged, literally and symbolically, the United States' almost completely uncritical support for Israel; to some extent, they were expressions of solidarity with the

Palestinians' struggle for self-determination. The aftermath of both events left the US government more politically isolated from the African and Islamic worlds than ever before.

Although the traumatic events of September 11 have pushed the black reparations issue temporarily into the background in the United States, the reality is that US and Western European imperialism ultimately will be forced to acknowledge the legitimacy and necessity of at least a limited reparations agreement. This movement also has international implications that link to issues of redress for colonialism: US policy makers will undoubtedly attempt to solidify their problematic relationships with African and Caribbean countries to preclude any possible strategic coalition between those nations and more radical Islamic states. The price for their diplomatic cooperation may be debt forgiveness and financial aid to assist in development projects. If African countries are successful in renegotiating their debt payments, such assistance may well be seen as compensation – whether implicit or explicit – for those nations' histories of colonial exploitation and slavery. In that case, the granting of some program of black reparations in the US also becomes more likely.

"Why Do They Hate Us?"

The recent bombing campaign against the people of Afghanistan will likely be described in future history books as the "US Against the Third World." The launching of military strikes against Afghan peasants does nothing to suppress terrorism and only erodes US credibility around the world. The question frequently posed in the media today, "Why Do They Hate Us?," can only be answered from the vantage point of the Third World's widespread poverty, hunger and economic exploitation. These are the new frontiers for the interrogation of the racialized other in the context of global apartheid.

The United States government cannot engage in effective multilateral actions to suppress terrorism because it has repeatedly illustrated its complete contempt for international cooperation. The United States owed $582 million in back dues to the United Nations, and it paid up only after the September 11 attacks jeopardized its national security. Republican conservatives still demand that the United States should be exempt from the jurisdiction of an International Criminal Court, a permanent tribunal now being established at The Hague, Netherlands. For the 2001 World Conference Against Racism, the US government authorized the allocation of a paltry $250,000, compared to over $10 million provided to the conference organizers by the Ford Foundation. Since the 1970s, the US has had an explicit policy of subsidizing terrorist movements against radical democratic and socialist governments – such as Renamo in Mozambique against the Frelimo government. For three decades, the US refused to ratify the 1965 United Nations Convention on the Elimination of Racism. Is it any wonder that much of the Third World questions our motives? The carpet-bombing of the Taliban seems to many observers to have less to do with the suppression of terrorism and more to do with securing future petroleum production rights in central Asia.

The official US delegation at Durban rejected the definition of slavery as "a crime against humanity." It refused to acknowledge the historic and contemporary effects of colonialism, racial segregation and apartheid on the underdevelopment and oppression of the non-European world. The world's subaltern masses represented at Durban sought to advance a new political discussion about the political economy of global apartheid – and the United States insulted the entire international community. Should we therefore be surprised that Palestinian children celebrate in the streets of their occupied territories when they see televised images of our largest buildings being destroyed? Should we be shocked that hundreds of protest marches in opposition to the US bombing of Afghanistan took place throughout the world?

The majority of dark-skinned humanity is saying to the United States that racism and militarism are exacerbating the world's major problems. Transnational capitalism and the repressive neoliberal policies of structural adjustment represent a dead-end for the developing world. We can only end the threat of terrorism by addressing constructively the routine violence of poverty, hunger and exploitation that character-izes the daily existence of several billion individuals on this planet. Racism is, in the final analysis, only another structural manifestation of violence. To stop the violence of terrorism, we must stop the violence of xenophobia, racialization and class inequality. To struggle for peace, to find new paths toward reconciliation across the international boundaries of religion, culture and color is the only way to protect our cities, our country and ourselves from the violence of terrorism.

Global Antiracism: Two Approaches

The World Conference Against Racism may be judged by history to have represented a dramatic turning point toward the construction of a global anti-racism. But to create practical, democratic instruments of social advocacy and capacity building – community-centered institutions that can make real changes in the material conditions and contexts of the lives of peoples of color – we must acknowledge two ideological tendencies within this anti-racist current: a liberal, democratic and populist tendency and a radical, egalitarian tendency. Both were present throughout the Durban conference, and they made their presence felt in the deliberations of the nongovernmental organization panels and in the final conference report. They reflect two very different political strategies and tactical approaches in deconstructing processes of racialization.

The liberal democratic tendency focuses on a discourse of rights, calling for civic participation, political enfranchisement and the capacity building of institutions to promote civic empowerment and multicultural diversity. This impulse seeks the reduction of societal conflict through the sponsoring of public conversations and multicultural dialogues. It seeks not a rejection of economic globalization, but its constructive engagement, with the goal of building political cultures of human rights. The most attractive quality of this liberal perspective is its commitment to multicultural social change without resorting to violence.

The radical egalitarian tendency of global anti-racists promotes a discourse about inequality and power. It seeks the abolition of poverty, the realization of universal housing, health care, and educational guarantees across the non-Western world. It is less concerned with abstract rights and more concerned with concrete results. It seeks not political assimilation in an old world order, but the construction of a new world from the bottom up.

These tendencies, which exist both in the United States and throughout the world in varying degrees, now define the ideological spectrum within the global anti-apartheid struggle. Scholars and activists alike must contribute to the construction of a broad front bringing together both the multicultural liberal democratic and radical egalitarian currents representing globalization from below. New innovations in social protest movements will also require the development of new social theory and new ways of thinking about the relationship between structural racism and state power.

TWENTY-ONE

REPARATIONS AND THE
POLITICS OF BLACK CONSCIOUSNESS

The next stage of the African-American freedom struggle, the demand for reparations, must become the new political consciousness of the great majority of our people, in order to win. Additionally, and equally important, is the role that scholars must play in contributing the socioeconomic and historical evidence that illustrates the central role of the US government and various state and local governments in creating the legal frameworks for the systemic exploitation of African-Americans, perpetrated by white corporations and throughout American society. When Professor Farah Jasmine Griffin and I coordinated the "Forty Acres a Mule" research conference in November 2002, our specific aim was to invite scholars to prepare academic papers that would contribute to the body of social science and historical data essential for constructing successful legal briefs.

There is, however, a political challenge that the black reparations campaign must address and overcome, if it is to become a truly mass movement. For decades, the demand for reparations has been largely pushed by black nationalist organizations and Afrocentric political groups. The most important of these forces has been N'COBRA, which has led an outstanding educational effort to build grassroots awareness and support for black reparations. Nationalist groups such as the Nation of Islam, the Black United Front, and December 12th have also contributed to this movement in different ways. Labor, most faith-based groups, women's organizations, legal aid groups, and civil rights groups like the NAACP and Rainbow-PUSH have remained almost completely outside of the process of black reparations mobilization. This inability to reach beyond the black nationalist sector has meant that the majority of African-Americans still do not fully understand why the demand for economic compensation is justified, nor why US government acknowledgement that "slavery was a crime against humanity" is a legal necessity.

In February 2002, CNN and *USA Today* commissioned the Gallup organization to conduct a national poll to assess public opinion on the issue. The poll results seemed to directly mirror the nation's parallel racial universes that are reproduced by structural racism. When asked whether "corporations that made profits from slavery should apologize to black Americans who are descendants of slaves," 68 per cent of African-Americans responded affirmatively, with 23 per cent opposed, while 62 per cent of all whites rejected the call for an apology and only 34 per cent supported it.

On the question of financial compensation, however, whites closed ranks around their racial privileges. When asked whether corporations benefiting from slave exploitation should "make cash payments to black Americans who are the descendants of slaves," 84 per cent of all whites responded negatively, with only 11 per cent supporting payments. A clear majority of African-Americans polled, by contrast, endorsed corporate restitution payments, by a 57 to 35 per cent margin, with 8 per cent expressing no opinion. When asked if the government should grant "cash payments" to blacks, 9 out of 10 white Americans rejected the proposal, while a strong majority of blacks favored it, by 55 to 37 per cent.

When black conservatives like Thomas Sowell, Shelby Steele and John McWhorter came out to attack reparations, it was not surprising. However, other prominent African-Americans embracing liberal and even progressive views have also expressed a variety of reservations about the black reparations demand. Writing in the urban issues magazine *City Limits*, educator Hakim Hasan warns that reparations represents a significant "danger, namely that black Americans, flush with compensation – we won! – would likewise avoid any sustained, collective introspection." Hasan grimly predicts that "if Martin Luther King's image can sell telephones ... then a Macy's Reparations Day sale, is not farfetched."[1] Progressive historian Robin D.G. Kelley raises similar reservations. Kelley fears that a pro-reparations campaign with its sights set solely on slavery risks becoming an excuse to quiet present-day discussions about racism and overlooking twentieth and twenty-first century racial injustices that have worked just as powerfully against people of color to produce white wealth at their expense.[2]

Wade Henderson, the executive director of the Leadership Conference on Civil Rights, has expressed support for the general concept of black compensation for enslavement and racial oppression, but opposes payouts to individuals. Henderson believes that any kind of financial reparations "[have] to go to some publicly chartered institution that is set up to eradicate the two most persistent problems black folks face: education and economic development."[3] *USA Today* columnist DeWayne Wickham is even more critical, declaring that the reparations movement "is in many ways a head without a body." He notes that three of the most prominent spokespersons for "the reparations cause" – Johnnie Cochran, Randall Robinson, and Charles Ogletree – did not speak at the Washington, DC demonstration held in August 2002. Wickham claims that reparations advocates have refused to address the Achilles' heel of the movement: "how the payout should be paid." He continues: "Instead of working to bridge this troubling gap of opinions, too many advocates of reparations continue to dance around it." Wickham warns that "their soft shoe on the payout question widens the divide over what should be done."[4]

The criticisms of Wickham, Henderson, Kelley and others have to be taken seriously and be convincingly addressed. First, and perhaps foremost, is the fact that white racism is structural in character and is largely grounded in institutional processes rather than in the behavior of individuals. Racial prejudice is reproduced within America's basic institutions – economic, educational, social, and political. The racial myths of white history are used to rationalize, explain away, and justify white supremacy and black inequality.

What reparations does is force whites to acknowledge the brutal reality of our common history, something white society generally has refused to do. It provides a historically grounded explanation for the continuing burden of racial oppression: the unequal distribution of economic resources, land and access to opportunities for social development, which was sanctioned by the federal government. Consequently, it is that same government that bears the responsibility of compensating those citizens and their descendants to whom constitutional rights were denied. Affirmative action was essentially "paycheck equality," in the words of political scientist and contributor to this issue, Ronald Walters; it created millions of job opportunities but did relatively little to transfer wealth from one racial group to another.

One-third of all African-American households today has a negative net wealth. The average black household's wealth is less than 15 per cent of the typical white household's. Most of our people are trapped in an almost bottomless economic pit from which there will be no escape – unless we change our political demands and strategy from what I have called in my writing "liberal integrationism" to a restructuring of economic resources, and the elimination of structural deficits that separate blacks and whites into unequal parallel racial universes. We live in the same country, we speak the same language, theoretically are governed by the same laws, but we encounter economic reality in fundamentally different ways. Reparations transforms the dynamics of the national racial discourse from an issue of handouts to paybacks. It parallels a global movement by people of African descent and other Third World people to renegotiate debt and to demand compensation for slavery, colonialism, and apartheid.

Wickham's argument that reparations advocates must articulate with one voice how and when the compensation should be paid is a seductive trap. Every social protest movement throughout history that has endeavored to achieve a broad strategic goal generates many different tactics and organizations to achieve it. It is only through the political struggle to win reparations – in the courtroom, in the media, at the grassroots level – that the specific reforms and measures for implementation take shape.

Economic reparations, the "payout question" that Wickham raises, could take a variety of forms, any of which could be practically implemented. I favor the establishment of a reparations social fund that would channel federal, state, and/or corporate funds for investment in nonprofit, community-based organizations, economic empowerment zones in areas with high rates of unemployment, and grants or interest-free loans for blacks to purchase homes or to start businesses in economically-depressed neighborhoods. However, there are other approaches to the reconstruction of black economic opportunity. Sociologist Dalton Conley has suggested processing "individual checks via the tax system, like a refundable slavery tax credit."[5] Major corporations and banks that were unjustly enriched by either slave labor or by Jim Crow-era discriminatory policies against African-Americans could set aside a portion of future profits in a trust fund to financially compensate their victims and their descendants. Universities whose endowments were based on the slave trade or on slave labor and/or companies that were unjustly enriched by racial segregation laws could create scholarship funds to give greater access to African-American students.

It would be dangerous and foolish for the proponents of reparations to quarrel among themselves over the best approach for implementation at this time. Over a generation ago, there were numerous divisions within the civil-rights movement that separated leaders and rival organizations. They all agreed on the general goal, the abolition of legal racial segregation, but espoused very different ways and tactics to get there. The same model should be applied to reparations. Any effort to impose rigid ideological or organizational conformity on this diverse and growing popular movement will only serve to disrupt and destroy it.

As the great revolutionary theorist Amilcar Cabral said, the greatest struggle of any oppressed people is not against their enemies; it's against their own weaknesses. That is the greatest struggle – the weaknesses of doubt and fear and uncertainty. The reparations demand is most liberating, I believe, for our young people – the next generation – because it has the potential to transform how black people see themselves, particularly in relationship to their own history. Part of this is understanding that the wages of slavery and segregation, for ghettoization and mass incarceration, must be paid.

Notes

1. Hakim Hasan, "Big Idea: Reparations Anxiety," *City Limits Monthly* (July/August 2002).
2. Ibid.
3. DeWayne Wickham, "Reparations-Payout Debate Undermines Support," *USA Today* (20 August 2002).
4. Ibid.
5. Hasan, "Big Idea: Reparations Anxiety."

TWENTY-TWO

KATRINA'S UNNATURAL DISASTER: A TRAGEDY OF BLACK SUFFERING AND WHITE DENIAL

Unquestionably, the September 2005 Hurricane Katrina was the largest natural disaster in US history. Yet, contrary to the assertions of President George W. Bush that no one could have "anticipated the breach of [New Orleans'] levees" and the massive flooding and destruction of one of America's historic cities in the wake of a major hurricane, the catastrophe we have witnessed was widely predicted for decades.[1] A 2002 special report of the New Orleans *Times-Picayune*, for example, warned: "It's only a matter of time before South Louisiana takes a direct hit from a major hurricane … Levees, our best protection from flooding, may turn against us." It predicted that such a disaster might "decimate the region" from flooding, and that in New Orleans, "100,000 will be left to face the fury."[2] That same year, in a *New York Times* editorial opinion, writer Adam Cohen predicted coldly: "If the Big One hits, New Orleans could disappear." A direct major hurricane strike, Cohen estimated, would certainly force Lake Pontchartrain's waters "over levees and into the city … there could be 100,000 deaths." Thousands "could be stranded on roofs, surrounded by a witches' brew of contaminated water."[3]

A natural disaster for New Orleans was statistically inevitable. But what made the New Orleans tragedy an unnatural disaster was the Federal government's gross incompetence and indifference in preparing the necessary measures to preserve the lives and property of hundreds of thousands of its citizens. The Federal Emergency Management Agency (FEMA), established in 1979, has been plagued for years with financial mismanagement, administrative incompetence and cronyism.

The litany of FEMA's bureaucratic blunders has been amply documented: its insistence that vital supplies of food, water, and medical aid were impossible to deliver to thousands of people stranded at New Orleans's downtown Morial Convention Center, though entertainers and reporters easily reached the site; its inability to rescue thousands of residents marooned on roofs and in flooded houses for days; the failure to seek deployment of active duty troops in large numbers until three days after Hurricane Katrina struck the Gulf Coast region. But the incompetence goes deeper than that. FEMA Director Michael Brown actually instructed fire departments in Louisiana, Mississippi and Alabama not to send emergency vehicles or personnel into devastated areas unless local or state officials communicated specific requests for them – at a time when most towns and cities lacked working telephones, fax machines, and internet access. Florida's proposal to send 500 airboats to assist rescue efforts was blocked by FEMA. Thousands of urgently needed generators, communications equipment, trailers, and freight cars of food went undelivered for weeks. Meanwhile, hundreds of dead bodies floated in New Orleans's streets and rotted in desolated houses. Millions of desperate Americans who attempted to phone FEMA's toll-free 800-number for assistance heard recorded messages that all lines were busy, or were disconnected.[4]

Even before Katrina struck, it was obvious that the overwhelming majority of New Orleans residents who would be trapped inside the city to face the deluge would be poor and working-class African-Americans, who comprised nearly 70 per cent of the city's population. As the levees collapsed and the city's Ninth Ward flooded, tens of thousands of evacuees were herded into the Superdome and Convention Center, where they were forced to endure days without toilets and running water, food, electricity, and medical help. Hundreds of black evacuees seeking escape on a bridge across the Mississippi River were confronted and forcibly pushed back into the city. One paramedic witnessing the incident stated: "I believe it was racism. It was callousness, it was cruelty."[5]

As the media began to document this unprecedented tragedy, the vast majority of New Orleans's victims were "the faces at the bottom of America's well – the poor, black and disabled," as reporters Monica Haynes and Erv Dyer of the Pittsburgh *Post-Gazette* observed. "The indelible television images of mostly black people living in subhuman conditions for nearly a week have prompted some to ask whether race played a role in how quickly or how not-so-quickly federal and state agencies responded in [Katrina's] aftermath."[6]

However, much of the media coverage cruelly manipulated racist stereotypes in its coverage. In one well-publicized example, the Associated Press released two photographs of New Orleans residents, wading through chest-deep water, carrying food obtained from a grocery store.

The whites were described as carrying "bread and soda from a local grocery store" that they found; the black man pictured was characterized as having "loot[ed] a grocery store."[7] A *London Financial Times* reporter, on 5 September 2005, declared New Orleans had become "a city of rape" and "a war zone," with thousands subjected to "looting" and "arson."[8] Administrators in Homeland Security and FEMA justified their lack of emergency aid by claiming that they had not anticipated that "people would loot gun stores ... and shoot at police, rescue officials and helicopters." The flood of racialized images of a terrorized, crime-engulfed city prompted hundreds of white ambulance drivers and emergency personnel to refuse to enter the New Orleans disaster zone. Television reports locally and nationally quickly proliferated false exposés about "babies in the Convention Center who got their throats cut" and "armed hordes" hijacking ambulances and trucks. Baton Rouge's mayor Kip Holden imposed a strict curfew on its facility that held evacuees, warning of possible violence by "New Orleans thugs."[9] That none of these sensationalized stories were true hardly mattered: as Matt Welch of the online publication *Reason* noted that the "deadly bigotry" of the media probably helped to "kill Katrina victims."[10]

The terrible destruction of thousands of homes and businesses, and relocation of over one million New Orleans and Gulf area residents, was perceived as a golden opportunity by corporate and conservative political elites who had long desired to remake the historic city. Even before the corpses of black victims had been cleared from New Orleans's flooded streets, corporations closely associated with George W. Bush's administration secured noncompetitive, multi-billion-dollar reconstruction contracts. Brown and Root, a subsidiary of Halliburton, for example, was awarded the contract to reconstruct Louisiana and Mississippi naval bases. Bechtel was authorized to provide short-term housing for several hundred thousand displaced evacuees. Shaw, the Louisiana engineering corporation, received lucrative contracts for rebuilding throughout the area. Bush waived provisions of the Davis-Bacon Act, allowing corporations to hire workers below the minimum wage. After Congress authorized over $100 billion for the region's reconstruction, Halliburton's stock price surged on Wall Street.[11] Local corporate subcontractors and developers who directly profited from federal subsidies set into motion plans for what local African-Americans feared could quickly become a gentrification removal of thousands of black households from devastated urban neighborhoods.

Behind the plans to "rebuild" New Orleans may be racially inspired objectives by Republicans to reduce the size of the city's all-black voting precincts. About 60 per cent of New Orleans's electorate is African-

American, which normally turns out at 50 per cent in local elections. All-white affluent neighborhoods have turnout rates exceeding 70 per cent. In the 1994 mayoral race, only 6 per cent of the city's white voters supported successful black candidate Marc Morial.[12]

African-American political analyst Earl Ofari Hutchinson speculated that "the loss of thousands of black votes" could easily "crack the thirty years of Black, and Democratic dominance of City Hall in New Orleans." The seat of black Democrat William Jefferson, who represents the city in Congress, could be in jeopardy. Even more serious, as Hutchinson observed, was that the massive African-American vote in New Orleans in 2000 and 2004 "enabled Democrats to bag many top state and local offices, but just narrowly. A shift of a few thousand votes could tip those offices back to Republicans."[13]

Nationally, most African-American leaders, public officials, and intellectuals were overwhelmed and outraged by the flood of racist stereotypes in the media, and their government's appalling inaction to rescue thousands of black and poor people. They observed that the most devastated sections of the city were nearly all-black and mostly poor. Local blacks had been largely ignored in preparations for evacuating the city.[14] Beverly Wright, the director of Xavier University's Deep South Center for Environmental Justice, expressed the general sentiment of most African-Americans by declaring: "I am very angry, and I really, really believe that [the crisis] is driven by race.... When you look at who is left behind, it is very disturbing to me."[15] Wright's viewpoint was echoed by many black intellectuals. For example, Harvard professor Lani Guinier observed, in the American society "poor black people are the throw-away people. And we pathologize them in order to justify our disregard."[16] Some reporters assigned to the Katrina crisis soon began to reflect these mounting criticisms. *Detroit Free Press* columnist Desiree Cooper drew parallels between the economic devastation of New Orleans and Detroit, noting, "the poverty rate in both cities rivals that of Third World nations. So as I watched the hurricane coverage with racism and poverty, creating the perfect storm, I couldn't help but think: If Detroit were underwater, no one would bother to rescue us either."[17]

By mid-September 2005, 60 per cent of African-Americans surveyed in a national poll believed that "the federal government's delay in helping the victims in New Orleans was because the victims were black." By contrast, only 12 per cent of white Americans agreed.[18] In response, the Bush administration unleashed its black apologists to deny any racial intent of its policies and actions. Secretary of State Condoleezza Rice insisted: "Nobody, especially the President, would have left people unattended."[19] Black conservative ideologue John McWhorter, a senior fellow at the Manhattan Institute, ridiculed the accusations of racism as "nasty, circular, [and] unprovable.... It's not a matter of somebody in Washington deciding we don't need to rush [to New Orleans] because they're all poor jungle bunnies anyway."[20]

African-Americans were stunned and perplexed by white America's general apathy and denial about the racial implications of the Katrina catastrophe. On a nationally televised fundraiser for the hurricane's victims, rap artist Kanye West sparked controversy by denouncing "the way America is set up to help the poor, the black people, the less well off as slow as possible."[21] Blacks were especially infuriated with the descriptions of poor black evacuees as "refugees" by officials and the media. black Congresswoman Diane Watson protested vigorously, "'Refugee' calls up to mind people that come here from different lands and have to be taken care of... These are American citizens."[22] But the racial stigmatization of New Orleans's outcasts forced many African-Americans to ponder whether their government and white institutions had become incapable of expressing true compassion for the suffering of their people. Prominent Princeton professor Cornel West, at a Columbia University forum sponsored by the Institute for Research in African-American Studies, asked whether "*black suffering* [his emphasis] is required for the preservation of white America."[23]

West's provocative query ought to be explored seriously. The US government and America's entire political economy were constructed on a racial foundation. Blacks were excluded by race from civic participation and voting for several hundred years; they were segregated into residential ghettoes, denied credit and capital by banks, and relegated to the worst jobs for generations. Over time, popular cultural and social attitudes about black subordination and white superiority were aggressively reinforced by the weight of discriminatory law and public policy. Psychologically, is the specter of black suffering and death in some manner reaffirming the traditional racial hierarchy, the practices of black exclusion and marginalization?

Even before Katrina's racial debate had receded from the media, the question of racial insensitivity was posed again by former Reagan Education Secretary William Bennett's remarks in a national radio broadcast. In early October 2005, Bennett announced to his radio audience: "I do know that it's true that if you wanted to reduce crime, you could – if that were your sole purpose – you could abort every black baby in this country, and your crime rate would go down." Perhaps covering his racial gaffe, Bennett immediately added, "That would be an impossible, ridiculous and morally reprehensible thing to do, but your crime rate would go down." *New York Times* columnist Bob Herbert interpreted Bennett's remarks as the central aspect of the Republican Party's "bigotry, racially divisive tactics and outright anti-black policies. That someone who's been a stalwart of that outfit might muse publicly about the potential benefits of exterminating blacks is not surprising to me at all ... Bill Bennett's twisted fantasies are a malignant outgrowth of our polarized past."[24] Bennett's repugnant statements, combined with most white Americans' blind refusal to recognize a racial tragedy in New Orleans, illustrate how deeply rooted racial injustice remains in America.

Has the public spectacle of black suffering and anguish evolved into what might be defined as a "civic ritual," reconfirming the racial hierarchy with blackness permanently relegated to a subordinate status? During the summer of 2005, the US Senate seemed to confirm Cornel West's hypothesis, as it was forced to confront the civic ritual of lynching. Between 1882 and 1927, over 3,500 blacks were lynched in the United States, with about 95 per cent occurring in the South. An unknown number of additional African-Americans were killed, especially in rural and remote areas where we have few means to reconstruct these crimes.

In Marion, Indiana, on 7 August 1930, a massive white mob stormed the jail in the local county courthouse, seizing two incarcerated African-American teenagers, Thomas Shipp and Abram Smith, who had been accused of raping a white woman. Within less than an hour, a festive gathering of several thousand white women and men armed with baseball bats, crowbars, and guns beat and then lynched the two black boys. A photograph of the Marion lynching that was reproduced in the book I co-authored with Leith Mullings, *Freedom*, depicts smiling young adults, a pregnant woman, teenage girls and a middle-aged man, pointing proudly to one of the dangling corpses.[25]

A third young African-American, a sixteen-year-old shoeshine boy named James Cameron, was also seized and beaten by the mob that night. Several men lifted Cameron up and a noose was slipped around his neck. Just at that moment, a local white man in the crowd pushed forward and declared that young Cameron was innocent. Years later, on 13 June 2005, speaking at a US Senate news conference, 91-year-old James Cameron recalled: "They took the rope off my neck, those hands that had been so rough and ready to kill or had already killed, they took the rope off my neck and they allowed me to start walking and stagger back to jail, which was just a half-block away."[26] Cameron, the only known survivor of an attempted lynching, had come to the Capitol as part of an effort to obtain a formal apology from the Senate for its historic refusal to pass federal legislation outlawing lynching. For decades, Southern senators had filibustered legislative attempts to ratify anti-lynching legislation, denouncing such bills as an unnecessary interference with states' rights. Prompted by the emotional testimony of Cameron and the family members and descendants of lynching victims, the Senate finally issued an apology for lynching – the first time in United States history that Congress has acknowledged and expressed regret for historical crimes against African-Americans – in a formal resolution. What was most significant, perhaps, was that only eighty-five of the one hundred US senators had co-sponsored the resolution when it came up for a voice vote. The fifteen senators who did not initially co-sponsor the bill were Republicans. Belatedly, seven senators subsequently signed an oversized copy of the senate's anti-lynching resolution, which was to be publicly displayed. The eight senators who still refused to concede an apology are Lamar Alexander (R–Tennessee); Thad Cochran (R–Mississippi), John Cornyn (R–Texas), Michael Enzi (R-Wyoming), Judd Gregg (R–New Hampshire), Trent Lott (R–Mississippi), John Sununu (R–New Hampshire), and Craig Thomas (R–Wyoming).[27]

Why the steadfast refusal to acknowledge the forensic evidence and the obvious human pain and suffering inflicted not only on the victims of racist violence, but also upon their descendants? Because, in a racist society – by this I mean a society deeply stratified, with "whiteness" defined at the top and "blackness" occupying the bottom rungs – the obliteration of the black past is absolutely essential to the preservation of white hegemony, or domination. Since race itself is a fraudulent concept, devoid of scientific reality, racism can only be rationalized and justified through the suppression of black accounts or evidence that challenges society's understanding about itself and its own past. Racism is perpetuated and reinforced by the historical logic of whiteness, which repeatedly presents whites as the primary (and frequently sole) actors in the important decisions that have influenced the course of human events. This kind of history deliberately excludes blacks and other racialized groups from having the capacity to become actors in shaping major social outcomes.

In this process of falsification, two elements are crucial: the suppression of evidence of black resistance, and the obscuring of any records of white crimes and exploitation committed against blacks as an oppressed group. In this manner, white Americans can more easily absolve themselves of the historical responsibility for the actions of their great-grandparents, grandparents, parents – and of themselves. Thus the destructive consequences of modern structural racism that can be easily measured by social scientists within contemporary US society today as well as the human suffering we have witnessed in New Orleans – can be said to have absolutely nothing to do with racism. Denial of responsibility for racism permits the racial chasm in America to grow wider with each passing year.

When the "unnatural disaster" of the New Orleans tragedy of race and class is examined in the context of American structural racism, the denial by many whites of the reality of black suffering becomes clear. It parallels the denial of the Turkish government of the massive genocide of the Armenian population committed by the former Ottoman empire in 1915–1916. It mirrors the repulsive anti-Semitism of those who to this day deny the horrific reality of the Holocaust during World War Two. Until the denial of suffering ceases, there is no possibility of constructing meaningful, corrective measures in addressing the racial chasm that continues to fracture the foundations of democratic life and a truly civil society in America.

Notes

1. Ted Steinberg, "A Natural Disaster, and a Human Tragedy," *Chronicle of Higher Education* 52: 5 (23 September 2005), 811–12.
2. John McQuaid and Mark Schleifstein, "Washing Away," five-part special series, *Times-Picayune* (23–27 June 2002).
3. Adam Cohen, "If the Big One Hits, New Orleans Could Disappear," *New York Times* (11 August 2002); also see Jon Nordheimer, "Nothing's Easy for New Orleans Flood Control," *New York Times* (30 April 2002).
4. Editorial, "Truly Clueless at FEMA," *Boston Herald* (8 September 2005); Editorial, "Political Appointments, Loss of Focus, Crippled Disaster Relief Agency," *USA Today* (8 September 2005); Tina Susman, "FEMA: Effort mired in bureaucratic hash," *Newsday* (11 September 2005); Jonathan S. Landay, Alison Young, and Shannon McCaffrey, "Was FEMA's Brown the Fall Guy?", *Seattle Times* (14 September 2005); Angie C. Marek, Edward T. Pound, Danielle Knight, Julian E. Barnes, Judd Slivka and Kevin Whitelaw, "A Crisis Agency in Crisis," *U.S. News and World Report* (19 September 2005); and Editorial, "FEMA: Just a Money Pit?," *Hartford Courant* (23 September 2005).
5. Andrew Buncombe, "'Racist' Police Blocked Bridge and Forced Evacuees Back at Gunpoint," *Independent* (11 September 2005).
6. Monica Haynes and Erv Dyer, "Black Faces are Indelible Image of Katrina," *Independent* (4 September 2005).
7. Aaron Kinney, "'Looting' or 'Finding'?", *Salon.com*, available at www.salon.com/new/features/2005/09/01/photo_controversy/.
8. Guy Dinmore, "City of Rape, Rumour and Recrimination," *Financial Times* [London], (5 September 2005).
9. David Caruso, "Disaster Official at NY Symposium: Planners didn't anticipate gun problem after Katrina," *Newsday* (12 September 2005).
10. Matt Welch, "The Deadly Bigotry of Low Expectations? Did the rumor mill help kill Katrina victims?", *Reason*, available at www.reason.com/links/links090605.shtml.

11. Katherine Griffiths, "Firms Linked with Bush get Katrina Clean-Up Work," *The Independent* (17 September 2005); and Scott Van Voorhis, "Katrina Boon to Builders," *Boston Herald* (6 September 2005).

12. Coleman Warner, "Primary Turnout Makes Black Vote Crucial in Runoff," *Times-Picayune* (7 February 1994).

13. Earl Ofari Hutchinson, "Katrina Wallops Black Voters," available from *hutchinsonreport@aol.com*.

14. Jonathan Curiel, "Disaster Aid Raises Race Issue: Critics say poor blacks not considered in planning for emergencies, evacuations," *San Francisco Chronicle* (3 September 2005).

15. Alex Tzon, "Katrina's Aftermath: Images of the Victims Spark a Racial Debate; some say authorities' response time is affected by the victims' skin color," *Los Angeles Times* (3 September 2005).

16. Lynne Duke and Teresa Wiltz, "A Nation's Castaways; Katrina Blew In, and Tossed Up Reminders of a Tattered Racial Legacy," *Washington Post* (4 September 2005).

17. Desiree Cooper, "Outrage, Carrying Mix in Katrina Response," *Detroit Free Press* (15 September 2005).

18. CNN, *USA Today* and Gallup poll, released 13 September 2005, cited in ibid. Other opinion polls confirmed that most black Americans believed that racism was behind the federal government's inaction to aid Katrina's victims. A Pew Institute poll, for example, indicated that 66 per cent of Blacks surveyed "felt the government would have reacted faster if the stranded victims had been mainly white rather than black." See Alex Massie, "Racial tensions simmer as blacks bear brunt of slow official response," *The Scotsman*, available at www.Scotsman.com/?id=1920892005.

19. Elisabeth Bumiller, "Gulf Coast Isn't the Only Thing Left in Tatters; Bush's Status with Blacks Takes a Hit," *New York Times* (12 September 2005).

20. Duke and Wiltz, "A Nation's Castaways."

21. Kanye West, quoted on "The O'Reilly Factor," Fox News Network (8 September 2005).

22. Robert E. Pierre and Paul Farhi, "'Refugee': A Word of Trouble," *Washington Post* (7 September 2005).

23. Cornel West remarks, "When Affirmative Action Was White," symposium, Institute for Research in African-American Studies, Columbia University, New York City (1 October 2005).

24. Bob Herbert, "Impossible, Ridiculous, Repugnant," *New York Times* (6 October 2005).

25. See Manning Marable and Leith Mullings, *Freedom: A Photographic History of the African American Struggle* (London 2002), p. 132.

26. Sheryl Gay Stolberg, "Senate Issues Apology Over Failure on Anti-Lynching Law," *New York Times* (14 June 2005).

27. "Eight U.S. Senators Decline to Cosponsor Resolution Apologizing for Failure to Enact Anti-Lynching Legislation," *Journal of Blacks in Higher Education Weekly Bulletin* (30 June 2005); Avis Thomas-Lester, "Repairing Senate's Record on Lynching," *Washington Post* (11 June 2005).

TWENTY-THREE

RACIALIZING JUSTICE, DISENFRANCHISING LIVES: TOWARD AN ANTI-RACIST CRIMINAL JUSTICE

Prison is a legitimate criminal sanction – but it should be used sensibly, justly, parsimoniously, and with due consideration for the principles of proportionality and respect for human dignity required by international human rights law. The incarceration of hundreds of thousands of low-level nonviolent drug offenders betrays indifference to such considerations.

Human Rights Watch, May, 2000[1]

Throughout the entire racial history of the United States, a series of state-sanctioned institutions excited that have "regulated" the African-American population, for the purpose of preserving white power and privilege. During the first two-and-a-half centuries of the black presence on the North American continent, the predominant mode of black oppression was enslavement. Blacks as a group were relegated outside of civil society; they were legally defined as private property, not citizens, and were largely excluded from legal and constitutional rights. After a brief experiment in biracial democracy known as "Reconstruction" (1865–1877), African-Americans were relegated to a subordinate economic and social status through the regime of Jim Crow segregation. Although technically free, the majority of blacks found themselves tethered to the land by sharecropping, debt peonage, "convict-leasing" and other forms of penury. Into the twentieth century, as millions of rural Southern blacks migrated to the industrial Northeast and Midwest, seeking employment and a better way of life, they quickly confronted a newer form of racial exclusion and stigmatization – the urban ghetto. Ghettoization once again relegated blacks to the margins of America's commercial, cultural and political life; through policies such as "redlining" by banks and financial institutions, blacks were denied credit and capital to purchase their own homes and businesses. They continued to encounter fierce discrimination in employment, and suffered from substandard schools, health facilities and housing. Each of these institutional barriers to racial access and opportunity reinforced the deep-seated cultural and psychological assumptions of black inferiority that millions of white Americans uncritically accepted as normative and customary.

American racial history was fundamentally altered by the dramatic events of 1954–1975, when an unprecedented series of civil demonstrations, legal maneuvers and political interventions challenged the legitimacy of Jim Crow segregation. A formation of civil-rights groups with widely divergent tactics and political ideologies – such as the National Association for the Advancement of Colored People (NAACP), the Congress of Racial Equality (CORE), the Southern Christian Leadership Conference (SCLC), and the Student Nonviolent Coordinating Committee (SNCC) – all contributed in different ways to barring segregation from public life. The pressure they exerted on the political establishment produced major legislative victories, such as the 1964 Civil Rights Act, and the 1965 Voting Rights Act. Presidents John F. Kennedy, Lyndon B. Johnson and Richard M. Nixon signed a series of Executive Orders establishing the principles of "affirmative action" and "equal opportunity," creating avenues for advancing minorities and women in both the public and private sectors. Under Johnson, new social welfare programs, public housing and health programs were extended to the poor, all of which reduced the percentage of blacks' poverty and narrowed the historic wage gap between African-Americans and whites. Indirectly, the hegemony of the civil-rights discourse had a positive impact on other public-policy debates, moving the nation to the left on a host of issues. The Supreme Court, for example, outlawed the imposition of the death penalty nationally, and ordered in a series of decisions new measures required by local law enforcement to protect the Constitutional rights of citizens accused of crimes (e.g. the *Miranda* decision).

The consequences of these political victories for the advancement of black freedom were numerous and, in retrospect, somewhat unanticipated. There was the rapid, unprecedented growth of an African-American professional, administrative, clerical and managerial class comprising, by 1980, nearly a quarter of the formal black labor force. This social group was the primary product of affirmative action and equal opportunity enforcement. Black entrepreneurs as a social category also quadrupled in size in less than two decades, as the federal government and cities adopted "minority economic set-aside provisions" guaranteeing a certain percentage of government contracts to minority and women vendors.

Within electoral politics, African-American representation in Congress soared, from five in 1964 to over thirty-five three decades later. Beginning in 1967, with the election of African-American mayors in Gary, Indiana, and Cleveland, black candidates won a string of impressive mayoral victories – in Los Angeles, Atlanta, Detroit, Newark, New Orleans, Philadelphia, Denver, and elsewhere. Such successes fostered the illusion by the 1970s that the nation, as a whole, had somehow managed to purge itself of the debilitating effects of white racism and black oppression. What went largely unexamined was the rapid growth of an urban class of black unemployed and low-wage workers whose material conditions were becoming increasingly worse. Millions of blacks and Latinos, trapped inside the rotting central cores of America's deindustrialized cities, lacked meaningful avenues of economic survival.

The historic turning point in how race was managed by the state occurred under the aegis of the Reagan administration, in 1981–1989. A conservative Republican, Ronald Reagan was deeply hostile to the policies of welfare state capitalism that had flourished under Johnson. In relatively short order, social welfare programs, food stamps, public housing, and job training programs were either eliminated or severely curtailed. A massive military expansion, designed to challenge and ultimately bankrupt the Soviet Union, was launched. Behind these policy initiatives was a political-philosophical approach that, two decades later, the world would come to know as "neo-liberalism." As famed urban geographer David Harvey has explained, the Reagan administration "emphasized that the role of government was to create a good business climate rather than look to the needs and well-being of the population at large." This meant, for example, "elaborate revisions in the tax code – mainly concerning depreciation on investments – [that] allowed many corporations to get away without paying any taxes at all, while the reduction of the top tax rate for individuals from 78 to 28 per cent obviously reflected the intent to restore class power." The strength of organized labor was systematically broken, as corporations were freed to jettison their pension obligations to employees. Harvey adds, "Worst of all, public assets were freely passed over into the private domain."[2]

The conservative politics of "neo-liberalism" required a fresh approach in dealing with African-American demands on the state. Internationally, the Reagan administration forged an informal alliance with the white-minority regime of apartheid South Africa, offered covert assistance to terrorists destabilizing the fragile independent African states of Mozambique and Angola, and in 1983, militarily invaded the black Caribbean island of Grenada. Domestically, the administration sought to end civil rights enforcement and to purge the US Civil Rights Commission of its liberal critics. These maneuvers were only partially successful. Americans, regardless of race, still retained a clear understanding of what the central debates had been about regarding the elimination of legal segregation, which was the result of mass, democratic protests, court challenges, and nonviolent, civil disobedience campaigns led by Martin Luther King, Jr., and many others. The majority of white Americans, at that time, still supported affirmative action and reforms such as race-sensitive scholarship programs to compensate blacks for generations of unfair exclusion from colleges. Dozens of major public school districts across the country continued to be under court-ordered desegregation sanctions. Moreover, the racial animus and hostility of the Reaganites precipitated new waves of black collective resistance in the 1980s: e.g., Harold Washington's remarkable mayoral victories in Chicago in 1983 and 1987; Jesse Jackson's "Rainbow Coalition" presidential campaigns of 1984 and 1988; the anti-apartheid campaign of 1984–87, which successfully broke the administration's "Constructive Engagement" strategy with South Africa, and initiated divestments by banks, corporations and universities from dealings with South Africa.

By the mid-1980s, however, the Reagan administration's approach toward the regulation of the urban black poor took a new tack. Justice Department officials encouraged local and state law enforcement officials to become "more aggressive" in efforts to combat urban crime. Municipalities began initiating massive street sweeps, and "buy and bust" operations in predominantly black, brown and poor neighborhoods. According to the research of Human Rights Watch, these "police activities have heavily targeted participants in street retail drug transactions in these neighborhoods. Not surprisingly, comparably few of the people arrested there have been white." Police and state highway patrol officers increased "racial profiling" – the "police practice of stopping, questioning, and searching minorities in vehicles or on the street based solely on their appearance."[3] The result of these policies directly contributed to a profound change in the *racial composition of Americans incarcerated in federal and state correctional facilities*. In 1979, for example, 39 per cent of all individuals admitted to state and federal prisons that year were African-Americans. By 1990, black Americans comprised 53 per cent of all prisoner admissions.[4]

Between 1982 and 1989, the overall number of prisoners in US correctional facilities rose from approximately 650,000 to one million. Conservatives insisted that this increase was the social cost of combating violent criminals and drug addicts who were threatening to destroy America's cities and suburbs. Yet crime statistics did not provide a rational explanation for this unprecedented growth. In the mid-1980s, violent crime rates across the board – that is, the national rates for murder, robbery, rape, burglary, etc. – peaked and began to decline. (The sole exception was an increase in the number of aggravated assaults nationally.) Nevertheless, the political rhetoric deploring "unchecked violent crime" accelerated; in the media, sensational stories usually highlighting black perpetrators of crime became ubiquitous. Hundreds of US cities and towns, with billions of dollars in federal assistance, greatly expanded local police agencies. Many established SWAT teams, or "Special Weapons and Tactics" squads, possessing paramilitary weaponry and armored vehicles, to combat the scourge of minority crime. Major cities like New York City developed plainclothes police squads such as the Street Crimes Unit, which conducted warrantless searches, stop-and-frisk operations and random racial profiling of blacks and Latinos, particularly in predominantly white neighborhoods. The Reagan administration, and later, the Republican administration of George H.W. Bush, praised such measures as a War on Drugs.

The hidden racial paradox in America's celebrated War on Drugs was that, throughout the 1980s and 1990s – when both powdered cocaine and crack cocaine were introduced and, for about a decade, proliferated in both urban and suburban markets – *the overwhelming majority of illegal drug abusers was white.* As of 1998, approximately 62 million white Americans had, at some point in their lives, consumed illegal drugs – marijuana, crack, powdered cocaine, heroin, etc.. Of that number, according to the Substance Abuse and Mental Health Administration (SAMHSA), 18.5 million whites had used powdered cocaine; 2.7 million had consumed it during 1998, with about 1.1 million abusing cocaine at least monthly. By contrast, only an estimated 8.2 million African-Americans had ever used illicit drugs in their lifetimes. Only 2.1 million blacks had ever tried powdered cocaine, with 1 million using crack at least once. If racial fairness existed in the policies and practices of law enforcement, one might reasonably expect that the racial demographics of those arrested and subsequently imprisoned for illicit drug sales and usage would conform with the general profile of users established by the Substance Abuse and Mental Health Administration. In short, millions of white illicit drug abusers somehow evaded, or avoided detection, surveillance, arrest and prosecution during the national War on Drugs.[5]

How did this happen? The illicit drugs of choice for white middle-class Americans were primarily marijuana and powdered cocaine in the 1990s. Despite the continued existence of federal, state and local laws against marijuana possession and sale, by 1996 only 4.3 per cent of all admissions to correctional facilities were the result of marijuana-related arrests. In most jurisdictions, district attorneys largely stopped

Table 1   Comparison of drug use and arrests by race, 1979–1998

Year	Black		White	
	% of current drug users	% of drug arrests	% of current drug users	% of drug arrests
1979	10.8	21.8	87.8	76.7
1985	12.4	30.0	86.6	68.9
1991	15.3	41.0	83.9	59.4
1995	16.2	36.9	82.7	62.1
1998	16.9	37.3	82.0	61.5

Source: Cited in "Punishment and Prejudice: Racial Disparities in the War on Drugs," *Human Rights Watch* 12:2 (May 2000), Table 18.

prosecuting first-time marijuana arrests. In the state of Michigan, for example, in 1996, marijuana offenders comprised barely 0.1 per cent of all drug-related admission to state prisons that year. Similar statistics for the low percentages of marijuana admissions to state prisons were recorded in North Carolina (0.05 per cent), Pennsylvania (0.4 per cent), Nevada (0.5 per cent), Wisconsin (0.5 per cent) and New York (0.6 per cent) in 1996.[6] The federal anti-drug authorities made the strategic decision to focus their activities not in the suburbs, where the numerical majority of illicit drug abusers lived, but in hardcore, central cities, in the most impoverished neighborhoods. According to a 1991–1994 national survey conducted by SAMHSA, of the US Department of Health and Human Services, African-Americans comprised approximately 16 per cent of admitted illicit drug dealers, and whites accounted for 82 per cent. Yet inexplicably, "the percentage of black drug arrests was at least double the percentage of blacks among current drug users. Whites, conversely, were under-arrested, that is, they constituted a smaller per cent of drug arrests than they did of drug users."[7] These trends continued throughout the 1990s. A 1998 SAMHSA survey found that "there were almost five times as many current white marijuana users as black and four times as many white cocaine users. Almost three times as many whites had ever used crack as blacks" – as shown in Table 1.

The War on Drugs quickly deteriorated into a race-conscious war on urban black and, to a lesser extent, Latino communities. Federal sentencing guidelines required significantly longer prison terms for drug abusers convicted of crack offenses, than for powdered cocaine.

Following the lead of New York State, which in the 1970s had adopted its draconian Rockefeller Drug Laws, state after state established mandatory-minimum sentencing laws for drug-related offenses, taking away discretionary powers from judges. In many jurisdictions, all-white juries were predisposed (or, due to the media, "preconditioned") to question or to dismiss evidence exonerating blacks accused of drug offenses.[8]

In almost every state, the numbers of prisoners grew beyond the capacities of correctional officials and facilities to manage them. The experience of New York State provides a typical example. From 1813 until 1981, New York State had constructed 33 state prisons, including Sing-Sing (Ossining) and Attica. In the following two decades, the state was forced to build another 38 correctional facilities. Nearly all of these prisons were located in predominantly white, rural areas in upstate New York, frequently hundreds of miles from major metropolitan areas. These facilities generated tens of thousands of new jobs for rural whites. Statewide, the prisoner population soared from 12,500 in 1971 to 71,000 by 1999. To pay for this massive prison expansion, New York's legislature reallocated hundreds of millions of dollars from the state's traditional subsidies to the State University of New York system (SUNY) and the City University of New York (CUNY) system. According to the Correctional Association of New York, and the Washington, D.C.-based Justice Policy Institute, between fiscal years 1988 and 1998, "New York's public universities have seen their operating budgets plummet by 29 per cent while funding for prisons has increased by 76 per cent. In actual dollars, that nearly has been an equal trade-off, with the Department of Correctional Sciences receiving a $761 million increase during that time while the state funding for New York's city and state university systems has declined by $615 million."[9]

The public policy trade-off between prisons and public colleges represented a double blow to black, Latino and low-income New Yorkers, who were disproportionately subjected to racial profiling, indiscriminate police sweeps, and drug-related arrests. CUNY had for decades been the primary institution of access and opportunity for first-generation minority and immigrant college students. Severe budgetary cuts forced university administrators to hike tuition costs significantly, placing education beyond the means of thousands of working-class students. The 1998 study of the Correctional Association of New York, and the Justice Policy Institute found: "There are more blacks (34,809) and Hispanics (22,421) locked up in prison than there are attending the State University of New York, where there are 27,925 black and Hispanic students." Between 1989 and 1998, "there were more blacks entering the prison system for drug offenses each year than there were graduating from SUNY with undergraduate, masters and doctoral degrees combined."[10] In 1995, Federal subsidies supporting Pell Grant financial aid to prisoners who were enrolled in college programs were terminated, and most states quickly followed suit. Despite substantial criminological evidence indicating that prisoners who enter educational programs have significantly lower recidivism rates, federal and state authorities were prepared to severely curtail, and in many cases eliminate, all college credit courses behind bars. By 1997, only 35 per cent of all prisoners released that year had ever enrolled in educational programs during their time of incarceration. Only 27 per cent had participated in vocational or job training programs to prepare them for gainful employment.[11]

Under the Democratic administration of President Bill Clinton (1993–2001), the essentially coercive model of racializing criminal justice and law enforcement constructed by Republicans was permitted to continue. Under Clinton's tenure, another 700,000 prisoners were added to the nation's correctional facilities. A series of popular films – "New Jack City," "Boyz in da Hood," "Juice," "Menace 2 Society" – popularized the image of the criminalized young black male. White juries, when confronted with circumstantial evidence of illicit drug use and sales in connection with African-American and Latino males, had little difficulty making the connections. This was particularly true in the US South, where the longstanding traditions of white supremacy and black oppression were still deeply engrained in the legal process. In Louisiana, for example, 73 per cent of all new admissions to that state's prisons by 1996 were African-Americans. In other formerly segregated and/or slave states, the patterns were similar: in Alabama, 64 per cent of all 1996 entering convicts were black; in Georgia, 65 per cent; Maryland, 79 per cent; North Carolina, 63 per cent; South Carolina, 68 per cent; and Virginia, 65 per cent. By 1996, in eleven states – including New Hampshire, Montana, Kansas, South Dakota, Wisconsin, Utah and Wyoming – the percentage of black prisoners represented more than six times their racial group's percentage of each state's population. In Minnesota and Iowa, African-American prisoners in 1996 constituted a proportion that was more than 12 times each state's share of their respective black populations.[12]

The national law enforcement drive to "incarcerate young blacks as a criminal class" in the 1990s reached absurd dimensions. In California, for example, in 1996, African-Americans in that state were statistically eleven times more likely than whites to be incarcerated in state prisons. In Texas, 2,575 per 100,000 African-Americans were imprisoned, compared to 224 per 100,000 whites, a twelve to one ratio. Other states had even higher ratios: in New Jersey, black rates of incarceration were thirteen

Table 2   Rates of incarceration to state prisons by race, per 100,000, nationally and in selected states, 1996

	Black	White	Black:White ratio
National	1,547	188	8:1
District of Columbia	2,720	81	34:1
Minnesota	1,383	59	23:1
Iowa	2,818	159	18:1
Wisconsin	2,210	131	17:1
Pennsylvania	1,681	108	16:1
Illinois	1,395	98	14:1
New Jersey	1,526	115	13:1
Texas	2,575	224	12:1
California	1,909	168	11:1
Idaho	951	265	4:1
Hawaii	579	219	3:1
Vermont	451	178	3:1

Source: Data of the Bureau of Justice Statistics, and the US Bureau of the Census, quoted in "Punishment and Prejudice: Racial Disparities in the War on Drugs," *Human Rights Watch* 12:2 (May 2000), Table 3.

times higher than those of whites; in Illinois, the racial ratio was fourteen to one; Pennsylvania, sixteen to one; Wisconsin, seventeen to one; Iowa, eighteen to one; Minnesota, twenty-three to one; and in the District of Columbia, a remarkable thirty-four to one – as shown in Table 2. To ensure that African-American and Latino criminals remained behind bars as long as possible, state after state toughened requirements for the successful completion of parole. In 1984, for example, 70 per cent of all former prisoners successfully completed parole, allowing them to reenter society. By 1998, only 45 per cent of all former prisoners were judged to have successfully completed the requirements of parole; 42 per cent were returned to prison.[13]

During the Clinton administration, federal and state law enforcement placed greater emphasis on the arrest and incarceration of black and Latina women, particularly nonviolent drug offenders. As a consequence, between 1990 and 1997, the female incarceration rate in the United

States nearly doubled, from 31 per 100,000, to 57 per 100,000. By 1997, African-American women were over eight times more likely than white women to be in prison – despite the fact that there were millions more white women who regularly used and sold illicit drugs than all women of color abusers combined. The vast majority of these new women convicts were the result of "anti-drug" mandatory-minimum sentencing laws, such as California's "Three Strikes and You're Out" law, requiring a life sentence after the third felony conviction. Between 1986 and 1996, the number of women nationally who were convicted and incarcerated on drug charges rose an astonishing 888 per cent.[14] The socially destructive consequences upon millions of African-American and Latino households by the imprisonment of thousands of mostly nonviolent, drug-offending women are not difficult to calculate. Tens of thousands of brown and black children were placed into foster care, or ended up in juvenile correctional facilities. Thousands of marriages and long-term relationships between partners were destroyed; working-class black and Latino households frequently went into ruinous debt to provide legal aid and financial help to relatives and children ensnared in the legal apparatus.

Perhaps the most terrible outrages of the racialized criminal justice system were borne by black and Latino children and young adults. In April 2000, the FBI, Clinton's Justice Department, and six major foundations released a study of the unequal justice experienced by black and Latino juveniles throughout the US. The statistical evidence was stunning, even to many criminologists and law enforcement officials. As of 2000, African-Americans under the age of eight comprised 15 per cent of their national age group, but comprised 26 per cent of all who were arrested by police. Once placed into the juvenile justice system, African-American youth and white youth experienced radically different legal experiences and outcomes, even when charged with identical crimes. Two-thirds of all whites were referred to juvenile courts, compared to less than one-third of all African-American youths. By 2000, black young people comprised over 40 per cent of all juveniles incarcerated in the nation's juvenile correctional facilities, and represented 58 per cent of all youths placed in adult prisons. For those young people who had never been to prison previously, African-American youths were nine times more likely than whites to be given time inside juvenile facilities. For young people charged with illicit drug-related offenses, *black youths were 48 times more likely than white youths to be sentenced to serve time inside juvenile correctional institutions.* The statistical probability that 48 times represents a racially-neutral or color-blind process of legal decision-making is nonexistent.[15]

In November 1994, conservative Republicans won majorities in both the US Senate and House of Representatives. The Clinton administration and the majority of Democrats, fearful of being pilloried by conservatives as "weak on crime," did little to halt this erosion of racial justice in the courts and correctional facilities. It was only in the late 1990s, as Democrats prepared for the 2000 national elections, that the dire political consequences of the War on Drugs, mandatory-minimum sentences, and selective prosecutions of black and brown drug offenders became clear. In 1998, the Sentencing Project, a non-profit research center in Washington, D.C., released a study surveying the impact of racialized mass incarceration upon the nation's political system. That year, 47 states, including the District of Columbia, prohibited prisoners from voting. In 32 states, former prisoners who had been released and were on parole were not permitted to vote. In ten states, including Florida, Mississippi and Alabama, former felons were excluded from voting for the remainder of their lives. Conservatively, the Sentencing Project calculated that about four million Americans as of 1998 had lost their constitutional right to vote, permanently or temporarily. In racial terms, roughly 13 per cent of all African-American males could not vote. Since 85 to 90 per cent of the black electorate supports Democratic candidates in national elections, the loss of several million potential voters represented a serious loss to the party's electoral base. From the vantage point of civil-rights organizations, the racialized processes of mass incarceration were, in effect, rolling back the effectiveness of the historic 1965 Voting Rights Act, which had been necessary to ensure that blacks, especially in the US South, had access to the ballot.[16]

In 1996, as founding director of Columbia University's Institute for Research in African-American Studies (IRAAS), I began lecturing annually at Sing-Sing Prison, in a Master's degree program in Theology for prisoners. All of the men involved in the program were either African-Americans or Latinos. As I became more directly involved in supporting educational programs for prisoners, and contributing to the legal defense of political prisoners, the vast scale of the racialized processes of mass incarceration, and their destructive impact upon the African-American community, became crystal clear. In 1999, IRAAS sponsored two educational conferences, both attracting hundreds of educators, criminologists, prisoners' rights advocates and students, to examine the racial dimensions of the US criminal justice system. Instrumental in this early stage of our work was a brilliant young student at Columbia Law School, Kristen Clarke, who subsequently worked for the US Justice Department. One of these conferences,

"Education, Not Incarceration," was held in a Harlem high school, and involved collaboration with over one dozen community-based organizations. IRAAS's newly established quarterly publication, *Souls: A Critical Journal of Black Politics, Culture and Society*, released an edited volume of papers largely generated by those conferences in its Winter 2000 issue.

In 2001, I proposed to the Open Society Institute (George Soros Foundation) a public policy and research project based at IRAAS, which was then called the "Africana Criminal Justice Project" (ACJP). Our larger objective was to develop a subfield within African-American Studies that would interrogate the interconnections between race, crime and justice. The Open Society Institute generously agreed to fund the initial stages of the project, from 2002 to 2004. As the project evolved, we identified four central goals: (1) To develop new scholarship on criminal justice issues within African-American Studies, and to promote collaboration and dialogue between Black Studies scholars, civil rights organizations, legal studies scholars, and prisoners' rights groups; (2) to produce scholarly research on the impact of the criminal justice system on African-American, Latino, low-income and immigrant communities; (3) To create new academic courses, educational resources and textbooks on these subjects; and (4) to explore the long-term consequences of racialization by the criminal justice system. In the pursuit of these objectives, ACJP was extremely fortunate to attract the invaluable leadership and contributions of a series of dedicated, young black intellectuals. From 2002 until 2004, Dr. Geoff Ward, currently a Professor of Sociology at Northeastern University, served as ACJP Coordinator. He was ably followed by Laurent Alfred, who had recently completed his law degree at Yale University, and who directed the project in 2004–2006. From fall 2006 to date (2009) the ACJP director has been Dr. Keesha Middlemass, an Assistant Professor of Political Science at Rutgers University, Newark. Under their leadership, ACJP organized two major national conferences: "Africana Studies Against Criminal Injustice: Research, Education, Action" in April 2003, and "Criminally Unjust: Young People and the Crisis of Mass Incarceration" in April 2005. Also, in November 2004, ACJP hosted a public symposium, "Chanting Down the Walls," focusing on ways that the arts could be employed to critique racial inequality within the criminal justice system. *Souls* published three edited volumes featuring conference papers and solicited research articles on race, crime and justice, in its Fall 2003, Winter 2004 and Spring 2006 issues. With the assistance of Dr. Mio Matsumoto, in 2003–2004, ACJP compiled a comprehensive, annotated bibliography of several hundred documents – including archival letters, scholarly articles, and papers – by African-

American intellectuals and writers since the mid nineteenth century on topics related to race, crime and justice.

The public recognition of ACJP's efforts in this field has been one of the most deeply gratifying experiences I have had during my three decade-long career as a university teacher and scholar. One of our most exciting and innovative efforts, initiated by Laurent Alfred in 2004, involved the development of an African-American Studies seminar inside New York City's Riker's Correctional Facility high school, mentoring young African-American and Latino incarcerated males. The seminar utilized spoken-word or hip-hop poetry as a vehicle for minority juveniles to express their experiences and feelings about being incarcerated, and the impact of the criminal justice system on their lives.

By the initial years of the twenty-first century, there was a growing recognition among broad sectors of the American public that the two-decade-long campaigns promoting the mandatory-minimum sentences, the eradication of educational, drug treatment and vocational training programs inside prisons, and other repressive policies were counterproductive and wasteful, both in dollar terms as in human lives. One reference illustrating this is the results from several opinion polls, respectively from 1994–1999 and 2000–2001. In a 1994 Gallup poll, 42 per cent of Americans agreed with the statement: "We need tougher approaches to crime," including longer prison sentences, additional police and restrictive paroles. A June 1995 Gallup poll also found that by a 55 to 38 per cent majority, most Americans were convinced that "mandatory-minimum sentencing laws" were a "good idea." By September 2000, however, a plurality of Americans polled, 45 to 38 per cent, believed that "judges should be able to decide" the length of sentences in felony conviction cases. An overwhelming majority of Americans polled in 2001 – 70 per cent – had concluded that the celebrated War on Drugs had been "more of a failure" than a success.[17]

But the years of demonizing and stigmatizing African-American youth as a criminal class left an enduring mark upon millions of white Americans, regarding their comprehension as to the necessary measures required to restore some measure of racial fairness – much less justice – to the American criminal justice system. According to a national survey conducted by Peter D. Hart Associates in September 2001, the African-Americans surveyed overwhelmingly supported "prevention, education and youth programs" (38 per cent) and "rehabilitation, education and job training programs" for prisoners (34 per cent) as the major elements for "how to deal with crime." Latinos somewhat agreed, but by a smaller margin: 46 per cent agreed with "prevention, education and youth programs," but only 13 per cent favored "rehabilitation" for prisoners. By contrast, only 34 per cent of whites supported "prevention, education, and youth programs," while 15 per cent endorsed "rehabilitation." Another 42 per cent of all whites surveyed believed that "more police on the streets" was the best method for "how to deal with crime." Another 22 per cent of whites (compared to only 10 per cent of blacks polled) favored "more punishment" and "longer prison sentences." The racial divide was the major demarcation in regards to how the American public perceived "alternatives to incarceration." For example, on the issue of whether juvenile offenders should be placed "in community prevention programs instead of prisons," 92 per cent of African-Americans but only 84 per cent of whites agreed. On the sentencing of nonviolent offenders into "community service and probation" instead of prisons, 82 per cent of blacks and 73 per cent of whites surveyed concurred. Regarding the necessity to "reduce prison sentences for nonviolent offenders," 74 per cent of African-American agreed, but only 60 per cent of white Americans were supportive.[18] In short, despite the fact that tens of millions of white Americans had consumed illicit drugs, and that white users outnumbered blacks by a margin of nearly three to one even with so-called inner-city drugs like "crack," most white Americans remained convinced that the evils of illicit drugs and the criminal underworld they engendered were largely the province of African-Americans. So long as this widespread, racial denial of reality existed among millions of whites, the prospects for fundamental reforms inside the criminal justice system remained bleak.

In 2002, I argued in *The Great Wells of Democracy: The Meaning of Race in American Life* that the racialized criminal justice system and the processes of mass incarceration had created the institutional context for a "New Racial Domain," a successor regime to the institutions of slavery, Jim Crow segregation, and ghettoization.[19] In 2006, I modified that thesis in *Living Black History*, suggesting that the racialized criminal justice apparatus formed one of three pillars in the New Racial Domain of race-neutral, color-blind inequality. The second pillar, mass unemployment, was structural, produced by neo-liberal public policies of abandoning the poor, and the pervasiveness of racial discrimination in urban labor markets, in which many black and Latino youth and young adults found it almost impossible to obtain gainful employment at living wages. The third institutional pillar, mass disenfranchisement, eliminated millions of blacks from electoral politics and civil society, and critically important, had the effect of reducing the Democratic Party's black voter bloc.[20] Under the ideological hegemony of neo-liberalism, racism seeks to present itself devoid of racial animus. The purging of millions of black voters from elections cannot appear to be inspired by racial intent. Therefore, under the New Racial Domain, black subordination, disenfranchisement and criminal stigmatization are presented as somehow attributable to the behavioral shortcomings and failures of African-Americans themselves. The challenge to Black Studies as a growing field of scholarship, and critical public policy analysis, is to dissect these institutional processes of racialized inequality, revealing them for what they are. Through education and practical public engagement, our scholarship must help to fashion democratic alternatives to how race, crime and justice are understood.

Racializing Justice, Disenfranchising Lives, published in 2007 and co-edited by ACJP director Dr. Keesha Middlemass and *Souls* managing editor Ian Steinberg, was the culmination of our efforts over nearly a decade. Because the processes of racialization transcend the particularity of the black American historical experience, extending in parallel ways to those of many Latinos, American Indians, Third World immigrants, Muslims and others defined outside of the racial rubric "non-Hispanic white," ACJP has been redefined as the "Anti-Racist Criminal Justice Project." America has never, in its long history, experienced a truly anti-racist criminal justice and penal system. Is it possible to imagine such a system, especially in the aftermath of the passage of the Patriot Act and other repressive legislation that followed 9/11? One fragile hope that nurtures my political optimism is the recognition of the impending social crisis that confronts this nation, due to its destructive policies of mass incarceration. As the Washington, D.C.-based Sentencing Project observed back in 1998, only 18 per cent of all prisoners with substance abuse problems received drug treatment while they were incarcerated. Roughly 16 per cent of all prisoners suffer from various types of mental illness, and only a small percentage receive treatment while behind bars. The median educational level of released prisoners – grade 11 – makes most incapable of securing stable, long-term employment. And most significantly, despite the massive construction of new prison facilities in the 1980s and 1990s, over 600,000 prisoners as of 1998 were being released annually – approximately 1,600 women and men every day.[21] Roughly six million Americans on any given day in 2007 find themselves within the US criminal justice apparatus – in jail or prison, on parole, probation or awaiting trial. Over two million Americans are confined inside correctional facilities. For the preservation of democracy and a civil society, the task of implementing major reforms within every aspect of policing, trials, incarceration and prisoner reentry is a great national responsibility that each of us share.

What would an anti-racist criminal justice strategy look like for the United States? Two prime objectives would be "restorative justice" and "democratic, civic capacity-building": to renew, from the margins, the aspirations and energies of millions of Americans, who are routinely denied employment, public housing, college loans and other opportunities due to prior felony convictions; to rebuild, within our political process, the involvement and confidence of millions of Americans who are now unfairly excluded from exercising their democratic, constitutional right to vote; to reenergize the power of millions of unemployed and under-employed and to incorporate former prisoners back into the economy, in part by establishing effective vocational training and educational programs inside every correctional facility, and by eliminating the state-sanctioned lists of prohibited jobs that ex-prisoners are denied the right to apply for; to revive by civic engagement the latent leadership and talents of millions of Americans who have been victimized by the New Racial Domain, whether through unemployment, unjust incarceration, or disenfranchisement. "Restorative justice" requires a therapeutic approach to jurisprudence, based on the availability of rehabilitation programs, constructive and creative alternatives that could begin the process of redirecting hundreds of thousands of nonviolent and drug-related offenders out of maximum security institutions. A truly anti-racist approach to crime would emphasize neighborhood courts, youth prevention programs, drug rehabilitation services, and non-confrontational policing strategies for most local crime. The articles in *Racializing Justice, Disenfranchising Lives* each present very different dimensions of the problems of race, crime and justice. But what underscores each of them is the intellectual conviction that justice cannot exist whenever and wherever institutional racism – the systemic inequality of an entire people justified by their race – endures.

Notes

1. "Punishment and Prejudice: Racial Disparities in the War on Drugs," *Human Rights Watch* 12: 2 (May 2000), p. 3.
2. David Harvey, *A Brief History of Neoliberalism* (New York 2005), pp. 48, 52.
3. "Punishment and Prejudice," p. 4.
4. Ibid., p. 8.
5. "Table 17. 'Drug Use Population Estimates for 1998,' compiled by the Substance and Mental Health Service Administration," in ibid.
6. Table 3. "Marijuana Offenders as Proportion of All Drug Admissions," compiled from 1996 data of the National Corrections Reporting Program, in ibid.

Table 3   New admissions to state prisons by race (1996 data)

	Black (%)	White (%)
National	51	47
Alabama	64	36
Florida	52	48
Georgia	65	34
Illinois	74	26
Louisiana	73	27
Maryland	79	20
Mississippi	70	29
New Jersey	72	28
New York	63	35
North Carolina	63	35
South Carolina	68	31
Virginia	65	34

Source: Data compiled by the National Corrections Reporting Program, cited in "Punishment and Prejudice: Racial Disparities in the War on Drugs," *Human Rights Watch* 12: 2 (May 2000), Table 2.

7. Ibid., pp. 20–21.
8. Ibid., p. 20.
9. Correctional Association of New York, and the Justice Policy Institute.
10. Ibid.
11. "Prisoners Re-Entering the Community," *The Sentencing Project* (Washington, D.C., 2002).
12. "Punishment and Prejudice," pp. 8–9.
13. Jeremy Travis, Amy L. Solomon, and Michelle Waul, *From Prison to Home: The Dimensions and Consequences of Prisoner Re-Entry* (Washington, D.C. 2001), p. 22.
14. "Punishment and Prejudice," p. 24.
15. Manning Marable, *The Great Wells of Democracy: The Meaning of Race in American Life* (New York 2002), pp. 158.
16. Ibid., pp. 159–60.
17. Peter D. Hart Associates, Inc., "The New Politics of Criminal Justice: Summary of Findings" (January, 2002). Data in the 2001 poll was compiled by Peter D. Hart Research Associates, on behalf of the Open Society Institute. From September 6–17, 2001, Hart Research conducted a national telephone survey of 1,056 adults, which included 101 black Americans and 151 Latinos. The majority of interviews, 863, were conducted prior to the September 11, 2001, terrorist attacks.

18. Ibid.

19. Marable, *The Great Wells of Democracy*, pp. 21–64.

20. Manning Marable, *Living Black History: How Reimagining the African-American Past Can Remake America's Racial Future* (New York 2006), pp. 215–21.

21. "Prisoners Re-Entering the Community," Fact Sheet, *The Sentencing Project* (Washington, D.C. 2002).

TWENTY-FOUR

BLACKNESS BEYOND BOUNDARIES: NAVIGATING THE POLITICAL ECONOMIES OF GLOBAL INEQUALITY

> The advance guard of the Negro people ... must soon come to realize that if they are to take their just place in the van of Pan-Negroism, then their destiny is <u>not</u> absorption by the white Americans. That if in America it is to be proven for the first time in the modern world that not only Negroes are capable of evolving individual men like Toussaint, the Saviour, but are a nation stored with wonderful possibilities of culture, then their destiny is not a servile imitation of Anglo-Saxon culture, but a stalwart originality which shall unswervingly follow Negro ideals.
>
> W.E.B. Du Bois, 1897[1]

On 5 March 1897, the newly formed American Negro Academy met for its inaugural sessions in Washington, DC. W.E.B. Du Bois, then a 29-year-old social scientist and recent Ph.D. graduate of Harvard University, delivered the second paper to this gathering of black American intellectuals, "The Conservation of Races," that would foreshadow much of his future life's work. The paper centered in part on the question of what constituted "blackness," or the construction of black identity within the challenging contexts of white dominated societies. Inside the United States, Du Bois argued, each African-American must struggle to determine "what, after all, am I? Am I an American or am I a Negro? Can I be both?" Du Bois then sought to delineate the boundaries between Africanity, race and citizenship, that constantly confronted black Americans:

> We are Americans, not only by birth and by citizenship, but by our political ideals, our language, our religion. Farther than that, our Americanism does not go. At that point, we are Negroes, members of a vast historic race that from the very dawn of creation has slept, but half awakening the dark forests of its African fatherland .... We are that people whose subtle sense of song

has given America its only American music, its only American fairy tales, its only touch of pathos and humor amid its mad money-getting plutocracy. As such, it is our duty to conserve our physical powers, our intellectual endowments, our spiritual ideals; as a race we must strive by race organization, by race solidarity …[2]

For Du Bois at this time, the boundaries of blackness were defined largely by aesthetics, culture, and the highly-charged construction of race. But as the twentieth century unfolded, Du Bois expanded his understanding about the common grounds that people of African descent shared throughout the colonial and segregated world. This led him to embrace the politics of Pan-Africanism, and efforts by black activists in the Caribbean, the United States and Africa itself to overthrow white minority regimes. Intellectually, it gave Du Bois a truly global concept of what today would be termed "Black Studies." Part of the mission of Black Studies as an intellectual project has been the remapping of collective identity and memory, in part by using Du Bois's criteria. But it should also combine theory with collective action, in the effort not simply to interpret but to transform the world, empowering black people in the process.

During the 1960s, when Black Studies Departments were first being launched within predominantly white academic institutions, an ideological debate subsequently developed over the appropriate geopolitical and cultural boundaries for what the study of "blackness" should comprise. Many prominent African-American cultural nationalists, such as Kwanzaa-founder Maulana Karenga, vigorously argued that Black Studies must trace its intellectual lineage back to classical Egyptian civilization. The black experience in the United States, in this Afrocentric interpretation, was a small subsidiary of a much grander African civilizational saga. Other Black Studies scholars noted the destructive effects of the transatlantic slave trade, and focused on the cultural and political resistance of African diasporic populations scattered across North and South America, the Caribbean, Europe and Asia, as the decisive elements in the making of the modern world. Scholars largely trained in the US often had a more parochial vision of Black Studies, emphasizing the local struggles waged by African-Americans to achieve political rights and equality against the American nation-state. As a measurement of the lack of theoretical and conceptual consensus among these scholars, departments and programs dedicated to Black Studies still call themselves by various names: "Afro-American Studies," "African-American Studies," "Africana Studies," "African and African-American Studies," "African Diasporal Studies," and "Comparative Race and Ethnicity Studies."

At Columbia University, when I founded the Institute for Research in African-American Studies (IRAAS) in July 1993, the precise name of the program was the result not of a theoretically-grounded academic discussion, but a pragmatic political compromise. The Institute of African Studies had been established in Columbia University's School of International and Public Affairs approximately a quarter century earlier, and its director and small faculty were deeply concerned that IRAAS would colonize and incorporate their curricula into our own program. The decision was made to keep African-American and Caribbean Studies distinctly separate from African Studies. Over subsequent years, as the fortunes of Columbia's African Studies Program rose and fell, I came to regret that decision administratively, as well as intellectually.

It is impossible to relate the full narrative of the experiences of people of African descent in the United States and throughout the Caribbean and the Americas without close integration and reference to the remarkable history of the African continent, its many peoples, languages and diverse cultures. The South Atlantic and especially the Caribbean were highways for constant cultural, intellectual and political exchange between people of African descent, especially during the past three centuries. Pan-Africanist-inspired social-protest movements like Marcus Garvey's Universal Negro Improvement Association and African Communities League (UNIA) started in Jamaica, but accelerated into hundreds of chapters across the United States as a mass movement, and then grew hundreds of new chapters throughout Central America and Africa. Documenting the UNIA's complex story by focusing solely on the events of one nation, like the United States, distorts the narrative, and cripples our understanding of fundamental events. Similarly, South Africa's Black Consciousness Movement of the 1970s and the brilliant protest writings of Stephen Biko cannot be interpreted properly without detailed references to the Black Power Movement in the United States during the 1960s, and to the influential speeches and political writings of Malcolm X of the US, and Frantz Fanon of Martinique.

"Blackness" acquires its full revolutionary potential as a social site for resistance only within transnational and Pan-African contexts. This insight motivated W.E.B. Du Bois to initiate the Pan-African Congress Movement at the end of World War I. George Padmore, Kwame Nkrumah, Du Bois, and others sponsored the Fifth Pan-African Congress in Manchester, England in October 1945, out of the recognition that the destruction of European colonial rule in Africa and the Caribbean, and the demise of the Jim Crow regime of racial segregation in the US, were politically linked. Any advance towards democracy and civil rights in any part of the black world objectively assisted the goals and political aspirations of people of African descent elsewhere. An internationalist perspective, from a historian's point of view, also helped to explain the dynamics of the brutal transnational processes of capitalist political economy – the forced movement of involuntary labor across vast boundaries, the physical and human exploitation of slaves, the subsequent imposition of debt peonage, convict-leasing and sharecropping in post-emancipation societies, and the construction of hyper-segregated, racialized urban ghettoes, from Soweto to Rio de Janeiro's slums to Harlem. As the 2008 edited volume, *Transnational Blackness: Navigating the Global Color Line* illustrates, the twentieth century was full of examples of "blackness beyond boundaries as praxis" – intellectual activists of African descent who sparked movements of innovative scholarship, as well as social protest movements, throughout Africa and the African Diaspora.

In 1900, Du Bois had predicted that the central "problem of the twentieth century" would be the "problem of the color line": the unequal relationship between the lighter versus darker races of humankind.[3] Du Bois's color line included not just the racially segregated Jim Crow South and the racial oppression of South Africa; but also the British, French, Belgian, and Portuguese colonial domination in Asia, the Middle East, Latin America, and the Caribbean among indigenous populations.[4] Building on Du Bois's insights, we can therefore say that the problem of the twenty-first century is the problem of global apartheid: the racialized division and stratification of resources, wealth, and power that separates Europe, North America, and Japan from the billions of mostly black, brown, indigenous, undocumented immigrant, and poor people across the planet. The term "apartheid" comes from the former white minority regime of South Africa: an Afrikaans word, it means "apartness" or "separation." Apartheid was based on the concept of *herrenvolk*: a "master race" that was predestined to rule all non-Europeans. Under global apartheid today, the racist logic of *herrenvolk* is embedded ideologically in the patterns of unequal economic and global accumulation that penalizes African, south Asian, Caribbean, Latin American and other impoverished nations by predatory policies.

Since 1979–80, with the elections of Ronald Reagan as US President and Margaret Thatcher as Prime Minister of the United Kingdom, America and Great Britain embarked on domestic economic development strategies that are now widely known by the term "neo-liberalism." Neo-liberal politics called for the dismantling of the welfare state; the end of redistributive social programs designed to address the effects of poverty; the elimination of governmental regulations and regulatory agencies in capitalist markets; and privatization, the transfer of public institutions and governmental agencies to corporations. Journalist Thomas B. Edsall has astutely characterized this reactionary process of neo-liberal politics within the United States in these terms: "For a quarter-century, the Republican temper – its reckless drive to jettison the social safety net; its support of violence in law enforcement and national defense; its advocacy of regressive taxation, environmental hazard and pro-business deregulation; its 'remoralizing' of the pursuit of wealth – has been judged by many voters as essential to America's position in the world, producing more benefit than cost."[5].

One of the consequences of this reactionary political and economic agenda, according to Edsall, was "the Reagan administration's arms race" during the 1980s, which "arguably drove the Soviet Union into bankruptcy." A second consequence, Edsall argues, was America's disastrous military invasion of Iraq. "While inflicting destruction on the Iraqis," Edsall observed, "Bush multiplied America's enemies and endangered this nation's military, economic health and international stature. Courting risk without managing it, Bush repeatedly and remorselessly failed to accurately evaluate the consequences of his actions."[6]

Significantly, Edsall's insightful analysis did not attempt to explain away the 2003 US invasion of Iraq and subsequent military occupation as a political "mistake" or an "error of judgment." Rather, he located the rationale for the so-called "war on terrorism" within the context of US domestic, neo-liberal politics. "The embroilment in Iraq is not an aberration," Edsall observed. "It stems from core [Republican] party principles, equally evident on the domestic front." The larger question of political economy, left unexplored by Edsall and most US mainstream analysts, is the connection between US militarism abroad, neo-liberalism, and macro-trends in the global economy. As economists such as Paul Sweezy, and Harry Magdoff noted decades ago, the general economic tendency of mature, global capitalism is toward stagnation. For decades, in the United States and Western Europe, there has been a steady decline in investment in the productive economy, leading to a decline in industrial capacity and lower future growth rates. Profit margins inside the US have fallen over time, and corporations have been forced to invest capital abroad to generate higher rates of profitability. There is a direct economic link between the deindustrialized urban landscapes of Detroit, Youngstown and Chicago, with the expansion of industries in China, Vietnam, Brazil and other Third World nations.

Since capitalist economies are "based on the profit motive and accumulation of capital without end," observed Marxist author Fred Magdoff, "problems arise whenever they do not expand at reasonably high growth rates."[7] Since the 1970s, US corporations and financial institutions have relied primarily on debt to expand domestic economic growth. By 1985, total US debt – which is comprised of the debt owed by all households, governments (federal, state, and local), and all financial and non-financial businesses, reached twice the size of the annual US gross domestic product (GDP). By 2005, the total US debt amounted to nearly "three and a half times the nation's GDP, and not far from the $44 trillion GDP for the entire world," according to Fred Magdoff.[8]

As a result, mature US corporations are forced to export products and investment abroad, to take advantage of lower wages, weak or nonexistent environmental and safety standards, and so forth, to obtain higher profit margins. Today about 18 per cent of total US corporate profits come from direct overseas investments. Partially to protect these growing investments, the United States has pursued an aggressive, interventionist foreign policy across the globe. As of 2006, the US maintained military bases in 59 nations. The potential for deploying military forces in any part of the world is essential for both political and economic hegemony.[9] Thus the Iraq War was not essentially a military blunder caused by a search for weapons of mass destruction but rather an imperialist effort to secure control of the world's second largest proven oil reserves; it was also the first military step of the Bush administration's neo-conservatives to remake the Middle East by destroying the governments of Iraq, Iran and Syria.

Although the majority of nations in the international community either openly opposed, or at least seriously questioned, the US military occupation of Iraq, the neo-liberal economic model of the United States has been now widely adopted by both developed and developing countries. Governments across the ideological spectrum – with the important exception of some Latin American countries in recent years – have eliminated social welfare, health, and education programs, reduced governmental regulations on business activity, and encouraged the growth of income inequality and entrepreneurship. Even non-capitalist countries like Cuba have revived the sex-trade-oriented tourism business, which has contributed to new forms of gender and racial prejudice in that country. As a result, economic inequality in wealth has rapidly accelerated, reinforcing traditional patterns of racial and ethnic domination.

A 2006 study by the World Institute for Development Economics Research of the United Nations University, established that, as of 2000, the upper 1 per cent of the globe's adult population (approximately 37 million people) averaged about $515,000 in net worth per person, and collectively controlled roughly 40 per cent of the world's entire wealth. By contrast, the bottom half of the planet's adult population (1.85 billion people) – most of whom are black and brown – owned only 1.1 per cent of the world's total wealth. There is tremendous inequality of wealth between nations, the UN report noted. The United States, for example, comprised only 4.7 per cent of the world's people, but it had nearly one-third (32.6 per cent) of global wealth. By stark contrast, China, which had one-fifth of the world's population, owned only 2.6 per cent of the globe's wealth. India, which has 16.8 per cent of the global population, controlled only 0.9 per cent of the world's total wealth. Within most of the world's countries, wealth was disproportionately concentrated in the top 10 per cent of each nation's population. It comes as no surprise that in the United States, for example, the upper 10 per cent of the adult population as of 2000 owned 69.8 per cent of the nation's total wealth. But surprisingly, Canada – a nation with much more liberal social welfare traditions than the United States – nevertheless still exhibited significant inequality: more than half (53 per cent) of Canadian assets, were owned by only 10 per cent of the population. European countries had similar or slightly lower levels of wealth inequality, such as Norway (50.5 per cent) and Spain (41.9 per cent).[10]

The most revealing finding of the World Institute for Development Economics Research was that similar patterns of wealth inequality have come to prevail throughout the Third World. In Indonesia, for example, 65.4 per cent of the nation's total wealth belonged to the wealthiest 10 per cent in 2000. In India, the upper 10 per cent owned 52 per cent of all Indian wealth. Even in China, where the ruling Communist Party still maintains vestiges of what might be described as an "authoritarian state socialism," the wealthiest 10 per cent owned 41.4 per cent of the national wealth.[11]

But even these macroeconomic statistics, as useful as they are, obscure a crucial dimension of wealth concentration, under global apartheid's neo-liberal economics. In the past quarter-century in the United States, where deregulation and privatization have been carried to obscene extremes, we are presently witnessing a phenomenon that the media has described as "the very rich" who are leaving "the merely rich behind." One study by New York University economist Edward N. Wolff found that one out of every 825 households in the United States in 2004 earned at least $2 million annually, representing nearly a 100 per cent increase in the wealth percentage recorded in 1989, adjusted for inflation. As of 2004, one out of every 325 US households possessed a net wealth of $10 million or more. When adjusted for inflation, this is more than four times as many wealthy households as in 1989. The exponential growth of America's "super-rich" is a direct product of the near-elimination of capital gains taxes, and the sharp decline in federal government income tax rates.[12]

Inside the United States, the processes of global apartheid are best represented by the "New Racial Domain," or NRD. The NRD is different from other earlier systemic forms of racial domination inside the US, such as slavery, Jim Crow segregation, and ghettoization, or strict residential segregation, in several critical aspects. These earlier racial formations, or exploitative racial domains, were grounded or based primarily, if not exclusively, in the political economy of US capitalism. Anti-racist or oppositional movements that blacks, other ethnic minorities, and white anti-racists built were largely predicated upon the confines or realities of domestic markets and the policies of the US nation-state. Meaningful social reforms such as the Civil Rights Act of 1964 and the Voting Rights Act of 1965 were debated almost entirely within the context of America's expanding, domestic economy, and influenced by Keynesian, welfare state public policies. The political economy of America's NRD, by contrast, is driven and largely determined by the forces of transnational capitalism, and the public policies of state neo-liberalism. From the vantage point of the most oppressed US populations, the NRD rests on an unholy trinity, or deadly triad, of structural barriers to a decent life. These oppressive structures are mass unemployment, mass incarceration, and mass disenfranchisement. Each factor directly feeds and accelerates the others, creating an ever-widening circle of social disadvantage, poverty, and civil death touching the lives of tens of millions of US people.[13]

Notes

1. W.E.B. Du Bois, "The Conservation of Races," *Occasional Paper No. 2* (Washington, D.C. 1898).
2. Ibid.
3. W.E.B. Du Bois, *The Souls of Black Folk*, (New York 2007), p. 8.
4. See W.E.B. Du Bois, "The Color Line Belts the World," *Collier's* 20 (October 1906), p. 20.
5. Thomas B. Edsall, "Risk and Reward", *New York Times* (5 December 2006).
6. Ibid.
7. Fred Magdoff, "The Explosion of Debt and Speculation," *Monthly Review* 58: 6 (November 2006), pp. 24–6.
8. Ibid.
9. The Editors, "US Military Bases and Empire," *Monthly Review* 53: 10 (March 2002), pp. 1–14.
10. Eduardo Porter, "Study Finds Wealth Inequality is Widening Worldwide," *New York Times* (6 December 2006).
11. Ibid.

12. Louis Uchitelle, "Very Rich are Leaving the Merely Rich Behind," *New York Times* (27 November 2006).

13. I have outlined in greater detail the political economy of the New Racial Domain in Marable, *Living Black History: How Reimagining the African-American Past Can Remake America's Racial Future* (New York 2006), especially in pp. 214–300.

TWENTY-FIVE

BARACK OBAMA, THE 2008 PRESIDENTIAL ELECTION AND THE PROSPECTS FOR A "POST-RACIAL POLITICS"

The historical significance of the election of Illinois Senator Barack Obama as president of the United States was recognized literally by the entire world. For a nation that had, only a half century earlier, refused to enforce the voting rights and constitutional liberties of people of African descent, to elevate a black American as its chief executive was a stunning reversal of history. On the night of his electoral victory, spontaneous crowds of joyful celebrants rushed into streets, parks and public establishments in thousands of venues across the country. In Harlem, over ten thousand people surrounded the Adam Clayton Powell State Office Building, cheering and crying in disbelief. To many, the impressive margin of Obama's popular vote victory suggested the possibility that the United States had entered at long last an age of post-racial politics, in which leadership and major public policy debates would not be distorted by factors of race and ethnicity.

Obama's election almost overnight changed the negative perceptions about the routine abuses of American power that were widely held, especially across the Third World. One vivid example of the recognition of this new reality was represented by a petulant statement by Ayman al-Zawahri, the deputy leader of the Al Qaeda terrorist network. Al-Zawahri contemptuously dismissed Obama as only the "new face of America," which only "masked a heart full of hate." Al Qaeda also released a video in which former Bush Secretaries of State Colin Powell and Condoleezza Rice, both African-Americans, as well as Obama, were denigrated "[in] the words of Malcolm X (may Allah have mercy on him) [as] 'house Negroes'." Malcolm X was favorably quoted for condemning the docile "house Negro who always looked out for his master." To Al Qaeda, Obama was nothing short of a "hypocrite and traitor to his race." America "continues to be the same as ever ...."[1] Despite Obama's concerted efforts to present himself as a presidential candidate "who happened to be black," both proponents and enemies like Al Qaeda were quick to freeze his identity to the reality of his blackness, for both positive and negative reasons.

To understand the main factors that contributed to Obama's spectacular but in many ways unlikely victory, it is necessary to return to the defining racializing moment in recent US history: the tragic debacle of the Hurricane Katrina Crisis of 2005, under the regime of President George W. Bush. It was not simply the deaths of over one thousand Americans, and the forced relocations of hundreds of thousands of people from their homes in New Orleans and across the Gulf of Mexico states-region who were disproportionately black and poor. The inevitable consequences of a natural disaster in New Orleans, a city below sea level, were not unexpected. Rather, it was the callous and contemptuous actions of the federal government – especially the Federal Emergency Management Agency (FEMA), which was plagued by cronyism and corruption – that directly contributed to blacks' deaths. The world witnessed on television for days the stunning spectra of thousands of mostly black and poor people stranded in New Orleans' downtown Morial Convention Center, into which FEMA's vehicles claimed it was impossible to send medical supplies, food and fresh water, even while media representatives and entertainers were easily able to drive to the center. States like Florida that proposed to send in five hundred airboats to assist with Gulf Coast rescue efforts were inexplicably turned away. Needed supplies such as electric generators, trailers and freight cars stocked with food went undelivered to starving, desperate evacuees. The overwhelming collage of tragic images pointed to the enduring blight of racism and poverty as central themes within the arrangements of institutional power within the United States.[2] By mid-September 2005, sixty per cent of all African-Americans surveyed were convinced that "the federal government's delay in helping the victims in New Orleans was because the victims were black." What was striking to minorities was that the overwhelming majority of white citizens remained convinced that their government was color-blind: only 12 per cent of whites surveyed agreed that the government's Katrina response was racially biased.[3]

The reality of racial injustice through governmental inaction was also reinforced among millions of black Americans by the results of the presidential elections of 2000 and 2004, both won by Republican George W. Bush. In 2000, there was substantial evidence that tens of thousands of African-American voters in Florida were deliberately excluded from exercising the franchise, through a variety of measures.

Thousands of Florida voters with misdemeanor convictions, for example, were illegally barred from voting. Thousands of black voters in specific districts were inexplicably barred from casting ballots. Four years later, a similar process of black voter suppression occurred in Ohio, which Bush narrowly won over Democratic presidential candidate John Kerry.[4] To many African-Americans the two controversial presidential elections and the Katrina tragedy cemented the perspective that the American system was hardwired to discriminate against the interests of people of African descent. If basic political change was possible, or even conceivable, it would probably not be through frontal assaults, similar to the bold challenges of Jesse Jackson's Rainbow Coalition presidential campaigns of 1984 and 1988. If meaningful change occurred at all, it would probably happen at the margins. Few anticipated the possibility that an African-American candidate, with relatively little experience at the national level, could capture the Democratic Party's presidential nomination, much less win election to the presidency.

Although the overall character of national black politics was in many respects defensive and deeply pessimistic, a growing minority trend within African-American leadership perceived the early years of the twenty-first century quite differently. For decades, prior to the early 1990s, there had been one iron-clad rule in American racial politics: that the majority of white voters in any legislative municipal or Congressional district would not vote for an African-American candidate, regardless of her or his ideology or partisan affiliation. There was an omnipresent glass ceiling in electoral politics limiting the rise of all black elected officials. Blacks could be elected to Congress or as mayors of major cities only if districts held high concentrations of minority voters. In the 1980s, progressive black candidates such as Harold Washington sought to circumvent this racial barrier by constructing multiracial coalitions as the base of their electoral mobilizations, reaching out to traditional liberal constituencies.[5] Other more conservative African-American leaders, such as Thomas Bradley, who was elected mayor of Los Angeles on his second try in 1972, and Philadelphia mayor Wilson Goode in the 1980s, won whites' support by deliberately downplaying their own ethnic affiliations and racial identities. They espoused a pragmatic, non-ideological politics that catered to local corporate interests and promoted urban concessions – even these moderate black officials could not depend on the electoral support of many whites, even in their own parties.

Political scientists first began observing the lack of reliability of pre-election polls for whites in races involving African-American candidates nearly three decades ago. In the 1982 California gubernatorial election, pre-election polls indicated that Democratic Los Angeles Mayor Thomas

Bradley would easily defeat Republican challenger George Deukmejian. After Bradley narrowly lost to Deukmejian, it became evident that a significant percentage of whites who had been predicted to support Bradley had voted for the Republican.[6] This so-called "Bradley effect" was subsequently documented in dozens of elections. For example, in 1989, Virginia Lieutenant Governor Douglas Wilder, a Democrat, announced his candidacy for the state's governorship. In many ways Wilder ran a campaign similar to that of Obama's two decades later. Wilder focused on issues largely devoid of racial overtones, such as economic development, the environment and public health. Opinion polls in the state showed Wilder maintaining a double-digit lead over a lackluster Republican candidate, Marshall Coleman. In Virginia's gubernatorial election, which Wilder managed to win but by less than one-half of one per cent of the total vote, white voters had overwhelmingly favored Coleman. Even more significantly, pollsters found that many white Virginians deliberately provided false information when revealing their voting intentions in polls. When whites were questioned about their gubernatorial preferences by a white pollster, Coleman defeated Wilder by 16 per cent. But when black pollsters were used for interviews, whites favored Wilder by 10 per cent over Coleman. Both the inconsistent pre-election polling information by whites, and the actual election returns appear to validate the "Bradley effect."[7]

The cases of Bradley and Wilder were in many ways mirrored by the 1989 mayoral election in New York City, which was won by an African-American Democrat, Manhattan Borough President David Dinkins. As noted by Andrew Kohul, the president of the Pew Research Center, the Gallup organization's polling research on New York City's voters in 1989 had indicated that Dinkins would defeat his Republican opponent, Rudolph Giuliani, by 15 per cent. Instead, Dinkins only narrowly won by 2 per cent. Kohul, who worked as a Gallup pollster in that election, concluded that "poorer, less well-educated [white] voters were less likely to answer our questions," so the poll didn't have the opportunity to factor in their views. As Kohul observed: "Here's the problem – these whites who do not respond to surveys tend to have more unfavorable view of blacks than respondents who do the interviews."[8]

In the multicultural nineties, as hip-hop began to define urban youth culture, and as President Bill Clinton proudly jogged around the White House after donning a Malcolm X cap, this racial barrier began to erode. A new generation of young African-American politicians – many of whom were lawyers, corporate executives, city administrators, educators, community organizers, and foundation officers – began seeking public office, first in municipal politics and then at statewide levels.

With few exceptions, they rhetorically offered a race-neutral language to advocate the interests of their constituencies – who happened to be white and Latino as well as African-American, middle class as well as working class, unemployed and poor, those without high school diplomas as well as those with professional and graduate degrees. Michael White, the mayor of Cleveland, Ohio, in the 1990s, was in many ways the model for post-black mayoral politics. Although ethnically black and a nominal Democrat, White was far more comfortable discussing tax abatements and incentives to attract corporate investment to inner city Cleveland, than leading a public protest march through the city's black neighborhood.

By the twenty-first century, hundreds of race-neutral, pragmatic black officials had emerged, winning positions on city councils, state legislatures and in the House of Representatives. Frequently they distanced themselves from traditional liberal constituencies such as unions, promoted gentrification and corporate investment in poor urban neighborhoods, and favored funding charter schools as an alternative to the failures of public school systems. A growing share of these new leaders were elected from predominantly white districts. In 2001, for example, according to the Joint Center for Political and Economic Studies, roughly 16 per cent of the nation's African-American state legislators had won election in predominantly white districts. By 2008, out of 622 black state legislators nationally, 30 per cent represented predominantly white constituencies. Between 1998 and 2008, about two hundred African-Americans defeated whites for municipal and state legislative races, even in some states, such as Iowa, Minnesota and New Hampshire, where black populations are small.[9] In November 2006, civil rights attorney Duval Patrick, employing campaign strategies drawn from Barack Obama's successful 2004 Senate bid, easily won the gubernatorial race in Massachusetts, a state with a 79 per cent white population.[10]

Ideologically, this new leadership group reflected a range of divergent views on social policy. The most prominent moderates within this cohort included: former Tennessee Congressman Harold Ford, who is currently leader of the centrist Democratic Leadership Council; and Newark, New Jersey Mayor Corey Booker. More ideologically liberal leaders in this group are: Barack Obama; New York Governor David Patterson; and Massachusetts Governor Duval Patrick. This is not to suggest that these politicians possess no strong ethnic roots or identity. All of these individuals are proudly self-identified as African-Americans. But strategically, none of them pursue what could be called race-based politics. None favor or would support a Black Agenda similar to that espoused by the March 1972 Gary, Indiana Black Political Convention.

Most probably would perceive even Jesse Jackson's Rainbow Coalition campaigns of the 1980s as too narrowly race- and ethnically-based, and too far to the left on economic policy.

Obama undoubtedly took most of these factors into account – the possibility of a "Bradley/Wilder effect" on whites' support of black candidates, African-American grievances surrounding the 2000 and 2004 presidential campaigns, the recent debacle of the Katrina Crisis, and the rise of the postracial politics of a new generation of black leaders – to construct his own image and political narrative essential for a presidential campaign. Early on in their deliberation process, the Obama pre-campaign group recognized that most white Americans would never vote for a *black* presidential candidate. However, they were convinced that most whites would embrace, and vote for, a remarkable, qualified presidential candidate *who happened to be black*. "Race" could be muted into an adjective, a qualifier of minimal consequence. So ethnically, Obama did not deny the reality of his African heritage; it was blended into the multicultural narrative of his uniquely American story, which also featured white grandparents from Kansas, a white mother who studied anthropology in Hawaii, and an Indonesian stepfather. Unlike black conservatives, Obama openly acknowledged his personal debt to the sacrifices made by martyrs and activists of the civil-rights movement. Yet he also spoke frequently about the need to move beyond the divisions of the sixties, to seek common ground, and a post-partisan politics of hope and reconciliation. As the Obama campaign took shape in late 2006–early 2007, the basic strategic line about race, therefore, was to deny its enduring presence or relevance to contemporary politics. Volunteers often chanted, in Hari Krishna-fashion, "Race Doesn't Matter! Race Doesn't Matter!" as if to ward off the evil spirits of America's troubled past.

Obama's strategic approach on race was indeed original, but coming at a time of hopelessness and pessimism among many African-Americans, there were doubts that the young Illinois Senator could actually pull it off. To some, Obama's multiracial pedigree raised questions about his loyalties to the cause of black people. Curiously, many of those with the loudest queries were African-American conservatives and Republicans, whose own *bona fides* on racial matters were often under fire. For example, conservative writer Debra Dickerson, author of *The End of Blackness*, declared in January 2007, that "Obama would be the great black hope in the next presidential race, if he were actually black."[11] Journalist Stanley Crouch took a similarly negative approach, arguing that while Obama "has experienced some light versions of typical racial stereotypes, he cannot claim those problems as his own – nor has he lived the life of a black American."[12] Juan Williams, conservative commentator on FOX News, warned that "there are widespread questions whether this son of a white American mother and a black Kenyan father really understands the black American experience."[13]

As late as December 2007, roughly one-half of all African-Americans polled still favored Hillary Clinton over Obama as their Democratic presidential candidate. Some of Obama's sharpest "racial doubters" were even from Chicago, his home base. Eddie Read, chair of Chicago's Black Independent Political Organization, for example, predicted that "nothing's going to happen" from the Democratic Senator's candidacy, because "he doesn't belong to us. He would not be the black president. He would be the multicultural president."[14]

Obama's ultimate victory over Hillary Clinton in the 2008 Democratic primaries began with his implacable opposition to the US invasion of Iraq. Back in 2002, Obama warned that "an invasion of Iraq without a clear rationale and without strong international support will only fan the flames of the Middle East, and encourage the worst, rather than the best, impulses of the Arab world, and strengthen the recruitment arm of Al Qaeda." Less noticed in this speech was Obama's appeal "to make sure our so-called allies in the Middle East, the Saudis and the Egyptians, stop oppressing dissent, and tolerating corruption and inequality, and mismanaging their economies so that their youth grow up without education, without prospects, without hope, the ready recruits of terrorist cells."[15] Like Malcolm X a generation earlier, Barack Obama's entry into national politics was associated with the Islamic world.

Even before the announcement of his candidacy for president, media conservatives resorted to Islamophobia to denigrate Obama. For example, on CNN's "Situation Room," on 11 December 2006, correspondent Jeanne Moos observed darkly: "Only one little consonant differentiates" Obama versus Osama, also noting that the candidate's middle name, Hussein, was shared with "a former dictator." In early 2007, Bernard McGuirk, then the executive producer of the Don Imus Radio Show, declared on air that Obama has "a Jew-hating name." Conservative radio commentator Russ Limbaugh repeatedly referred to the candidate as "Osama Obama."[16]

Religious bigotry and intolerance, even more than traditional racism, was the decisive weapon to delegitimize Obama. The 17 January 2007 issue of *Insight* magazine, for example, claimed that Obama "spent at least four years in a so-called madrassa, or Muslim seminary, in Indonesia." Writing in the *Chicago Sun-Times*, columnist Mark Steyn then claimed that Obama "graduated from the Sword of the Infidel grade school in Jakarta."[17] On FOX News, former liberal-turned-reactionary

Juan Williams argued that Obama "comes from a father who was a Muslim and all that ... Given that we're at war with Muslim extremists, that presents a problem."[18] The truth of Obama's background was that his biological father, while being raised as a Muslim, was an atheist like Obama's mother. Obama's stepfather was not deeply religious. The two elementary schools Obama attended, one Catholic, the other predominantly Muslim, were not madrassas. In 2007, CNN correspondent John Vause traveled to Indonesia, investigated the charges, and established the truth about Obama's religious and family background. Yet despite this, the "madrassa myth" linking Obama to Islamic terrorist cells continued to be promoted on television and especially over the internet.[19]

As the Democratic caucuses and primaries began, however, Obama quickly established the ability to win a surprisingly large share of whites' votes. He consistently won majorities among all voters under 30, voters earning over $50,000 annually and college-educated voters. After the South Carolina Democratic primary, where Bill Clinton's racially insensitive remarks alienated thousands of voters, the African-American electorate swung decisively behind Obama.

The most damaging controversy involving race to erupt during Obama's quest for the Democratic presidential nomination involved the politics of faith: the media's re-broadcasting of provocative statements by the candidate's former minister, the Reverend Jeremiah Wright of Chicago's Trinity United Church of Christ. A major center for social justice ministry in Chicago, Trinity's activist program was not unlike that of other progressive African-American churches involved in the civil-rights movement in the 1960s, or the anti-apartheid campaign against white South Africa during the 1980s. Yet even before the controversial videos of the Reverend Wright's speeches surfaced, some white conservatives had attempted to equate Trinity Church's theological teachings with the black separatism of the Nation of Islam.[20]

Obama's response to the Reverend Wright politics of faith controversy was a masterful address, "A More Perfect Union," delivered in Philadelphia's Constitution Center on 15 March 2008. Obama began by reminding his audience that American democracy was "unfinished" at its founding in 1787, due to "this nation's original sin of slavery." Obama declared that despite his rather unusual personal history and mixed ethnic background, "seared into my genetic makeup [is] the idea that this nation is more than the sum of its parts – that out of many, we are truly one."[21]

Obama's great strength is his ability to discuss controversial and complex issues in a manner that conveys the seeking of consensus, or common ground. His Philadelphia address reminded white Americans that "so many of the disparities that exist in the African-American community today can be directly traced to inequalities passed on from an earlier generation that suffered under the brutal legacy of slavery" and Jim Crow segregation. But he also acknowledged the anger and alienation of poor and working-class whites, people who do not live especially privileged lives, who feel unfairly victimized by policies like affirmative action. Obama criticized Reverend Wright's statements as "not only wrong but divisive, at a time when we need unity; racially charged at a time when we need to come together to solve a set of monumental problems ... that are neither black or white or Latino or Asian, but rather problems that confront us all."[22]

Another astute dimension of Obama's "A More Perfect Union" speech was his repeated referencing of US racial history, while simultaneously refusing to be defined or restricted by that history. For blacks, Obama asserted, the path forward "means embracing the burdens of our past without becoming victims of our past ... it means binding our particular grievances – for better health care, and better schools, and better jobs – to the larger aspirations of all Americans."[23] In the context of electoral politics and public policy, Obama's argument makes perfect sense. In America's major cities, for example, there's no explicitly "Latino strategy" for improving public transportation, or a purely "African-American strategy" to improve public health care. Obama did not deny that racial disparities in health care, education, employment and other areas existed. But by emphasizing a "politics of hope," he implied that any real solutions must depend on building multiracial, multiclass coalitions that could fight to achieve change.

Although Obama finally secured his party's presidential nomination, religious and racial stereotypes and intolerance were again deployed by many opponents to derail his campaign. In mid-September 2008, for example, a Pew Research Center survey revealed that millions of Americans held grossly erroneous views about Obama's religious and ethnic background. Despite the extensive news coverage earlier in the year concerning the Reverend Wright controversy, and Obama's repeated affirmations about his deeply-held Christian beliefs, only one-half of all Americans believed the Democratic candidate was a Christian. Thirteen per cent stated that Obama was a "Muslim," and another 16 per cent claimed they "aren't sure about his religion because they've heard 'different things' about it." On a number of fundamentalist Christian radio stations, and conservative Christian websites, Obama has been described as the possible "anti-Christ." As journalist Nicholas D. Kristof observed, "Religious prejudice is becoming a proxy for racial prejudice. In the public at least, it's not acceptable to express reservations about a candidate's skin color, so discomfort about race is sublimated into concerns about whether Mr. Obama is sufficiently Christian."[24]

What animated the fear and loathing of Obama by some terrified whites was also the recognition that America is fundamentally changing ethnically and racially. Demographically, the white majority population is rapidly vanishing. Latinos, blacks, Asians and Native Americans combined, will outnumber Americans of European descent by 2042, earlier than predicted. By 2050, racialized groups will account for 54 per cent. Already, in cities like New York, Chicago, Los Angeles and Atlanta, whites have been a "minority group" for years, but they still have exercised decisive power, especially in government and economically. So the emergence and election of a racial minority candidate like Obama was inevitable. A majority of white Americans now recognize that the traditional racial project of "white supremacy," is no longer sustainable, or even in the best interests of the nation. Nevertheless, a significant minority of whites are still dedicated proponents of both racialization and religious intolerance, as central tools in the continuing perpetuation of a racist America.

On 4 November 2008, the US electorate made its decision by electing Barack Obama its first African-American president, by a popular vote of 52 per cent. Obama's victory rested in part on nearly unanimous (95 per cent) support provided by African-Americans, who voted in record numbers. Almost as impressive, however, was the broad, multiethnic, multiclass coalition the Obama forces were able to construct from Jewish voters (78 per cent), Latinos (67 per cent), young voters age 18–29 (62 per cent) and women voters (58 per cent). Obama's victory sparked hundreds, perhaps even thousands of spontaneous street demonstrations involving millions of celebrants across the nation.

Although Obama's core constituencies provided him with the essential foundations of his triumph, equally essential was his ability to attract millions of moderate Republicans and independents, many of whom had voted for George W. Bush in 2000 and/or 2004. Throughout the 2008 campaign Obama explicitly refused to attack the Republican Party per se, focusing his criticisms either on his presidential opponent John McCain, or against the extremist right-wing of the party. Obama's campaign had astutely recognized the partisan shift in voter attitudes that had taken place in the wake of disasters such as the Katrina Hurricane Crisis and the Iraq War. Obama's post-black, race-neutral rhetoric reassured millions of whites to vote for a "black candidate."

For example, according to the Pew Center for The People and The Press, in 2004 one-third of all registered voters (33 per cent) identified themselves with the Republican Party, compared to 35 per cent of registered voters favoring Democrats, and 32 per cent claiming to be independents. In 2004, Republicans trailed Democrats in their support from 18- to 29-year-olds, but only by 4 per cent (29 vs. 33 per cent). Republicans won pluralities over Democrats among all white registered voters (38 vs. 30 per cent), voters with BA and BS degrees (38 vs. 30 per cent), voters earning more than $75,000 annually (40 vs. 29 per cent), white Southerners (43 vs. 28 per cent), white Protestant voters (44 vs. 27 per cent), and a clear majority among white evangelical Christian voters (53 vs. 22 per cent).[25]

Four years later, just prior to the Democratic National Convention, the Pew Center conducted a similar national survey of registered voters and found major gains made by the Democrats in many important voter identifications. One major shift occurred among youth voters age 18–29, who favored Democrats over Republicans (37 vs. 23 per cent), with another 40 per cent identifying themselves as independents. Republican support in union households fell slightly, from 26 per cent in 2004 to only 20 per cent in 2008. Hispanics, who in 2004 had favored Democrats over Republicans, but only by a 44 vs. 23 per cent margin, had become more partisanly Democratic (48 vs. 19 per cent). But what was perhaps most striking was the growing defection of the intelligentsia and educated class from the Republicans. The 2008 Pew survey indicated that registered college graduates, who vote generally at rates above 80 per cent, favored Democrats over Republicans (34 vs. 29 per cent). For registered voters with postgraduate and professional degrees the partisan bias towards Democrats was even wider (38 vs. 26 per cent, with 36 per cent independents).[26]

The 2008 Pew survey also made clear that the United States, in terms of its political culture and civic ideology, had become a "center-left nation," rather than a "right-center nation," as it had been under Ronald Reagan. Sixty-seven per cent of registered voters surveyed about their views on affirmative action, favored such policies that had been "designed to help blacks, women, and other minorities get better jobs and education." Sixty-one per cent agreed that the US government should guarantee "health insurance for all citizens, even if it means raising taxes." A majority of registered voters believed that abortion should either be "legal in all cases" (18 per cent) or "legal in most cases" (38 per cent). Over 70 per cent of those surveyed believed "global warming" was either a "very serious" or "somewhat serious problem." And over 80 per cent favored "increasing federal funding for research on wind, solar and hydrogen technology."[27] This was a rationale for long-overdue governmental action, along the lines proposed by Obama, not for laissez-faire and the Reaganite mantra of "government-is-the-problem."

On nearly every college campus by the early fall, it became over-whelmingly clear that Obama had won the enthusiastic support of both students and faculty. In a comprehensive national survey of over 43,000 undergraduates conducted by CBS News, UWIRE and the *Chronicle of Higher Education* in October, 2008, the Obama–Biden ticket received 64 per cent support vs. 32 per cent for McCain–Palin. When asked to describe their "feelings about your candidate," 55 per cent of the Obama-backers "enthusiastically" supported him, compared to only 30 per cent of McCain's supporters. By significant margins, college students described Obama as "someone you can relate to" (64 per cent), who would "bring about real change in Washington" (70 per cent), and who "cares about the needs and problems of people like yourself" (78 per cent).[28]

Although nearly one-half (48 per cent) of all students surveyed had never voted in a presidential election, a significant percentage of them had become involved in one of the national campaigns primarily through the internet. Twenty-three per cent surveyed had signed-up to be a candidate's fan on a social networking site; 28 per cent had "visited a candidate's Facebook or MySpace page"; 65 per cent had browsed a candidate's official website; and 68 per cent had seen a video of their favorite presidential candidate on YouTube. Small numbers had partici-pated in more traditional ways. Thirteen per cent had volunteered to help their candidate by canvassing or by doing voter registration. Nearly one-fourth had personally attended a rally featuring their candidate, with another 31 per cent recruiting friends to join their campaign.[29]

It was the conservative British news magazine, *The Economist*, that identified the critical brain gap that contributed to McCain's electoral downfall. "Barack Obama won college graduates by two points, a group George Bush won by six points four years ago," the publication noted. "He won voters with postgraduate degrees by 18 points." *The Economist* observed that Obama even carried by six points households above $200,000 annually. McCain's core constituency, by contrast, was "among uneducated voters in Appalachia and the South." In the view of *The Economist*, "The Republicans lost the battle of ideas even more comprehensively than they lost the battle for educated votes, marching into the election armed with nothing more than slogans."[30]

On the issue of racialization, the most underreported story connected with Barack Obama's presidential victory has been the disturbing spike in racial hate crimes across the US. On 25 November 2008, representa-tives of seven major civil-rights groups met with the media presenting evidence of hundreds of racist incidents and hate crimes leading up to, and following, the election of Obama. These include a cross burning on the lawn of one New Jersey family, and the random beating of an

African-American man on Staten Island by white teenagers, who cursed him with racial epithets and "Obama." The groups involved – the Leadership Conference on Civil Rights, the National Council of La Raza, the Asian American Justice Center, the National Urban League, the National Association for the Advancement of Colored People, the Anti-Defamation League and the Mexican American Legal Defense and Education Fund – all condemned the recent hate crimes.

"At a time when we as a nation are celebrating our demonstrated diversity" with Obama's election, stated NAACP Washington D.C. Bureau Director Hilary Shelton, "there are unfortunately those who are still living in the past filled hatred, fear and division." Marc Morial, National Urban League Director, called upon the Justice Department to "become more aggressive in prosecuting hate crimes ... As a country, we've come a long way, but there is still more change needed."

What can be anticipated from an Obama administration, especially as it relates to the Middle East, and more broadly the Islamic world? From his major speeches on international policy, Obama deeply believes in the nationalistic, world supremacist mission of the United States. In his speech, "The American Moment," delivered at the Chicago Council of Global Affairs on 23 April 2007, Obama declared that "the magical place called America" was still "the last, best hope on Earth." He "reject[ed] the notion that the American moment had passed." The most disturbing line of Obama's address was his assertion that the US had the right to launch unilateral and preemptive attacks on foreign countries, a position not unlike that of Bush and Cheney. "No president should ever hesitate to use force – unilaterally if necessary to protect ourselves and our vital interests when we are attacked or imminently threatened," Obama stated. "We must also consider using military force in circumstances beyond self-defense," Obama also argued, "in order to provide for the common security that underpins global security ..."[31] This is a geopolitical worldview that directly challenges the interests of both the Third World and most Islamic nations.

In fairness, Obama never claimed to be an ideologue of the left. He promised a post-partisan government and a leadership style that incorporated the views of conservatives and liberals alike. This political pragmatism – which is also reflected in the new, post-racial black leadership Obama represents – is a rejection of radical change, in favor of incremental reform. As Obama explained in 2006: "Since founding the American political tradition has been reformist, not revolutionary. What that means is that for a political leader to get things done, he or she should ideally be ahead of the curve, but not too far ahead."[32] Malcolm X at the end of his life sought to overturn capitalism, not to reform it; Obama apparently seeks to achieve Keynesian changes but within our existing, market-dominated political economy.

Such criticisms in no way are intended to minimize the significance of Obama's victory, and the continuing importance of electoral politics, voting, and using all the tools of electoralism for oppressed people in the United States. The Obama victory will be of great assistance in waging the struggle for racial justice. But electoral politics is not a substitute for social protest organizing in neighborhoods and in the streets.

A new, anti-racist leadership must be constructed to the left of the Obama government, that draws upon representatives of the most oppressed and marginalized social groups within our communities: former prisoners, women activists in community-based, civic organizations, youth groups, from homeless coalitions, and the like. Change must occur not from the top down, as some Obama proponents would have it, but from the bottom up. The growing class stratification within African-American and Latino communities has produced an opportunistic, middle-class leadership elite that in many important ways is out of touch with dire problems generated by poverty, unemployment and mass incarceration. We must reconnect the construction of leadership by addressing and solving real-world problems of racialization that challenge everyday people's daily lives. The Obama victory has the potential for creating a positive environment for achieving dramatic reforms within public policy, improving the conditions for the truly disadvantaged – but only if it is pressured to do so. Obama may be successful in standing outside of the processes of racialization, but for millions of minorities, race and class inequality continue to define their lives, and only collective resistance will lead to their empowerment.

Notes

1. Mark Mazzetti and Scott Shane, "Al Qaeda Offers Obama Insults and a Warning," *New York Times* (20 November 2008).
2. See Manning Marable and Kristen Clarke, eds., *Seeking Higher Ground: The Hurricane Katrina Crisis, Race, and Public Policy Reader* (New York 2008).
3. CNN, *USA Today* and Gallup poll on Hurricane Katrina Attitudes, 13 September 2005; and Desiree Cooper, "Outrage, Carrying Mix in Katrina Response," *Detroit Free Press* (15 September 2005).
4. See Michael Powell and Peter Slevin, "Several Factors Contributed to 'Lost' Voters in Ohio," *Washington Post* (25 December 2004); and Jamal Watson, "Blacks File Lawsuit in Ohio, Claim Disenfranchisement in Election," *Amsterdam News* (16–22 December 2004).
5. See Manning Marable, "How Washington Won: The Political Economy

of Race in Chicago," *Journal of Intergroup Relations* 11: 2 (Summer 1983), pp. 56–81.

6. See Raphael J. Sonenshein, "Can Black Candidates Win Statewide Elections," *Political Science Quarterly* (Summer 1990).

7. See Judson Jefferies, "Douglas Wilder and the Continuing Significance of Race: An Analysis of the 1989 Gubernatorial Election," *Journal of Political Science* 23 (1990), pp. 87–111.

8. Andrew Kohut, "Getting it Wrong," *New York Times* (10 January 2008).

9. Rachel L. Swarns, "Quiet Political Shifts as More Blacks are Elected," *New York Times* (13 October 2008).

10. On Duval Patrick, see Scot Lehigh, "Patrick's Stunning Victory," *Boston Globe* (30 September 2006); and Kirk Johnson, "In Races for Governor, Party May Be Secondary," *New York Times* (4 November 2006).

11. Debra Dickerson, "Color-blind," *Salon* (22 January 2007), www.salon. com/opinion/feature/2007/01/22/obama.

12. Stanley Crouch, "What Obama Isn't: Black Like Me," *New York Daily News* (2 November 2006).

13. John K. Wilson, *Barack Obama: His Improbable Quest* (Boulder, CO 2008), pp. 57–58.

14. Peter Wallsten, "Would Obama Be 'Black President'?" *Los Angeles Times* (10 February 2007).

15. Paul Street, *Barack Obama and the Future of American Politics* (Boulder, CO 2008), pp. 156–9.

16. John Wilson, *Barack Obama*, pp. 93–4.

17. Ibid., pp. 95–6.

18. Ibid., pp. 96–7.

19. Ibid., pp. 98–9.

20. Ibid., pp. 73–4.

21. Barack Obama, "A More Perfect Union," public speech, 15 March 2008, Philadelphia, PA, www.barackobama.com/2008/03/18/ remarks_of_senator_barrack_obam_53.php.

22. Ibid.

23. Ibid.

24. Nicholas D. Kristof, "The Push to 'Otherize' Obama," *New York Times*, September 22, 2008.

25. "A Closer Look At the Parties in 2008," Report of the Pew Research Center for the People and the Press, August 22, 2008.

26. Ibid.

27. Ibid.

28. Elyse Ashburn, "Poll: Students Less Engaged Than Thought," *Chronicle of Higher Education* 55: 10 (31 October 2008); and "College Students and the Presidential Election," *Chronicle of Higher Education* 55: 10 (31 October 2008).

29. Ibid.

30. "Lexington: Ship of Fools," *The Economist* (15 November 2008).

31. Street, *Barack Obama and the Future of American Politics*, pp. 156–160.

32. Ken Silverstein, "Obama, Inc.: The Birth of a Washington Machine," *Harper's* (November 2006).

INDEX